JOHN DONNE IN THE NINETEENTH CENTURY

John Donne in the Nineteenth Century

DAYTON HASKIN

OXFORD
UNIVERSITY PRESS

OXFORD
UNIVERSITY PRESS

Great Clarendon Street, Oxford OX2 6DP

Oxford University Press is a department of the University of Oxford.
It furthers the University's objective of excellence in research, scholarship,
and education by publishing worldwide in

Oxford New York

Auckland Cape Town Dar es Salaam Hong Kong Karachi
Kuala Lumpur Madrid Melbourne Mexico City Nairobi
New Delhi Shanghai Taipei Toronto

With offices in

Argentina Austria Brazil Chile Czech Republic France Greece
Guatemala Hungary Italy Japan Poland Portugal Singapore
South Korea Switzerland Thailand Turkey Ukraine Vietnam

Oxford is a registered trade mark of Oxford University Press
in the UK and in certain other countries

Published in the United States
by Oxford University Press Inc., New York

British Library Cataloguing in Publication Data

Data available

Library of Congress Cataloging in Publication Data

Data available

Typeset by Laserwords Private Limited, Chennai, India
Printed in Great Britain
on acid-free paper by
Biddles Ltd., King's Lynn, Norfolk

ISBN 978–0–19–921242–2

1 3 5 7 9 10 8 6 4 2

For Margaret, Thomas, Peter, and Helen

Contents

List of Illustrations

Abbreviations

DNB	*The Dictionary of National Biography*
ELH	*ELH: Journal of English Literary History*
JDJ	*The John Donne Journal: Studies in the Age of Donne*
JEGP	*Journal of English and Germanic Philology*
MLQ	*Modern Language Quarterly*
MP	*Modern Philology*
N&Q	*Notes and Queries*
OED	*The Oxford English Dictionary*
PMLA	*Publications of the Modern Language Association*
SEL	*Studies in English Literature, 1500–1900*
SP	*Studies in Philology*
UTQ	*University of Toronto Quarterly*

Brief Notes to the Reader

In the chapters that follow references to *The Variorum Edition of the Poetry of John Donne*, gen. ed. Gary A. Stringer (Bloomington, IN: Indiana University Press, 1995–), are generally given (within parentheses) in the text. In making reference to individual volumes of the *Variorum* in the discursive sections of the book and in reproducing the titles of the volumes in the notes, because users of this tool are familiar with the practice of designating them by Arabic numerals, I have in these places retained that form of designation. However, page references, given in parentheses or in a footnote, follow the usual style of designating volume number in lower-case Roman numerals.

As a general rule, I place in italics the title of *The Variorum Edition* whenever referring to something that has already been published. I use the phrase the Variorum, or the Donne Variorum, without italics to refer to the large collaborative project that Gary Stringer initiated in the 1980s. In practice it has not always proved easy to distinguish clearly between the two.

In making reference to Donne's poems, I have ordinarily followed the form and spelling of the titles as they appear in the master list print-ed in *The Variorum Edition*. Where accurate representation of another's treatment of a poem requires it, I have deviated from this practice. An example is the elegy called in the *Variorum* 'On his Mistress' but known to many readers under headings that propose that the poet's wife or mis-tress had sought to accompany him 'disguised as a page'. Sometimes in citing the text of Donne's poetry it has proved necessary to quote from the particular edition with which a given reader or group of readers was work-ing. In writing about Coleridge's marginalia on Donne's Third Satire, for instance, I quote from the 1669 edition, into a copy of which he wrote his commentary.

Quotations of materials published before the twentieth century general-ly come from the earliest printed version of a book or article. When it is pertinent to quote a different version, I do so. For instance, in citing Izaak Walton's *Life of Donne*, I usually cite the edition of 1675 because it was the final edition on which Walton himself worked. At relevant moments I cite the edition published by Thomas Zouch (1796), however, since Zouch mediated the 1675 edition to many nineteenth-century readers. In working with critical and biographical materials, I have consistently attempted to compare earlier and later versions of books and articles that have been reprinted, in order to find whether any notable change was made. Where I have found a significant alteration, as with David Masson's discussion of Donne in his biography of Milton, I have attempted to discover the grounds for revision and to gauge, insofar as it is possible, the impact of the change.

Preface

> It is one of the illusions of our age that Donne was invented by Mr. Eliot.
>
> —G. M. Young, in the *London Mercury* (1936)

One September evening, walking out of the Loeb Drama Center at Harvard where the British actor Alec McCowen had just given a one-man show, I overheard a fellow theatre-goer confide to his companions, 'I never knew Donne was a preacher!' He was not so much confessing ignorance. He was expressing astonishment and delight and, I take it, gratitude for a segment of the program during which we had been treated to cuttings from John Donne's sermons. I have felt a kindred gratitude to him, whoever he was, for having helped to set me on a path that led to writing this book.

Hearing the pleasure and surprise in the voice of that anonymous patron of the theatre raised for me one of three foundational questions that have contributed a good deal to my conception of this project. By way of introducing the first, I should explain that I had seen McCowen in other productions. These included a spirited creation of the libertine Lucio in *Measure for Measure*, a solo recitation of the complete Gospel according to St Mark, and a haunting performance as the probing psychiatrist in one of the earliest productions of *Equus*. At the Loeb that evening McCowen was performing a personal tribute to popular theatrical entertainment. He called it *Shakespeare, Cole and Company*. His material comprised a dazzling array of favorite passages, most of them drawn from the Bard, some from more recent work, including that of Cole Porter. He held everything and brought everyone together by weaving in genial commentary. Here he gave a bit of explanation about how a certain scene works. There he offered some self-effacing personal history about how he had stumbled into an inspired interpretation of a classic role. As the evening wore on and the actor was able to count on increased intimacy with the audience, he set the stage to recite a passage from a sermon preached in a time of plague. He framed his selection by acknowledging that, with the spread of HIV, many of us have lost persons we have held dear. He added that the AIDS virus has struck a number of persons who have given their lives to the theatre. Whatever autobiographical implications his observations may have entailed were not spelled out.

That members of the audience should have been talking animatedly about the sermon just after the show seemed fitting at the time, as it does now in memory. Both the cutting and Donne himself came as a surprise. There had been nothing in the printed program, nor in the actor's previous remarks, that predicted a dramatic ascent into the pulpit of St Paul's Cathedral—or that intimated that there was to be a serious departure from light entertainment. McCowen introduced the materials poignantly, and Donne's remarks sounded an intimate resonance as the lines between the actor and the preacher disappeared. In putting together the script, McCowen had been able to count on there being members of the audience who would know Donne as a love poet. This helped to make the passage from the sermon challenging in just the right ways, and provided an emotional climax. The preacher that McCowen created, who acknowledged his auditors' fears of the plague and at the same time showed himself intent on speaking words of consolation, might just have been someone who had experimented freely with sex and then been required, by a dire turn of events, to take a more discreet public stance. He seemed still to have, as Lucio says of the Duke in *Measure for Measure*, 'some feeling for the sport.'

The question raised for me by the theatre-goer's spontaneous declaration depended, as these things do, on some peculiarities of my own angle of vision. For some time, I had been making descents into the book-stacks in Harvard's Widener Library, trying to learn what nineteenth-century readers had seen—and not seen—in early modern poetry. In particular I had been paying attention to the love lyrics of a writer whom A. S. Byatt would make into a Galeotto in her novel, *Possession*, where Donne's poetry facilitates the coming together of two Victorian poets whose brief idyllic love affair becomes the object of intense postmodernist sleuthing. I already understood dimly that something like a textual erotics was at work in the Victorians' reading of Donne. I had been intrigued by the fact that poetic lines about how love makes one little room an everywhere and about forgetting the He and She are implemented in *Middlemarch* as chapter-mottoes. What caught my imagination in the remark 'I never knew that Donne was a preacher' depended upon my awareness that George Eliot identified the author of those passages as Doctor Donne. That is, she took it for granted that her contemporaries knew him as a character in the book that was regarded as the masterpiece of English biography: 'A preacher in earnest, weeping sometimes for his auditory, sometimes with them', as Izaak Walton told them in his charming story about the former Dean of St Paul's, 'always preaching to himself like an angel from a cloud, but in none; carrying some, as St Paul was, to heaven in holy raptures, and enticing others by a sacred art and courtship to amend their lives: Here picturing a vice so as to make it ugly to those that practiced it, and a virtue so as to make it be beloved even by those that loved it not.'[1] The note of surprise in 'I never knew Donne was a preacher!' had become possible because few people read Walton any longer. By a radical change in the cultural frameworks in which Donne is lodged, the writer of passionate poetry now has a decided priority over the subject of Walton's hagiographical narrative. That transformation is the subject of this book.

When McCowen gave his performance, I already had to hand an unprecedented body of material in which I could begin to explore questions about when and how this reversal in Donne's identity had taken place. A few years earlier I had accepted an invitation to work on the project that would create *The Variorum Edition of the Poetry of John Donne*. The large goals of this variorum are principally two: to produce a new text of Donne's poems, based on careful scrutiny of all the major editions and all the seventeenth-century manuscripts, and to provide a comprehensive history of the commentary on all of Donne's poems. To me were allocated the twin tasks of creating a record of how each of fifty-four lyrics was interpreted between 1800 and 1900 and of composing a history of the interpretation of the Songs and Sonnets during the period. Finding all the books and articles in which Donne's poetry had been discussed for a hundred years was a challenging task; scholarship on the nineteenth-century revival turned out to be spotty, and often it proved misleading.[2] Fortunately, a previously obscure dissertation on the history of Donne's reputation written at the University of Uppsala proved a bibliographical godsend for the period from 1779 to 1873. Working primarily at Harvard, and also at Yale's Sterling Library and at the British Library, I scoured hundreds of old books and periodicals to augment the bibliography that I had culled out of earlier studies. In addition to 350 or so items about Donne previously listed in Raoul Granqvist's industrious dissertation and elsewhere, I turned up more than 150 new items.

Twenty years on it seems remarkable that as recently as the 1980s one could have easy access to Widener's extensive holdings from the nineteenth century. The sort of work that I was doing then—making my way row by row through subterranean book-stacks, pulling down old tomes from shelf after shelf, looking through hundreds of volumes to see whether this or that

---

[1] Izaak Walton's *Lives of Dr. John Donne*, etc., is quoted here from the edition by Thomas Zouch (York, 1796); most nineteenth-century editions of Walton's *Lives* were based on Zouch.

[2] At the time when the Variorum project began, the principal bibliographical resources for the study of Donne's place in nineteenth-century literary history were as follows: Geoffrey Keynes, *A Bibliography of Dr. John Donne, Dean of Saint Paul's*, 4th edn (Oxford: Clarendon, 1973); A. J. Smith (ed.), *John Donne: The Critical Heritage* (London: Routledge and Kegan Paul, 1975); and Raoul Granqvist's Uppsala dissertation, published as *The Reputation of John Donne, 1779–1873* (Stockholm: Almqvist and Wiksell, 1975).

one contained some reference to Donne—can no longer be carried out. Lest this sound like pure nostalgia, I must acknowledge that much of this scouring before we had electronic search engines was not only drudgery but literally dirty work. Most of it was undertaken in the summer time, and the library had no air-conditioning. The books were dusty. Many were crumbling. Occasionally the bindings had come apart. Tiny corners of pages, some of them folded down perhaps by readers a hundred years previously, kept falling out, leaving a random trail of scraps. If there were a cadre of secret Library Police, I thought to myself, they would have little trouble tracking me down. Someone might tell me to stop handling so many old books.

In the event, still more drastic measures were taken. They were executed impersonally, with no direct embarrassment for anyone. Even before major renovations commenced at Widener in the 1990s, the library accelerated the removal of thousands of old books into storage off-site. No one can browse any longer as I once did, when in, say, two hours' time you could make a preliminary examination of dozens of artifacts and note down whether the contents of each of these items was 'pertinent' or 'not pertinent' to the history of reading Donne's Songs and Sonnets. Of course theoretically all the books are still available. If you know in advance just what to look for, you can access the relevant title through an electronic database and order it up. Say you've noticed that in 1819 an editor named Ezekiel Sanford published out of Philadelphia a series of *Works of the British Poets*. Although the database does not tell you which poets are included, you can summon from the Depository (one by one) all twenty-five volumes. The next day, once you charge out each volume individually for use within the library, it is possible to look through them all until you find whether your poet is included. It is completely impractical, however, to perform this operation for thousands of books and periodicals. And forget about serendipitous discoveries from desultory browsing.

By the time I began the next phase of my research, when I systematically examined every known published reference to Donne that I had found, the mass of materials had grown so large that more often than not I felt relieved (and a bit guilty for that) when an item could be dismissed as 'not pertinent.' Having clear criteria that allowed me to ignore large amounts of material, I made photocopies of the writings that were directly pertinent to the Songs and Sonnets. During a sabbatical leave I annotated each article and book in which there was any discussion of Donne's love poetry. On the basis of my annotations, I composed a history of how each of the Songs and Sonnets had been interpreted. Later I reread my photocopies in chronological order and wrote a general history of Donne's love poetry in the period. The results are to become available whenever the relevant parts of the *Variorum* are at last published. (At the time I am writing, three and a half of the projected eight volumes have appeared in print.[3])

This work for the Variorum project began in a general climate of literary studies when deconstructionist and new historicist critics were calling attention to what had been deferred, repressed, and made invisible during the period when a New Critical approach to Donne had been favored. As I started taking an interest in questions about how 'Donne' had come popularly to denominate a poet rather than a preacher, contemporary critical perspectives offered hope that I could discern questions that had gone unasked or that remained unexplored. It became evident that the procedures that had enabled me to ignore masses of published evidence were tied to assumptions that could not account for the most conspicuous material finding that my research had turned up: that something like three-quarters of the pages I had photocopied had been published between 1890 and 1900. I was going to have to re-examine many items that I had dismissed as 'not pertinent.' Once my research took this decisive turn towards exploring nineteenth-century literary culture, with increasing frequency I began to seek out three kinds of materials that I had hitherto tried to ignore: Donne's prose, nineteenth-century editions of his writings, and biographical narratives. As my project came more and more to differ in scope and in perspective from the Variorum, it also began to differ from previous accounts of the Donne revival. These accounts evinced three principal limitations: (1) they tended to treat the poetry in isolation from the prose and the biography; (2) they broke off in the early 1870s, leaving unexamined the period when writing about Donne intensified; and (3) they told the story of Donne's recovery as if his emergence as a major poet had been inevitable.[4]

---

[3] *The Variorum Edition of the Poetry of John Donne*, gen. ed. Gary A. Stringer (Bloomington, IN: Indiana Univ. Press, 1995–); Vol. 6: *The Anniversaries and the Epicedes and Obsequies* (1995); Vol. 8: *The Epigrams, Epithalamions, Epitaphs, Inscriptions, and Miscellaneous Poems* (1995); Vol. 2: *The Elegies* (2000); Vol. 7, Part 1: *The Holy Sonnets* (2005).

[4] See Kathleen Tillotson, 'Donne's Poetry in the Nineteenth Century (1800–1872)', in *Elizabethan and Jacobean Studies Presented to Frank Percy Wilson in Honour of His Seventieth Birthday* (Oxford: Clarendon, 1959), 307–26; Roger Sharrock, 'Wit, Passion and Ideal Love: Reflections on the Cycle of Donne's Reputation', in Peter Amadeus Fiore (ed.), *Just So Much Honor: Essays Commemorating the Four-Hundredth Anniversary of the Birth of John Donne* (University Park, PA: Pennsylvania State Univ. Press, 1972), 33–56; cf. Smith (ed.), *Critical Heritage* (1975). A second volume of *John Donne: The Critical Heritage*, ed. A. J. Smith and Catherine Phillips (London: Routledge, 1996), purports to cover the period from 1873 to 1923.

Helpful exceptions to the general cutting short of accounts of the Donne Revival include Roland B. Botting, 'The Reputation of John Donne during the Nineteenth Century', *Research Studies of the State College of Washington*, 9 (1941), 139–88, and Joseph Duncan, *The Revival of Metaphysical Poetry, The History of a Style, 1800 to the Present* (Minneapolis, MN: Univ. of Minnesota Press, 1959).

Another aspect of the climate of literary and cultural studies in the late twentieth century provided just the right sort of challenge: Donne's stock was on the decline, and it was no longer possible to write as if his aesthetic greatness had been bound to reassert itself at last. One need not fully embrace the apocalyptic premise of Wallace Shawn's play, *The Designated Mourner*, according to which everyone on earth who could read John Donne's poetry is now dead, to see that the circuitous history of reading Donne cannot be exhausted in a triumphal narrative meant to demonstrate the superiority of a modernist sensibility.[5] The cult that emerged in the 1920s has long since spent itself and given way to productive and unproductive kinds of skepticism about the value of reading Donne. In order to appreciate the historical contingencies by which Donne came to be regarded as a major author, it is helpful to adopt a provisional agnosticism in the face of truth-claims about his greatness, even though privately (as it were) one regards many features of his writing as remarkable. The history of contingencies that I have to recount shows clearly enough that readers have repeatedly placed unnecessary and undesirable limits on how Donne's work can be understood.

Reading *Possession* provoked a second foundational question. My attempts to learn what 'Donne' had meant to various readers—and writers—had showed me that for most of the nineteenth century his name referred to a biographical subject whose poetry was only incidental to his enduring significance. Donne, as he appears in Byatt's book, belongs to twentieth-century literature teachers and to fictional nineteenth-century poets, not (as the record in Victorian publications has it) to readers interested in his marriage and concerned about a Jacobean preacher's place in English history. In the Victorian plot of *Possession* Donne's love poems are central to the dynamics of the relationships between its male protagonist, Randolph Henry Ash, and the two principal women in his life, his spouse, Ellen, and his lover, Christabel Lamotte. The latter parts of the narrative reveal that in 1889, during the weeks before he passed away, Ash was obsessed with Donne's poems and quoted them 'to the ceiling.' He took a particular interest in 'A Valediction Forbidding Mourning.' This poem was connected in his memory to Lamotte, with whom he had discussed it, and to their month-long tryst some thirty years earlier. In a letter in which Ash had discreetly declared his wish that they might find a limited time and space to be together, he had told her as well that he had the words of John Donne before him as he wrote. In this way Ash prodded Lamotte (much as Robert Browning did Elizabeth Barrett) to begin reading Donne. It seems to have been Lamotte, however, who initiated discussion of the implications of the passage in the 'Valediction' that refers

---

[5] Wallace Shawn, *The Designated Mourner* (London: Faber and Faber, 1996), 53.

to the 'inter-assured' mind of two lovers. Another letter in which she tells of having read 'your Donne' suggests that they may have been reading 'The Ecstasy' as an injunction to express their love bodily. If Byatt's narrator assigns these poems by Donne the work of recalling to a dying poet a central though well hidden episode from his past, she assigns another poem an even more decisive role in projecting the future. Ash repeatedly reads 'The Relic' to the woman with whom he has never consummated their marriage, proposing that it is 'our poem, Ellen, ours, yours and mine.' They seem, in fact, to share a mutual hope that in or beyond the grave their hands will at last touch the seals that for forty years they forbore to touch and that they will at last know difference of sex. Ellen does what she can to prepare for this possibility. On her husband's tombstone she has inscribed Donne's words 'One short sleep past we wake eternally.' Later she sees to her own burial in a common grave with him—taking along a bracelet of bright hair and a packet of papers that teaches a future generation something miraculous about love.[6]

For all this, the relations between Byatt's book and Donne's poetry are more thoroughgoing. Donne emerges in *Possession* not only as a poet who wrote movingly of ideal love but as one who—already in the nineteenth century—was a powerful spokesman for cynicism about love. Of the fictional Ash's poems, one that is supposed to be among his best known is called 'Mummy Possest.' Its title comes from 'Love's Alchemy.' Its inspiration, we learn, is both the precursor poet and a disillusioning experience that Ash had the last time he and Lamotte were together. Byatt includes 'Mummy Possest' in its entirety, in a move that would seem to deliver the *coup de grâce* to the notion that it was the moderns who discovered the potential in Donne to be rendered integral to English poetic tradition. Yet, since this poem was written by Byatt herself, its presence helps to make good the claim that modernist poets discovered 'the metaphysicals': for all Byatt's reading of Donne through spectacles that she borrows from Coleridge and Browning and George Eliot, there is nothing in extant Victorian poetry quite like her poem's engagement with Donne.

Byatt's quite fictional revelation of a poetic John Donne who figured largely but secretly in Victorian literary culture thus reminded me to think harder about what escaped the surface record of how Donne was read. The intensity with which *Possession* invites readers to imagine what the Victorians may have seen in Donne, while it pushes us to read between the lines of the commentary on the love poems enshrined in the published record, unsettles assumptions about what we know, and can know, concerning past readers' experiences.

---

[6] A. S. Byatt, *Possession: A Romance* (London: Chatto and Windus, 1989; New York: Random House, 1990).

There were after all many experiences that the Victorians regarded, rightly or wrongly, as not to be spoken of. Inevitably, this recurrent phenomenon became an explicit part of my subject, since Donne's Victorian editors and biographers all worked within a literary culture that, as the infamous controversy about editing Thomas Carlyle's *Reminiscences* made plain, increasingly looked upon the silences in past records as potentially rich objects for interpretation and speculation.

In attempting to isolate and to evaluate the modes of assimilating Donne that were prevalent in nineteenth-century literary culture, I have been helped by Stephen Gill's clear exposition, in *Wordsworth and the Victorians*, of what a very different poet may have meant in a comparable period. About half of Gill's book is devoted to the creative engagement of Tennyson and Arnold, George Eliot and others with the poetry of Wordsworth. That a book about Donne's nineteenth-century afterlife cannot afford proportionate attention to this feature of literary history helps to account, I think, for two things: the readiness with which the idea that T. S. Eliot discovered Donne was credited in the twentieth century and the brilliance with which, shadowing Browning, Byatt's Henry Ash is imagined as having invented the modernists' Donne in a distinctly Victorian key. The bold intertextuality by which Byatt connects her fictional poet to Donne points up a telling contrast between my study and recent books about what the Victorians saw in and did with the poetry of the Romantics.[7]

While Wordsworth's poetry was readily available in countless Victorian editions, Donne's was slow to make its way back into print. The editors responsible for printing Donne's work therefore feature more largely in this book than do the editors of Wordsworth in Gill's study. They made it possible for Victorian readers to suppose that it might be worth trying to assimilate a profoundly unsettling and challenging writer. In some cases, by denying the authenticity of certain poems and by claiming others as Donne's, they radically altered the picture of the author available to their contemporaries. Yet, because subsequent editors established that most of what, for instance, A. B. Grosart added to the canon is not actually Donne's work, little consideration has previously been given to the impact that these materials had on late Victorian readers. This neglect is not so beneficial for developing an accurate understanding of Donne as we might suppose; it distorts our understanding of how the history of reading Donne continues to affect what we attend to in

---

[7] See Stephen Gill, *Wordsworth and the Victorians* (Oxford: Clarendon, 1998); Andrew Elfenbein, *Byron and the Victorians* (Cambridge: Cambridge Univ. Press, 1995); and James Najarian, *Victorian Keats: Manliness, Sexuality, and Desire* (Basingstoke and New York: Palgrave, 2002).

his life and writings. Just as it is misguided, say, for art historians who compile inventories of antique artworks known in the Renaissance to omit from consideration works that modern scholars have shown to be misattributions or forgeries, so the assumption that the Victorians had the same Donne available to them that we do creates a debilitating misperception.

By attending to the ways in which editors and readers dealt not only with Donne's poetry but with his prose and with his biography, we can begin to carry out a task that the *Variorum* itself will not accomplish: an integration of textual, critical, and biographical perspectives. This book therefore explores the process by which 'Doctor Donne' was transformed from a subject of hagiography: for some readers, into the irreverent and rebellious figure who was constructed at the *fin de siècle* out of images and voices in the satires, elegies, and more cynical lyrics; for others, into an exalted love poet who became the object of a cult in the century that followed; for many more readers than there had been for two hundred years, into a fascinating writer, who seemed a perpetual puzzle. En route to its attempt to show how the word 'Donne' came at last to refer to a body of writing to which Walton's narrative was increasingly irrelevant, the book also pays considerable attention to forces of resistance to reviving Donne's poetry, among them forces that embody ambivalence about and fascination with human sexuality.

From the point of view of those who fostered the cult of Donne in the 1920s and 1930s, that there is now appearing a *Variorum Edition of the Poetry of John Donne* would perhaps seem unsurprising. It is nonetheless, or it should be, astonishing. What other poet has virtually disappeared from readers' ken for more than two centuries and then been promoted, retrospectively, to so large a place in English literary history? By contrast with the situation of other early poets who have been accorded variorum status, through the eighteenth century and most of the nineteenth no comparable body of commentary accrued to Donne's poems. The background to the rediscovery of Donne thus provokes larger questions than the enabling limitations of the present book make it possible fully to pursue here. To what extent is endurance as a biographical subject, for instance, a necessary precondition for a neglected writer's work later to be installed in a prominent place in accounts of literary history?

The book takes up other questions. Granted that a writer's afterlife occurs partly in the private experiences of readers, partly in published work by editors and by critics, is the institutional basis offered by the classroom also necessary to make a writer 'canonical'? Or is it rather, as Christopher Ricks has proposed, that 'the most important and enduring rediscovery or reinvention of a book or of a writer comes when a subsequent creator is inspired

by such to an otherwise inexplicable newness of creative apprehension'?[8]
Did Donne come to be considered a normative writer because critics who
were themselves creative writers (Ben Jonson, Coleridge, T. S. Eliot) made
significant pronouncements about his writings? because industrious editors
got his texts right and made them available? because perceptive critics secured
attention for his achievements? because teachers put him on the syllabus?
These questions about the relative importance of different modes of Donne's
afterlife came into focus relatively late in the project, when a lead that looked
like a brief detour opened into a highway that raised questions that I hadn't
anticipated.

The detour took me into the Harvard Archives in the Pusey Library. What
I found there contributed to the final shape that the book has taken because
it helped to focus a third question about conditions of possibility. This
question occurred to me not by chancing to witness another's epiphany or by
encountering a provocative fictional narrative but more inwardly, as I became
restless with the stacks of photocopies I had been fingering. The question
took concrete form after a rereading of T. S. Eliot's contribution in 1931 to
the tercentenary anniversary of Donne's death, which he called 'Donne in
Our Time.' Like Virginia Woolf in her essay, 'Donne after Three Centuries',
Eliot ignored the Victorian background to the modernist glorification of a
precursor.[9] When I first read his essay, I must have dismissed it as irrelevant
to my purposes. In the rereading, I noticed that the piece begins with a
disarming personal tribute to Le Baron Russell Briggs, the teacher who
introduced Eliot to Donne's poetry in his freshman English course. Still,
carrying out so much of my research at Harvard, where Eliot had been a
student, it did not immediately occur to me to question whether in the early
twentieth century a college freshman was likely to encounter Donne in the
curriculum anywhere else. Gradually, having noticed that in the front matter
to his edition Herbert Grierson referred to having first attempted to teach
Donne in 1907, I realized that I could no longer simply take for granted
the situation at Harvard. The resources of the university, its libraries and
archives and pedagogical traditions, were not merely a convenient window
onto my subject: they were an integral part of it. What I found in Pusey's
archives made me understand that Widener's holdings in nineteenth-century
criticism and that the Houghton Rare Book Library's unique collection of
Donne materials had been the groundwork that facilitated Donne's entrance

---

[8] Christopher Ricks, *Essays in Appreciation* (Oxford: Clarendon, 1996), 339.
[9] T. S. Eliot, 'Donne in Our Time', in Theodore Spencer (ed.), *A Garland for John Donne
1631–1931* (1931; repr., Gloucester, MA: Peter Smith, 1958), 1–19; Virginia Woolf, 'Donne
after Three Centuries' (c.1932), in *Collected Essays*, ed. Leonard Woolf (London: Hogarth, 1967),
i. 32–45.

into the curriculum; the collections at Harvard had made possible not just *my* study of Donne but studies by thousands of students who had come along a hundred years earlier. Had they attended other colleges, these students would not have been reading Donne's poetry. What were the implications, then, of Eliot's having not thought it unusual that he had first encountered Donne in a freshman English course?

So I began to explore in archival materials how Donne was taught and studied at Harvard for nearly two decades before Eliot matriculated in 1906. I also made a study of the process by which James Russell Lowell and Charles Eliot Norton created the earliest American editions of Donne's poetry; confirmation of the importance of their editorial work came when I noticed that Grierson acknowledged that, had he known their Grolier Club edition when he began editing Donne, he probably would have abandoned his project as superfluous.[10] Working with the unique annotations and artifacts that Lowell and Norton had left behind made me increasingly curious about when and how their university had acquired its rich collection of Donne materials. The book that has made its way into your hands differs considerably from the one I first envisaged writing therefore in that it moves towards chapters about 'Donne at Harvard' and about how Donne became an 'academic subject.' It does so because readers and editors and teachers working in and around Boston played a decisive role in the larger story I have to tell, about how the subject of Walton's biographical narrative was displaced by a writer whose works seem worth reading in their own right.

The assumptions that tell us that as an academic subject Donne belongs not to the history department or the divinity school but to 'English' were created relatively late in the nineteenth century. The placement of Donne within English literature prepared for and survived the coming of modernism, which, when it was combined with Practical Criticism and New Criticism, promoted certain aspects of 'Donne' to unprecedented heights of reputation and popularity. As the essays by Woolf and Eliot reveal, modernism proposed that Donne speaks to us directly across the centuries; and it claimed him as its own. That is why, until the Variorum project got under way, the standard bibliographies available to scholars took 1912 (the date of Grierson's edition) as the starting point of Donne studies, and why for so long in popular accounts of literary history and in debates about the canon, it remained curiously axiomatic that Eliot discovered Donne.[11] It is not the business of the

---

[10] Herbert J. C. Grierson, Introduction, *The Poems of John Donne*, 2 vols. (Oxford: Clarendon Press, 1912), ii, p. cxiii n.

[11] The invaluable bibliographical work of John R. Roberts takes as its starting point the date of Sir Herbert Grierson's edition of Donne's *Poems*: see *John Donne: An Annotated Bibliography*

book to refute the popular misconception. What I aim to do is to chart that large and complex terrain that made Donne 'discoverable.'

While the book culminates in a study of literary culture during the last two decades of the nineteenth century, I want to acknowledge that a certain falling off of interest took place before the 1920s. Good reasons could be adduced for extending this study to include the two decades before 1921 when Grierson published the anthology called *Metaphysical Lyrics and Poems of the Seventeenth Century*, of which Eliot's essay on 'The Metaphysical Poets' was ostensibly a review.[12] Treating Grierson and Eliot and the other modernist poets who made Donne a decisive precursor, however, warrants sustained study in its own right. Aware as I am that editors of the *Variorum Edition* have announced a forthcoming volume that will cover the whole history of Donne's reputation as a poet, I aim here to provide an account of a key episode in that history: how, by the end of the nineteenth century, interest in Donne's poetry became by far the most intensive that it had been since the middle of the seventeenth, so that it had ceased to be likely that one might overhear the exclamation, 'I never knew Donne was a poet!'

I should like to suggest what may be gained, and what we ought not to expect to gain, from my version of the history of Donne in the nineteenth century. I do not think that there is much in this book that will be of direct methodological relevance to the problems in reading Donne that readers have today. The frameworks brought to bear on any particular writer not only change over time; they can never again be the same as those that have existed in the past. This is not to say that we cannot learn anything by examining the ways in which previous readers have produced their interpretations. What we learn has chiefly to do with the cultural assumptions and interests that have generated diverse and often highly contradictory constructions of the author. In Chapter 1 I will argue that this is what is of greatest interest in a variorum commentary. Here I will simply observe that it often enhances the pleasures of reading to compare what we see and feel with what others have seen and felt. I offer this distillation of how others have read Donne, a subject just intractable and intriguing enough to have engaged me for

of Modern Criticism 1912–1967 (Columbia, MO: Univ. of Missouri Press, 1973); *John Donne: An Annotated Bibliography of Modern Criticism 1968–1978* (Columbia, MO: Univ. of Missouri Press, 1982); *John Donne: An Annotated Bibliography of Modern Criticism 1979–1995* (Pittsburgh, PA: Duquesne Univ. Press, 2004).

   [12] Eliot's essay now known as 'The Metaphysical Poets' first appeared as a review of Grierson's *Metaphysical Lyrics and Poems of the Seventeenth Century, Donne to Butler* (Oxford: Clarendon, 1921) in the *Times Literary Supplement*, 1031 (10 Oct. 1921). Cf. the coda in Anne Ferry's *Tradition and the Individual Poem: An Inquiry into Anthologies* (Stanford, CA: Stanford Univ. Press, 2001), 247–50.

several years, as much in gratitude to the librarians who are preserving old books as in defiance of their assumption that it's acceptable to bury those books off-site, to make room for the latest interpretations. The dead merely bury the dead: this book attempts to drive a cart and a plow over their bones.

1

Introduction: The Variorum as a Window onto Cultural History

[I]t is doubtful, whether a copy ... of ... Donne's poems will be extant at
the close of the nineteenth century, if nature, united with a correct and
elegant taste, continue to be cultivated and progressively improved.

— *The European Magazine and London Review* (1822)

In the 1880s, during the planning stages of two monumental projects of
collaborative scholarship, the *Dictionary of National Biography* and the *Oxford
English Dictionary*, no one would have imagined that a century later an
international group of scholars would be launching a *Variorum Edition
of the Poetry of John Donne*. Granted, the prediction that Donne's poems
would disappear from the face of the earth was not coming true. Still,
there was not a single poem by Donne in *The Golden Treasury*; and what
the periodical writer who made the prediction in 1822 had added seemed
quite plausible, that Donne's name would 'travel down to posterity, while
antiquarian research continues to hoard up the useless lumber of ancient
times.' Even among those who had begun to read Donne's poetry with care,
many were not sanguine about its prospects. William Minto concluded as
shrewd an essay on the subject as anyone had ever written by remarking that
'Donne belongs to the class of failures in literature—failures, that is to say,
for the purpose of making an enduring mark, of accomplishing work which
should be a perpetual possession to humanity.' This was a provocation. Its
ironic perspective comes through subtly as Minto explains that Donne is
damned by virtue of his 'invincible repugnance to the commonplace' and
because there is so much in his verse that 'does not accord with our ideas of
refinement and culture.'[1]

---

[1] M.M.D., 'Essay on the Genius of Cowley, Donne and Clieveland', *European Magazine and
London Review*, 82 (1822), 112; William Minto, 'John Donne', *The Nineteenth Century*, 7 (May
1880), 862–3.

To some extent it was the late Victorian rejection of conventional ideas about 'refinement' and 'correct taste' that made Donne newly valuable. By the 1890s Minto's essay was widely read and cited amidst an explosion of writing on Donne. One startling thing that the *Variorum* has begun to make clear is that, for a large proportion of Donne's poems, critical scrutiny began in earnest in the Victorian period. When the volume devoted to the Songs and Sonnets appears, we will see that in the last decade of the nineteenth century commentary on the love poetry proliferated dramatically. There is no need, however, to await the complete *Variorum* to begin examining this phenomenon in relation to other features of literary and cultural history.

Admittedly, the Donne Variorum is taking much longer to complete than anyone originally envisaged, just as the *OED* and *DNB* did. Understandably, reviewers have so far paid a good deal of attention to what is innovative in the work on the text: the textual editors, acting in response to Donne's having circulated his poems in manuscript, are creating an unprecedented genealogical edition. Their work takes more seriously than ever before the fact that Donne saw little of his poetry through the press and seems not to have kept an archive of his poems. On the basis of the first three volumes to be published, reviewers concluded that, when it is complete, the *Variorum* will constitute a 'landmark' edition. It has already changed the way that Renaissance and early modern poetry in English will be edited hereafter.

Reviewers have not given us to suppose that comparably dramatic fruits can be ascribed to the compilation of commentary. However convenient the gathering of commentary is, few readers find that the *Variorum* offers the sorts of pleasures that are sometimes to be had from desultory excursions through the pages of the *DNB* and *OED*. Among reviewers the most incisive critic of the commentary has been Speed Hill, himself a textual editor who finds romance in the *Variorum*'s introductions to the texts of the various poems. Hill has called attention to the recurring absence of an original holograph on which to base the text of each poem and has explained the theoretical and practical grounds on which we ought to find this intriguing. Not only do the recurring reports of a 'lost original holograph' suggest an example of what is commonly called the death of the author; they confirm the importance of the hypothesis of an author-function. Yet at the same time they raise historical and biographical questions that recent theory has inhibited scholars from pursuing. 'When so many copies, many of them quite careful ones, were prepared and preserved', Hill asks, 'were the authorial or scribal originals simply discarded, as of no further value (as would have been true of printer's copies, which ordinarily do not survive)? Or did a deeply embarrassed Dean of Paul's commit Jack's poems to the fire?'[2] These are not the sorts of questions that the editors of the *Variorum* have so far taken up, and they don't seem likely to do so in future volumes.

Turning to the work of the commentary editors, Hill observes that, having decided to limit themselves to recording the history of published commentary on the poetry, they do not attempt to make the sort of definitive progress that the textual editors have been achieving. Nor do they seek, as they themselves emphasize, 'to interpret the criticism nor to examine the various epistemological constructs that have shaped it' (vi, p. xli). This self-imposed limitation tends to leave even knowledgeable and sympathetic readers unsatisfied. Hill points out that the commentary 'does not inexorably lead to confident decisions as to what a poem means.' The *Variorum* does not settle interpretative disputes once and for all; it leaves things 'inconsistent, contradictory, and fundamentally unparseable.' In fact, for all the editors' industry, 'the data will not cohere.'[3] This criticism rightly implies that merely objective reporting leaves wide open the work of interrogating the record and of bringing together literary criticism and textual scholarship. Some first-fruits of the kind of work that the *Variorum* makes possible have appeared elsewhere, for instance in Claude Summers's moving Presidential address to the John Donne Society on 'Donne's 1609 Sequence of Grief and Comfort.'[4] In order for the makers of the projected Volume 1 of the *Variorum* to write an illuminating account of 'The Historical Reception of Donne's Poetry from the Beginnings to the Present', they will need to be able to rely on a good deal more scholarship of this sort. The drudgework of compiling commentary needs to be superseded by studies that explore the myriad ways in which Donne has been implicated in literary and cultural history. This will require a radically different frame of mind from those with which we have been accustomed to thinking about a variorum. We need, first, not to project illegitimate expectations about what a variorum is good for and, second, to find advantages in the limitations that the editors of the Donne Variorum have imposed upon their enterprise. Precisely because the editors have not sought to provide timeless 'correct' interpretations, we can scan the assembled history of the text and the commentary to get glimpses of critical moments when the interests and aims of one interpretative community

[2] See Claude Summers, review of *The Variorum Edition of the Poetry of John Donne*, Vol. 6, in *Early Modern Literary Studies*, 1/3 (Dec. 1995), 6.1–10; Brian Vickers's reviews of Vol. 6 and of Vol. 8, respectively, in *Analytical and Enumerative Bibliography*, new ser., 10 (1999), 37–42; 107–11; W. Speed Hill, 'The Donne Variorum: Variations on the Lives of the Author', *Huntington Library Quarterly*, 62 (1999), 451.

[3] Hill, 'The Donne Variorum', 453.

[4] Claude J. Summers, 'Donne's 1609 Sequence of Grief and Comfort', *SP*, 89 (1992), 211–31. See also Diana Treviño Benet, 'Sexual Transgression in Donne's Elegies', *MP*, 92 (1994), 14–35.

have come into conflict with those of another.[5] This is to say that the Donne *Variorum* serves as a window onto literary and cultural history rather than as a final arbiter that fixes meaning. It enables us to take an intelligent interest in criticism from earlier eras, which, if we approached it with conceptions of literary culture that have been defined chiefly by our current interests, we might otherwise dismiss as 'wrong' or uninteresting.

WHAT CAN WE DO WITH A VARIORUM?

A generation ago, when the first two volumes of the Milton *Variorum Commentary* appeared, the editors were able to regard the text of Milton's poems as having been so well handled in the Columbia edition as not to require fresh scrutiny or revision. Milton had, after all, provided for his work to make its way through the press. This state of affairs seemed to imply that interest in theories of interpretation ought neither to be fed nor constrained with page after page of textual variants painstakingly gathered, sorted, and displayed. Rather, the editors took it to be their task to create a selected history of commentary on the poems. They sought to sift competing bits of commentary, to adjudicate among them, and, when possible, to settle difficult matters by providing 'correct' interpretations.

The first two volumes of the Donne *Variorum* to appear in print—Volume 6 containing the Anniversaries and Epicedes and Obsequies and Volume 8 containing the Epigrams, Epithalamions, and miscellaneous poems—already established their large differences from the Milton *Variorum Commentary*, conspicuously in the sustained attention that they accord to textual matters. The texts of Donne's poems occupy fewer than one hundred pages in these two volumes. More than seventy-five pages are given to reporting a history of textual transmission and to explaining the basis on which a copy-text for each poem has been chosen. Nearly three hundred pages are filled with evidence of textual variants, all of them reported according to an elaborate scheme of abbreviation that makes available a maximum of information in a minimal amount of space. This makes a powerful demonstration of the radical difference between Donne, who generally did not see his poetry through the press, and the likes of the self-crowning laureates, Spenser and Milton and Ben Jonson.

The manifest differences in approaching poetic texts between the Milton Variorum and the Donne Variorum ought not to overshadow, however-er, profound differences between the two projects in the presentation of

⁵ See Stanley Fish, *Is There a Text in This Class? The Authority of Interpretive Communities* (Cambridge, MA: Harvard Univ. Press, 1980), 16.

commentary. To a large extent, Milton's editors worked according to an ideal that would make meaning determinate and produce settled readings.[6] By contrast, Donne's editors provide summary and paraphrase without explicit evaluation. (Of course, the amount of space given to the views of various critics does entail intelligent evaluation.) To appreciate the value of these quasi-empiricist procedures, we need to take a long view that holds out the prospect of integrating the textual and critical histories.

As it has turned out, the first volumes of the *Donne Variorum* show that the textual editors have exploited some unprecedented possibilities of their own historical moment to report on the numerous seventeenth-century artifacts known through the work of Peter Beal and others to contain Donne materials. Their work has a much broader base than any previous edition. Moreover, they have made bold to claim, on the basis of their collations of the artifacts, that traces of authorial revisions can be discerned in the Epigrams and Epithalamions. In the subsequent volumes on the Elegies and on the Holy Sonnets they have made good on their promise to provide illustrations of how the poet went about reshaping his verses. In light of a rationale that has broadened the whole business of criticism to include the constitutive contributions of editors and textual critics, we can already conclude that the data presented in the *Variorum* have helped to shake off an inhibition, which was partly induced by antifoundationalist tendencies in recent literary theory, according to which readers felt obliged to consider questions of authorial intention beyond the pale of legitimate interest.[7]

One principal work for Donne Studies as the volumes of the *Variorum* continue to be published is to bring together its textual scholarship, which has wrought some striking discontinuities with the past, and its record of criticism. The massive amount of data about the texts needs to be sifted with a recognition, heightened by attention to the commentary, that everyone always reads Donne in physical artifacts that help to constitute their literary experience. Nonetheless, the *Variorum* is radically limited when it comes to helping us imagine the experience of reading the poetry in any of the editions. Its reporting is necessarily fragmentary, requiring and enabling users themselves to collaborate in the imaginative work of reconstructing any text that differs from the one that the textual editors have created. It also leaves us to carry out on our own the task of contextualizing the commentary on which

---

[6] See Fish, 'Interpreting the Variorum', which first appeared in *Critical Inquiry*, 2/3 (1975–76) and was reprinted, along with 'Interpreting "Interpreting the Variorum"', in *Is There a Text*, 147–80. After a long hiatus, the Milton Variorum went back into business late in the 1990s, under the general editorship of Albert C. Labriola: see *Milton Quarterly*, 32 (1998), 135–6.

[7] See the thoughtful 'Reflections on Scholarly Editing' by G. Thomas Tanselle in *Raritan*, 16/2 (Fall 1996), 52–64.

it reports. Arranging the commentary in chronological order is not the same thing as placing the criticism in historical contexts. It is altogether beyond the scope of the *Variorum* to tell us about how the criticism fits into the diverse interpretative communities in which it was produced, assimilated, refuted, and ignored.

THE IMPORTANCE OF THE VICTORIAN PERIOD IN THE HISTORY OF READING DONNE

As this is a book about how Donne came to be lodged, often uneasily, in inter-pretative communities that formed and shifted and sometimes dissolved, it is precisely within its scope to notice how oddly the *Variorum*'s straightforward chronicle of commentary sorts with its bold textual scholarship, especially since the editors are giving us a text that has never been seen by the critics whose work is reported. It is noteworthy, moreover, that in the pages devoted to verbal variants the *Variorum* shows that the five Victorian editions on which it reports were strikingly different from one another. One might have thought that the creation of the *Variorum* would assure us once and for all that we need not seriously attend to editions that antedate the New Bibliography of the early twentieth century. The case is just the opposite. By listing verbal variants from selected modern editions, the *Variorum* invites readers to scrutinize them. It prints the dots that we can connect to discern the process by which the need for a variorum text was discovered. It also suggests the foundation on which a variorum would be created. It shows how little the Victorians understood, and what they were learning, about the transmission of Donne's texts. These points warrant exploring and will be taken up in due course elsewhere in this book. Each chapter to follow includes detailed discussion of the work of one or more Victorian editors, since the editions contributed centrally to the transformation whereby Donne came to be known again as a writer.

Occasionally, and only indirectly, the *Variorum* alerts us to how thorough-going the assumption was during the twentieth century that the Victorians had little to offer for understanding Donne. Consider for instance a salient contradiction in the record as it appears in Volume 6. The commentary editors report, without contradicting it, Frank Manley's claim that the Anniversaries, having been 'largely forgotten' in the eighteenth century, were even more invisible in the nineteenth (vi. 359). Elsewhere, however, they record com-ments on these poems by George Henry Lewes (1838), Ralph Waldo Emerson (1841), Algernon Swinburne (1876), Charles Eliot Norton (1895), George

Saintsbury (1896), and an anonymous writer in the *Quarterly Review* (1897). Some of this commentary made large claims for the value of these poems and for Donne as a poet.

In fact even those who conceived the Variorum had little idea when the project began about how extensive nineteenth-century interest in Donne was and how intensive it became. As recently as the mid-1990s, when they composed a General Introduction to appear in each volume, the editors observed only abstractly that previous bibliographical work by A. J. Smith and John Roberts left 'entirely uncovered the periods 1890–1911 and 1979-present' (vi, p. xli and viii, p. xlvi). With respect to the earlier of these two periods this is a remarkable understatement. Smith's *Critical Heritage* volume of 1975 is so narrowly trained on interpretations of Donne's poetry that it is impossible to fathom why readers were taking an interest in it. It says virtually nothing about numerous editions of Izaak Walton's *Life of Donne* that began appearing in 1796 and multiplied through the whole course of the nineteenth century. It reports on only four items from the 1880s and breaks off short of the succeeding decade when the name 'Donne' came increasingly to stand for a remarkable body of love poetry. Tucked quietly away on a single page in Volume 6 of the *Variorum* one finds a brief observation that in the 1890s there were 'as many critical references to' the Epicedes and Obsequies as there had been 'during the entire preceding part of the century' (vi. 537). What's nowhere attempted is an explanation of the grounds on which Donne's poems suddenly commanded unprecedented critical attention.

When we turn to the poems that appear in Volume 8 and encounter first the Epigrams, it is striking that while there has been little writing about these poems, they were nonetheless once held in relatively high esteem.[8] Proportionately, the nineteenth century accounts for a good bit of the commentary, especially in the editions of A. B. Grosart, E. K. Chambers, and Norton. By contrast with the Epigrams, there's a good deal of commentary on the Epithalamions, much of it concerned to place the poems in a temporal scheme that separates Donne's youth from his maturity and even more of it dedicated to their metrical properties. There's so much commentary on the Valentine's Day epithalamion, almost all of it positive in its estimation of the poem, that one may be inclined to credit Gosse's claim that this was the most popular of all Donne's writings in the nineteenth century, although there are other candidates. The section devoted to reporting on the Somerset epithalamion shows clearly that long before Arthur Marotti and others writing in the 1980s directed attention to the economic and political

---

[8] As the *Variorum* indicates (viii. 284–5), this point was already recognized by Wesley Milgate (1950).

circumstances in which Donne wrote his poems, this was a prominent concern of late nineteenth-century critics, many of whom deplored Donne's having compromised himself by participating in the poetry of patronage.[9] Attempts to exculpate Dr Donne from the charge of having behaved like a toady or having acted indecently became widespread. Grosart's desire to save Donne from disrepute is nowhere more pronounced than in his decision not to print *A Sheaf of Miscellany Epigrams*, the English poems ascribed to Jasper Mayne that were purportedly based on Donne's Latin epigrams. The *Variorum* is the first edition of Donne's poetry ever to include these poems; it prints them in an appendix to Volume 8 and provides a history of the controversy surrounding them. Grosart expressed his 'satisfaction' at having become convinced by 'multiplied external and internal proofs' that the *Sheaf* was an 'imposture' (*Variorum*, viii. 473). Chapter 5 will examine in greater detail this episode in the history of editing Donne's poetry.

What's notable here is that the reports in the *Variorum* display the eagerness with which others lined up behind Grosart. In the 1870s a great deal of scholarly energy was expended to dismiss these poems. Much of it claimed to be a matter of protecting Donne's good name. An unspoken purpose was also at work.[10] Grosart and others were intent on keeping in place Walton's sketchy picture of Donne's youth, according to which he had spent the late 1580s in Oxford and Cambridge, and on preserving Walton's narrative about a conversion to Protestantism on purely intellectual grounds. Critical writing from the 1870s on the Latin epigrams reflects a growing general interest in Donne's youth that had been heralded by a piece submitted in 1857 to *Notes and Queries* by one J.Y. This correspondent was seeking to learn more about an unaccountably 'obscure portion of Donne's biography.' He pointed out that, 'If these *Epigrams* are undoubtedly Donne's, it is remarkable that Walton should be silent on this eventful period', since the *Sheaf* 'was published between the first and second editions of his *Life of Donne*.'[11]

Freed from the constraints that the commentary editors have imposed upon themselves, it is possible also to take an interest in the still more lavish attention directed to Donne in the 1890s, when two new editions appeared, followed by the first book-length treatments of Donne ever published. The *Variorum* has made it timely to examine the functions and effects of the myth according to which 1912 has been used to mark the starting point of Donne studies. Some of

---

[9] Arthur Marotti, *John Donne, Coterie Poet* (Madison, WI: Univ. of Wisconsin Press, 1986).
[10] See the important work of Dennis Flynn, which suggests some ways in which these poems may bear a profound relation to Donne's upbringing as a Catholic: 'Jasper Mayne's Translation of Donne's Latin Epigrams', *JDJ*, 3 (1984), 121–30; *John Donne and the Ancient Catholic Nobility* (Bloomington, IN: Indiana Univ. Press, 1995), 140–6, 183–94.
[11] J. Y[eowell], *N&Q*, 2nd ser., 4 (1857), 49.

these effects are evinced in the programmatic—and practical—decision of the editors of the *Variorum* to isolate Donne's poetry from the rest of his œuvre. Others appear in an account of the history of Donne's literary reputation that, without investigating the record of how Walton's *Life of Donne* has actually been read, proposes to tell us how it has influenced the marketing of Donne's works since the Restoration and eighteenth century.[12]

In *The Emergence of the English Author*, working with the concepts of an author-function and of cultural capital, Kevin Pask has sought to assimilate Donne to four other poets: Chaucer and Sidney, Spenser and Milton. He proposes that in the years just after his death Donne was a 'name' author whose 'life-narrative' served as a marketing tool for the publishers of his 'works.' Pask must acknowledge, of course, a number of anomalies: that Donne really became an 'author' only after the publication of his *Poems* in 1633; that 'Donne's incorporation into literary history' owes a good deal to Ben Jonson's dicta about the harshness of his numbers and the difficulty of his verses; and that in the life that Walton contributed as an introduction to the *LXXX Sermons* Donne's identity as a poet does not figure prominently. Rather than examining these anomalies,[13] Pask fabricates a plot according to which there occurred a 'radical transformation of the Renaissance divine into a Restoration libertine' (7). His narrative suppresses the dramatic fact, now made plain in the *Variorum*, that there was no body of commentary on Donne's works in the seventeenth, eighteenth, and nineteenth centuries comparable to what was amassing on the works of Chaucer and Spenser and Milton. In order to make the story seem plausible, Pask subsumes the history of reading Walton's biography within a larger, more familiar narrative about 'the emergence of discursive secularization ... in the seventeenth and eighteenth centuries.' He then claims that 'despite its own best efforts to shore up Donne's religious authority, the *Life of Donne* was increasingly read after the Restoration not as the life of a divine but as a "life of the poet"' (113). The 'cultural authority' of Walton's book, he says, 'no longer derived from its original status as an ecclesiastical narrative' (113); its authority derived instead from an autonomous literary system. This account gets us more than a little bit ahead of ourselves. Having left unexamined literary and cultural history between Samuel Johnson and T. S. Eliot, Pask has quite overlooked the independent popularity of Walton's *Lives* all through the nineteenth century when the *Life* of Donne was disconnected from his writings and circulated as a charming story about religious conversion and romantic love.

---

[12] Kevin Pask, *The Emergence of the English Author: Scripting the Life of the Poet in Early Modern England* (Cambridge: Cambridge Univ. Press, 1996), chap. 4.

[13] Pask, 115, 127; see, however, Pask's brief statement about Sidney and Donne's difference from the others, 7.

The elegy that Walton contributed to the 1633 edition of the *Poems* praised Donne's verse in terms that suggested he had written most of his poetry before Walton was even born (in 1593). It also emphasized the activity of writing and its effects, rather than the finished products themselves:

> Did his youth scatter *Poetrie*, wherein
> Was all Philosophie? Was every sinne,
> Character'd in his *Satyres*? made so foule
> That some have fear'd their shapes, & kept their soule
> Freer by reading verse? Did he give *dayes*
> Past marble monuments, to those, whose praise
> He would perpetuate? Did hee (I feare
> The dull will doubt:) these at his twentieth yeare?[14]

Once Walton took over from Sir Henry Wotton the task of writing Donne's life as an introduction to the sermons, his organizing ideas required him to downplay his subject's early poetic output still further. In the *Life*, he reserved his most sustained treatment of the poetry until the moment in his narrative when, having left Dr Donne in his bed waiting to die, he inserts several paragraphs that invite the reader to share something like his subject's death-bed reflections. The discussion of Donne's having written poetry is placed immediately after a complex evaluation of Donne's marriage. This juxtaposition came to exert a profound influence on what readers found in Donne's poetry. By deflecting attention from the possibility that 'The Canonization' provides a defense of the poet's own marriage, it kept readers of that poem, even those who were most keen on finding hidden autobiography in the poet's lyrics, from finding the poem biographically revealing. Only at the very end of the nineteenth century did anyone propose that Walton himself had provided the information that makes such a reading possible.[15] Because Walton did not label his remarks as the interpretation of particular poems, this influential section of the *Life of Donne*, although it was once well known, is not likely to be noticed in any volume of the *Variorum* devoted to specific poems. 'His marriage', Walton wrote, 'was the remarkable error of his life';

an error which though he had a wit able and very apt to maintain Paradoxes, yet, he was very far from justifying it: and though his wives Competent years, and other reasons might be justly urged to moderate severe Censures; yet, he would occasionally condemn himself for it: and doubtless it had been attended with an heavy Repentance, if God had not blest them with so mutual and cordial affections, as in the midst of

---

[14] *Poems, By J. D. with Elegies on the Authors Death* (London, 1633), 382–3.
[15] The case is presented in my article, 'A History of Donne's "Canonization" from Izaak Walton to Cleanth Brooks', *JEGP*, 92 (1993), 17–36.

their sufferings made their bread of sorrow taste more pleasantly then the banquets of dull and low-spirited people.[16]

It was within this section where the dying Donne is made out, as it were, to be preparing for his eternal reckoning that Walton placed his most extended treatment of the poetry. Again, he takes away with one hand as he gives with the other:

The Recreations of his youth were *Poetry*, in which he was so happy, as if nature and all her varieties had been made only to exercise his sharp wit, and high fancy; and in those pieces which were facetiously Composed and carelesly scattered (most of them being written before the twentieth year of his age) it may appear by his choice Metaphors, that both *Nature* and all the *Arts* joyned to assist him with their utmost skill.

Even as he praised Donne's wit by proposing that his poetic achievements had been casually tossed off at an early age, Walton provided grounds for not taking the poems very seriously. In fact, he offered anyone inclined to read the love poems as revealing something about the youth of a man whom he had designated 'a second St. *Austine*' a means for reconciling them to the larger theme:

It is a truth, that in his penitential years, viewing some of those pieces that had been loosely (God knows too loosely) scattered in his youth, he wish't they had been abortive, or, so short liv'd that his own eyes had witnessed their funerals: But, though he was no friend to them, he was not so fallen out with heavenly Poetry as to forsake that: no not in his declining age; witnessed then by many Divine Sonnets, and other high, holy, and harmonious Composures. Yea, even on his former sick-bed he wrote this heavenly *Hymn*, expressing the great joy that then possest his soul in the Assurance of Gods favour to him when he Composed it.

When Walton proceeds to quote 'An Hymn to God the Father', in which Donne conspicuously puns upon his own name, he rounds out his intertwined treatment of Donne's erratic love-life and loosely scattered poetry. He skillfully sets up the possibility that readers might see also in the speaker's claim to have 'more' sins Donne's own pious confession that his earthly love for Anne More had long diverted him from his heavenly calling. These passages quoted from Walton's *Life* were among the best known parts of the book throughout the nineteenth century; and they contributed little to spreading abroad a picture of Donne as a libertine.

For all this, there is some truth in the claim that Donne was transformed into a libertine. The only Restoration edition of Donne's *Poems* did print

---

[16] This and the following quotations are from *The Lives of Dr. John Donne, Sir Henry Wotton, Mr. Richard Hooker, Mr. George Herbert, Written by Izaak Walton*, 4th edn (London, 1675), 52–3. Cf. 38.

some 'libertine' verses for the first time.[17] Moreover, the *Poems on Several Occasions* published by Tonson in 1719, which was based on the 1669 edition, did contain a greatly abbreviated version of Walton's *Life*. Walton had worked on this book through the course of thirty-five years. After the fourth edition was published in 1675 no new edition appeared until 1796, when Thomas Zouch—emboldened by widespread enthusiasm for *The Compleat Angler*—brought out an annotated version of Walton's *Lives*. Through the next six decades the popularity of the *Life of Donne* in particular grew steadily. The *National Union Catalogue* lists more than forty editions from the 1800s, about half of them from the 1830s, 1840s, and 1850s. Many of these were based on Zouch's work, others on the work of John Major. The annotations in these editions displayed relatively little interest in Donne's having written poetry. In 1831 William Godwin, taken with the 'originality, energy, and vigor' of Donne's writing, remarked in exasperated admiration that he 'is left undisturbed on the shelf, or rather in the sepulchre; and not one in an hundred even among persons of cultivation, can give any account' of Donne as a writer, 'if in reality they ever heard of his productions.' In short, through the first four decades of the nineteenth century Donne was known not as a writer but as the subject of Walton's narrative.[18]

The pitting of a 'libertine in wit' against the exemplary hero of Walton's *Life* presupposes a dichotomy between two competing Donnes so familiar to twentieth-century readers as to seem a permanent feature of the record and a plausible heuristic device for charting the history of Donne's reputation. Yet this dichotomy, although it is frequently sponsored by quotations from the letter of 1619 in which the author of *Biathanatos* differentiated between 'Jack Donne' and 'Doctor Donne', was only gradually teased out of the record in the Victorian period, in large measure to account for the fact that what 'Donne' meant to readers of poetry was quite different from what this name meant to readers who were chiefly interested in biographical narratives. The distinction, though it was sometimes made early in the nineteenth century, became firmly established only after the editions of the poetry that appeared in the mid-1890s made two important innovations in the presentation of Donne's poetry: independently of one another, each removed from the title-page for the first time since 1654 all reference to the author's having been 'Doctor' Donne, and each restored the Songs and Sonnets to the pride of place they had been accorded in 1635. What Pask has presented as an account of Donne in the long

---

[17] See Ernest W. Sullivan, II, '*Poems*, by J.D.: Donne's Corpus and His Bawdy, Too', *JDJ*, 19 (2000), 299–309.

[18] William Godwin, *Thoughts on Man, His Nature, Productions, and Discoveries* (London: Effingham Wilson, 1831), 84; see also, 'Gallery of Poets. No. 1.—John Donne', *Lowe's Edinburgh Magazine*, 1 (1846), 228.

eighteenth century is above all a tribute to cultural work that was performed by interpreters of Donne in the late nineteenth century.

In view of the longer history of who 'Donne' has been thought to be, it is helpful to isolate two separate and profoundly related Donne revivals in the nineteenth century. The first phase belongs to the Romantic and early Victorian periods. While it by no means dismissed the poetry, it did not revive a poet as such. It promoted interest in a hallowed figure of considerable intelligence and learning and creativity, who occasionally gave vent to his creative powers by writing verses. His life was thought to be much more interesting than his poetry.[19] He was remembered, thanks not only to Walton but to Anna Jameson, especially for his romantic marriage. Writing in 1829, she retold the 'Story of Dr. Donne and His Wife' in a form that was then frequently reprinted for the next seventy years: 'Dr. Donne, once so celebrated as a writer, now so neglected, is more interesting for his matrimonial history, and for one little poem addressed to his wife' (she was referring to the elegy 'On his Mistress') 'than for all his learned, metaphysical, and theological productions. As a poet, it is probable that even readers of poetry know little of him, except from the lines at the bottom of the pages in Pope's version, or rather translation, of his Satires, the very recollection of which is enough to "set one's ears on edge".'[20] The First Revival, which was inspired by the story of a talented man who eventually became an eloquent preacher, came to a focus in an edition of the sermons. This was the six-volume edition called *The Works of John Donne, D.D., Dean of Saint Paul's, 1621–1631. With a Memoir of His Life*, edited by Henry Alford and published in 1839.[21] Its appearance owed a good bit to a few lovers of Elizabethan poetry and of old divinity, including Wordsworth and Coleridge, who encouraged Alford in a labor that, because it was chiefly concerned to revive Donne's prose, will scarcely merit notice in the *Variorum*.

In the next three chapters Alford's edition receives attention as the center-piece of the First Revival. It made the first major step in the transformation of Walton's biographical subject back into a writer. By the 1830s the number of Donne's readers was growing. The best of them, above all Coleridge, were no more constrained by facile dichotomies between youth and age, immorality and respectability, poetry and preaching, religion and secularism, than good

---

[19] Thomas Campbell, *Specimens of the British Poets; … and an Essay on English Poetry*, 7 vols. (London: John Murray, 1819), iii. 73; quoted by Henry Hart Milman, *Annals of S. Paul's Cathedral* (London: John Murray, 1868), 324.

[20] [Anna Brownell Murphy Jameson], *The Loves of the Poets*, 2 vols. (London: Henry Colburn, 1829), ii. 94–5.

[21] *The Works of John Donne, D.D., Dean of Saint Paul's, 1621–1631. With a Memoir of His Life*, ed. Henry Alford, 6 vols. (London: John W. Parker, 1839).

readers ever are. They held Walton's *Life* in regard as a moving narrative without allowing its intellectually lightweight author's indifference to Donne's theology and to most of his poetry utterly to curtail their interests. As Evert Duyckinck, writing in 1841, put it: 'Donne has not received the same attention from editors, that has been given to many of his contemporaries; perhaps the neglect in this studious biographical age is the best compliment that could be paid to the life by Walton.' Yet even as he was making this remark Duyckinck pored over Donne's writings, the sermons as well as the verse, and concluded, 'We like to read the theology of Donne, by the light of his early love poems. The sincerity of his affection, is remarkable in both.'[22] Twelve years later, as editor of *The Literary World*, he published Coleridge's marginalia on Donne's poetry. As one decade succeeded another in that era that came to speak of itself as 'the nineteenth century', more and more interest was accorded to Donne. A good deal but by no means all of it came from figures—Lewes and George Eliot, Edmund Gosse and his mentor Minto, Norton and his friend Leslie Stephen—who would help to construct and enforce the narrative about a progressive secularization in Western culture in relation to which readers are accustomed to thinking about the history of Donne's reputation. Drawing partly on data being made available in the *Variorum* and yet moving well outside its boundaries, I have begun to suggest some reasons that both the life and the writings of Donne resist easy induction into that familiar paradigm. This chapter ends therefore not with a conclusion but with a hypothesis: as the aims of a self-consciously secular interpretative community collided with the interests of readers who were looking into the writings because they valued the Dr Donne mediated to posterity by Walton, a larger, more fluid interpretative community emerged. Its members found in Donne an intriguing site at which to explore their own cultural contradictions. The various interpretations of the poems now being reported in the *Variorum* attest to a struggle over the identity and significance of John Donne that took on an unprecedented urgency at the end of the nineteenth century. Because it involved a cultural investment that has continued to produce interest for more than a hundred years, that struggle has made the history of Donne's reputation a much more important subject than anyone could have imagined before it began.

[22] Evert A. Duyckinck, 'Dr. Donne', *Arcturus*, 2/1 (June 1841), 19, 26, respectively.

2

Doctor Donne

For every individual reader of the poems of John Donne, there have probably been a hundred readers of the exquisite 'Life' of him, by Izaak Walton. Unprefaced by this 'Life', no edition of Donne's poems ought ever to have appeared.

—*Lowe's Edinburgh Magazine* (1846)

In the early nineteenth century there were three overlapping interpretative communities in which Donne's name had currency. One was made up of readers who, although they were familiar with Dr Donne from Pope's satires and Johnson's *Life of Cowley*, dismissed his poetry without actually reading it. Another consisted of a growing number of admirers of Izaak Walton's *Lives*, of which 'The Life of Dr John Donne' proved the most popular. There were also the writers whom we now call the Romantics, several of whom read Donne's sermons and poems with pleasure, often in one another's company. In bringing out an edition of the *Works* in 1839 Henry Alford and John W. Parker sought to unite the interests of these three groups and to make available a more ample picture of the writer than any living person had glimpsed.

Even in the 1840s, when Walton's *Lives* was at the height of its popularity, it must have been an exaggeration to maintain that there were one hundred times as many readers of the 'Life' as there were of Donne's *Poems*. Almost certainly it was an exaggeration with respect to the long record dating back to the early seventeenth century. Yet the anonymous essay from *Lowe's* tells us a good deal. Launching the new periodical's attempt to provide an alternative to the attacks on poets that readers had come to expect from the *Quarterly Review* and the *Edinburgh Review*, it stood first in a series that was to concern 'less familiar, but worthy English poets.'[1] It also sought to manage the 'lascivious' matter that actual readers of the poems were sure to encounter.

---

[1] 'Gallery of Poets. No. 1.—John Donne', *Lowe's*, 1 (1846), 228 n. For the history of Walton's biographical work on Donne, see David Novarr, *The Making of Walton's Lives* (Ithaca, NY: Cornell Univ. Press, 1958), chaps. 1–4.

The passage quoted here was the opening of the essay. The first sentence, like the title, eschewed the 'Doctor' and simply employed the poet's Christian name. The contrary-to-fact wish implied in the second sentence carries significant implications for understanding what was then the past, the present, and the future of Donne's poetry. It reminds us that no seventeenth-century edition of the *Poems* was accompanied by a life of the author. The writer's insistence that the poetry be read in conjunction with Walton's portrait shows that the situation which George Saintsbury would later describe, whereby people thought Donne worth their notice chiefly because Walton had written about him,[2] was already beginning to give way to one in which 'Donne' would be considered essentially a poet and someone might register surprise at learning that he had also been a preacher. In short, the passage registers a prescient sense of issues taking on new shapes at mid-century, when the project for which Alford's edition of the *Works* (1839) was to be the centerpiece failed to take hold, and understanding Donne's place in literary and cultural history became a much more engaging problem than anyone had thought it a century earlier.

Alford's decision to edit the sermons was not an appendage to a widening interest in the poetry. Nor was it an outgrowth of the Oxford Movement, which is often assumed to have stimulated renewed interest in Donne as a religious writer.[3] Parker's willingness to publish a six-volume *Works* owed a good deal, however, to the legacy of consistently religious concerns displayed by several leading Romantic writers, in whose works Robert Ryan has traced a wide range of contributions to religious politics between 1789 and 1824. For 'approximately three decades, the decades in which Romantic poetry flourished', Ryan argues, 'religion in England seemed to abandon its character as a guarantor of social stability and to become, as it had during the sixteenth and seventeenth centuries, a force for potentially revolutionary change.' He shows how Blake and Wordsworth and other writers consciously attempted to influence, sometimes by subversion and sometimes by revision, the process by which the national religion was being transformed. Even the writings of Byron, Keats, and the Shelleys, whether readers admired them or reproached them, were widely thought to carry authority in religious matters.[4]

Ryan's demonstration that the Romantics made continuing attempts to offer prophetic interventions against the encrustations of religious and political

---

[2] *The Lives of John Donne,* etc., The World's Classics (London: Oxford Univ. Press, 1927), p. xvii.

[3] Cf. Raoul Granqvist, *The Reputation of John Donne 1779–1873* (Stockholm: Almqvist and Wiksell, 1975), 108–10.

[4] Robert M. Ryan, *The Romantic Reformation: Religious Politics in English Literature, 1789–1824* (Cambridge: Cambridge Univ. Press, 1997), 18, and 6, respectively.

power provides a decisive context for understanding the revival of interest in certain of Donne's writings. It helps to make sense, for instance, of the fact that Charles Lamb and Thomas De Quincey held the *Metempsychosis* in high regard. It lays bare the reactionary bias of those who thought that by omitting *Pseudo-Martyr* from his edition Alford failed to include Donne's most important work. Ryan's study also invites renewed exploration of the marginalia that Coleridge wrote into two different copies of Donne's *LXXX Sermons* and into Charles Lamb's copy of Donne's *Poems*. The full complement of these marginalia on Donne, now available in the Bollingen edition, represents a significant part of his massive contribution to 'the Romantic Reformation.' Many annotations on Donne further illustrate that 'Coleridge came to understand himself primarily as a theologian and only secondarily as a poet or a writer of fictions.'[5] They also reveal a deep affinity with Donne. The kindred practices of both writers open up questions about how far conventional distinctions between theology and fiction are helpful in explaining the kinds of cultural work that their writings are capable of performing.

By contrast with the boldness in Coleridge's reading of Donne, the genial presentation of Donne's poetry in *Lowe's* seems almost a throwback to eighteenth-century literary antiquarianism. In 1823 antiquarian interest had issued into the first periodical article ever devoted to Donne's poetry, the piece in *The Retrospective Review* sometimes credited with saving the poet from oblivion, which Donne's reputation as a scholar and a preacher never could have accomplished. By 1846, however, Donne was of practically no interest to antiquarians. The Percy Society declined the opportunity to print his Songs and Sonnets, even when they were offered the chance to include Coleridge's marginal annotations. A few years later the Society was out of business, and Donne was on his way to being known once again as a poet.[6]

DR DONNE'S POETICAL WORKS

Some thirty years ago, with prodigious resourcefulness, Raoul Granqvist assembled nearly all the most significant data for generating a portrait of what Donne looked like in print during the late eighteenth and early nineteenth centuries. Donne was known principally through the following sources: (1) the editions of Alexander Pope's *Works*, where Satires II and IV were often printed along with 'translations' of them; (2) Samuel Johnson's *Life of Cowley*, in which Donne was made to stand as the head of the metaphysical school of

---

[5] Ibid. 10.   [6] Granqvist, *The Reputation of John Donne*, 67.

poets and in which excerpts from his poems served to illustrate features of the metaphysical style; (3) biographical dictionaries, in which Donne was included chiefly because he had been a writer and in some of which it was acknowledged that, although his poems were virtually unread, still 'the name of Dr. Donne is now more generally known as a poet than in any other capacity'; and (4) three collections of English poetry in which Donne was included, those of John Bell (1779), Robert Anderson (1793), and Alexander Chalmers (1810).[7] These editions were, like the only other eighteenth-century edition of Donne's poems (Tonson's, 1719), based on the last seventeenth-century edition; they were unlike all the seventeenth-century editions in that they were prefaced by a life of the author. Most of what was printed in the biographical dictionaries and editions owed a good bit to what, after 1796, became a fifth major—and increasingly the leading—representation of Donne in print, Walton's *Life*, which promoted an interest that had little to do with his having written poetry.

Donne had not been included in the series for which Dr Johnson therefore did not write his life. What is less well known is that Walton's *Lives*, which had long been out of print, was one of Johnson's favorite books. In fact, Boswell reveals that in 1774 the Great Cham had called for Walton's *Lives* to 'be benoted a little' and that he subsequently contributed to plans for a new edition, urging that all the seventeenth-century editions be collected. Johnson also proposed that the new editor compile 'a critical catalogue' of all the works of the different persons whose lives were written by Walton.[8] Meanwhile, the entry in the *Biographica Britannica* had begun to supplement Walton's information about Donne's family. It called attention to his prose writings, especially *Biathanatos* and *Pseudo-Martyr*, 'which contains an unanswerable confutation of the Papal Supremacy.' It also located a basis for paying attention to Donne that suggests how much the popularity of Walton's version may have owed to its affinities with the novel:

There is something in the private character of Dr. Donne which attaches the mind, and renders the contemplation of it pleasing and interesting even at the present day. This arises from the story of his marriage, the difficulties in which that event involved him, and the amiable sensibilities which he appears to have displayed in all the relations and circumstances of Life.[9]

These remarks hinted at the principal grounds on which many readers would look into Donne's poetry. By the 1840s newly printed copies of Walton's *Lives* largely displaced the other media through which Donne had been known.

[7] Andrew Kippis, 'Donne', in *Biographica Britannica*, 2nd edn (London: John Nichols, 1793), v. 336, 337.
[8] James Boswell, *Life of Johnson* (London: Oxford Univ. Press, 1953), 566–7, 627, 694; cf. also 563, 798.
[9] Kippis, 'Donne', 337.

At the turn from the eighteenth to the nineteenth century the new editions of the British poets that included Donne had all offered biographical information adapted from Walton. John Bell's edition printed the poems in three volumes, the first of which contained an engraving of 'John Donne, D.D.', made by Thomas Cook in 1778.[10] Bell prefaced the poetry with the penultimate version (1670) of Walton's *Life*, probably because it did not contain the long account of Donne's vision of his wife while he was at Paris, which was commonly thought to be the most prominent instance of the author's naive credulity. The brief 'Life' that appeared fourteen years later in Anderson's *Complete Edition of the Poets of Great Britain* offered a more radical revision of Walton. It traced Donne's ancestry back to his maternal grandfather, Heywood the Epigrammatist, and it cited Ben Jonson's remark that this lineage made him 'originally a poet.' Placing Donne at Lincoln's Inn well in advance of his twentieth year, it offered a perspective that has at various times been revived: Donne 'divided his studies between law and poetry' and 'about this time, he composed most of his love poems, and other levities and pieces of humour, which sufficiently established his poetical reputation, and procured him the acquaintance of all those of his own age, who were most distinguished for acuteness of wit, and gaiety of temper.'[11] In treating the rest of Donne's life, Anderson removed all reference to the central struggle around which Walton had organized his story, Donne's long resistance to taking holy orders. His breezy account sent Donne readily and easily into the church: shortly after his return from the Continent with Sir Robert Drury, Donne was persuaded by King James to take holy orders, and straightaway he began mouthing sermons full of 'the pedantry of the times.' Lining up behind the dominant literary theorists of the day, Anderson sought to endorse the superior refinement of modern culture. He distanced his view of the poetry from that of Donne's contemporaries, 'all' of whom 'seem to have rated his performances beyond their just value.' He repeated the characteristic charges against the unnaturalness of Donne's thought and 'the carelessness of his versification.' He cited Dryden, Pope, and Johnson to clinch the case according to which Donne, for all his 'wit' and 'prodigious richness of fancy', was uncouth and almost altogether lacking in dignity.

This is the view that persisted in literary handbooks for decades, unmitigated by the insights of the writers for the *Retrospective Review*, *Arcturus*, *Lowe's*, and other periodicals in which the reading of Donne's poems was recommended.

[10] *The Poets of Great Britain Complete, from Chaucer to Churchill*, ed. John Bell (Edinburgh: Mundell, 1779). For a helpful study of this series, see Thomas F. Bonnell, 'John Bell's *Poets of Great Britain*: The "Little Trifling Edition" Revisited', *MP*, 85 (1987), 128–52.

[11] Anderson, 'Life of Donne', *A Complete Edition of the Poets of Great Britain* (London: James Evans, 1793), iv. 3.

Henry Hallam's *Introduction to the Literature of Europe,* for instance, dismissed Donne as the founder of a metaphysical school of poetry that showed a love for 'vicious novelties' and failed utterly to conform to 'sound principles of criticism' or to participate in the 'diffusion of classical knowledge.' Hallam pronounced Donne 'the most inharmonious of our versifiers' and sought to dissuade potential readers by pronouncing that 'it would perhaps be difficult to select three passages that we should care to read again.'[12] It was not Donne's reputation as a poet but fascination with his life's story that prompted readers to look into his poems.

THE ZOUCH EDITION OF WALTON'S *LIVES*

Although Thomas Zouch (1727–1815) played a decisive role in establishing the priority of Walton's *Life of Donne,* his work has received little attention, and estimates of its value have been decidedly negative. When in 1796 Zouch brought out the first new edition of the *Lives* in more than a hundred years, the book was a handsome folio volume, beautifully produced and replete with learned annotations. Zouch provided a good deal of new biographical information, especially about the various persons mentioned in the narrative. Yet R. C. Bald dismissed Zouch's work on the grounds that his annotations made little contribution to the history of writing Donne's life.[13] What Bald failed to appreciate was the decisive role played by Zouch in remaking Donne into a subject of interest and in creating the conditions for the publication of a six-volume edition of his *Works.* Zouch's project was part of an explosion of interest during a 'studious biographical age' that redefined Donne in broader terms than either Walton or Anderson had been thinking.[14] His work met with success, and he found that a less expensive edition was called for. This was published in a smaller format in 1807. Half a dozen years later the bibliographer Philip Bliss endorsed the opinion that there was not 'a life written with more

---

[12] Henry Hallam, *Introduction to the Literature of Europe in the Fifteenth, Sixteenth, and Seventeenth Centuries,* 4 vols. (1837; repr., Paris: Baudry's European Library, 1839), iii. 284.

[13] R. C. Bald, *John Donne: A Life* (Oxford: Oxford Univ. Press, 1970), 15. Zouch's edition of the *Lives* was published at York, in 1796. Subsequent references to this edition are given parenthetically.

[14] Notices of Donne appeared in *The Biographical Magazine* (1776), the *Nouveau Dictionnaire Historique* (1779), *The Biographical Magazine, Containing Portraits* (1794), the *Encyclopædia Britannica* (1797), the *Universal Biographical Dictionary* (1800), Aiken's *General Biography* (1802), *A New Biographical Dictionary* (1802), and many other publications of this sort. See also Joseph W. Reed, Jr., *English Biography in the Early Nineteenth Century 1801–1838* (New Haven, CT: Yale Univ. Press, 1966), 24 n. See also Granqvist, 55 n., 60–1.

advantage to the subject, or more reputation to the writer' than the first of the *Lives* in the volume, and pronounced that 'Donne's life written by Walton, and enlarged with notes and extracts by Dr. Zouch, is in the hands of every reader.'[15] The *Life* was incorporated into Christopher Wordsworth's *Ecclesiastical Biography* in 1810, and reappeared there in subsequent editions. Granqvist has listed twenty-three editions by Zouch or based on Zouch's work that appeared by the mid-1860s and another dozen dependent upon the editorial work of John Major.[16]

While Granqvist depicted Zouch as a moralizing pedant and proposed in particular that he was complicit with Walton in belittling and suppressing Donne's secular life, such charges are difficult to credit. Zouch appended to Walton's 'Life' a bibliography of virtually all Donne's writings, including much information about when the *Poems* had been published; right down to the end of the nineteenth century many readers relied on this information. Zouch's numerous biographical notes acknowledged a historical distance of more than a hundred years, during which knowledge of the persons with whom Donne had mixed and the historical circumstances in which he had lived had been considerably blurred, especially by partisan loyalties.

What is surprising is that, even though Zouch himself accepted Johnson's estimate of Donne as a poet, his edition of Walton sparked new interest in the poetry. Unfortunately, the first volumes of the *Variorum* to be published have not helped us to recognize this. The commentary editors have missed some opportunities to notice Zouch's work. Where Walton had written only of Donne's relations with Sir Robert Drury, Zouch explicitly identified Elizabeth Drury as the subject of the *Anniversaries* (45 n.) and would seem to deserve acknowledgment in the section that reports the earliest commentary on 'Donne, the Drurys, and Patronage' (vi. 284–5). Certainly Zouch's claim that the 'Obsequies upon the Lord Harrington' was written by Donne as 'his last poem' before taking holy orders (56 n.) should have been reported as the earliest extant comment on the 'Date and Circumstance' of the poem (vi. 612). And with respect to the St Valentine's Day epithalamion, Zouch provides the relevant background to the fact that in 1852 a writer in Dickens's *Household Words* could allude to the opening lines confident that they were well known

[15] Philip Bliss (ed.), *Athenæ Oxonienses. An Exact History of All the Writers and Bishops Who Have Had Their Education in the University of Oxford*, by Anthony à Wood, 3rd edn, 4 vols. (London: F. C. and J. Rivington, et al., 1813–20), ii. (1815) 504, 505. The opinion had been previously expressed by John Hales.

[16] 'Doctor John Donne', *Ecclesiastical Biography; or Lives of Eminent Men, Connected with the History of Religion in England*, 6 vols. (London: F. C. and J. Rivington, 1810), iv. 403–79. See Raoul Granqvist, 'Izaak Walton's *Lives* in the Nineteenth and the Early Twentieth Century: A Study of a Cult Object', *Studia Neophilologica*, 54 (1982), 247–61.

(viii. 373): glossing Walton's report of Donne's visit to the Queen of Bohemia, Zouch had printed the first eight lines of the poem (68 n.).[17] The passage was quoted again in the piece in *Lowe's*. Future volumes of the *Variorum* are likely to notice Zouch's comments on 'An Hymn to God the Father' and 'The Bait.' Walton had quoted the divine poem in full; and as Zouch acknowledged that it 'is not ... embellished with poetical beauties', he directed readers 'desirous of forming a just opinion of ... metaphysical poets' to the *Life of Cowley* (77 n.). He concurred with Walton that 'The Bait' offers evidence that Donne 'could make soft and smooth verses' (76 n.).

Elsewhere, Zouch provided some annotations with more architectonic significance. His note on the Latin poet Prudentius, to whom Walton had compared Donne because they both wrote divine hymns at an advanced age, raised a key question about the shape of Donne's career:

Aurelius Prudentius Clemens, a Christian poet of the fourth century, was a native of Spain. He spent the earlier period of his life in more active scenes, distinguishing himself as an advocate at the bar, a soldier in the camp, and lastly as a courtier in the Imperial Court. He attempted not to write verses until he was advanced in years .... Gyraldus observes, that in his works there is more of religious zeal, than of the beauties of poetry, *Melior omnino Christianus est quam Poeta.* (83 n.)

If, as Walton might have said, it is altogether preferable to be a Christian than a poet, Zouch was in no sense hostile to poetry; nor did he begrudge Donne's having written it. Apropos of Walton's report that Donne responded to his wife's death by saying 'For then, *as the grave is become her house,* so I would hasten to make it mine also, *that we two might there make our beds together in the dark'* (64), Zouch contributed to a burgeoning fascination with Donne's marriage to Anne More by citing analogues from *Romeo and Juliet* and from Euripides's *Hippolytus*, where Theseus laments the death of Phaedra. At the same time he sought to limit the ease with which readers might slip into biographical interpretations of the poetry. Glossing a passage in which Donne declines Bishop Morton's offer of a benefice on the grounds that there had been 'some irregularities' in his earlier life, Zouch pronounced, somewhat defensively:

There is not the least reason to suppose that Mr. Donne ever disgraced his character by any act of immorality. He probably mixed more in the world than he thought consistent with the profession of a clergyman: He had not given that valediction to the pleasures and amusements of life, which he deemed requisite. When he devoted his time to the study of poetry, he chose subjects for his pen, which at a later period of life appeared to him too trifling and ludicrous. (41 n.)

---

[17] 'Dumbledowndeary', *Household Words*, 117 (19 June 1852), 312. The author has been identified as George A. Sala; see *Household Words: A Weekly Journal 1850–1859*, ed. Anne Lohrli (Toronto: University of Toronto Press, 1973), 95.

This was to call attention to one of the most powerful aspects of Walton's interpretation of Donne—and one that became increasingly controverted.

Through the first half of the nineteenth century it was common for writers on Donne to observe two dominant 'faults', one poetic, the other personal. Anna Jameson was more explicit than most in suggesting a connection between them. 'The events of Donne's various life, and the romantic love he inspired and felt', she wrote, 'make us recur to his works, with an interest and a curiosity, which while they give a value to every beauty we can discover, render his faults more glaring,—more provoking,—more intolerable.'[18] The faults that she was willing to enumerate included 'a most perverse taste, and total want of harmony', chilling 'pedantry' and disgusting 'coarseness', and the fact (as she took it) that Donne had spent his youth in 'dissipation' (ii. 95). No details were spelled out. Rather the burden of her chapter was to rehearse 'as true and touching a piece of romance as ever was taken from the page of real life' (ii. 94).

Walton had characterized Donne's passion for Anne More as 'a flattering mischief, that ... carries us to commit Errors with as much ease as whirlwinds remove feathers.' Famously he designated the marriage as 'the remarkable error of his life.'[19] This language suggested to Mrs Jameson that Donne's tenderness of conscience must have been owing in large measure to his experience of marriage. She emphasized the 'sad, and almost sordid misery and penury' experienced by Donne's family in the years following the secret wedding (ii. 102). This interpretation of Walton had been made explicit by Zouch and became decisive in Chalmers's biographical sketch, which drew heavily upon Donne's letters to show that, by the time he went into the church, he 'had relinquished the follies of youth, and had nearly outlived the remembrance of them by others.' Donne's youth had not been 'disgraced' by any 'flagrant turpitude', Chalmers claimed, and in any event after his marriage 'he appears to have become of a serious and thoughtful disposition, his mind alternately exhausted by study, or softened by affliction.' From 1607, when Donne declined Dr Morton's offer of a benefice, he consistently 'displays that character for nice honour and integrity which distinguished ... all his future life, and was accompanied with a heroic generosity.'[20]

The connection that readers had been invited to make between Donne's impulsive passion and his scruples about taking holy orders came clear in Robert Williams's novel of 1838, *Shakspeare and His Friends*, where, with

---

[18] *Loves of the Poets*, 2 vols. (London: Colburn, 1829), ii. 95–6.

[19] Quoted here from the 1675 edition of *The Lives of Dr John Donne; Sir Henry Wotton;* etc., 16, 52, respectively.

[20] Alexander Chalmers (ed.), *The Works of the English Poets from Chaucer to Cowper*, 21 vols. (London: J. Johnson et al., 1810), v. 121, 123, 119, respectively.

a cavalier regard for historical accuracy worthy of comparison with Tom Stoppard's script for *Shakespeare in Love*, the essence of Walton's story is concentrated into a few months' time. Master Donne, freshly returned to the Mermaid from his imprisonment, has already received the offer of a benefice from Dr Morton, even before he is reconciled to Sir George More. He has declined it, he informs Sir Walter Raleigh, on account of 'scruples against entering the priesthood, because I am not of that holy disposition methinks it should require.' This elicits from Raleigh a prescient remark that anticipates Donne's eventual prominence as Walton's Dr Donne: 'I do most truly believe you would do the church infinite honour .... I wish all were as conscientious and as worthy.' Yet, as Raleigh, Shakespeare, Ben Jonson and all the 'chiefest wits' of the time go on to indulge in a sumptuous meal, Donne's coarseness is characteristically intermixed in the portrait. Williams has him denounce the use of forks as a new fangled 'atheistical invention' out of Italy, a 'flying in the face of Providence', which, Donne is made to say, gave men fingers precisely to lay hold of meat.[21] By contrast, Jonson and 'Master Shakspeare' are drawn both as more truly witty and more refined.

WORDSWORTH

For readers familiar with the standard complaints about Donne's poetry Williams's sketch of his table manners must have made a kind of sense: 'Donne's numbers', as Chalmers had put it, 'are certainly the most rugged and uncouth of any of our poets.'[22] To dress Donne as a figure of respectability would require concentration on other parts of the record, not only the portrait supplied by Walton but the line of cultural history to which the *Lives* contributed, including the mature work of the leading poet of the era. By the 1830s there was no writer better able to endorse the rugged and uncouth than Wordsworth. His sonnet in praise of 'Walton's Book of Lives' was inducted as front matter in many mid-nineteenth century editions of those *Lives*. The editors who thus capitalized on Wordsworth's cultural authority, and the readers who fell under its spell, did not necessarily understand the depth and scope of Wordsworth's interest in Donne.

About the time when the *Lyrical Ballads* first appeared in print, Wordsworth seems to have read Donne's poems in Anderson's collection. He copied the

---

[21] [Robert F. Williams], *Shakspeare and his Friends; or, 'The Golden Age' of Merry England*, 3 vols. (London: Henry Colburn, 1838), iii. 175–6, 194.

[22] Chalmers, *Works of the English Poets*, v. 124.

opening of 'Death be not proud' into a manuscript in which he was working on *The Ruined Cottage*.[23] Years later, in 1833, he persuaded Alexander Dyce to include this poem in *Specimens of English Sonnets*: it is 'so eminently characteristic of his manner', he wrote, 'and at the same time so weighty in thought, and vigorous in the expression, that I would entreat you to insert it, though to modern taste it may be repulsive, quaint, and laboured.' Early and late, Wordsworth's interest in Donne was partly antiquarian, partly formal, above all religious, and more theological than Walton's had been. In 1807 he bought a copy of the *LXXX Sermons*. About two years later Coleridge began writing annotations into the margins of the book; many of them posited Donne as a worthy antagonist in thinking through the history of the doctrines of the Trinity and the Redemption. Like Coleridge, Wordsworth returned to the volume from time to time because he found it challenging. In 1830 he remarked, apropos of reading one of Donne's sermons, 'I prefer this Writer because he is so little likely to be explored by others; and is full of excellent matter, though difficult to manage for a modern audience.'[24]

Wordsworth generally thought of Donne in the religious and cultural terms that he came to associate with Walton's *Lives*, rather than as a figure of importance in the history of English poetry. What he valued in Donne and Hooker, Wotton, Herbert, and Sanderson was something for which Walton had specially chosen them as representatives, a breadth of vision that was in no way compromised by their having conformed to the established church. The praise for Donne in the *Ecclesiastical Sketches* first published in 1822 (and later renamed *Ecclesiastical Sonnets*) is characteristically submerged—and the more intriguing for its being framed in terms that Wordsworth twice employed in sonnets praising Milton.

It was uncommon to be thinking of Donne in relation to Milton. It was not unusual for Wordsworth, however, given his having shared the reading of Donne's sermons with Coleridge and given his interest in the potential of the sonnet form. In the *Ecclesiastical Sketches* he was aiming to combine the narrative shape of the old sonnet cycle from Elizabethan times with the national and public perspectives that Milton had shown the form to be capable of bearing. He was extending a precedent set by Milton, who in several sonnets had displaced erotic love with a sublimated love of a patriotic or religious nature. As Wordsworth's remarks about 'Death be not proud' attest,

[23] See Duncan Wu, *Wordsworth's Reading 1770–1799* (Cambridge: Cambridge Univ. Press, 1993), 48.

[24] *The Letters of William and Dorothy Wordsworth*, 2nd edn, *V: The Later Years Part II 1829–1834*, rev. Alan G. Hill from the 1st edn by Ernest de Selincourt (Oxford: Clarendon Press, 1979), 604–5, 257, respectively.

he knew that Donne had partly anticipated Milton in making the sonnet a weighty and vigorous vehicle for a public defense of prophetic religion. Still, where he acknowledged that Donne's verses could seem 'repulsive, quaint, and laboured', Wordsworth admired Milton's sonnets for evincing 'an energetic and varied flow of sound crowding into narrow room more of the combined effect of rhyme and blank verse than can be done by any other kind of verse.'[25] The *Ecclesiastical Sketches* were both formally and thematically consonant with the earlier defenses of the sonnet in 'NUNS fret not at their convent's narrow room' and 'SCORN not the Sonnet.' Their treatment of the Restoration period looked back upon the middle of the seventeenth century as a time when the nation had 'felt the weight of too much liberty', and 'when a damp | Fell round the path of Milton', who nonetheless made the sonnet 'a trumpet' from which to blow 'Soul-animating strains.' Precisely as a prophetic writer Milton remained for Wordsworth long after 1807, as Ryan makes clear, 'his model—the national religious poet who had been shaped, like himself, by experience of radical politics and who had gone on to become the moral conscience of his generation.'[26]

The political and religious vision that informs Wordsworth's sequence is moderate, tolerant, generous, and full of sympathy. It affirms what was good in monastic life and praises the reformers. It recognizes Milton and Walton as contemporaries and sees them both as working to foster the nation's spiritual health. In Wordsworth's view, what joined Walton and Milton was their having both lived in a period marked by 'wantonness' and 'Circean revels' presided over by 'Charles the Second' (sonnet III of the 3d series), when England was 'sink[ing] | Into a gulf' as 'bigotry ... swallow[ed] the good name, | And ... life-blood' of the nation. The Poets who 'loathed' this 'misery [and] shame' and the Historians who shrunk from that condition were more sensitive than the contemporary writers castigated in the 'London, 1802' sonnet for their 'selfish' partisanship. Milton's political commitment had made him a traveller 'on life's common way', and his heart had embraced 'lowly duties.' Wordsworth's was an original conception of Milton, one that recalled his having been a schoolmaster, and one that envisaged personal virtue as a source of public good. Similarly, when Wordsworth brought Milton back in the *Ecclesiastical Sketches* to counter the 'Circean revels' presided over by Charles I's untaught and undisciplined son, he emphasized a corner of the record in which Milton's choice of a universal theme for *Paradise Lost* aligned

[25] Christopher Wordsworth, *Memoirs of William Wordsworth*, ed. Henry Reed, 2 vols. (Boston: Ticknor, Reed, and Fields, 1851), i. 286 n.

[26] Ryan, *The Romantic Reformation*, 99; see also 5, 13–18, 33–7, 99–100. Quotations of Wordsworth's poetry are from *The Poetical Works of William Wordsworth: Miscellaneous Sonnets, etc.*, ed. E. de Selincourt and Helen Darbishire, 2nd edn (Oxford: Clarendon, 1954).

him, surprisingly, with those other lovers of a light beyond partisan heat, the Cambridge Platonists:

Latitudinarianism

Yet Truth is keenly sought for, and the wind
Charged with rich words poured out in thought's defence;
Whether the Church inspire that eloquence,
Or a Platonic Piety confined
To the sole temple of the inward mind;
And One there is who builds immortal lays,
Though doomed to tread in solitary ways,
Darkness before and danger's voice behind;
Yet not alone, nor helpless to repel
Sad thoughts; for from above the starry sphere
Come secrets, whispered nightly to his ear;
And the pure spirit of celestial light
Shines through his soul–'that he may see and tell
Of things invisible to mortal sight.'

In the 1822 edition of *Ecclesiastical Sketches* and in the editions published after 1839, 'Walton's Book of Lives' follows immediately after this poem. It picks up the imagery of 'celestial light' and transports it outward from the 'inward mind' and solitary 'soul' back to the 'starry sphere', where it is in full public view and can serve, even more than 'lonely tapers', as a 'guide.' At the same time the 'very names' of Walton's heroes, which are present with a special sort of power for their not being explicitly enunciated in the poem, are 'like stars' dwelling 'apart':

Walton's Book of Lives

There are no colors in the fairest sky
So fair as these. The feather, whence the pen
Was shaped that traced the lives of these good men,
Dropped from an Angel's wing. With moistened eye
We read of faith and purest charity
In Statesman, Priest, and humble Citizen:
Oh could we copy their mild virtues, then
What joy to live, what blessedness to die!
Methinks their very names shine still and bright;
Apart—like glow-worms on a summer night;
Or lonely tapers when from far they fling
A guiding ray; or seen—like stars on high,
Satellites burning in a lucid ring
Around meek Walton's heavenly memory.

The omission of the names of Walton's five subjects is consistent with Wordsworth's characteristic practice in this period. In the years after Waterloo, when he wrote about Wellington without naming him, Wordsworth took an increasingly active interest in biography. In 1820 he published a prose biography of a rural priest, Robert Walker, and yet in 'The River Duddon' sonnet series he withheld the proper name even as he praised Walker as a 'Teacher' and 'Pastor', just as he had done in the seventh book of *The Excursion* where he celebrated Walker's 'temperance' and 'industry' and 'constant motion.'[27] Similarly, in the Walton sonnet, the 'mild virtues' of the quiet heroes are trumpeted only in the heavily accented opening of the penultimate line. The imagery is visual rather than aural: they shine 'bright' and yet 'meekly' in an inward paradise, the 'heavenly memory' that is the monument both to 'the lives of these good men' wrought by this 'humble Citizen' and to later readers' appreciation for Walton's achievement.

Just as Wordsworth worked with the language of *Paradise Lost* in 'Latitu-dinarianism', so here he borrowed from the very book he celebrated. Walton had said that Donne was 'always preaching to himself, like an angel from a cloud, but in none.' He had emphasized Donne's 'charity' to prisoners and to poor scholars and portrayed him as 'a shining light among his old friends.' He painted Hooker, moreover, as 'mild and humble' and also 'meek.'[28] 'Meek' likewise appeared in the *Life of Donne*, where Walton applied it first to Donne's reluctance to enter the ministry and then, still more curiously, to Moses:

In the first and most blessed times of Christianity, when the clergy were looked upon with reverence, ... those only were then judged worthy the ministry, whose quiet and meek spirits did make them look upon that sacred calling with an humble adoration and fear to undertake it; which indeed requires such great degrees of *humility*, and *labour*, and *care*, that none but such were then thought worthy of that celestial dignity; and such only were then sought out, and solicited to undertake it. This I have mentioned, because forwardness and inconsideration could not in Mr. Donne, as in many others, be an argument of insufficiency or unfitness; for he had considered long, and had many strifes within himself, concerning the strictness of life and competency of learning required in such as enter into sacred orders; and doubtless, considering his own demerits, did humbly ask God with St. Paul, 'Lord, who is sufficient for these things?' and with meek Moses, 'Lord, who am I?'   (55)

Walton's deployment of the word 'meek' proved sufficiently troubling that Zouch's gloss attempted to explain it away: 'A reader, who hath considered with attention the history of Moses, as recorded in the sacred writings, will

---

[27] See Eric C. Walker, 'Wordsworth as Prose Biographer', *JEGP*, 89 (1990), 330–44.

[28] These and other verbal borrowings were pointed out by Abbie Findlay Potts in her notes on *The Ecclesiastical Sonnets of William Wordsworth: A Critical Edition* (New Haven, CT: Yale Univ. Press, 1922), 283.

not easily acknowledge the propriety of applying the quality of *meekness* to this great leader of the Israelites. He seems rather to have been susceptible of a warmth of temper.' Zouch then quotes a learned exegete who proposed an alternate translation for the Hebrew of Numbers 12:3, according to which the sacred text 'gives a sense entirely different ... and more consistent with the character of Moses. "He was highly favoured with answers (from God) above all the men which were upon the face of the earth."' What Zouch missed is that in his Christmas sermon for 1627 Donne himself had considered in some detail the saying according to which Moses had been called '*the meekest man upon earth.*'

For Wordsworth 'meekness' was one of a constellation of words to be rescued from popular disdain and made newly serviceable for promoting sympathetic understanding. Early on in the *Sketches*, writing of the Druids and of the early Christians, he made bold to use the term 'meek' in connection with 'doctrines' that have from his own time to ours been commonly thought to represent a threat to autonomous poetic creativity:

> Haughty the Bard: can these meek doctrines blight
> His transports? wither his heroic strains?[29]

These questions, posed when Wordsworth was fifty-one, seem already to acknowledge the charge, which gathered force through the rest of his life, according to which he was said to have become a reactionary. This influential view of Wordsworth's career was sealed when, in the year after the first volume of *The Recluse* was published and only a few months before he wrote his influential article on Donne, William Minto wrote for *The Nineteenth Century* on 'Wordsworth's Great Failure.' Minto proposed that after 1807 Wordsworth's attempt to write a great philosophical poem had blighted his poetic work. Further dissemination of this interpretation came with the entry on Wordsworth that Minto contributed to the eleventh edition of the *Encyclopædia Britannica.*[30]

The sonnet on 'Clerical Integrity' that follows 'Walton's Book of Lives' shows a quality of imaginative boldness that the Arnoldian tradition in which Minto was writing has obscured. This poem is an integral part of Wordsworth's prophetic redefinition in the *Sketches* of what was enduringly significant in seventeenth-century English religion. Instead of projecting the encrusted denominationalism of contemporary politics onto the past,

[29] See Wordsworth's sonnet, 'Trepidation of the Druids', *Poetical Works*, iii. 343.
[30] 'Wordsworth's Great Failure' originally appeared in *The Nineteenth Century*, 26 (1889), 435–51. Its enduring significance is attested by its being the only nineteenth-century criticism chosen for inclusion in *Wordsworth's Mind and Art*, ed. A. W. Thomson (Edinburgh: Oliver and Boyd, 1969), 10–27.

Wordsworth pointed a way forward by endorsing integrity wherever it can be discerned. He did not accept the facile inference that because Donne had taken orders in the church his life was necessarily at cross purposes with those of earnest dissenters who were (according to Milton's phrase) 'church-outed by the prelates.' Knowing the story of Donne's penury in the years after his marriage, Wordsworth recognized an experiential kinship between him and the nonconformist ministers who were ejected after the Restoration: 'Nor shall the eternal roll of praise reject | Those Unconforming.' Like Walton's Donne, who paid for his marriage by suffering separation from his beloved and imprisonment and poverty, these exiles were 'voluntary prey | To poverty, and grief, and disrespect' who 'cast the future upon Providence', just as Milton's Adam and Eve did. In short, in the third series of *Ecclesiastical Sonnets*, where Wordsworth expressed his greatest praise for the 'name' of Donne without ever mentioning it, he did so in terms that moved beyond the partisanship so characteristic of the seventeenth century. In their treatment of ecclesiastical history these poems, almost silent as they are about the civil wars, project a broader, more tolerant vision of English religion than Milton or Donne, Walton or even Richard Baxter had been able to foster.

Wordsworth's rationale for this breadth of vision may be seen in a letter of 1824 to Walter Savage Landor, who had written him that he was 'disgusted at all things treating of religion.' Wordsworth's return letter, of 21 January, began with an expression of frustration at how long he had been waiting for the publication of Landor's *Imaginary Conversations*. When Landor's work appeared it contained, inter alia, a conversation in which Walton was made to discuss a passion that, allegedly, Donne had conceived in his early twenties for a young 'damsel' who inspired some of his early trifles. (This conversation will be taken up in Chapter 5.) It was another of the conversations, however, from which Robert Southey had recently read aloud, that seems to have prompted Wordsworth to write in the letter:

All religions owe their origin or acceptation to the wish of the human heart to supply in another state of existence the deficiencies of this, and to carry still nearer to perfection whatever we admire in our present condition; so that there must be many modes of expression, arising out of this coincidence, or rather identity of feeling, common to all Mythologies.

Then Wordsworth went on to address directly his friend's aversion to religion, enlisting ideas that had recently informed his representation of Donne and Milton, and of Walton and the Restoration dissenting ministers:

This leads to a remark in your last, 'that you are disgusted with all books that treat of religion.' I am afraid it is a bad sign in me, that I have little relish for any other—even in poetry it is the imaginative only, viz., that which is conversant [with], or turns upon infinity, that powerfully affects me,—perhaps I ought to explain: I mean to say that, unless in those passages where things are lost in each other, and limits vanish, and aspirations are raised, I read with something too much like indifference.[31]

The implications for public behaviour lodged in these remarks are consistent with the fact that Wordsworth steadfastly resisted giving his unqualified support to any of the religious parties who in the next twenty-five years of his life sought to appropriate the cultural authority of his name. This resistance had implications for Wordsworth's poetic practice. It also helps to clarify his significance for the first Donne Revival, which for all the religious language in Dr Donne's poetry made little of the poems. In February, 1840, just months after Henry Alford had brought out his edition of Donne's *Works*, Wordsworth wrote to him that he had long been reluctant to write explicitly and frequently about 'the mysteries of Christian faith, not from a want of a due sense of their momentous nature; but the contrary. I felt it far too deeply to venture on handling the subject as familiarly as many scruple not to do.'[32] The proximate occasion of Wordsworth's letter was his reception of an essay on his poetry that Alford had just contributed to a regional periodical. His correspondent's article set out a 'distinction' that rang true to Wordsworth between 'religious poetry and versified religion': 'The former', Alford wrote, 'ranges at a distance from the subject, and brings the mind and feelings into unconscious and comely subjection, clearing the temple, as it were, of intruders, before the solemn music of spiritual truth bursts on the ear of the soul; the latter hitches into doggrel, better or worse, the deepest solemnities of our faith, talks in texts, and descants on doctrines; forbids the gentle and inquiring, disgusts the practised ear of taste, and furnishes laughing matter for the trifling.'[33] Alford's remarks about 'versified Religion' go some distance towards explaining how he had handled some of Donne's 'trifling' poems in his edition. Keenly interested in poetry himself, Alford was quite aware that he had very different ideas about it from Donne's.

ALFORD'S EDITION AND THE ROMANTIC REFORMATION

It is worth exploring how an interest in Donne developed within the career of Henry Alford (1810–71), because, with the exception of Coleridge, Alford gave more time to reading Donne than probably any other person who lived

---

[31] *Letters, IV: The Later Years, 1821–1828*, 2nd edn (1978), 243–5.
[32] *Letters, VII: The Later Years, 1840–1853*, 2nd edn (1988), 23.
[33] See Alford's 'Wordsworth', *Dearden's Miscellany*, 3 (Feb. 1840), 108.

in the first half of the nineteenth century. Alford came to Donne early. He spent a good part of his twenties making his way through the corpus, and chose to make an edition of Donne's sermons the first serious literary labor of his adult life. He then turned to a different sort of editorial work, in which he eventually distinguished himself. In 1839, as editor of a newly founded Nottingham periodical called *Dearden's Miscellany*, he wrote a series of essays called 'Chapters on Poetry and Poets.' Among these were two on Wordsworth (the second examined 'London, 1802' in detail) and, later, others on Byron and Keats. The first of the essays on Wordsworth worked toward a sustained discussion of 'The Excursion', a poem 'full of quiet beauty and touching descriptions of the human heart' in which the poet, despite the critics' charge that he is 'without Christianity', is said by Alford to have 'done more than most divines who have written, to bind up the charities and feelings of this our human life ... with religious faith.' The passage to which Wordsworth responded favorably in his letter appeared in the conclusion of the essay, immediately following Alford's praise for the poet's having tactfully avoided enunciating 'the lofty mysteries of our creed by their theological appellations.' In the essay that followed, Alford proposed that in Wordsworth's hand the sonnet, drawing from 'common life and everyday feelings and sights' to make 'sparkling jewels', could be seen to belong 'to the very highest class of Poetry.'[34]

What Alford did not say of course was that for some time he had been writing sonnets himself. During his time at Cambridge, where he was an undergraduate and later a Fellow at Trinity, he had found himself 'surrounded with professors of religion', as he said, 'many of them neither moral nor religious.'[35] He recoiled from the chilling brutality that he observed in many instructors' behavior. He made a good friend, however, in Christopher Wordsworth, the poet's brother; and he found community first in W. M. Thackeray's essay club and then in the Cambridge Apostles. His best friends in these years included Arthur Hallam, Alfred Tennyson, and James Spedding. In their company he took to literary pursuits, renewing his religious aspirations by writing verse. *The School of the Heart and Other Poems* reprinted many short pieces that Alford had published before his twenty-second birthday. In August 1835, he sent his verses to Christopher's brother as 'some acknowledgment ... [of the] many

[34] See 'Wordsworth', 106–8; 'Wordsworth's Sonnets', *Dearden's Miscellany*, 3 (Apr. 1840), 245. Later correspondence between Wordsworth and Alford included an exchange on sonnets. In a letter of 6 Mar. 1844, Wordsworth wrote to Alford about additions he had made to the *Ecclesiastical Sonnets* of still unpublished poems on the English liturgy. Concerning the importance ascribed by nineteenth-century readers to 'The Excursion' on the grounds that it was a religious poem, see Ryan, *The Romantic Reformation*, 34–6, 80–1, 100–18.

[35] Alford's letters are quoted by Augustus J. C. Hare, in *Biographical Sketches* (London: George Allen, 1895), 99–100.

trains of thought in which your own influence may be traced', and William replied politely.[36] Three years later, during the period when he was preparing Donne's *Works* for the press, Alford and his wife were entertained at Rydal Mount by Mrs Wordsworth.

In editing Donne it had been no part of Alford's original intention to include any of the poetry. He claimed in the Editor's Preface that he had begun reading Donne's sermons in 1831 and that he immediately recognized that 'their republication [was] ... highly desirable', well in advance of discovering that the *Table Talk* of Coleridge provided encouragement for his project. At first he had considerable difficulty finding a publisher. Eventually John W. Parker took on the project, and Alford expanded his original intention to provide a selection of the sermons in four volumes. Parker enabled him to offer them all in six, and others of Donne's writings to boot. In the final volume Alford printed a number of Donne's poems. It was consistent with his conception of Donne as a preacher that he selected for inclusion the *Divine Poems* and a few other poems of a 'theological ... stamp.' He avoided what he considered the 'misrepresentation' of Donne's 'genius' found in his copy-text, the 1633 edition, with its 'strange jumble of subjects' and disorderly arrangement, 'where Hymns and Love-elegies ... are recklessly placed in company.' Given what we know from his own poetic theory, we can infer that Alford regarded such poems as 'The Funeral' and 'The Relic', 'The Flea' and 'The Canonization', which contain religious language wittily turned to what he considered 'trifling' uses, as inconsistent with his aims. Alford did not wish Donne's youthful secular verse erased from the record, however. In fact, he called for 'the whole Poems' to be 'well edited' and recommended that 'the Satires especially would repay the labour.'[37]

The basis of Alford's enthusiasm for Donne's sermons comes clear in his own poetry, which locates an ideal in the era that Walton had celebrated. *The School of the Heart* won early approval from John Henry Newman, who seems to have had no particular interest in Donne.[38] Apart from the title poem (which includes a section headed by an epigraph from Donne's 'Obsequies upon the Lord Harrington'), much of the volume is filled out with youthful autobiographical sonnets. One is designated 'Written in an Interval of Melancholy Foreboding Respecting the Church'; Alford, in a manner

[36] See Peter Allen, *The Cambridge Apostles: The Early Years* (Cambridge: Cambridge Univ. Press, 1978), 136–8; Wordsworth, *Letters VI: The Later Years 1835–1839*, 2nd edn (1982), 94. Alford's letter is quoted in the footnote.

[37] Alford, Editor's Preface, *The Works of John Donne, D.D., Dean of Saint Paul's, 1621–1631. With a Memoir of His Life*, 6 vols. (London: John W. Parker, 1839), i, pp. v–vii; 'Life of Dr. Donne', i, p. xxiv.

[38] See *The Letters and Diaries of John Henry Newman, V: Liberalism in Oxford January 1835 to December 1836*, ed. Thomas Gornall, S.J. (Oxford: Clarendon, 1981), 377.

reminiscent of the address to Milton in 'London, 1802', invokes the memory
of Herbert and Crashaw, who 'set our smouldering energies on flame.' The
sonnet on the facing page shows that Alford had adopted another perspective
that would come a century later to be associated with the claim that a
'dissociation of sensibility' had set in during the later seventeenth century: its
theme is the belatedness of current piety, which has no 'song of praise' to offer
the Lord 'in these latter days' that has not already been 'sung' in 'ages' past.[39]
Even before Alford decided to edit Donne's sermons he had made a break with
the narrow evangelical piety in which he had been schooled. He was caught
up in the growing enthusiasm for English divinity of the late sixteenth and
seventeenth centuries that was abroad at the time of his ordination and that
prompted him in the early months of his married life to read Hooker with
his bride.

Despite many faults in his edition of Donne, Alford went on to have
a distinguished career as a scholar. He worked towards an integration of
religious and literary pursuits that he could not have imagined during his
early months in Cambridge. Having recognized during several months spent
in Bonn in 1847 the superiority of German textual criticism of the New
Testament, he went on to make his name in biblical studies as a first-
rate textual scholar. He brought out a variorum edition of the Greek New
Testament in which he gave the various readings in more detail than English
readers had ever seen. Some features of this edition made it influential for
the next half century: along with the various readings, it provided glosses for
many words with reference to Hellenistic usage, and Alford printed all this
information in a form meant to give the user the grounds for coming to an
independent judgment about the readings and the senses of the words. We
might suppose that it was in virtue of his first editing project that Alford
was subsequently able to work out interpretative canons that resemble those
embraced by the editors of the Donne Variorum. Alford freely confessed,
however, that in editing Donne's poetry he had not known what he was
doing. The more profound connection between Alford and Donne lies in their
common interest in fostering respectful tolerance among diverse interpretative
communities. Once he distanced himself from Anglo-Catholicism, Alford was
appointed Dean of Canterbury. He also became one of the early members of
the Metaphysical Society. From 1866 to 1870 he served as the first editor of *The
Contemporary Review*. His new periodical published many articles on religious
poetry and a number of distinguished theoretical essays on the function of
poetry in an age of unbelief. It gained a reputation for fair-minded inquiry into

[39] Henry Alford, *The School of the Heart and Other Poems*, 2 vols. (London: Longman and
Co.; Cambridge: J. and J. J. Deighton, 1835), i. 36–7.

the great intellectual conflicts of the day and numbered among its contributors Matthew Arnold, John Ruskin, Walter Pater, Herbert Spencer, and Thomas Huxley.[40]

For his Donne scholarship, Alford has always been judged harshly: through his mature career his first literary endeavor as a graduate of Cambridge was an embarrassment to him. Almost as soon as the Donne edition appeared, it elicited a testy letter to the editor of *The British Magazine and Monthly Register* from 'A Lover of Old English Divinity and Literature', who pointed out many errors and pronounced it 'not a worthy companion to Mr. Keble's Hooker.' The writer was another young clergyman, J. C. Robertson, who, having invested in the six volumes, was using them to study Donne in detail. A year later Robertson wrote for *The Gentleman's Magazine* an elaborate set of 'Notes on the Life and Works of Dr. Donne.' Based on study of the Loseley manuscripts and research in the British Museum, these 'Notes' augmented what was known about Donne from Walton, Zouch, Major, and the makers of biographical dictionaries. There will be occasion in Chapter 4 to examine some of the particulars. Here, it is sufficient to note that Robertson's strictures established the bad name of Alford's edition to which subsequent editors have routinely referred.[41] In the 1870s Grosart condemned it as 'a literary *fiasco*.'[42] In the 1890s Gosse reported that Alford had 'bitterly lamented the publication of this edition.'[43] Alford's own memoirs make but the briefest mention of the Donne project, and he claims (against what he had written in the preface to the edition) that it had been 'undertaken at the request of Mr. Parker.'[44] Among the few critics in the twentieth century who deigned even to refer to Alford's edition, Evelyn Simpson pronounced its representation of Donne's poems as 'worthless.'[45]

The first volumes of the *Variorum* enable us to reopen consideration of Alford's work as an editor of the poetry. Virtually all the poems that appear in Volume 6, on the *Anniversaries* and funeral verses, were included by Alford. This tells us something about what parts of Donne's poetry seemed to him

[40] See the entry on Alford, written by W[illiam] H[enry] F[remantle], in *DNB*, 22 vols. (Oxford: Oxford Univ. Press, 1917), i. 282–4.

[41] [J. C. Robertson], 'The Rev. H. Alford's Edition of Donne', *The British Magazine and Monthly Register of Religious and Ecclesiastical Information*, 15 (1839), 534–7; *The Gentleman's Magazine*, new ser., 16 (1841), 25–32.

[42] Alexander B. Grosart, Preface, *The Complete Poems of John Donne, D.D.*, The Fuller Worthies' Library, 2 vols. ([London: printed for private circulation], 1872–3), i, p. xiv.

[43] Edmund Gosse, Preface, *The Life and Letters of John Donne Dean of St. Paul's*, 2 vols. (London: Heinemann, 1899; repr., Gloucester, MA: Peter Smith, 1959), i, p. x.

[44] *Life, Journals and Letters of Henry Alford, D.D.*, ed. [Frances Alford] (London: Rivingtons, 1873), 112.

[45] Evelyn M. Simpson, *A Study of the Prose Works of John Donne*, 2nd edn (Oxford: Clarendon, 1948), 286.

most compatible with Walton's portrait of a man whose own life had become a 'holy dying.' Attending to the tables in the *Variorum* that report verbal variants from modern editions, it is clear that many readings found in Alford are eccentric, especially in his text of *The Second Anniversary*, where more than half a dozen variants are utterly unique to his edition. Yet this fact contains a surprise: although Alford was just beginning to learn about editing, he did not slavishly reproduce his copy-text. He managed to locate a number of points at which the received texts needed attention; and he contributed to a growing desire, which along with Coleridge he was one of the first to articulate, for a new edition of the complete poems.[46]

With respect to the poetry, Alford made one especially inspired editorial innovation: his romantic assumptions about the importance of a return to origins contributed to his decision to make the edition of 1633 his copy-text. Alford thereby broke a hundred-and-twenty-year line of editorial practice according to which each edition after that of 1669 had been based chiefly on a predecessor in a sequence of transmission that preserved old errors and introduced new ones. The fact that wherever he could Alford used 1633 as his copy-text meant that, where 1633 was good, Alford was good, almost despite himself. His versions of the 'Elegia', the 'Elegy on the Lady Markham', and especially the 'Elegy upon the Death of Mrs. Bulstrode' ('Language, thou art too narrow') are generally superior to all the previous modern editions. In view of the collations performed half a century later by C. E. Norton and E. K. Chambers, and then more extensively by Grierson, we can say at the very least that Alford made an inspired guess when he fixed on the seventeenth-century edition that is in many respects superior to all the others. Rather than joining the chorus that has castigated him for suppressing much of Donne's poetry, allegedly on the grounds of some moralizing prudery, we can acknowledge that he contributed materially to a growing interest in Donne's poetry by bringing together with the sermons a large offering of the poems, including (from the love poems) 'The Bait', 'A Valediction Forbidding Mourning', and 'The Will.'

DONNE'S LOVE POETRY AND COLERIDGE'S MARGINALIA

The views expressed in the article in *Lowe's* are indicative of a new fascination with the poetry of Dr Donne, which the author sought carefully to delimit. In

---

[46] Occasionally Alford's edition of the poetry showed flashes of editorial genius. In printing the verse letter 'To Mr. B.B.', he proposed that the printed word 'nurse' was an erroneous transcription of 'Muse.' This shrewd proposal is confirmed by several manuscripts.

keeping with Pope's admiration for the poet's vitality, with Zouch's goal of placing Walton's subject in his historical milieu, and with Alford's selection of poems that seemed fittingly to come from the pen of a great preacher, the anonymous essayist praised the satires and the funeral poems. Yet in a gesture likely to play into Mrs Jameson's promotion of the idea that Donne had been a great lover, he quoted from 'A Valediction Forbidding Mourning', 'The Good Morrow', 'The Ecstasy', and 'The Blossom', aiming 'to sharpen the appetite of the lover of poetry, and send him to their source.' Among these four poems, the first named was well known. Dr Johnson had called attention to it when he remarked that 'it may be doubted whether absurdity or ingenuity has the better claim' to its comparison of parting lovers to a pair of compasses.[47] A more positive estimate descended from Walton, who quoted it in full, though inaccurately from memory it seems, in his third revision. The other three lyrics were little known, rarely quoted, and hardly ever commented upon in print. This was the case with the great majority of poems that had first been designated 'Songs and Sonets' in the 1635 edition, a designation that had long since been ignored as critics came to speak dismissively of Donne's 'amatory verses' as part of the youthful works that, according to Walton, Donne himself had dismissed. Few writers were persuaded that these poems belonged among those to which Ben Jonson referred when he remarked that the poet wrote 'all his best pieces err he was 25 years old.'[48]

Nonetheless, a tendency was gaining force to divide the love poems into two distinct categories: those to be preserved because of their exalted portrayal of love and those that deserved consignment to oblivion. When G. H. Lewes praised 'The Good Morrow' as indicative of the sincerity of Donne's passion and Margaret Fuller quoted 'The Ecstasy' to help illustrate her 'ideal of love and marriage',[49] they contributed to a rejection of Alford's claim that in Elizabethan times the women who appeared in love poems were often imaginary. The quasi-Wordsworthian norm by which the poet ought to speak sincerely in his own voice meant that admirers of Donne discreetly averted their eyes from the more lascivious and cynical lyrics. With the exception of the song 'Go, and catch a falling star' and of Coleridge's marginal comments on 'The Flea', 'Woman's Constancy', and 'The Indifferent', most of the lyrics

---

[47] 'Cowley', in *Lives of the English Poets* (1779–81), ed. George Birkbeck Hill, 3 vols. (Oxford: Clarendon, 1905), i. 34.

[48] *Ben Jonson*, i: *The Man and His Work*, ed. C. H. Hereford and Percy Simpson, 11 vols. (Oxford: Clarendon, 1925–52), 135.

[49] [George Henry Lewes], 'Donne's Poetical Works', *The National Magazine and Monthly Critic*, 2/9 (Apr. 1838), 377. Fuller's essay was first published in *The Dial* (Boston) for July 1843, under the title of 'The Great Lawsuit—Man *versus* Men; Woman *versus* Women.' It was expanded and reprinted as *Woman in the Nineteenth Century* (New York: Greeley and McElrath, 1845); see 55.

that do not offer an edifying picture of romantic love went largely unremarked until the 1890s.

By rights Donne's more licentious lyrics should have been omitted from Chalmers's edition, not on the grounds that they were unbecoming of Dr Donne, but simply due to the prevailing idea of good taste. Chalmers explained that 'licentious language', although it was sometimes used even by 'some of our most eminent poets', had been one of his criteria for omitting materials.[50] This declaration gave rise to an exchange, printed in Leigh Hunt's *The Reflector*, on the question, whether it was 'justifiable to reprint the Pruriencies of our Old Poets.'[51] Hunt's interlocutor, Barron Field, objected to Chalmers's omissions on the grounds that an editor should 'reprint his authors without mutilation or castration.' Field argued that works by Skelton and Carew, which Chalmers had omitted, are part of the historical record, and that an editor had no more right to suppress them 'than we have to shoot our neighbour's dog because it may do the public mischief.' Hunt took the more stringent position that an editor has a 'sacred duty' to omit prurient passages. He gave himself the last word, approving Chalmers's censorship, since editors ought not to 'perpetuate the vices that we condemn.' Donne's poems were not 'castrated' in Chalmers's collection, however, and they did not bear mention in the exchange. Chalmers may have managed to overlook Donne's potentially offensive poems as readily as he invited his readers to overlook them when he proposed that by his marriage Donne had redeemed himself for having toyed in his youth with 'sentiments of men whose morals are not very strict.'[52] The issue remained a lively one for Field, however. In the same period when he was debating with Hunt about poetic pruriencies, he was making his transcript of Coleridge's marginal notes from Lamb's copy of the 1669 *Poems*. When thirty years later he sought to get the Percy Society to publish an edition of the *Songs and Sonnets* and to include in it Coleridge's marginalia, he aptly identified what continued to trouble other readers, the frank sensuality of many of the amatory verses.

Increasingly, there were signs that a casual dismissal of Donne's poems, however 'loosely' they may have been 'scattered', would no longer be countenanced. Lewes defended Donne's use of conceits in his love poetry: 'there is a law in Nature', he argued, 'and consequently it becomes a canon in criticism,

---

[50] Chalmers, Preface, *Works of the English Poets*, i, p. vii.
[51] *The Reflector* 1/2 (1811), 365–74. In the article Hunt's interlocutor is designated as 'A.' In a copy in the British Library, the authors are identified, in pencil, in the Table of Contents. See also Kenneth E. Kendall, *An Index to Leigh Hunt's Magazine, The Reflector* (Gainesville, FL: [printed privately], 1970), 18. Field contributed a number of other articles to *The Reflector* in 1812, including one on Shakespeare and several on legal subjects. The quotations that follow can be found on 365, 370, and 373, respectively.
[52] Chalmers, *Works of the English Poets*, v. 123.

that the *language of passion is ever extravagant*.'[53] The article in *Lowe's* offered a further defense of extravagance. Proposing that it had been one of the principal benefits of the Reformation that writers were freed from the 'false shame which Romanism had attached to the contemplation of the sexual relations', its author argued that Donne's licentious verses, although they were not good poems, were not to be ignored or suppressed on the grounds that they were unworthy of the subject of Walton's *Life*. Rather, they required precisely to be read along with it, since it 'supplies a commentary upon the writings ... which could ill have been dispensed with.'[54] Similarly, Evert Duyckinck, reading the sermons and the love poems alike, remarked that 'Donne never was a profligate, or a libertine' and that to 'hold his life up to the vulgar sot or rake, as an illustration of the converting power of religion, is to misunderstand not only Donne, but the spirit of Christianity itself.'[55]

At least as well as Duyckinck, who in 1853 published most of Coleridge's marginalia on the poetry, Field understood that his friend's views provided the best introduction to Donne that a reader could find.[56] It was he who broached the question whether Donne's licentious verses ought to be reprinted, and he who sought to show that Coleridge had effectively answered it. When in the course of the preface that he wrote for the Percy Society Field referred to the indecencies in many of Donne's poems, he not only took up an issue in which he had a long-standing interest; he also identified what remained a primary issue for interpreters of Donne's poetry for the remainder of the century and beyond. For his part, Field admitted that he was leaving out of his transcript one poem on the grounds of 'indelicate obscurity' (p. viii; he omitted 'Farewell to Love' without naming it). He nonetheless included many poems that were later deemed offensively licentious by others.

Strikingly, Field isolated the annotations that Coleridge had written next to 'Woman's Constancy' and 'The Indifferent' and displaced them to the front of the collected marginalia. His doing so might suggest that he violated some intimate connection between these comments and the poems that were their

---

[53] 'Donne's Poetical Works', 377.

[54] In *The Mind and Art of Coventry Patmore* (London: Routledge and Kegan Paul, 1957), J. C. Reid confidently ascribed this article to Patmore (249–52, 333). Some implications of this ascription have been explored by Granqvist, *Reputation*, 148, 151–5. The *Lowe's* article is quoted here from pages 229 and 228, respectively. For the purposes of this argument, it matters little who was the author.

[55] 'Dr. Donne', *Arcturus* 2/1 (1841), 26.

[56] Field's preface and transcript are quoted with permission from 'The Songs and Sonnets of Dr. John Donne: With Critical Notes by the late Samuel Taylor Coleridge', MS Eng 966, Houghton Library, Harvard University. Field wrote the principal part of the obituary of 'Samuel Taylor Coleridge, Esq.' for *The Annual Biography and Obituary: 1835*, xix (London: Longman et al., 1835), 320–61. (For identification of the author, see the *National Union Catalogue*, Pre-1956 Imprints, clxxi. 531.)

proximate occasions. Neither 'Woman's Constancy' nor 'The Indifferent' was the object of much detailed commentary at any time before the twentieth century; and one advantage of noting that Coleridge wrote the annotations next to these particular poems is that it shows how differently he was reading them from the way in which biography-hunters, seeking to augment or overturn Walton's portrait, came to read them later in the century. Field's rearrangement does, however, show that the object of Coleridge's attention was the poetry.

Tellingly, Coleridge proposed that Donne's poetry is metrically sophisticated. The first point that a reader of Lamb's book would encounter in the initial annotation inside the front cover is that reading Donne's lines, unlike reading those of Dryden and Pope, has nothing to do with counting syllables: 'to read Donne you must measure *Time*, & discover the *Time* of Each word by the Sense & Passion.'[57] Moreover, Coleridge intuited that Dr Johnson, having spoken disapprovingly of the *discordia concors*, had recognized Donne's remarkable talent without fully appreciating it. Coleridge understood the 'combination of dissimilar images', indeed the 'discovery of occult resemblances in things apparently unlike', to be a mark of imaginative power. From his perspective, there were basic similarities between metaphysical wit and the secondary Imagination, which 'dissolves, diffuses, dissipates, in order to recreate; or where this process is rendered impossible, yet still at all events it struggles to idealize and to unify.'[58]

What Coleridge most valued in Donne was a vital capacity for creation, a teeming energy that could not be accounted for by the detached scrutiny that Johnson had applied to 'metaphysical' poetry. Coleridge believed that Donne was a poet of Imagination, but he qualified his praise in view of the poet's willfulness, which, to his way of thinking, compromised Donne's ability to discover truth in poetry. He wrote out his praise of Donne and his reservations specifically for Lamb, and some of them presuppose a common understanding of the nature of the greatness of Shakespeare as the poet who came closest to expressing truth completely and provided the norm against

---

[57] Unless otherwise indicated, the marginalia are quoted from *The Collected Works of Samuel Taylor Coleridge*, xii: *Marginalia II*, ed. George Whalley (London: Routledge and Kegan Paul; Princeton, NJ: Princeton Univ. Press, 1984), 213–338. In an unpublished thesis, Helen Kathryn Sterling concluded that Coleridge's most unqualified praise for Donne's poetry had to do with its rhythm. Coleridge, she explained, assumed that if there were a difficulty in ascertaining the rhythm either the printer or the reader was at fault. Quoted with permission from 'Unpublished Marginalia by Samuel Taylor Coleridge in a Volume of John Donne's Poetry', MA thesis (University of Nevada, 1954), 34.

[58] See 'Cowley', i. 20; and *The Collected Works of Samuel Taylor Coleridge: Biographia Literaria*, ed. James Engell and W. Jackson Bate, 2 vols. (London: Routledge and Kegan Paul; Princeton, NJ: Princeton Univ. Press, 1983), chap. 13; i. 304.

which all other poets were to be judged. It is no accident that Coleridge should have come to appreciate Donne in the context of his own 'most joyous and abiding friendship', as George Whalley observed. The 'dominant tone' of the annotations 'is set by Coleridge's sense of Lamb's imaginative presence. His perceptions are heightened by affection and by the certainty of sympathetic response.' Some of the annotations are astonishingly candid. These include ones that suggest that it was 'through certain of Donne's poems [that] the encouraging and restoring virtue of love seems to have come to him.'[59] It seems likely, moreover, that the poems of vital sexual energy occasioned Coleridge's most exalted appreciations of Donne. What chiefly informs the annotations on 'Woman's Constancy', 'The Indifferent', and 'The Canonization' is the fact that they transcend the moralizing concerns that through the rest of the century nearly all other commentators voiced in the face of such poems. In his note on 'The Indifferent', for instance, Coleridge contrasts Cowley with Donne on the grounds that Donne far surpasses his imitator not in the 'populousness' or 'activity' that appears in their poems but precisely in '*vigor*.' Although the note was written alongside the first stanza of the poem—

> I can love both fair and brown,
> Her whom aboundance melts, and her whom want betrayes,
> Her who loves lovers [sic] best, and her who sports and playes,
> Her whom the country form'd, and whom the Town,
> Her who believes, and her who tries;
> Her who still weeps with spungie eyes,
> And her who is dry Cork, and never cries;
> I can love her, and her, and you and you,
> I can love any, so she be not true,[60]

Field shrewdly recognized that it constitutes a general introduction to Donne's poetry. In Coleridge's view, Donne's characteristic quality was an exuberant creativity that would 'squander ... golden Hecatombs on a Fetisch, on the first stick or straw met with at rising!' Coleridge admired 'this pride of doing what he likes with his own', and remarked that Donne was 'fearless of an immense surplus to pay all lawful Debts to self-subsisting Themes that rule, while they create, the moral will.'[61] '[T]his', he emphasizes, 'is Donne', the poet who acted on the basis of a 'purse-proud Opulence, of innate Power!'

[59] Whalley, 'The Harvest on the Ground: Coleridge's *Marginalia*', *UTQ*, 38 (1968–9), 273–4; 265–7. Cf. Sterling, 'Unpublished Marginalia', 6.

[60] This passage is quoted from the edition (1669) annotated by Coleridge.

[61] The publication of this annotation in *The Literary World* (1853) added the word 'cannot' between 'they' and 'create.' This error was reproduced in other transcriptions and has been corrected in Whalley's edition of the *Marginalia*. For the quotation that follows, see *Marginalia II*, 219–20.

What Coleridge praised in Donne is closely akin to what William Hazlitt had already begun to praise in Shakespeare, a 'natural' power of creativity that was not to be chastened by the deadening conceptions of ordinary morality. Such a power, which Hazlitt (but not Coleridge) would find in *Measure for Measure*,[62] showed that Shakespeare was not a copier of Nature, but a 'co-worker with nature, a collaborator with her rich treasures and abundant variety.' The power that celebrated the 'teeming foison' of the natural world was as 'indifferent' to merely conventional morality as the speaker in Donne's poem. It enabled the poet to see various sides of a question, and to adopt opposing viewpoints. Its complexity and variety ensured that it would transcend ordinary rules and categories, even the faculties of perception. From this perspective, Hazlitt judged Shakespeare, who seemed on the surface the least moral of writers, to be the writer *par excellence* to be read by the Society for the Suppression of Vice.[63] He would deliver readers from that narrow didacticism that indulges the tendency to glean moral lessons from literary works.

Hazlitt himself, however, was one of the great resisters of Donne's writing. As late as 1818 he did not know Donne's poems. When he finally read them, he found nothing much to admire.[64] The annotations that Coleridge made on 'The Indifferent' and 'Woman's Constancy' are nonetheless reminiscent of Hazlitt's 1805 'Essay on the Principles of Human Action: Being an Argument in Favour of the Natural Disinterestedness of the Human Mind.' They seem, moreover, to anticipate Hazlitt's remarks on Shakespeare's wealth of imaginative power in the Lecture of 1818 on Shakespeare and Milton. Some of Coleridge's insight into the dramatic power of Donne's imagination as he expressed it in his note on 'Woman's Constancy' may be owing to Hazlitt. When in a later annotation Coleridge proposed that the title of the poem ought to be 'Mutual Inconstancy',[65] he acknowledged that the poem could be spoken by either a man or a woman.

Although 'Woman's Constancy' precedes 'The Indifferent' in the 1669 edition and Coleridge's comment is written nearer the front of Lamb's copy,

[62] For Hazlitt's views on the play, see *The Complete Works of William Hazlitt*, ed. P. P. Howe, 21 vols. (London: Dent, 1930–4), iv. 345–9; for Coleridge's, see *Literary Remains*, ed. Henry Nelson Coleridge, 4 vols. (London: Pickering, 1836–9), ii (1836), 122–4. What Coleridge found 'hateful' about the play was chiefly the travesty of justice entailed in Angelo's escaping punishment. Quotations from Hazlitt are from Howe's edition.

[63] See the account in John L. Mahoney, *The Logic of Passion: The Literary Criticism of William Hazlitt* (1978; repr., New York: Fordham Univ. Press, 1981), 48–59; quoted from 48. Cf. Herschel Baker, *William Hazlitt* (Cambridge, MA: Belknap Press of Harvard Univ. Press, 1962), 278; cited in Mahoney, *Logic of Passion*, 51–2. See also Hazlitt, *Works*, v. 283.

[64] Hazlitt, 'On Dryden and Pope', *Works*, v. 83; 'On Cowley, Butler, Suckling, etc.', *Works*, vi. 51–3.

[65] *Marginalia II*, 18.

his annotation seems to presuppose the ideas about 'profound ... Thinking', 'Will-worship', and 'pride' expressed a few pages later:

After all, there is but one Donne! & now tell me yet, wherein, *in his own kind*, he differs from the *similar* power in Shakespere? Sh. was all men potentially except Milton—& they differ from him by negation, or privation, or both. This power of dissolving orient pearls, worth a kingdom! in a health to a Whore! this absolute Right of Dominion over all thoughts, that Dukes are bid to clean his Shoes, and are yet honored by it!—But, I say, in the Lordliness of opulence, in which *the* Positive of Donne agrees with *a* Postitive of Shakespere, what is it that makes them *homoi*sousian, indeed; yet not homoousian?

In Coleridge's eyes Shakespeare was the closest of all writers to expressing the synthesis of truth that would reflect all the 'self-subsisting Themes that rule, while they create, the moral will.'[66] He could do virtually anything that any other writer, save Milton, could do. Donne could equal Shakespeare in one respect and was therefore 'of like essence' with the Supreme Poet but not of one essence with him.

It would be superficial to arrest consideration of this comment by fixing on the conspicuous displacement of theological categories to a discussion of English poetry, as if the passage were of interest chiefly as evidence for an emerging natural supernaturalism. By 1811 Coleridge had been carefully studying the controversies about the Trinity from the period of the early church, which had been renewed in the seventeenth century. In fact, many of the annotations that he made in Wordsworth's copy of Donne's *LXXX Sermons* concerned Trinitarian theology. That interest was not displaced into aesthetic concerns in the marginalia on Donne's *Poems*. Reading one of Donne's Lenten sermons some years later, Coleridge returned directly to the language of similitude used by theologians and preachers to discuss the two natures of Christ, and he took Donne to task for a certain timidity about depicting a thoroughgoing union of humanity and divinity in Jesus.

Not uncharacteristically, this marginal annotation addresses Donne as if he were present. It poses a battery of rhetorical questions to the preacher. In the course of them Coleridge asks something that applies to the bifurcation of Jack Donne and Doctor Donne as much as it does to the two natures of Christ: 'what can we mean by Original Sin relatively to the *flesh*, but that Man is born with an animal life, and a material organism that renders him *temptible* to evil, that tends to dispose the life of the *Will* to contradict the Light of the Reason. Did Paul by ομοιωμα [sic] mean a deceptive resemblance?'[67] In light of these imaginings and convictions, and in relation to the history of theological

---

[66] Ibid. 218–19. Cf. Sterling, 'Unpublished Marginalia', 48–9.   [67] *Marginalia II*, 315.

reflection on the Trinity and the Redemption, we can see that in the marginal note on 'Woman's Constancy' Coleridge was adapting theological categories to insist upon the existence of 'but one Donne.' The term *homoousian* had been used in the Nicene Creed to express the relations of the Father and Son in the Godhead. It was originally meant to exclude relegating the Son to the dubious status that He was given by the Arians. Many Origenists preferred the term *homoiousian*, in order to allow for sharper distinctions within the Godhead. Their term was discarded from normative theology but proved useful to Coleridge for suggesting that Donne was the real thing, but nonetheless not wholly identifiable with his incomparable older contemporary. This Donne was 'of like essence with' the Shakespeare whom Hazlitt would later describe as being 'all that others were or that they could become', who 'had in himself the germs of every faculty and feeling, ... [and] could follow them by anticipation, intuitively, into all their conceivable ramifications, through every change of fortune or conflict of passion, or turn of thought.' Donne, whose 'Positive' thus agreed with 'a Positive of Shakespere', lacked the extraordinary range of the Bard who 'was all men potentially except Milton.' Yet the Donne who wrote the amatory lyrics was like the Shakespeare of whom Hazlitt said, 'When he conceived of a character, whether real or imaginary, he ... entered into all its thoughts and feelings.'[68] In love with life, as Coleridge took Shakespeare to have been, Donne might be said to have taken as much delight in conceiving the speaker of 'Woman's Constancy' or 'The Apparition' as the speaker of 'The Anniversary' or 'The Canonization.' Coleridge's proclamation that there is 'but one Donne' was not so much an answer to those who sought to reconcile Donne's youth and maturity as it was a recognition of Donne's utterly unique individuality and a denial that the parts of Donne's life could be separated the way that many Christians, including at times Donne himself, sought to separate the divine from the human nature in Christ.

When Coleridge remarked that 'The Canonization' was one of his 'favorite poems', he was in part acknowledging Donne's ability to create a character like Antony, who lost the world for love. He was also noticing, as he says, that Donne's poems can be read as wholes; and he was aware that such well-wrought urns were created by the poet, that this was the remarkable accomplishment. In view of the theological language that he enlisted to describe Donne's relations to Shakespeare, however, it is also possible to conclude that Coleridge favored 'The Canonization' on other grounds as well, including the bold fusion of religious and erotic language that was anathema to Alford. The writer of marginal glosses in the *Poems* and in the *Sermons* recognized that love and religion were the two great passions of Donne's life, and he taught Duyckinck to

<hr />

[68] Hazlitt, *Works*, v. 47–8.

read these works in light of one another. For the rest of the nineteenth century, however, few others proved capable of reading with this sort of religious imagination. In the case of Donne, the interpretative timidity of most readers owed a good deal to a poverty of theological sophistication. Even and perhaps especially the editors of Donne who were themselves clergymen—Alford and Augustus Jessopp and Grosart—were unable to bring Coleridge's theological insights to bear on the reading of Donne's poetry.

3

A Thinker and a Writer

Do you know Donne? I should like to have some more talk with you about
him. He was one of those over-metaphysical-headed men, who can find
out connections between everything and anything, and allowed himself
at *last* to become a clergyman, after he had (to my conviction, at least)
been as free and deep a speculator in morals as yourself. (I am talking to
Shelley, you see, Marina—but you are one flesh.)

—Leigh Hunt, letter to Percy and Mary Shelley (1819)

In the English-speaking world of the 1830s, most readers, if they knew of John
Donne at all, knew chiefly about the life portrayed by Walton: Donne's lineal
descent from Sir Thomas More by way of his mother's family, his romantic
marriage and its trying aftermath, his reluctance to take holy orders and his
eloquence as a preacher, his grief upon the death of his wife, and his holy
dying. By the early 1840s the situation was changing. More of Donne's own
writing was available in print than at any time since the mid-seventeenth
century: almost all the extant sermons, 130 prose letters, nearly one hundred
poems, three new editions of the *Devotions upon Emergent Occasions*, and
an unprecedented volume of nearly 300 pages titled *Selections from the
Works of John Donne, D.D.* Interest in Donne began to owe something to
a festering impatience with Walton's having cavalierly dismissed the poetry
and with his having failed to appreciate Donne as a restless and probing
thinker.

The revival of Donne as a writer began as a logical complement to Walton's
portrait, and yet it threatened to constitute an alternative to it. The best readers
were able to interpret Donne's works with a remarkable independence of the
spell cast on others by the *Life*. This was especially true of Coleridge, who
rarely seems to have thought about Donne in the terms disseminated in the
editions of Walton. In commenting on Donne's poetry, he dwelt often upon
matters of versification and sometimes upon matters of form. In annotating
the sermons, he frequently wrestled with Donne's ideas and sought as often

to criticize as to express admiration.[1] Still, there was something profoundly biographical about Coleridge's interest in Donne, a man who had not only 'allowed himself at *last* to become a clergyman', as Hunt put it, but who had left behind, as Walton attested, notes on more than fourteen hundred authors.

Significantly, the proximate stimulus for republishing Donne's sermons was the publication of Coleridge's *Literary Remains*, particularly volume iii with its notes on various authors. Here readers found many intriguing quotations from Donne's sermons and a body of commentary that took the preacher's ideas seriously. Coleridge saw in Donne a kindred worker from another era, whose contributions to philosophical and religious thought and to the native poetic tradition could be recovered only by entering into the sorts of interpretative labors that informed Donne's own writings.[2] The signs of Donne's active reading to be found in his writings offered a model for open-minded inquiry. They showed an inspiring willingness to tackle difficult materials. These precedents attracted even readers who were themselves unable to emulate Donne's practice. The most prominent instance was Alford, who claimed to have found in Coleridge's fascination with Donne an effective justification for his project.

The front matter for *The Works of John Donne, D.D.* contains a telling contradiction. In the body of the Editor's Preface Alford expresses thanks to Henry Nelson Coleridge for 'permission to reprint the valuable notes of the late Mr. Coleridge' on Donne's sermons. A footnote shows, however, that Alford changed his mind and decided not to print the marginalia after all. Without revising the text of his preface, he simply alleged that printing them as notes 'would impair much of their freshness and character.'[3] His reluctance to devise ways to include them was of a piece with what he acknowledged as his own 'inadequacy, especially in antiquarian learning, to the task of giving a complete edition of Donne, as old authors are now edited.' The suppression of these materials also made a radical change in the nature of the 'experiment' (i, p. v) his edition was to set in motion, testing 'how far the present English public are desirous to retrieve the treasures of divinity and eloquence contained in the writers immediately following the Reformation' (p. viii). Without having Coleridge's dialogue with Donne ready to hand, most people who encountered the *Works* were unlikely to be looking to Coleridge to challenge their notions

---

[1] Jerome C. Christensen has proposed that this was generally characteristic of Coleridge's marginal annotating. See 'Coleridge's Marginal Method in the *Biographia Literaria*', *PMLA*, 92 (1977), 928–40.

[2] See Anthony John Harding, '"Against the stream upwards": Coleridge's Recovery of John Donne', in Lisa Low and Anthony John Harding (eds.), *Milton, the Metaphysicals, and Romanticism* (Cambridge: Cambridge Univ. Press, 1994), 204–20.

[3] Henry Alford, Editor's Preface, *The Works of John Donne, D.D.*, 6 vols. (London: John W. Parker, 1839), i, p. viii. Subsequent references are given in parentheses.

about reading Donne. Alford's timidity in omitting the marginalia had effects
that were nearly as significant as the publisher's behest that he print more of
Donne's writings than just the sermons.

THE RE-EMERGENCE OF DONNE AS A PROSE WRITER

Even before 1840 a few readers had been casting a shrewd eye upon Donne's
writings, especially his sermons. Thomas De Quincey pronounced Donne
'the first very eminent rhetorician in the English Literature' and singled him
out among public speakers, in an era when preachers could rely on their
auditors to exert themselves intellectually, for his 'extraordinary compass of
powers.' In De Quincey's view, Donne 'combined what no other man has
ever done—the last sublimation of dialectical subtlety and address with most
impassioned majesty.' This was to be concerned with Donne's substance
as well as his style, and there were others who looked to Donne chiefly
as a thinker. We don't know whether Hunt ever managed to have 'more
talk' with the Shelleys about him. It is curious, however, that Mary Shelley
had already in her account of 'the modern Prometheus' bestowed the name
Walton upon the credulous reporter of Frankenstein's life story. In 1831, her
father referred to Donne as 'the most deep-thinking and philosophical of our
poets', remarked that '[e]very sentence that Donne writes, whether in verse
or prose, is exclusively his own', and proposed that 'passages may be quoted
from him that no English poet may attempt to rival, unless it be Milton and
Shakespear.'[4]

Clearly, the philosophical and theological spectrum within which Donne
was of interest was wider and less partisan than the Tractarianism of the Oxford
Movement.[5] It was also more challenging than most devotees of Walton were
prepared to reckon with. The quality of interest in Donne's writings displayed
by Coleridge and De Quincey, Hunt and Godwin helps us to imagine the
climate in the late 1830s in which a London publishing house with close ties to
Cambridge University acceded to Alford's proposal to republish a selection of
the sermons. In Coleridge's *Table Talk* of 1830 the question had been raised,
'Why are not Donne's volumes of sermons reprinted at Oxford?' and in the

---

[4] [De Quincey], 'Elements of Rhetoric', *Blackwood's Magazine*, 24 (Dec. 1828), 892; *The Correspondence of Leigh Hunt*, ed. [Thorton Leigh Hunt], 2 vols. (London: Smith, Elder, 1862), i. 149; there is no mention of Donne in published letters from the Shelleys in the ensuing weeks; William Godwin, *Thoughts on Man, His Nature, Productions, and Discoveries* (London: Effingham Wilson, 1831), 4, 83, 84.
[5] Further evidence for this point may be found in Chapter 4.

Quarterly Review for 1837 a reviewer quoted some of Coleridge's recently printed remarks on Donne and amplified the question:

Surely the character of some of his juvenile *poems* cannot be the reason! Donne's Life is placed in a cheap form in the catalogue of the Society for Promoting Christian Knowledge, and deservedly so in every respect. Why does Oxford allow one hundred and thirty sermons of the greatest *preacher*, at least, of the seventeenth century—the admired of all hearers—to remain all but totally unknown to the students in divinity of the Church of England, and to the literary world in general?[6]

The question became more insistent in the following year, when a new edition of the *Table Talk* appeared and volume iii of the *Literary Remains* made available most of the annotations that Coleridge had written into the margins of the *LXXX Sermons*. Notably, there was not much call for renewed interest in Donne's religious poetry. Apart from 'A Hymn to God the Father' (which appeared in Walton) and 'Death be not proud', the *Divine Poems* were little read. Coleridge did not annotate the religious poetry in any of the extant volumes that contain marginalia. Hunt, when he compiled *The Book of the Sonnet*, omitted Donne's work on the grounds that the piety displayed in the Holy Sonnets, 'though sincere, was not healthy' and 'does not do justice to the Divine Goodness.'[7]

   In 1838, Alford at last found a publishing house willing to reprint Donne's sermons. John W. Parker had his shop in the West Strand. In the 1830s he and his son were publishing books on a wide variety of subjects in history, science, world literature, and many other fields, including the abolition of the African slave-trade. Titles on their list ranged from *Elizabethan Religious History* to *Notes on Indian Affairs*. By the 1840s their house was actively involved in promoting Christian socialism. It had also become an official printer for Cambridge University Press, for which it brought out books aimed at persons of modest income.[8] Publishing Donne was a large undertaking,

---

   [6] See *The Collected Works of Samuel Taylor Coleridge*, xiv: *Table Talk II*, ed. Carl Woodring (London: Routledge; Princeton, NJ: Princeton Univ. Press, 1990), 105; *Quarterly Review*, 59/18 (July and Oct. 1837), 6.

   [7] 'An Essay on the Sonnet', *The Book of the Sonnet*, ed. Leigh Hunt and S. Adams Lee, 2 vols. (Boston: Roberts Brothers, 1867), i. 78. Annotating 'On the Blessed Virgin Mary', mistakenly ascribed to Donne in Anderson's *British Poets*, Coleridge expressed surprise at 'so full an assertion of the Virgin's *Immaculate Conception*': see *The Collected Works of Samuel Taylor Coleridge*, xii: *Marginalia I*, ed. George Whalley (London: Routledge and Kegan Paul; Princeton, NJ: Princeton Univ. Press, 1980), 43–4. Subsequent references from *Marginalia II* (1984) in Volume xii appear in parentheses.

   [8] See the catalogue of 'New Works Published by John W. Parker' bound into the back of vol. vi of *The Works of John Donne*. On the publishing house generally, see the account by Dennis R. Dean in Patricia J. Anderson and Jonathan Rose (eds.), *Dictionary of Literary Biography*, cvi: *British Literary Publishing Houses, 1820–1880* (Detroit: Bruccoli Clark Layman, 1991), 233–6.

more ambitious than anything for which Alford had hoped at first. Yet one of Alford's editorial principles immediately qualified Donne's work for inclusion among the sorts of projects in which the Parkers were interested: Alford modernized the spelling and punctuation of Donne's sermons, bringing them into general conformity with standard nineteenth-century usage and making them accessible to the growing number of literate persons.[9]

The result was the only edition that had ever been called Donne's *Works*. Its six volumes included 158 sermons, the *Devotions*, the prose letters, and a large number of poems consistent with the religious emphasis of the project. The edition was dedicated to the Bishop of Lincoln, John Kaye, who as Regius Professor of Divinity at Cambridge had revived the custom of public lectures and recalled theological students to the study of the Fathers of the church. His lectures on Tertullian, Justin Martyr, and Clement of Alexandria were being turned into books, and the books were running through several editions.[10] Alford's Donne turned out to be as unlike Kaye's own scholarship, much of which remained unsurpassed through most of the nineteenth century, as it was unworthy of the expectations that Coleridge's marginalia had raised. Almost as soon as it appeared there were complaints that since many of Donne's writings were not contained in the edition the title was misleading. Still, its appearance prompted Oxford to move at last, and in 1840 D. A. Talboys brought out a volume of *Selections* from Donne, which excerpted in order, but without identifying their provenance, passages from volume i of Alford's edition right through volume vi. Talboys often collaborated with the London house of William Pickering, which was Coleridge's publisher. Pickering himself was a devotee of seventeenth-century divines and the publisher of the Aldine British Poets, in which Donne's poetry did not appear. His business was at its peak in the 1830s and 1840s, and he was a major supplier of scholarly books to the British Museum and the Bodleian Library. While he was printing Coleridge's *Literary Remains* he was also bringing out an edition of George Herbert's works.[11] In 1840 he published in a single volume a more handsome and somewhat more accurate edition of Donne's *Devotions* than Parker had. In the

John W. Parker needs to be differentiated from the Oxford publisher John *Henry* Parker, who in 1840 began publishing 'The Library of Anglo-Catholic Theology', in which Donne's works were not included.

[9] Alford cut many words and phrases from Donne's Latin quotations of Scripture and of the Fathers and Doctors of the church. It is difficult to isolate consistent criteria used for the cuts, but one criterion that he often used was that, when Donne provided a close translation into English of a Latin phrase, he could omit the Latin.

[10] For Kaye's career and reputation, see the entry by Edmund Venables in *DNB* (London: Smith, Elder, 1892), xxx. 252–3.

[11] See Bernard Warrington, 'William Pickering', in *British Literary Publishing Houses, 1820–1880*, cvi: *Dictionary of Literary Biography*, 245–50.

following year Talboys published the third edition of the *Devotions* to appear in as many years. By the first years of Queen Victoria's reign, therefore, many of Donne's writings were available, and much more widely available. What has been aptly said of Coleridge as the new Bollingen editions of *his* works are being published was, *mutatis mutandi*, true in the 1840s of Donne: that, for those who cared to notice, a 'new image of this complex and controversial writer' was emerging, and 'the figure ... is not a poet who dwindled into a philosopher' — or a theologian — 'but a thinker who happened to be a poet.'[12]

The emergence of a more complex picture of Donne based on wider familiarity with his writings owed something to ideas articulated by Wordsworth about the biographies of writers. Wordsworth's reluctance to have his own life written is well known and was hardly unique. It showed up in his correspondence with Alford, and was in keeping with a conviction that he expressed on a number of occasions, with a relish for its irony, that 'it is writers who least need their lives written.' In discussing Milton's epitaph on Shakespeare, for instance, Wordsworth proposed that the 'mighty benefactors of mankind ... do not stand in need of biographic sketches' since their works, by inscribing their 'character' in the 'memories' of posterity, have already done this for them. A biography added to the work of a good writer would be superfluous and might even be counterproductive. In his *Letter to a Friend of Robert Burns* (1816), he insisted that the works of poets, 'if their words be good, ... contain within themselves all that is necessary to their being comprehended and relished.'[13] This prescription, while it helps to explain the emergence of ways of thinking about Donne not heavily dependent upon Walton, contributed as well to a project that proved compelling to many: the attempt to uncover Donne's secret life. Some workers on this project simply sought to use Donne's writings to fill in gaps in the narrative of his life. Others quoted them to undermine Walton's guiding interpretation. Walton, after all, had said that Donne's *Devotions* contained his 'most secret thoughts.' And Wordsworth, for all his strictures against writing the biographies of poets, wrote poetry that inevitably encouraged the hunters of biography. He even claimed, in one of his defenses of the sonnet, that Shakespeare in *his* sonnets had 'unlocked his heart.' The remainder of this chapter will sketch the principal lines of the more ample portrait of Donne that began to emerge in the marginalia of Coleridge and will examine the results of Alford's experiment.

[12] See H. J. Jackson, ' "Turning and turning": Coleridge on Our Knowledge of the External World', *PMLA*, 101 (1986), 848.

[13] The phrase quoted here comes from Eric C. Walker, 'Wordsworth as Prose Biographer', *JEGP*, 89 (1990), 341; for a more ample discussion of the materials quoted below, see 341–2. See *The Letters of William and Dorothy Wordsworth*, ed. Ernest de Selincourt, 2nd edn, revised by Mary Moorman and Alan G. Hill (Oxford: Clarendon, 1970), iii. 287 n.

The three chapters that follow will document an intensification of interest in Donne's biography that was set in motion as readers began to consider Walton's portrait in closer relation to Donne's own writings.

COLERIDGE'S READING OF DONNE, 1796–1834

It turned out to be important that Walton had not been much interested in Donne as a thinker. Much of what he wrote had little impact on what readers actually found in Donne's writings. As Hunt's letter to the Shelleys suggests, good readers came to both the prose and the poetry with a remarkable independence. This was above all the case with the person who inspired James Gillman's *Life of Coleridge*, a book that, because it was modeled on Walton's *Lives*, gave the mistaken impression that its subject had been a great admirer of Walton.[14] Coleridge, although he was familiar with information that Walton supplied, rarely seems to have thought about Donne in the terms disseminated in the editions of the *Lives*. In annotating two separate copies of the *LXXX Sermons*, both times he prescinded from marking the introductory life of the author. As a passage from his own *Lay Sermons* (1817) makes plain, Coleridge was interested in differences that had emerged in religious thinking between the seventeenth century and the present, and especially he was attentive to the conditions in which sermon literature is or is not widely read:

[T]hink likewise on the large and numerous editions of massy, closely printed folios: the impressions so large and the editions so numerous, that all the industry of destruction for the last hundred years has but of late sufficed to make them rare .... [O]n the single shelf so filled [with such volumes] we should find almost every possible question, that could interest or instruct a reader whose whole heart was in his religion, discussed with a command of intellect that seems to exhaust all the learning and logic, all the historical and moral relations, of each several subject.[15]

The extent and independence of Coleridge's reading of early modern literature continues to become clearer with the publication of all the extant marginalia and the gradual assimilation of the *Collected Works*. Coleridge read Donne through the whole course of his adult life, at times within the field of that interest in older poets which he shared with Charles Lamb, at times within the adjacent and still broader field of his wide reading and extensive

---

[14] See B. R. McElderry, Jr., 'Walton's *Lives* and Gillman's *Life of Coleridge*', *PMLA*, 52 (1937), 412–22.

[15] *The Collected Works of Samuel Taylor Coleridge*, vi: *Lay Sermons*, ed. R. J. White (London: Routledge and Kegan Paul; Princeton, NJ: Princeton Univ. Press, 1972), 198.

annotation of seventeenth-century divines. As early as 1796, when he acquired Anderson's *British Poets*, he was interested in Donne as a witty thinker and logician, and he considered him the earliest satirist to have written in English. He wrote lines that echo 'The Bracelet', 'A Valediction Forbidding Mourning', and 'To E. of D.'; and he resolved also to write satires in the manner of Donne. He made good on this resolve both in a verse letter to Thomas Poole and in the verses 'On Donne's Poetry', which survive in various forms from different periods in his life and may have been first drafted as early as August of 1798:

> With Donne, whose muse on dromedary trots,
> Wreathe iron pokers into true-love knots;
> Rhyme's sturdy cripple, fancy's maze and clue,
> Wit's forge and fire-blast, meaning's press and screw.[16]

Coleridge continued reading Donne's poems after the first publication of the *Lyrical Ballads*, quoting from the eclogue for the Somerset epithalamion in 1800, making notes on the Elegies and Verse Letters in 1803, reading Donne again during his stay with the Wordsworths in December 1803 and January 1804, and thinking of *Metempsychosis* as he read *Pseudodoxia Epidemica* in 1808. It was probably not until 1809 that he began writing marginal commentary into the pages of Wordsworth's copy of the *LXXX Sermons*. This reading later emboldened him defiantly to write into a copy of *Shakespeare's Plays* one of his pithier appreciations. In response to an annotation by Warburton proposing that the '*jingles*' of Polonius are reminiscent of Dr Donne's sermons, Coleridge wrote, 'I have (and that most carefully) read Dr. Donne's Sermons and find none of these Jingles.' (The contrast between Donne and Shakespeare's prating exponent of old saws then gives way to a distillation of Coleridge's intuition about why Donne had been a successful preacher: 'The great art of an orator is to make whatever he talks of appear of importance, this indeed Donne has effected with consummate skill.'[17]) In March of 1811 he read *Biathanatos* and around this time he left conspicuous evidence that he had been most carefully reading Donne's poems as well. Many of the annotations that he wrote into Lamb's copy of the 1669 edition took seriously 'Poems where the Author *thinks* & expects the Reader to do so' (*Marginalia II*, 221). Beyond annotating Donne's poems, he made a number

---

[16] 'On Donne's Poetry' is quoted here from the version written into Chalmers's edition as reported in *The Collected Works of Samuel Taylor Coleridge*, xii: *Marginalia II*, ed. George Whalley (London: Routledge and Kegan Paul; Princeton, NJ: Princeton Univ. Press, 1984), 16. 'On Donne's First Poem' (dated 1796) is quoted from *The Literary Remains of Samuel Taylor Coleridge*, ed. Henry Nelson Coleridge (London: William Pickering, 1836), i. 148.

[17] Quoted from *Coleridge on the Seventeenth Century*, ed. Roberta Florence Brinkley (Durham, NC: Duke Univ. Press, 1955), 205.

of comments on the prose letters and on the elegies on the author's death that had been included in the volume. Also numbered among these marginalia are three defenses of his having 'bescribbled' his friend's book, the last of which recording a date on which he perhaps returned it to its owner: 'I shall die soon, my dear Charles Lamb! and then you—will not be vexed that I had bescribbled your Books. 2 May, 1811.' It was in this period as well that Coleridge's interest in Donne as a poet of negation must have come clear to him, although it remained hidden to others until 1973. In a notebook in which he transcribed his playful lines 'On Donne's first Poem' (the 1669 *Poems* opened with 'The Flea')—

> Be proud, as Spaniards! and Leap for Pride, ye Fleas
> Henceforth in Nature's *Minim* World Grandees,
> In Phœbus' Archives registered are ye—
> And this your Patent of Nobility.
> No Skip-Jacks now, nor civiller Skip-Johns,
> Dread Anthropophagi! Specks of living Bronze,
> I hail you one & all, sans Pros or Cons,
> Descendants from a noble Race of *Dons*.
>
> What tho' that great ancestral Flea be gone
> Immortal with immortalizing Donne—
> His earthly Spots bleach'd off as
> Papists gloze,
> In purgatory fire on Bardolph's Nose … .

—he followed up with drafts of 'Limbo' and 'Ne Plus Ultra.'[18] In view of the complex relations among these materials we can infer that the poems in which Donne sought to imagine utter nothingness—especially 'To Mr. T. W.' ('Haste thee harsh verse'), 'A Nocturnal upon St. Lucy's Day', and the Second Anniversary—were even more important to Coleridge than his marginalia suggest.

Coleridge's twin interests in Donne as a writer of prose and of verse continued after the publication of the *Biographia Literaria*, in which Donne is briefly mentioned amidst remarks about 'the characteristic faults of our elder poets.' In February of 1818, he announced a lecture that he intended to give on 'Dante, Donne, and Milton' and wrote to H. F. Cary that 'the middle name will, perhaps, puzzle you.' In the event, the surviving notice does not mention Donne, and no notes pertaining specifically to this lecture

---

[18] *The Notebooks of Samuel Taylor Coleridge*, iii: *1808–1819 Text*, ed. Kathleen Coburn (London: Routledge and Kegan Paul; Princeton, NJ: Princeton Univ. Press, 1973), 4073–4. See John A. Hodgson, 'Coleridge, Puns, and "Donne's First Poem": The Limbo of Rhetoric and the Conceptions of Wit', *JDJ*, 4 (1985), 181–200.

are known. In *Literary Remains* H. N. Coleridge borrowed materials from elsewhere to create an impression of the lecture: Donne marginalia from a copy of Chalmers, notes on Milton and Dante that seem actually to have been used for Lectures 4 and 5 in the following year. Although we don't know what Coleridge was planning or what he actually said, we needn't be as puzzled as the writer of the letter imagined the great translator of Dante would be, and as the latest editors of the *Lectures* assume we will remain. We know that already in the 1790s Coleridge had admired Donne as a demanding satirical writer who relished the exposure of vice and hypocrisy. In the same period that he was writing satire after the manner of Donne he was also reading Milton's controversial prose.[19] That prose, strenuous and often satirical as in *Colasterion* ('the place of punishment'), not only bears stylistic affinities to parts of the *Inferno*, but was seen by Coleridge to have been anticipated in Donne's satires. Where the 1669 *Poems* gave the lines from Satire III,

> On a huge hill,
> Cragged, and steep, Truth stands, and he that will
> Reach her, about must, and about it goe:
> And what the hills suddenness resists, win so,
> Yet strive so, that before age, deaths twilight,
> Thy Soul rest, for none can work in that night.
> To will implyes delay, therefore now do:
> Hard deeds, the bodies pains; hard knowledge to
> The minds indeavours reach; and mysteries
> Are like the Sun, dazling, yet plain to all eyes.

Coleridge had underlined in Lamb's copy the words 'can' and 'will' and 'do.' He went on then to sort out the demanding syntax: 'The body's pains reach hard deeds; & likewise so do the mind's Endeavours reach hard Knowledge' (*Marginalia II*, 228). What he attended to here accords closely with the symbolism of the opening canto in the *Inferno*—and with what he himself thought about the process and benefits of reading Donne's sermons. It also squares with what he wrote at the head of the Satire in Lamb's book: 'If you would teach a Scholar in the highest form, how to *read*, take Donne, and of Donne this Satire. When he has learnt to read Donne, with all the force & meaning which are involved in the Words—then send him to Milton—&

---

[19] See *The Collected Works of Samuel Taylor Coleridge*, vii: *Biographia Literaria*, ed. James Engell and Walter Jackson Bate (London: Routledge and Kegan Paul; Princeton, NJ: Princeton Univ. Press, 1983), Part I, 23; *Letters of Samuel Taylor Coleridge*, ed. Earl Leslie Griggs, 6 vols. (Oxford: Clarendon, 1956–71), iv. 827. See *Literary Remains*, 1 (1836), 148–50. Cf. *Marginalia I*, 280 n., and *Collected Works*, v: *Lectures 1808–1819 On Literature II*, ed. R. A. Foakes (London: Routledge and Kegan Paul; Princeton, NJ: Princeton Univ. Press, 1987), 184–6.

he will stalk on, like a Master, *enjoying* his Walk' (Ibid. 225–6). It was not unusual for readers of Donne's satires to be thinking of them as doing religious work. George Godfrey Cunningham, in his *History of England in the Lives of Englishmen* (1834), displaced Donne from his Ecclesiastical Series to his Literary Series and quoted Satire III to illustrate Donne's 'conviction of the right and duty of private judgment in matters of faith.' Even Landor, disgusted as he was with religious writing, imagined Walton explaining that Donne had 'ordered' his satires 'to officiate as he would his curate, and perform half the service of the church for him.'[20]

The marginalia on Donne that Coleridge wrote into the copy of Chalmers may date from the period when he was giving his lectures on European literature, or they may be as late as 1829, when, according to Baron Hatherly, he was 'seized with a fit of enthusiasm for Donne's poetry.' Sometime after 1830 Coleridge himself recorded in a notebook his joyful reading of a number of Donne's love lyrics. Late in 1831 and at the start of 1832, it seems, he annotated his own copy of the *LXXX Sermons*, almost all of the notes concerning different sermons from those that he had annotated in Wordsworth's copy. According to Willmott, during Coleridge's last visit to Cambridge in 1833, he praised the sermons for their display of 'a depth of intellect', 'nervousness of style', 'variety of illustration' and 'power of argument', and he provocatively proposed that 'Donne's poetry must be sought in his prose.'[21] When the marginalia on the sermons were published in 1838, however, they appeared as a single series of notes without any indication that Coleridge had been reading and thinking and writing about Donne's prose over a period of more than two decades. Still, they helped Alford to find a publisher, and they proved an integral part of the first demonstration in literary history that publishing one's own marginalia was a possibility. As Heather Jackson has revealed, there was a sustained interest in these materials through much of the nineteenth century; and their repeated publication 'permanently changed the conditions and therefore the conventions of the writing of marginal notes', above all by making them more like familiar letters. As editors took more care to indicate when, and in what circumstances, Coleridge had written his annotations, readers were better able to appreciate one of the ways in which he himself used them, that is, as a grounds on which to discern, in relation to repeated readings of particular

---

[20] *Marginalia II*, 225–8; Cunningham is quoted here from the 1853 edn (London and Edinburgh: A. Fullarton), iii. 241; Landor, 'Izaac Walton, Cotton, and William Oldways', *Imaginary Conversations of Literary Men and Statesmen*, 2nd ser. (London: James Duncan, 1829), ii. 538.

[21] For the remark by Baron Hatherly, see *Coleridge on the Seventeenth Century*, 529; R. A. Willmott, 'S. T. Coleridge at Trinity', in *Conversations at Cambridge* (London: John W. Parker, 1836), 15.

works, how he had changed and as a means for testing whether he had made 'moral and intellectual progress.'[22]

That Coleridge found as much to criticize as to praise in Donne's sermons was in the twentieth century quite well understood, above all by Evelyn Simpson, whose *Study of the Prose Works of John Donne* lines up a number of illustrations of this fact.[23] To passages she singled out as instances of strong criticism of Donne's philosophy or theology, it may be added that Coleridge criticized Donne for crediting an old story according to which Jews kept 'in readinesse the blood of some Christian, with which they anoint the body of any that dyes amongst them' (*Marginalia II*, 274), for tastelessly dwelling at length on the material conditions of 'Mary's pregnancy & parturition' (Ibid. 273), and for giving the 'worst Sermon on the best text', St. Paul's declaration (in I Corinthians 15:26) that 'the last enemie that shall be destroyed, is death' (Ibid. 314). Coming to matters nearer the heart of theology, in his marginalia on Donne's Candlemas sermon on Matthew 5:16, Coleridge can be seen to take back praise as soon as he has recorded it: having written next to one passage 'the heroic Solifidian, Martin Luther, himself would have Subscribed, hand and heart' (Ibid. 298), his dynamic mind reversed field to register disappointment at the way Donne's argument subsequently unfolded. The remark is consistent with what we have seen in the marginalia on a Lenten sermon, where Coleridge judged that Donne lacked the imaginative boldness fully to credit the unity of the divine and human natures in Christ:

Donne was a truly great man; but he did not possess that full, steady, deep yet comprehensive Insight into the nature of Faith and Works, which was vouchsafed to Martin Luther. But Donne had not attained to the reconciling of distinctity with unity—ours yet God—God, yet ours.   (Ibid. 299–300)

While he respected Donne's stylistic achievements, Coleridge only rarely annotated Donne's writings as those of a superior thinker. In a marginal note on a sermon in which Donne had bestowed praise on a learned man for 'acknowledg[ing] that he had somewhat more to learn of Christ, then he knew yet', he designated the passage as '*pure gold*' and congratulated himself on having independently expressed the same idea. Characteristically, he then made Donne an ally as he extracted some practical implications: 'Without being aware of this passage in Donne I had expressed the same conviction, or rather declared the same experience, in the Appendix to my first "Lay Sermon"—or Statesman's Manual. | O if only one day in a week, Christians

[22] See H. J. Jackson, 'Writing in Books and Other Marginal Activities', *UTQ*, 62 (1992–3), 221–2, 226.
[23] Evelyn M. Simpson, *A Study of the Prose Works of John Donne*, 2nd edn (Oxford: Clarendon, 1948), 287–90.

would consent to have the Bible as the only Book—& their Ministers labor to make them find all substantial good of all other books in their Bible' (Ibid. 320).[24] The passage is important on at least three counts. First, it is directly related to a characteristic feature of preaching by Donne and other seventeenth-century divines that Coleridge valued most highly: the harnessing of formidable learning for the task of biblical exposition. Second, it shows Coleridge writing within a living theological and hermeneutical tradition, seeking creatively to exercise fidelity to its ever-unfolding truth. Third, it looks towards future moments of assessment by a wider audience, as the annotator virtually cites his own writings so that others might follow up on his claim. These annotations are quite different from the marginalia written into Wordsworth's copy of the sermons and show that Coleridge had entered into a markedly different interpretative community. In the earlier marginalia Coleridge, in the familiar mode of rationalist debunkers, criticized the 'sort of sophism … peculiar to the Christians' (Ibid. 253) which amounts to a kind of hypocrisy. In particular, he remarked upon 'the use, w[hi]ch the Xtian Divines make of the very facts in favor of their own religion, with which they triumpha[ntly] batter that of the Heathen', pointing out that when it comes to 'anthropomorphitism' in representing the divinity 'the Heathen Philosophers … tell us as plainly as Donne or Acquinas can do, these are only accomodations [sic] to human modes of conception' (Ibid. 254–5). The later marginalia are indicative of the perspective from which he read Donne after he had read more widely in the writings of Richard Baxter, Jeremy Taylor, and other seventeenth-century divines and had realized, as he put it in a letter of 1819, that rationalism was a 'Dry Rot in the timbers' of a vital community.[25]

RE-EVALUATING ALFORD'S EDITION

In the early Victorian period the quality of interest taken in Donne's writings by a few intelligent readers dovetailed with the popularity of Walton's *Lives* to create the conditions for a revival of Donne as a writer. Increasingly, Donne's sermons were assumed to have continuing relevance for the church and, as Alford hoped, for 'English literature in general' (i, p. v). In this climate of expectation Alford and Parker published the largest quantity of Donne's writings ever gathered into a single edition. The works actually published were

---

[24] Cf. Coleridge's expression of his 'reverence for Dr Donne', even as he seeks to correct Donne's views, *Marginalia II*, 300.

[25] See *Collected Letters of Samuel Taylor Coleridge, iv: 1815–1819*, ed. Earl Leslie Griggs (Oxford: Clarendon, 1959), no. 966.

those thought likely to speak directly to current spiritual and ecclesiastical needs. What the edition excluded was much of the poetry, most of the juvenilia, and virtually all of the controversial prose. The assumption that Donne's religious writings could speak for themselves also meant that the edition was only lightly annotated. The modest front matter, such as it was, included a 'Life of Dr. Donne' with a critical notice of his works, together with two pages of 'particulars respecting Dr. Donne's children' (i, pp. xxvii–xxviii). Alford summarized and silently revised Walton to accommodate Donne to a popular audience. Instead of dwelling on Donne's reluctance to go into the church, Alford developed details from Walton's opening pages and emphasized that as a young man Donne had converted to the reformed church on purely rational grounds. Of Donne's marriage to Anne More he simply said that it was 'rather unfortunately brought about, than itself unfortunate' (i, p. xii). Even after the wedding cost him his prospects, Alford's Donne was steadily sought after by men of influence in the church and at court, so that there was no real struggle with scruples but rather a steady progress into a clerical career, in which 'he was raised to comparative affluence' (i, p. xvi).

From the first appearance of Alford's edition it was clear that it would not fully serve the purposes of readers eager to inform themselves about the old divinity. J. C. Robertson pointed out 'blunders and deficiencies', wrong dates, and typographical errors, especially in printing Donne's Latin. More substantially, he lamented that Alford had not included *Pseudo-martyr* and complained that, for all the editor's training at Cambridge and his freedom from venal aims, since Alford had failed to take the pains to provide the apparatus necessary for informed reading, the edition amounted to no more than a reprint. '[T]he republication of our great old divines in these times is a matter of very high importance,' he urged. 'Their writings are a noble part of our inheritance as a church and as a nation; we are daily becoming more and more aware of their value.' He observed, however, that 'the appearance of one new edition makes it unlikely that any other will be called for, for many years to come, and therefore we are positively *wronged*', he concluded, by the publication of an edition that 'takes away from us who are now living almost all hope of ever seeing a better.' Alford defended himself only weakly, protesting that he had never meant to be 'a commentator.' He proposed that the 'main object' of the edition—'opening the treasures of Donne's eloquence and theological reading to the public'—would be accomplished, despite 'the casual errors of his editor.'[26] This rationalization contained a measure of truth.

---

[26] See the exchange in *The British Magazine and Monthly Register*, 15 (1839), 534–7; 16 (1839), 60–1.

During the twentieth century, Alford's edition was more maligned than it was in the nineteenth. In the 1950s, preparing a new edition of Donne's sermons, George Potter and Evelyn Simpson made a grudging acknowledgement of the existence of Alford's as the only other complete edition since the publication of the three folios in the seventeenth century. Their California edition, conceived and executed at a time when it was customary to denigrate the benighted Victorians, enshrined an apotheosis of Donne and looked condescendingly upon those who had failed to appreciate his prowess. Indeed, the edition celebrated the twentieth-century Donne revival as a decisive proof of the superiority of a modernist sensibility that had effected 'a major revolution in the practice of poetry' and made us 'feel the force of our turning against the Victorian valuation of him.' Donne is 'rightfully ours', Willard Farnham pronounced in the Foreword to the tenth and final volume of *The Sermons of John Donne*, 'because he is a poet with *angst* and his *angst* is somehow deeply like our own.'[27] The standard Victorian view of Donne was assumed to have been epitomized in Alford's having left out 'some passages which he thought might be objectionable to Victorian taste' (x, p. viii) and in Donne's having been altogether omitted from Palgrave's *Golden Treasury of the Best Songs and Lyrical Poems in the English Language* (1861). Theodore Gill claimed that Alford 'expurgated' the sermons for 'nineteenth-century readers.' He proposed, moreover, that Potter and Simpson offered Donne's sermons in a form 'clearly closer to the author's intention than in any earlier publication', even the 1640 'folio', and judged that their 'superlative scholarship' produced 'in a very real sense, *first* editions of Donne's sermons.'[28]

While no one would deny that the California edition of Donne's sermons is vastly superior, the energetic denigration of Alford's edition ought to give us pause. Like Bald ignoring the importance of Zouch's work for reviving interest in Donne's biography, Potter and Simpson made little effort to examine the circumstances in which Alford's edition was created or to gauge the effects that it helped to produce. Anyone who actually dusts off Alford's edition can see that the insinuation that he was a bowdlerizer is based on an utterly superficial acquaintance with it, and the claims of the California editors about the superiority of their edition were overstated. In Alford's introduction he conscientiously mentioned that when he first began his project, before the Parkers agreed to print all Donne's extant sermons, he had 'contemplated' a 'selection' and had, in the sermons he had already prepared for the press,

---

[27] Willard Farnham, Foreword, *The Sermons of John Donne*, ed. George R. Potter and Evelyn M. Simpson, 10 vols. (Berkeley and Los Angeles: Univ. of California Press, 1953–62), x, pp. viii, ix. Subsequent references for quotations from this edition appear within parentheses.

[28] Theodore Gill (ed.), *The Sermons of John Donne: Selected and Introduced* (Canada: Meridan Books, 1958), 27, 284.

omitted 'one or two passages containing allusions, common at the time when they were delivered, but likely to offend modern readers.' He went on to say that the omissions were no more than these one or two and to assure readers that they were getting all the rest of the sermons in 'their original unmutilated form' (i, p. vi). Close inspection shows that Alford had cut two passages from the last of the seven Christmas sermons, the one not marked in its heading for a particular year. One cut is about fifteen lines long. It is a striking passage in the course of which Donne observes that while the Scriptures often ascribe various body parts to God they never say that God has 'shoulders.' Donne then suggests that this involves a tacit recognition that 'shoulders are the subjects of burdens, and therein the figures of patience, and so God is all shoulder, all patience' and in the person of Christ 'suffers patiently a quotidian Crucifying' through 'our dayly sins' (ix. 135–6). A second omission is much briefer and comes from the peroration. Alford omitted Donne's reference to the 'joy' of Christian martyrs as 'such a joy, as would worke a liquefaction, a melting of my bowels' (154). In the King James Bible, 'bowels' regularly appeared as the translation for the Hebrew *meim*. Even after Donne's death, it continued to be used in English to refer to the seat of pity and strong emotion, as in the title Richard Sibbes's commentary on the Song of Solomon, *Bowels Opened*, and in Bunyan's remark that 'bowels becometh pilgrims.' When Alford suppressed the passage he was acknowledging what he had reason to suppose his readers might not know: that there had been a marked change in the dominant sense of the word. This cut was consonant with Alford's concern for, and later his participation in, the first major revision of the language of the Authorized Version.[29]

While Potter and Simpson edited each of Donne's sermons in conformity with prevailing editorial standards for accurate transcription, they took an extraordinary liberty in arranging the collection. Whereas Alford followed the order of arrangement in the seventeenth-century folios, Potter and Simpson broke up the sermons and constructed a putative chronology for them. They had to admit, and did so belatedly in the last volume, that the *LXXX Sermons* had been arranged according to 'a definite plan' (x. 402–3). That plan organized forty-nine sermons according to the rhythms of the liturgical year, beginning with seven Christmas sermons, then following with sermons for Candlemas Day, Lent, Easter, etc. Although the editors admitted that 'Donne himself may have devised the arrangement' (x. 403), Peter McCullough has provided grounds for supposing that the liturgical groupings were the work of John Donne, Jr., who followed the precedent set in Lancelot Andrewes's

---

[29] But cf. the Christmas sermon for 1628, where Alford retains the words 'bowels' and 'embowelled.'

XCVI Sermons.[30] Potter and Simpson found this structure inconvenient for their own plan, which was to illustrate Donne's 'development.' What they failed sufficiently to emphasize in promoting this idea is that the texts published in the folios were not sermons that Donne had written out and then delivered, nor were they transcripts. Donne's typical method, as Walton had explained, was to prepare notes from which he preached. Some sermons were written for publication later, presumably with the help of the notes. In such circumstances, Donne was likely to have omitted or curtailed what was topical and to emphasize ideas that he assumed would have enduring value and that would be of interest to wider, and later, audiences.

The invocation of a fiction of the writer's development by Potter and Simpson implicates their work more profoundly in a Romantic and expressive theory of literature than Alford's was. In a number of ways it distances their edition, for all its trappings of frequent italics and old spellings, from seventeenth-century practice. It obscures for current readers some things evident to earlier readers who knew the sermons in the folios or in Alford's edition: not only the dominant principle of organization, but the spherical patterns created by returning again and again to Christmas, before moving on to Candlemas, then to Lent, etc. More subtly, it tends to hide one of the most striking features of the sermons, Donne's odd and challenging choices of the texts—and subjects—on which he preached. If we take the eight surviving Christmas sermons as an example, we note first of all that the sermon for 1621 was not included in *LXXX Sermons*; because it was grouped with two other sermons on John 1:8 in *Fifty Sermons*, it appeared relatively late in Alford's edition. Eager to illustrate the preacher's supposed development, however, Potter and Simpson present it as Donne's 'manifesto' as a preacher (iii. 36–7) and single out its theme of light as a norm against which to measure all the other Christmas sermons. With this arbitrary canon, they judge the others mostly as failures. The sermon of 1622 is quietly buried in the fourth volume of their edition, and they have nothing to say about it except that it 'is not particularly noteworthy.' About its prominence as the introduction to Donne's preaching in 1640 and 1839 there is no mention at all (iv. 38). The editors make the sermon for 1627 seem an egregious and impertinent discourse when they speak of its 'perversity and aridity' (viii. 27; cf. viii. 11) and pronounce that 'as a Christmas sermon it is a complete disappointment', since it is not about the life of Jesus (viii. 12). The sermon for 1628, which

---

[30] On Walton's appreciation of ways in which Donne's life could be understood as a 'counterpointing' of time and eternity, see W. Gerald Marshall, 'Time in Walton's *Lives*', *SEL*, 32 (1992), 429–42. On the arrangement of Donne's *LXXX Sermons*, see Peter McCullough, 'Donne and Andrewes', *JDJ*, 22 (2003), 184–7.

Coleridge greatly admired, 'is not an eloquent sermon', they say, and 'by no means a characteristic Christmas sermon'; for Donne 'regards Christ, not as the babe of Bethlehem, but as the Suffering Servant of Isaiah, despised and rejected of men, and crucified in history by man's unbelief' (viii. 27). Even with respect to the sermon for 1624, which contains the oft-quoted passage about God's boundless mercy in which Donne proposes that while in 'paradise, the fruits were ripe, the first minute, … in heaven it is alwaies Autumne' and God's 'mercies are ever in their maturity' (vi. 172), a passage that Potter and Simpson must admit to be 'one of [the] most exquisite passages' in all Donne's sermons—even here, they instruct readers to expect 'a number of dull and tedious pages' (vi. 14–16).

Potter and Simpson's handling of Donne's Christmas sermons makes it difficult for readers to imagine how these materials were read in the editions of 1640 and 1839. The group of seven, which as seven stands as 'the holy Ghosts Cyphar of infinite' and marks the meeting of eternity and time, has been separated and redistributed.[31] The new chronological framework erects linear and diachronic time as the norm and belittles cyclical and synchronic conceptions of time. It accommodates, moreover, the complex liturgical sense of multiple times superimposed onto one another into a fullness of time, to the rather more dull secular perspective according to which Christianity is a religion that flourished in the past. This latter perspective is readily compatible with sentimental ideas about the old-fashioned 'traditional' Christmases of one's childhood and with the Anglo-Catholic assumptions (borrowed, as McCullough shows, from Lancelot Andrewes and T. S. Eliot) that bedevil Potter and Simpson's introductions to the Christmas sermons. It makes it more difficult than ever to imagine that Donne's Christmas sermons may have been attractive and engaging to their first audiences because the texts on which he chose to preach were often surprising, his subjects unconventional, and his approaches deeply challenging. Rather than showing his perversity, Donne's chosen texts provoke reflection on everyone's need to make intelligent, imaginative choices about what to read and how to read it.

The gap between Coleridge's regard for the seven Christmas discourses and Potter and Simpson's denigration of them helps us to understand some reasons that Alford's edition, even on his own terms, was not a wholly successful 'experiment.' While the young editor's casual and often inaccurate scholarship

---

[31] See Sermon XXVII, in *Fifty Sermons* (London, 1649), 237. For a trenchant critique of popular assumptions about Donne's 'development' as a preacher, see P. G. Stanwood, 'Donne's Earliest Sermons and the Penitential Tradition', in Raymond-Jean Frontain and Frances Malpezzi (eds.), *John Donne's Religious Imagination: Essays in Honor of John T. Shawcross* (Conway, AR: UCA Press, 1995), 366–79.

earned his edition its reputation as 'a literary *fiasco*', more likely the edition did not achieve the modest goals that Alford set for it because of profound cultural changes that made Donne seem quaint, irrelevant, or merely puzzling to readers who picked up the first volume and began reading the Christmas sermons. With his wide reading in the seventeenth century, Coleridge was aware of great differences between the festive celebration of Christmas in Tudor and Stuart times on the one hand and the lukewarm observance characteristic of his own lifetime, when, partly in the wake of the puritan suppression of the feast, traditional customs had fallen into desuetude. Although *The Times* made no mention of the occurrence of Christmas between 1790 and 1835, by the time Alford's edition appeared, the situation was changing. The 1830s witnessed a resurgence of interest in the holiday, and through the middle decades of the century an idealized Christmas that was supposed to have been kept in 'merrie olde England' was newly fashioned. Its construction depended precisely upon the fiction that it was a vestige of a golden age. The ideal was expressed in a growing body of Christmas literature, much of it as revealing of Victorian anxieties about political instabilities and a lack of social harmony as it is about the customs of the season. The constructed longing for Christmases of old took on an almost definitive narrative form in *A Christmas Carol*, first published in 1843. Dickens had been contributing to the nostalgic idealizing even earlier, in the description of Christmas at Dingley Dell in *Pickwick Papers* (1836), while on the American side of the Atlantic Washington Irving's depiction of 'Old Christmas' in his *Sketch Book* offered the sort of imagery of roaring fires and horse-driven coaches en route to Grandmother's house still typical of many illustrations of the season. Once the appeal of Christmas became sentimental, as in Dickens's reduction of it to a metaphor for human sympathy, once people took it for granted that it was a family holiday, a time for indulging children with trees and presents from Santa Claus, that is, once it became 'traditional', the possibility was virtually obliterated that a significant number of persons would achieve understanding and find pleasure in a body of Christmas sermons that emphasize mortality and regularly associate the Nativity with the Day of Judgment.

In the early Victorian period Donne was partly sought out, like the traditional Christmas, as an object of nostalgia. Some hoped to find in him an exemplary precursor and, as Walton had depicted him, a father of the English Church. It seemed appropriate and promising that the new edition of his *Works* should begin not with 'Metempsychosis' or 'The Flea', but with the Christmas sermons. Yet however much the sermons may have had to offer to Anglican theology, they cannot have been much help to the newly active promoters of the 'old-fashioned' Christmas. Far from being full of 'traditional Christmas spirit', the Christmas sermons on which Coleridge had bestowed concentrated attention were long and learned and replete with intellectual challenges. Preached on surprising texts that concerned old Simeon's intense consciousness of his mortality or Moses's frustration that his preaching was met with obstinate silence, rather than predictable ones that fed a fascination with legends about the childhood of Jesus, they suggested ways of keeping the season that would have been as uncongenial to the Bob Cratchit family as they were to Scrooge himself.

A CODA

In the short run, the publication of the *Works of Donne* was a stimulus to other publishers. The simplicity of Alford's presentation of the material seems to have assuaged fears that they would have to give in to the necessary evil, as Dr Johnson had designated it, of publishing books replete with annotations. This largely guaranteed that few readers would exercise on Donne's writings the sort of historical imagination necessary to understand them. Neither the 1840 and 1841 editions of the *Devotions* nor the 1840 *Selections* contained much explanatory apparatus. In the volume of *Selections* prepared for general readers, the anonymous editor made no attempt to identify the sources of the excerpts and merely bestowed on most passages pious editorial headings, such as 'God's Mercy Immeasurable' and 'Summary of Religious Duties.' Occasionally, the headings were more inviting, capturing something striking from Donne's own language, especially headings for passages about death: 'How? A Hateful Monosyllable'; 'Life Not a Parenthesis'; 'This Life a Preface.' Most of the poems printed near the back of the volume were freely retitled, in accord with editorial practices then prevailing among the makers of poetic and other anthologies. An excerpt from the verse letter to Henry Goodyere beginning 'Who makes the past a pattern' is titled 'Improvement', and an excerpt from the Second Anniversary 'Human Ignorance.' Among the sonnets 'This is my play's last scene' is named 'Thought on Death', 'At the round earth's imagined corners' is called 'Repentance', and 'Batter my heart' has become, in accord with a pervasive editorial timidity, 'Prayer for Grace.'[32] Nor did the new editions of the *Devotions* carry any sign that their makers had experienced Donne—or expected their readers to experience his writings—with the sort of imaginative boldness characteristic of Coleridge's annotations. In this sense, we can say that the conspicuous short-term success of Alford's edition ensured its long-term failure to promote intelligent reading.

[32] *Selections from the Works of John Donne, D.D.* (Oxford: Talboys, 1840).

Within a generation Alford's experiment to find out 'how far the present English public are desirous to retrieve the treasures' of old divinity demonstrated that there was no body of readers with the learning, the historical imagination, and the motivation necessary to fulfill the expectations voiced by the annotator of the *LXXX Sermons*, who had called for a new edition. In 1868 Donne's learned successor at St Paul's, Dean Milman, pronounced that Coleridge, who had 'delighted to wander in the wide and intricate mazes of Donne's theology', had capriciously carried 'admiration' too far. Having himself surveyed 'the massy folios of Donne's sermons', Milman confessed without any sense of irony or shame that he was unable to imagine how Donne, even if his style of delivery had been 'graceful and impressive', could have held 'a London congregation enthralled, unwearied, unsatiated.' While acknowledging that Donne's listeners attended 'not only with patience but with absorbed interest' and that they were often moved to tears, Milman judged Donne's sermons 'interminable disquisitions, ... teeming with laboured obscurity, false and misplaced wit, fatiguing antitheses.'[33]

Yet if Donne's sermons secured neither the quantity nor quality of attention that Alford had sought for them, in a biographical age that was sometimes studious, often cavalier, and occasionally prurient there were other materials in the *Works* that proved to be of enduring interest. Tellingly, it was the prose letters rather than the sermons that were made to speak for Donne.

---

[33] Henry Hart Milman, *Annals of S. Paul's Cathedral* (London: John Murray, 1868), 328–9.

4

Letters

The best history of a writer is contained in his writings—these are his
chief actions. ... Biographies are generally a disease of English literature.

—George Eliot, *Letters*

Of the thousands of decisions, large and small, taken in the nineteenth century
by persons seeking to make Donne's writings available in print, few were as
influential as certain moves made in the late 1830s by the publisher and the
editor of *The Works of John Donne, D.D.* John W. Parker offered six volumes,
instead of the requested four, for a new edition of the sermons. His liberality
made it possible to include the sermons in their entirety. It also necessitated a
number of decisions that the aspiring editor had not expected to make. Among
these the most important was what to do with the additional space. Alford chose
to include works that had a conspicuously biographical interest: the *Devotions*,
which according to Walton contained Donne's 'most secret thoughts', poems
mostly on religious subjects, especially holy dying, and virtually all the letters
in prose and in verse. As it turned out, the prose letters became the most
widely read section of the *Works*. As productions of a figure known in Britain
chiefly through a narrative about his life, the letters of Dr Donne took their
place with other epistolary collections to which Victorian readers turned for
instruction and entertainment. While the sermons of an obscure writer were
almost stillborn, the letters spoke to a 'desire for windows that open on the
private lives of the famous',[1] as it has been called in a helpful study of how
published collections of personal letters were read in the period. Through the
rest of the century, this desire sent readers to look into Donne's poetry as
well. Curiosity about a figure known first apart from his writings provided a
decisive hermeneutical criterion that profoundly affected what readers would
find when they looked, as increasingly they did, into the 'works.'

---

[1] Rosemarie Bodenheimer, *The Real Life of Mary Ann Evans: George Eliot, Her Letters and
Fiction* (Ithaca, NY: Cornell Univ. Press, 1994), 12. The epigraph for this chapter is the first
passage quoted from George Eliot in the book, p. xiii.

TWO MODELS FOR READING LETTERS

Two principal traditions of reading personal letters were available to readers
in the English-speaking world. One approached them chiefly as artifacts, the
other predominantly as personal expressions. The differing emphasis of each
is summed up in the preface to a collection of *Letters of Eminent Persons*,
which contained three letters by Donne and was published in the same year
and by the same publisher as Alford's edition: 'The letters composing the
present volume', Robert Willmott explained, 'have been chiefly selected either
for their inherent beauty, or for the sake of the persons, and the subjects to
which they relate.' In the one tradition a letter was considered primarily a
verbal construction, a piece of social conduct emanating from a pen. Often
it did not matter who the writer had been; the purpose of the collection
within which the letter was incorporated was to illustrate effective letters of
varying kinds. In the other tradition, inasmuch as readers were seeking details
about the experience of someone whom they already knew by reputation, the
connection of a letter with a particular writer was of the utmost importance.
Willmott's acknowledgment that few of the letters he had selected were by
persons whose 'names' had 'not become familiar to our lips as household
words'[2] points to the fact that in practice the two traditions are often only
notionally separable. They coexist and overlap, sometimes even comfortably.
Both traditions informed the way in which Willmott presented the materials
he selected from Donne: 'All the characteristics of the poetry and the prose
of Donne will be found in his letters; the same eccentricity of expression,
originality of thought, and liveliness of illustration, surprise the reader in
every page. ... But his letters are also interesting as developements [*sic*] of
personal feelings, and descriptions of his situation and prospects. Many of
them were written amid the perplexities into which an improvident marriage
had plunged him.'[3]

Of course these ways of reading letters were already operable when Donne's
personal correspondence was first put into print. The volume published 1651
and titled *Letters to Severall Persons of Honour* was ascribed to 'John Donne
sometime deane of St Pauls.' The words on the title page did not necessarily
presuppose interest in the letter-writer. In fact, the habit of looking to letters
as exemplary pieces of writing provided a rationale for the editor's taking no
particular care to produce a chronological arrangement. That some readers

---

[2] Robert Aris Willmott (ed.), *Letters of Eminent Persons: Selected and Illustrated* (London:
John W. Parker, 1839), 13.
[3] Ibid. 50.

regarded the identity of the original writer as irrelevant is suggested by the analogous case of the elegy, 'The Expostulation', variously ascribed to Donne and to Ben Jonson. In Samuel Sheppard's *The Marrow of Complements* (1655) this poem was identified as the work of one 'R. L.' and printed as a prose letter. The editor offered it as an example for use in a particular set of circumstances: 'The Lover finding himself abus'd by her who promis'd him Marriage (she deserting him and electing another) may thus vent himselfe.'[4]

A mixture of rhetorical and personal grounds for publishing Donne's letters was already evident in the earliest editions of *Poems by J.D.*, which contained epistles in prose as well as verse. The editions of 1633 and 1635 show that the editors were handling personal letters both as artifacts and as carriers of biographical information. Some letters seem to have been chosen more for their exemplary writing, others because they show something about Donne's life. The idea that a writer's letters could offer models inspired the earliest printed collection, the group included in 1633, as David Novarr has shown, 'not for what they tell of Donne's life and insights, not as informal and personal revelations of the writer', but simply as 'examples of epistolary elegance.'[5] Several contained reflections upon the nature and function of personal letters, and this feature of the writing continued to command attention. Coleridge's praise for one addressed to Henry Goodyere epitomizes this way of reading: 'A noble Letter ... in which Friends communicate to each other the accidents of their meditations, and baffle absence by writing what, if present, they would have talked.'[6] The orientation displayed in this marginal comment had been common from the Stuart era onward. Its continuing currency in the Victorian period encouraged editors to make collections that would offer a model of character for emulation. It was on these grounds that personal letters had become established as a literary form, and the tradition provided a background against which the epistolary novels of the eighteenth century were written.

Because this tradition sustained the habit of reading the assertions in letters as 'truths of character', it also helped to promote the idea that a writer's correspondence is personally revealing. By 1635 looking to Donne's letters for personal information was already being encouraged, as the editors of the second edition of the *Poems* inserted four additional prose letters to emphasize

---

[4] See Ernest W. Sullivan, II, *The Influence of John Donne: His Uncollected Seventeenth-Century Printed Verse* (Columbia, MO: Univ. of Missouri Press, 1993), 44–6. The passage quoted here appears (44) in italics.

[5] David Novarr, *The Making of Walton's Lives* (Ithaca, NY: Cornell Univ. Press, 1958), 36, 35, respectively. For the quotation that follows, see 38.

[6] *The Collected Works of Samuel Taylor Coleridge*, xii: *Marginalia II*, ed. George Whalley (London: Routledge and Kegan Paul; Princeton, NJ: Princeton Univ. Press, 1984), 232. Subsequent references from *Marginalia II* (1984) in volume xii appear in parentheses.

the importance of Donne's having become a divine. As Novarr has observed, the newly incorporated letters seemed to 'counteract the licentiousness of some of the poems now added for the first time.' Whether the model operative in 1633 is to be regarded in the terms that Donne presents Truth in the third Satire, as the elder twin of falsehood, the sequence by which the letters were augmented from 1633 to 1635 could not easily have taken place in reverse. Within the practice of reading his letters as performances, that is, as artifacts worthy of rhetorical analysis, were the seeds of reading them as documents containing personal revelations by the performer. It was Walton who helped readers to realize this potential when, with an editorial liberty that he acknowledged, he created composite letters for inclusion in *The Life and Death of Doctor John Donne*. By the high Victorian period it may have looked to believers in Progress that this sequence in the reading of Donne's letters had gone against the tide of cultural history. Writing for *The Nineteenth Century* an account of letter-writing from ancient Egypt to the penny-post, Augustus Jessopp proposed that for more than a thousand years of Western history an 'almost universal intolerance of anything that bordered on freedom of thought and freedom of speech' had made people 'afraid of expressing their real sentiments' in letters and that it was only in 'the Renaissance that men began to unbosom themselves again.' Jessopp celebrated the 'fathomless ocean of letters' written in the late Elizabethan period and proposed that regarding letter-writing as 'a graceful accomplishment', which he dated to the reign of King James I, came about from a reassertion of repressive social forces.[7] Although Jessopp had by this time written two substantial accounts of Donne's life, his essay made no mention of Donne's letters, over which he had been poring for more than thirty years. He knew quite well that in his own time the sequence by which interest in Donne's writings had once led readers to look into his life had been reversed. Himself an avid reader of the letters made available by Alford, he mined them precisely with a view to augmenting the biographical picture sketched by Walton.

Relatively few readers seem to have been adept at reading Donne's letters simultaneously for their rhetorical achievements and their personal revelations. Significantly, two of the best, Coleridge and George Eliot, were themselves accomplished writers. Alongside letters found in Lamb's 1669 edition, Coleridge wrote marginal comments that show how deftly he moved back and forth between two complementary ways of reading. One letter, headed 'To the Countess of Bedford', he identified as 'a truly elegant Letter, and a happy

---

[7] Augustus Jessopp, D.D., 'Letters and Letter-Writers', repr. in *Studies by a Recluse in Cloister, Town, and Country* (London: T. Fisher Unwin; New York: G. P. Putnam's Sons, 1893), 245–6, 249.

specimen of that dignified Courtesy to Sex and Rank, of that white Flattery, in which the Wit unrealizes the Falsehood, and the sportive exaggeration of the Thoughts blending with a delicate tenderness faithfully conveys the Truth as to the Feelings' (*Marginalia II*, 236). While the emphasis here is on the witty performance, the observation comes to rest with a judgment about an emotional veracity that expresses itself precisely through hyperbole. Similarly, the marginal criticism of Donne's letter 'To the La. G.' shows that Coleridge was thinking about both the strategies of writing and the writer who devised them. His comment was directed to a passage in which, according to the edition he had to hand, Donne had written 'Madam, my best treasure is time, and my best imployment of that (next my thoughts of thankfulness for my Redeemer) is to study good wishes for you.' Again, Coleridge's evaluation of the letter extends to a judgment about the character of the writer: 'the thoughts played upon are of so serious a nature, and the exception in the Parenthesis so aweful, that the Wit instead of carrying off aggravates the Flattery—and Donne must either have been literally sincere, or adulatory to extravagance, & almost to Blasphemy' (Ibid. 233). What Coleridge did not know was that the editor who first printed this letter in 1635 had altered what Donne wrote, inserting in the parentheses a thought that is quite foreign to the tone and content of the rest of the letter. (This seems to have been part of a concerted editorial attempt to make Donne seem more pious.[8]) Although Coleridge did not have the textual resources to be able to identify the editorial corruption, he heard the false note and showed by his response that he knew the passage was out of keeping with Donne's characteristic writing.

Elsewhere, commenting on the late letter in which Donne confessed his 'desire ... that I might die in the Pulpit', Coleridge offered another observation that shows how he read in both traditions simultaneously: 'This passage seems to prove', he remarks, 'that Donne retained thro' life the main opinions defended in his Biothanatos—at least, this *joined* with his dying command that the Treatise should not be destroyed tho' he did not think the Age ripe for its Publication, furnishes a strong presumption of his perseverance in the defensibility of Suicide in certain cases' (*Marginalia II*, 235–6). Suggesting familiarity with another letter, the one in which the writer had distinguished between Jack Donne and Dr Donne,[9] Coleridge seems to endorse the idea that there was a hiatus separating the life into two parts. Yet the annotation shows that Coleridge, who in another marginal comment concluded that 'After all, there is but one Donne!' (Ibid. 218), was skeptical about that distinction. The

---

[8] Novarr, *Making of Walton's Lives*, 42–3.

[9] In *Letters to Severall Persons of Honour* (London, 1651), 21–2; in *The Works of John Donne, D.D., Dean of Saint Paul's, 1621–1631. With a Memoir of His Life*, ed. Henry Alford, 6 vols. (London: John W. Parker, 1839), vi. 373.

sentence ultimately substitutes for Walton's focus on Donne's life a concern with Donne's afterlife as a writer.

While the two traditions of letter-reading were not mutually exclusive, they sometimes collided. Each had a different center of gravity. The tradition that tended to define letters as a mode of social conduct and to promote self-conscious performance in writing continued to prompt readers to notice passages that seemed unusual or exemplary. Robert Southey, for instance, excerpted a remark that Donne had made in a letter about how he had sifted the materials for one of his sermons: 'As Cardinal Cusanus writ a book *Cribratio Alchorani*, I have cribrated, and re-cribrated, and post-cribrated this sermon.'[10] Entries from the early 1840s in the journals of Henry David Thoreau show that he especially admired Donne's verse letters for the thoughts they inspire. Having read through all Donne's poems in Chalmers's collection, Thoreau concluded that

Donne was not a poet—but a man of strong sense—a sturdy English thinker—full of conceits and whimsicalities, hammering away at his subject—be it eulogy or epitaph—sonnet or satire with the patience of a day laborer, without taste, but with an occasional fine distinction or poetic phrase. He was rather *Doctor* Donne, than the *poet* Donne. His letters are perhaps best.[11]

That is, Thoreau specially valued the epistles because they reveal the groping of a hard-working 'thinker', whose 'real life' (to borrow the phrase felicitously chosen to describe the experience of George Eliot) was lived largely by a patient practice of the art of writing. He looked to Donne for ideas and for striking means of expression. His way of reading accorded well with principles that George Eliot would articulate in one of her letters, when she insisted that the writings of a writer are 'his chief actions', and that she wished for no biography of her recently deceased spouse.[12]

The energies that went into attempts to dampen interest in biography suggest that the tradition that looked to letters for intimate personal revelations was gaining force. Southey, besides copying out striking passages, made excerpts of confessional statements, such as 'I am the worst present man in the world', a passage reminiscent of I Timothy 1:15 and perhaps revealing only as much as the familiar claim to be 'chief of sinners' by Bunyan, Cromwell, and dozens of others. Southey transcribed, moreover, the whole of the famous letter

[10] *Southey's Common-Place Book*, 4th ser., ed. John Wood Warter (London: Longman, Brown, 1850), 621. Cf. *Letters* (1651), 308.

[11] Henry D. Thoreau, *Journal*, ii: *1842–1848*, gen. ed. John C. Broderick (Princeton, NJ: Princeton Univ. Press, 1984), 83. Thoreau's reading of Donne, which began at Harvard, is discussed further in Chapter 7.

[12] *The George Eliot Letters*, ed. Gordon S. Haight, 9 vols. (New Haven, CT: Yale Univ. Press, 1954–78), vii. 230.

to Goodyere, beginning 'Every Tuesday I make account that I turn a great hour-glass, and consider that a week's life is run out since I writ.'[13] This was the best known of all Donne's letters, though readers knew it chiefly by way of the version printed by Walton:

'tis now Spring, and all the pleasures of it displease me; every other tree blossoms, and I wither: I grow older and not better; my strength diminisheth and my load grows heavier; and yet, I would fain be or do something; but, that I cannot tell what, is no wonder in this time of my sadness; for, to chuse is to do; but, to be no part of any body, is as to be nothing; and so I am, and shall so judge my self, unless I could be so incorporated into a part of the world, as by business to contribute some sustentation to the whole.

When Walton incorporated these words into his account of how Donne had at last contributed to the English nation and church, his providential narrative served as a larger context that transformed their meaning. Many nineteenth-century readers seem to have taken for granted the validity of this perspective and to have directed their best attention to the next passage, in which they found an extraordinary self-revelation:

This I made account, I began early when I understood the study of our Laws: but was diverted by leaving that and imbracing the worst voluptuousness, *an hydroptique immoderate desire of humane learning and languages*: Beautiful ornaments indeed to men of great fortunes; but mine was grown so low as to need an occupation: which I thought I entred well into, when I subjected my self to such a service as I thought might exercise my poor abilities: and there I stumbled, and fell too: and now I am become so little, or such a nothing, that I am not a subject good enough for one of my own letters.[14]

The revelatory power of this passage seemed great because it was assumed that Donne had intended his letter to be read only by a limited audience. Its appearance in print violated his intention and held out a forbidden pleasure.[15] In a book published by Parker five years after Donne's *Works*, Richard Cattermole pointed out that this and other letters from the period when Donne was living at Mitcham 'exhibit most affectingly a gloomy picture of family distress.' Cattermole then used them to create a more dramatic plot than Walton had offered. The letters were made to yield up evidence of the

[13] *Common-Place Book*, 4th ser., 621; 1st ser. (New York: Harper and Brothers, 1849), 250. Southey transcribed the letter in the modified form that appears in Walton. Cf. *Letters* (1651), 48–52; Alford (ed.), *Works of John Donne*, vi. 320–2. This letter was also printed by Willmott, 52–4.

[14] Walton, *The Lives of Dr John Donne, Sir Henry Wotton, Mr Richard Hooker, Mr George Herbert*, 4th edn (London, 1675), 26–7. The two long passages appeared, with the exception of the words printed in italics here, in italics; that is, I have reversed the procedure.

[15] Cf. Bodenheimer, *Real Life of Mary Ann Evans*, 3.

'deplorable condition' and 'lowest depth of depression' into which Donne had to fall before embracing at last his true vocation.[16]

   This is an aspect of Donne's 'real life' in which George Eliot took an active interest, and she thought about the letter to Goodyere over the course of many years. During the period when she was composing *Middlemarch*, for instance, she was not only reading *Paradise Lost* with George Henry Lewes, but reading Johnson's *Life of Milton*, Hippolyte Taine's *History of English Literature*, Walton's *Life of Donne*, and Donne's *Letters*. The jottings she made in her notebooks suggest that Taine's remark that Donne had spoiled his gifts stimulated her interest in his life. As if to answer Taine with a Miltonic criterion found in the sonnets 'How soon hath time ... 'and 'When I consider how my light is spent', Eliot recorded signs of Donne's fascination with the idea of using his talents and making his learning socially productive. From the letter to Goodyere, she copied out a remark that bears on her own long-standing struggle with ambition:

The Eagle were very unnatural if because she is able to do it, she should perch the whole day upon a tree, staring in contemplation of the majesty & glory of the sun, & let her young Eglets starve in the nest.[17]

This passage has been cited as evidence that Eliot saw Donne as a male writer who insisted on the importance of childrearing as a woman's 'natural role.'[18] It is unlikely that Eliot transcribed the passage for this reason. Donne was, after all, comparing himself to the mother eagle. Moreover, Eliot thought of Donne precisely as a writer who dared to dissolve conventional boundaries between the sexes. When in *Middlemarch* she first brings him onto the stage, he is the author of lines from 'The Undertaking' that stand as the epigraph for Chapter 39:

> If, as I have, you also doe,
>   Vertue attired in woman see,
> And dare love that, and say so too,
>   And forget the He and She;

---

[16] *The Literature of the Church of England Indicated in Selections from the Writings of Eminent Divines*, 2 vols. (London: John W. Parker, 1844), i. 121.

[17] *George Eliot's* Middlemarch *Notebooks: A Transcription*, ed. with an Introduction by John Clark Pratt and Victor A. Neufeldt (Berkeley, CA: Univ. of California Press, 1979), 146–7, 63, respectively. In the quotation from Donne's letter, I have silently emended the faulty transcription of the decisive word 'able' as 'unable.' The editors have also mis-cited the relevant volume number of Alford's edition; the accurate reference is vi. 320. Taine's view of Donne is considered below, in Chapter 5, and his view of Donne's place in literary history in Chapter 8.

[18] Gillian Beer, *George Eliot* (Bloomington, IN: Indiana University Press, 1986), 13. Quotations from *Middlemarch* are from the edition by David Carroll (Oxford: Clarendon, 1986), based on the 1874 edition, which was the last corrected by the author.

And if this love, though placed so,
  From prophane men you hide,
Which will no faith on this bestow,
  Or, if they doe, deride:

Then you have done a braver thing
  Than all the Worthies did,
And a braver thence will spring,
  Which is, to keep that hid.

This chapter illustrates the profound emotion that Dorothea Brooke feels about the quiet work that she does among poor cottagers. The chapter motto affords the narrator the opportunity to suggest an important component of Dorothea's attractiveness to Will Ladislaw, the man she will marry in defiance of the codicil to her dead husband's will: Ladislaw appreciates 'a certain greatness' in her 'eloquence', which while 'nature … intended' it 'for men', is quite lacking in her uncle's 'masculine consciousness' and 'stammering condition.' Eliot's invocation of Donne at the head of this chapter suggests that, rather than seeing in the passage from Donne's letter an attempt to curtail women, Eliot, who was herself fascinated with what it might mean to 'forget the He and She', found there the expression of an eminently natural duty shared by women and men alike. It was an obligation that Donne had been prone to thinking he had violated, and one about which Eliot herself often worried. 'Therefore I would fain do something,' Donne went on to write in the letter (quoting now not from Walton but from Alford's edition),

but that I cannot tell what, is no wonder. For to choose, is to do: but to be no part of any body, is to be nothing. At most, the greatest persons, are but great wens, and excrescences; men of wit and delightful conversation, but as moles for ornament, except they be so incorporated into the body of the world, that they contribute something to the sustentation of the whole.   (vi. 321)

Dorothea's aspirations to 'contribute something to the sustentation of the whole' are voiced in another chapter where the narrator provides a motto from Dr Donne. Nearer the end of the novel, in Chapter 83, Dorothea and Ladislaw meet in a library (as they had in Chapter 39) and they are, in a dramatic flash of lightning, suddenly each 'lit … up for the other.' The epigraph consists of four lines from 'The Good-morrow', a poem that Lewes used to express his conviction that 'soul-lit eyes' show love to be the essence of paradise:

And now good-morrow to our waking souls
Which watch not one another out of fear;
For love all love of other sights controls,
And makes one little room, an everywhere.

This is the chapter that ends with Dorothea's eager embrace of poverty.[19] No sooner have she and Will agreed that 'We can never be married' than Dorothea shows that she is willing to risk everything for love. Her declaration that 'I don't mind about poverty—I hate my wealth' was not likely to remind Victorian readers of 'The Canonization', a poem that was not much known. It is reminiscent, however, of Walton's story about Donne's having lost his position and of living with his wife in impecunious misery for many years after their secret marriage. Walton's conclusion to that story—

God ... blessed them with so mutual and cordial affections, as in the midst of their sufferings, made their bread of sorrow taste more pleasantly than the banquets of dull and low-spirited people

—suggests that Lewes and Eliot saw in Donne's remarkable love for his wife a model of the Miltonic 'paradise within.' More than a mere compensation for the losses of position and of money that would accompany Dorothea and Will's marrying, the good-morrow into which their souls were waking might be their 'happier Eden.'

After George Eliot lost such a paradise herself, she went back to reading Donne's poetry. A reason for this is intimated in a brief passage from Walton about Donne's grief after the death of his wife, which she had copied out at the time she was composing *Middlemarch*: 'She being now removed by death, a commeasurable grief took took [sic] as full a possession of him as joy had done .... Thus he began the day, & ended the night; ended the restless night & began the weary day in lamentations.'[20] After Lewes's death, in November, 1878, Eliot turned often to poetry. She read and reread *In Memoriam*. She also marked, in a 1633 edition of Donne's *Poems* lent to her by Barbara Bodichon, the lines 'For love, all love of other sights controules, | And makes one little roome an every where.'[21] These lines had been written by a man who had also known despair. In his letters he had often been as self-recriminating as Eliot herself was, and she knew that he had written a treatise justifying suicide. Yet he had overcome despair and self-reproach. He had defied social convention in his marriage, had scorned fame in declining

[19] Gordon S. Haight, 'George Eliot's "eminent failure", Will Ladislaw', in *This Particular Web: Essays on Middlemarch*, ed. Ian Adam (Toronto: Univ. of Toronto Press, in association with the Faculty of Arts and Science of the University of Calgary, 1975), 33. For Lewes's article on Donne, see above, Chapter 2.

[20] Quoted from *George Eliot's* Middlemarch *Notebooks*, 63–4. Eliot was quoting from an undated nineteenth-century edition of Walton's *Lives*, 43.

[21] See Gordon S. Haight, *George Eliot: A Biography* (Oxford: Oxford Univ. Press, 1968), 516. For J. W. Cross's letter to Mme Bodichon, accompanying the volume upon its return, see *Letters*, ix. 326–7.

to publish his poems, and had nonetheless known '*une grande* passion' and achieved posthumous recognition. The writings that he left behind showed how he did manage to use his learning and his talents.

THE LETTERS AS SOURCES FOR BIOGRAPHY-HUNTERS

Coleridge and George Eliot were unusual in their ability to read Donne's letters as telling autobiographical acts in their own right. Most other readers looked to the letters as windows onto facts and events that would fill out a knowledge of Dr Donne's life. Alford largely accommodated the assumptions of those who regard such documents as transparent bearers of information. Using the *Letters to Severall Persons of Honour* as his copy-text, Alford brought their spelling and punctuation into conformity with nineteenth-century usage. He took far more editorial liberty with them, however, than he did with the sermons. He sorted the letters into two rough categories according to what he thought he knew about their dates of composition. Then he radically rearranged the majority of them according to a putative chronology. The first letter he printed bears the internal date of 12th December 1600. It is headed '*To my good Friend G. H.*', and a footnote identifies the addressee as George Herbert. (Alford thus egregiously displayed his incompetence: in 1600, at age seven, George Herbert was hardly in a position to receive such a letter.) Next, he printed a letter to Henry Goodyere and proposed the date 1605. Eighty more letters followed, extending down to the one, dated 15 January 1630, to Mrs Cokain, which had appeared last in the 1651 edition. Then Alford gathered into a second category headed 'Letters of Uncertain Date' another forty-eight letters, beginning with four that had appeared at the front of the volume in 1651.

The attempt to place as many letters as possible into a chronology had far-reaching consequences, not all of them consistent with Alford's likely intentions. It contributed to a growing expectation that eventually a con-cordant synthesis of Donne's life and writings would be achieved. It also introduced a model of editorial agency largely discontinuous with the one operative in the early printed editions and in Alford's first five volumes: whereas Alford retained for the sermons the traditional liturgical and aesthetic groupings (e.g., Christmas sermons, sermons on the penitential psalms), he redistributed most of the letters into a rudimentary narrative framework. In this way, he arrogated to himself what an astute critic of collections of letters identifies as 'one of the central prerogatives of the author, that of conceiving and implementing a coherent organization.'[22] Given that Donne was an object of a flourishing biographical interest, Alford thus helped to feed a 'curiosity', as R. C. Bald put it more than a century later, that would 'be satisfied only by the bringing together of every scrap of relevant information which has survived.'[23]

Alford's tendency to suppress the possibility of valuing Donne's letters as entertaining rhetorical performances set in motion a trajectory that continued well into the twentieth century. It is effectively at work in what is now considered the standard biography, *John Donne: A Life* (1970). In Bald's view, it is not the task of a writer's biographer to present and explore what Wordsworth and George Eliot regarded as the subject's 'chief actions.' Rather the biographer looks to personal letters to provide material that will 'enrich the drab official records' (11). Assuming that Donne's letters also offer a key to understanding the 'development' of his 'mind' (10), Bald identifies three Victorian scholars as his principal predecessors in constructing a plausible narrative out of the letters and other records: Thomas Edlyne Tomlins, the editor of the 1852 *Life of Donne* in the 'Contemplative Man's Library for the Thinking Few'; Jessopp, who wrote the entry on Donne for the *Dictionary of National Biography*; and Gosse, whose 'services to the reputation of Donne' have been 'many and great' (18). Bald dismisses the work of Zouch, ignores altogether the editions of Major, refers to Alford's volumes only in passing (as an obstacle to Jessopp's aspirations for a better edition), and seeks to distance his own method from the excesses of Gosse's belief that the erotic poems tell Donne's secret history.

The scholarly pedigree that Bald constructs masks significant changes in the history of reading personal letters. He acknowledges that Donne's letters often constitute 'brief essays', that they 'differ strikingly in kind from those familiar to the present-day writer or reader', and that they were not arranged in chronological order by the seventeenth-century editors (3). He also registers his frustration that the letters often bear titles different from what modern editorial practice would impose: 'In the *Collection* attributed to Sir Toby Mathew ... many of the letters are headed by captions like "A Letter of much kindness from one friend to another"' (4). Instead of probing the grounds of these differences, however, he reports them along with other alleged obstacles (such as the fact that the recipients are not always identified and that so many letters are undated) to what he considers his real work. Accepting the popular idea that personal letters should provide intimate and revealing glimpses of

[22] English Showalter, Jr, 'Authorial Self-Consciousness in the Familiar Letter: The Case of Madame de Graffigny', *Yale French Studies*, 71 (1987), 129.

[23] R. C. Bald, *John Donne: A Life* (Oxford: Oxford Univ. Press, 1970; repr., with corrections, Oxford: Clarendon, 1986), 1. Subsequent references are given within parentheses.

the personal life of a writer, as those of, say, Charlotte Brontë and James Joyce often seem to do, he altogether fails to explore the implications of the other quite different idea about the value of letters.

THE NEED FOR A 'MODERN' BIOGRAPHY

In the months following the publication of Alford's edition, another young clergyman trained at Cambridge began to define the contours of the project that would require a modern biography of Donne. The new agenda whereby scholars would need to embrace the 'very unpoetical work' of setting 'Isaak Walton right in his chronology and facts' was announced by J. C. Robertson. Having called attention to a few salient deficiencies in Alford's edition, such as the meagerness of annotation and the lack of an index, Robertson suggested that the value of the newly published 'works' lay principally in the light they could throw on the life. The time had come to illustrate 'how entirely the helps towards the biography of the Dean which are contained in his own writings have hitherto been overlooked.'[24] As it happened, however, the letters found in Alford's edition provided rather little information on two matters about which readers interested in Donne wanted to know more, his marriage and his change of ecclesiastical allegiance.

To begin the new work, Robertson drew heavily upon the letters, both those made available by Alford and earlier ones of which Alford seems to have been altogether ignorant. Two years before the *Works* appeared, in *The Loseley Manuscripts*, A. J. Kempe printed papers from the home of the More family into which Donne had married. The volume included 'Original Letters relating to the clandestine marriage', and Kempe presented them both as compositions that 'exhibit great depth and originality of thought, clothed in forcible and appropriate expression' and as documents relating 'chiefly ... to the romantic passage' of Donne's life.[25] Robertson largely avoided exploring the latter possibility and sought instead to raise a number of factual questions

---

[24] [J. C. Robertson], 'The Rev. H. Alford's Edition of Donne', *The British Magazine and Monthly Register*, 15 (1839), 534–7; 'Notes on the Life and Works of Dr. Donne', *The Gentleman's Magazine*, new ser. 16 (July to Dec. 1841), 25. This is the same James Craigie Robertson (1813–82) noted in the *DNB*, as confirmed by the information that he had been at Boxley, Maidstone, given in *Alumni Cantabridgienses, Part II: From 1752 to 1900* (1953), v. 323. The piece in *The Gentleman's Magazine* was submitted from Boxley. Robertson had overlapped with Alford at Trinity; in 1859 he was made a canon of Canterbury, two years after Alford had been named Dean.

[25] Alfred John Kempe (ed.), *The Loseley Manuscripts* (London: John Murray, 1836), 321, 325, 323, respectively.

about the lives of John and Anne Donne as told by Walton. He proposed that the letters show that Donne had first gone to work as Egerton's secretary late in 1597; that the marriage had taken place in December 1601; that the husband had made at least two visits to Paris (and thus that most of the letters that Alford sought to connect with the earlier visit had been written during the latter); and that Anne had not died just after her husband had received the degree of D.D. at Cambridge but had lived for another three and a half years. Although he wished to correct Walton on these and other points, Robertson protested that he understood quite well the many merits of *The Life of Donne* and proclaimed that he was desirous of bestowing upon Walton, had he been capable, a sonnet in praise of his work.

The precedent set by Robertson gave rise a decade later to the most thoroughly annotated edition of *The Life of Donne* ever published. The title page announced simply that the annotations were the work of 'an antiquary.' Early in the twentieth century he was identified as Tomlins,[26] a man who was trained in the law and who had been writing for the Shakespeare Society on topics such as the text of the plays, the Curtain Theatre, and the Restoration nursery of actors and actresses. Tomlins's new edition of Donne's *Life* was published by Henry Kent Causton and, while it acknowledged the work of Zouch half a century earlier, it presented itself as a response to 'the taste and the requirements of the present day.' Unlike the editions of the five *Lives* that descended from Zouch and Major, this one printed only the first of Walton's compositions. The aim announced in the preface was to make Donne's *Life* popular; yet the book was heavy with footnotes. Sometimes as little as two lines of Walton's text appeared on a page. Tomlins quoted frequently, and often at length, from the letters. He seems to have been interested in nearly everything he could learn about Donne. He documented Donne's fascination with poisons and his interest in burial customs, and he gave details of his finances. He was also well aware of the subjects in which there was general interest, including the extent to which Donne's youth had in fact been dissolute, whether his marriage had actually been the remarkable error of his life, how he had made a transition from Catholicism to Protestantism, and whether his poetry deserved the negative estimation that had been fixed upon it.

---

[26] [Thomas Edlyne Tomlins] (ed.), *The Life of John Donne, D.D. Late Dean of St. Paul's Church, London,* by Izaak Walton, with some original notes by an Antiquary (London: Henry Kent Causton, [1852]). For the identity of the antiquary, see *N&Q*, ser. 10/6 (1906), 228–9, 338. Unfortunately, Jessica Martin seems not to have known about this important edition when she was composing *Walton's Lives: Conformist Commemorations and the Rise of Biography* (Oxford and New York: Oxford Univ. Press, 2001).

As for Donne's marriage, the popular account in Anna Jameson's *Loves of the Poets* attests that even before the Loseley manuscripts were published there had been a palpable desire to reverse Walton's designation of it as an error. Kempe invited readers of the marriage letters to find in them confirmation of Walton's account—and in terms that made it compatible with the idea that the marriage had been an 'error' only insofar as those in power had been able for a time to punish the young husband. Donne's letter of 2 February 1601 to Sir George More is said 'remarkably to confirm the correctness' of Walton's observation that the removal of Anne from the Lord Chancellor's house was a precaution taken too late, since 'faithful promises' were already 'interchangeably passed as never to be violated.' This was to evoke sympathy for the newly-wed couple and for their sufferings in the years after Donne lost his position, even as Kempe's appeal to a 'Providence' that 'soon after bettered their condition' served further to bolster Walton's emphasis on the 'mutual and cordial affections' with which God 'blest them ... in the midst of their sufferings.'[27] Tomlins's annotations served in part to consolidate Mrs Jameson's version of the story. In the longer term, however, they created the possibility of reasserting Walton's negative estimate of the marriage—and without the saving grace of subsuming the story within a larger providential pattern. Tomlins provided elaborate notes on members of Anne More's family and its house and used the marriage letters and some poems to fill in several 'circumstances which Walton forbore to tell.' In particular, he read 'The Perfume' and 'On his Mistress' ('By our first strange and fatal interview') as revealing details of the courtship. Similarly, as if to make better Walton's claim about 'mutual and cordial affections', he proposed that the song 'Sweetest love, I do not go' was composed on the same occasion to which Walton had ascribed 'A Valediction Forbidding Mourning', Donne's farewell to his wife at his departure for the continent with Sir Robert Drury. Nonetheless, he took very seriously a letter that Donne had written from the fireside next to his wife, which was well known from the Zouch editions. In that letter Donne wrote that he had to 'labour to disguise' his having 'transplanted [Anne] into a wretched fortune', and Tomlins explicitly opened the possibility that Donne had worked hard to resist the conclusion that his marriage was an error: 'Unwilling, undesirous ... to acknowledge a fact that might be taken to reflect on his choice [of Anne] rather than on the circumstances by which it was attended', Donne 'appears to have been fully sensible', he remarks, 'that his apparent prospects in life had been in a moment, cut short, by that, his own

---

[27] Izaak Walton, *The Lives of Dr. John Donne*, etc., 4th edn. (London, 1675), 52; see Kempe, *The Loseley Manuscripts*, 322–3.

act.' To confirm this perspective, he then quoted from the letter of 1612 to Sir Henry Wotton in which Donne wrote, presumably referring to the aftermath of the wedding, '*I died ten years ago.*'[28] In this way he made available a darker interpretation of the marriage.

In 1855 still another discussion of the marriage appeared, in an unlikely place: when Jessopp brought out an edition of Donne's *Essays in Divinity*, he introduced it with a sixty-four page essay modestly titled 'Some Notice of the Author and His Writings.' His first reference to Walton's treatment of the marriage was sarcastic and suggested that it needed wholesale revising: Donne 'committed what one has called "the great error of his life"—he married!'[29] Jessopp could confidently rely on his readers' approval of a marriage made 'for love only', and he proceeded to offer a lengthy year-by-year narrative that placed issues of public importance at center stage. So wholly was Jessopp committed to writing about Donne's life that he readily conceded that '[n]othing like an allusion to these Essays occurs in any of Donne's letters' (p. xliii). His lengthy introduction offered barely a word about the very works that he was ostensibly introducing.

We will turn momentarily to Jessopp's extensive treatment of Donne's choice of religion. Here, reflecting on his rather jejune treatment of the marriage, we should note that in his concern to direct attention to Donne's public station, he proposed what has since proved an extremely influential interpretation of the grounds for Egerton's dismissal of his secretary. Knowing little of Donne's father and nothing, apparently, of the long-standing connections between Donne's mother's family and the Percys and other members of the court, which dated back to the days of Queen Elizabeth's education,[30] Jessopp ascribed to Donne a 'low birth.' He urged that 'distinctions of class' (p. xix) had been the decisive factor in constituting the wedding as an 'offence ... of enormous magnitude.' Without stopping to question how Donne had been able to enlist the Earl of Northumberland as an emissary to his new father-in-law, Jessopp proposed that the core problem must have been that 'a tradesman's son ... presumed to love the niece of the Lord Chancellor of England, and not only to love, but to woo and win her without leave or license from queen or subject.' In offering this interpretation the biographer's

[28] [Tomlins] (ed.), *Life of John Donne, D.D.*, 24, 23–4, 50, and 56, 47, respectively. The quotations from Donne are from Letter XXVIII in Alford's edition (vi. 332) and Letter XLVII (vi. 359).
[29] 'Some Notice of the Author and His Writings', *Essays in Divinity by John Donne, D.D.*, ed. Augustus Jessopp (London: John Tupling, 1855), p. x. Subsequent references appear in parentheses.
[30] The Heywoods' relations with members of the court are recounted by Dennis Flynn, *John Donne and the Ancient Catholic Nobility* (Bloomington, IN: Indiana Univ. Press, 1995).

own sympathies shone through clearly. Donne had been 'imprisoned by a mere tyrannical exercise of arbitrary power' (p. xxi). After he heroically won his release, he 'loved his wife with a deep and noble affection which never flagged, his letters abound with tender allusions to her, he never remembered how much his love had cost himself, nor ever allowed himself to forget how much it had brought upon her' (p. xxii). Despite what Tomlins's edition of Walton had suggested, Jessopp—like the vast majority of readers—was eager to place a positive construction on the marriage. He did not go so far as Alice King would, when in 1881 she published an essay describing Donne's married life as 'one long floating down a sunny river.'[31] He was deeply invested, however, in seeing Donne's commitment to his family as the grounds for all his subsequent searches for a livelihood and the justification for his worldly 'ambition.' Regarding the letters as affording 'insight into Donne's life and character which is to be obtained nowhere else' (p. lxxi), Jessopp valued in particular those from the period after Bishop Morton offered Donne a living in the church. In these he found a devotion to the life of the mind, only 'occasional despondency' (p. xxv), and above all Donne's 'standard of what a clergyman's life and qualifications ought to be', which 'was higher than he believed he had the ability or learning to attain to' (p. xxvii). In light of what he discerned in the letters, including ones to Lord Rochester and Lord Hay in which Donne 'announced his intention of obeying the king, and of eventually taking holy orders' (p. xl), Jessopp interpreted evidence that Donne was still seeking secular preferment in 1614 as a sign that he had felt the need for temporary secular employment in order to underwrite the continuing studies that would fit him for the church. Jessopp regarded the *Essays in Divinity* as fragments written as part of Donne's preparation for the ministry and never intended for publication. He invited readers to find in them the 'modes of thinking of a theologian whose education had given him all the benefits of a severe training in polemical and scholastic learning, and whose religious prejudices had veered round from Romish asceticism till they became rather in favour of the Puritanical school.' Ultimately, he presented them as 'the private utterances of a man who had passed through severe mental conflicts' and who 'had drunk somewhat deeply at most of the then known fountains of knowledge', so that he had been able to approach the Scriptures 'with the accumulated learning of centuries to help him in his task' (pp. xliii–xliv). Concerned as he was with Donne's public career, Jessopp's account quietly relegated the love-story to the background.

---

[31] 'John Donne', *Argosy* [London], 32 (1881), 301.

'ROMAN' CATHOLICISM

Besides looking to the letters to learn more about his marriage, in the aftermath of Catholic Emancipation (1829) and amidst increasing Irish immigration, readers looked into the letters to learn more than *The Life of Donne* told about the Catholicism of Donne's youth. Although Walton acknowledged that Donne's mother had sought to provide him with a Catholic education, he said nothing about his father's religion and the account was ambiguous about the extent to which Donne had ever been a convinced Catholic. Walton did claim that when Donne entered into his eighteenth year, he 'had betrothed himself to no Religion that might give him any other denomination than *a Christian*.' He went on prominently to announce that '[a]bout the nineteenth year of his age' Donne began 'seriously to survey, and consider the Body of Divinity, as it was then controverted betwixt the *Reformed* and the *Roman Church*.' Even as he located the decisive conversion of Donne's life in the long-delayed decision to take holy orders, Walton drew upon what Donne had said about his Catholic heritage in the preface to *Pseudo-Martyr*, where he presented himself as 'deriued from such a stocke and race, as, I beleeue, no family ... hath endured and suffered more in their persons and fortunes, for obeying the Teachers of Romane Doctrine, then it hath done.' In the mid-seventeenth century, when amidst civil and religious turmoil autobiographical conversion narratives were multiplying exponentially, Walton thus suggested that Donne had experienced an intellectual conversion that had resulted from open-minded scrutiny of the evidence: 'indeed, truth had too much light about her to be hid from so sharp an Inquirer; and, he had too much ingenuity'—the word was already a kind of mantra when Walton used it in 1640—'not to acknowledge he had found her.'[32] Coming as it does near the start of the narrative, the passage was in some measure meant to render benevolent Walton's envisaged readers, all of whom were Protestants of some stamp or other and upon whom he wished to impress the piety and authenticity of the leaders of the established church *avant le déluge*.

By the early nineteenth century, readers of Walton readily believed that Donne had been a convert to Protestantism. Zouch, in glossing the passage about Donne's 'ingenuity', contrasted his inquiry, which had been pursued with 'preparatory knowledge' and 'humble diffidence', with that of Alexander Pope, who claimed to have reviewed the controversies when he was

---

[32] Walton, *Lives* (1675 edn.), 13–14; *Pseudo-Martyr* (London, 1610), 'An Advertisement to the Reader', sig. I^r. On 'ingenuity', see Robert A. Greene, 'Whichcote, Wilkins, "Ingenuity", and the Reasonableness of Christianity', *Journal of the History of Ideas*, 42 (1981), 227–52.

fourteen and to have been unable to make up his mind. This left readers to draw the inference that Pope's adult Catholicism lay on the ignorant foundation of implicit faith, whereas Donne's faith had been informed and reasonable. Southey made capital of the idea when he introduced Donne in his *Select Works of the British Poets*: 'A serious, dispassionate, humble, and religious examination ... terminated in his sincere and dutiful conversion to the Protestant faith.' Robertson opened another possibility, however, when he questioned whether Donne had ever been an actual papist. He seems to have drawn a certain inspiration for this perspective from the letter to George More in the Loseley manuscripts in which Donne forcefully denies what he has heard rumored about his 'loving a corrupt religion.'[33] Similarly, the 1846 article in *Lowe's* assumed that Donne had been little affected by his Catholic background. Its author, while he emphasized the 'lofty extraction' Walton had documented when he had told of Donne's 'masculine' descent from 'a very ancient family in Wales' and of his mother's having belonged to 'the family of the ... learned Sir Thomas More, some time Lord Chancellor', made no mention of Donne's parents' religion. (No one at this time seems to have known that Donne's father had been Catholic, or that his mother's two brothers had been Jesuits.) He ascribed Donne's interest in Catholicism to the influence of 'friends ... of the Romish persuasion' and went on to present Donne's poetry as an instance of an 'enhanced ... poetic liberty' among Protestant writers after the Reformation. Reformed religion, he claimed, for a time 'extinguished that false shame which Romanism had attached to the contemplation of the sexual relations', although 'the poisonous taint' that 'yet lurked in [Catholic] doctrine' reasserted itself in the next era.[34]

The annotations in Tomlins's edition of the *Life of Donne* were more even-handed on the question whether Donne had been a Catholic. On the one hand, they contributed to the presumption that the religion of Donne's family held no abiding sway. Tomlins quoted the long letter in which Donne seeks to console his mother on the death of his sister, which opens with a curious detachment on the part of the writer. Even as Donne appeals to Christian beliefs that he shares with his mother, he speaks of the deaths of his father and his siblings almost as if they were only his mother's losses: 'My most dear Mother ... when I consider so much of your life as can fall within my memorie and observation, I find it to have been a sea under a continuall tempest. ... All those children (for whose maintenance his [i.e., Donne's father's] industrie provided, *and for whose education you were so carefullie and so chargeablie*

---

[33] Robert Southey, *Select Works of the British Poets* (London: Longman, Rees, etc., 1831), 714; Robertson, 'Notes', 25; Kempe, *The Loseley Manuscripts*, 334.
[34] 'Gallery of Poets. No. I.—John Donne', *Lowe's Edinburgh Magazine*, 1 (1846), 228–9.

diligent) [God] hath now taken from you.' Later in the letter, at the conclusion of his promise to 'provide for' his mother 'as for my own poore wife and children', Donne expressed gratitude for '*that education* which must make my fortune.'[35] Tomlins italicized these two passages, and they were commonly read as illustrations of filial piety and gratitude, even as their silence about the religious grounds and dimensions of Donne's education by Catholics lightly veiled a distancing from his mother's Catholicism that endeared him to English Protestants.

Elsewhere, however, Tomlins documented Donne's great familiarity with Catholic doctrines and Jesuit practices. This tended to shift the emphasis from the idea that Donne had converted on purely rational grounds and to create a new focus on the uniquely useful purposes Donne served for English Protestantism, because he had been intent, from *Pseudo-Martyr* to the mature sermons, on exposing on the basis of first-hand knowledge the fallacies and wickedness of Catholicism. At the same time, Tomlins dismissed the idea that in the nineteenth century Catholics could not be loyal subjects, pointing out that the 'Universal Catholic Church' so called had 'long since ... adopted the celebrated declaration of the Gallican clergy, "that the power which Jesus Christ had given to St. Peter, and his successors, related only to spiritual things" .'[36]

When Jessopp published his extensive biographical sketch three years later, he was not disposed to treat the subject of Donne's Catholicism with a liberal's magnanimity. Over the next forty years he would come to understand that the sort of 'mere tyrannical exercise of arbitrary power' that he had blamed for imprisoning Donne after his wedding had had dire consequences for many Catholics under the Elizabethan penal laws. He would edit for the Camden Society (1879) a seventeenth-century document written by the warden of the Fleet, which plainly showed how 'the legislation of Queen Elizabeth against the Catholics' worked to enrich those who imprisoned 'the Recusant Gentry, whose obstinate nonconformity subjected them to heavy fines.'[37] In his entry on Donne for the *Dictionary of National Biography* (1888) he would mediate the sad history of Donne's brother Henry, who in 1593 had been caught with a priest in his chambers and been allowed to die in the Newgate prison. Jessopp's most successful book would be his study of the Walpole family, *One Generation of a Norfolk House*, which began by calling attention to 'that strange phase of the conflict with Rome which was exhibited in the latter half of Queen

---

[35] [Tomlins] (ed.), *Life of John Donne, D.D.*, 13–14 n. Tomlins quoted the letter from *A Collection of Letters, made by Sr Tobie Matthews K^t* (London, 1660), 323–7.

[36] [Tomlins] (ed.), *Life of John Donne, D.D.*, 73 n.

[37] Introduction, *The Œconomy of the Fleete: An Apologeticall Answeare of Alexander Harris (Late Warden There) unto XIX Articles Sett Forth Against Him by the Prisoners*, ed. Augustus Jessopp (Westminster: Camden Society, 1879), p. xiv.

Elizabeth's reign.' Jessopp acknowledged that 'for the most part historians have slurred over [it] … carelessly' and explained that he had undertaken to write the book because even the most reputable ones had ignored the persecution. His own careful 'inquiries' over fifteen years, he explained, led him to dwell on 'matters which … were but little known to us of the Church of England.' At the back of the volume he appended a remarkable list of books from the sixteenth and seventeenth centuries that readers were not likely to find preserved in any library and which he had purchased (as he hinted) at considerable prices; he pointed out that '[i]t was at the peril of a man's life that he ventured three hundred years ago to be in possession of some of the books which this list contains.'[38] The courage with which Jessopp undertook to learn about the situation of Elizabethan Catholics, and the imaginative sympathy that he allowed to their plight, were in marked contrast to the views that had colored his presentation of the life of John Donne in the preface to the *Essays*.

In the period of 'the Protestant Crusade', when 'Anti-Catholicism was an integral part of what it meant to be a Victorian',[39] it was unimaginable to virtually everyone writing on Donne that his having come from a Roman Catholic family should be a grounds for sympathizing with him. This tended to be true even in the seat of Anglo-Catholicism, which had changed dramatically since Coleridge first asked the question, why are not Donne's sermons printed at Oxford? Coleridge himself had been unsympathetic to the developing rapprochement between Rome and Canterbury. For him, it was not sufficient to discredit the papal church by applying the label 'Roman Catholic', which exercised its protest through a biting oxymoron. 'N.B. Instead of the Roman Catholic *read* throughout, in this and all other works; & every where and on all occasions,' he wrote in his marginalia on Richard Field's *Of the Church* (1635),

unless where the duties of personal courtesy forbid, *say* the Rom*ish* Anti-catholic Church—Rom*ish* to mark that the corruptions in Discipline, Doctrine and Practice do for the worst and far larger part owe both their origin & their perpetuation to the Court and local Tribunals of the City of Rome, & are not & never have been the catholic (i.e. universal) Faith of the Roman Empire or even of the whole Latin or Western Church—and Anti-catholic because no other Church acts on so narrow and excommunicative a principle, or is characterized by such a jealous Spirit of Monopoly and Particularism, counterfeiting Catholicity by a negative Totality, and heretical

---

[38] Augustus Jessopp, *One Generation of a Norfolk House: A Contribution to Elizabethan History* (1878), quoted from the 3rd edn. (London: T. Fisher Unwin, 1913), 13.

[39] See John Wolffe, *The Protestant Crusade in Great Britain, 1829–1860* (Oxford: Clarendon Press, 1991); D. G. Paz, *Popular Anti-Catholicism in Mid-Victorian England* (Stanford, CA: Stanford Univ. Press, 1992), quoted here from 299. Cf. also Frank H. Wallis, *Popular Anti-Catholicism in Mid-Victorian Britain*, Texts and Studies in Religion, 60 (Lewiston, NY: Edward Mellen Press, 1993).

Self-circumscription—cutting off, or cutting herself off from, all the other members of Christ's Body.[40]

In the mid- and late-1830s, after John Keble's sermon on 'National Apostasy', the answer to the question about the publication of Donne's sermons was that Oxford had become a hotbed of 'Anglo-Catholicism', whereas the author of *Pseudo-Martyr* and the preacher of Gunpowder Plot sermons had been someone who distanced himself from Catholicism and used his learning to detail its corruptions as a threat to the monarch and the nation. Newman's *Lectures on the Prophetical Office of the Church* (1837) associated 'what is called Anglo-Catholicism' with 'the religion of Andrewes, Laud, Hammond, Butler, and Wilson.' Apart from the two volumes issued by Talboys in the early forties, Donne seems rarely to have been noticed in Oxford, where the church's spiritual independence from the Erastian establishment was increasingly emphasized.[41] While it was true, as Coleridge had remarked, that Donne had sometimes been able to say better things for the Catholics than they could say for themselves, Donne was not revived or read as an Anglo-Catholic alternative to a line of visionary Protestant writers extending from Spenser through Milton and Bunyan to the Romantics.[42] He was of interest in the ecclesiastical and political contexts of the twenty-five or thirty years after Catholic Emancipation (when Walton's *Lives* were at the height of their popularity) chiefly as

[40] Quoted from the Bollingen edn., xii, *Marginalia II*, 673–4. Coleridge dated this entry 12 Mar. 1824.

[41] Newman's *Lectures on the Prophetical Office of the Church* are quoted here from *The Via Media of the Anglican Church*, 2 vols. (London: Longmans, Green, 1901), i. 17. Cf. Peter Benedict Nockles, *The Oxford Movement in Context: Anglican High Churchmanship, 1760–1857* (Cambridge: Cambridge Univ. Press, 1994), 53. James Burns, who sold books for John Henry Parker of Oxford and who had by the late 1830s himself become the leading publisher for the younger generation of High Churchmen, published volumes of extracts from 'approved' English divines that generally did not include Donne. Thomas Chamberlain, for example, a student of Christ Church, Oxford, published with Burns *A Help to Knowledge, Chiefly Religious, in Extracts* (new edn., 1840). The volume included passages from Bishops Burnet, Hall, Jewel, Ken, Sanderson, Stillingfleet, Taylor, and Wilson (inter alia); from George Herbert, Sir Thomas Browne, and an especially large number from Richard Hooker and Thomas Fuller. There was nothing, however, from Donne. On the Tractarians' neglect of Donne, see John Griffin, 'Tractarians and Metaphysicals: The Failure of Influence', *JDJ*, 4 (1985), 291–301.

[42] Since T. S. Eliot, writers on literary history have made commonplace a bifurcation between a high church 'line of wit' and a dissenting line of vision. See for example, Harold Bloom, *The Visionary Company: A Reading of Romantic Poetry* (1961; rev. and enlarged edn., Ithaca, NY: Cornell Univ. Press, 1971); Joseph Anthony Wittreich, Jr., *The Romantics on Milton: Formal Essays and Critical Asides* (Cleveland, OH: Press of Case Western Reserve University, 1970). It is surprising that in exploring Coleridge's highly independent reading of Donne, Anthony John Harding should have given so much credit to this tendentious reading of literary history; see ' "Against the Stream Upwards": Coleridge's Recovery of John Donne', in Lisa Low and Anthony John Harding (eds.), *Milton, the Metaphysicals, and Romanticism* (Cambridge: Cambridge Univ. Press, 1994), 204–5.

an unassailable representative of a Protestantism redefining itself over against 'Roman Catholicism.' No one writing on Donne saw him as a crypto-Catholic, or even as a writer who, having known the sufferings of Catholics first-hand, had much sympathy for his former co-religionists. Nor did the *Library of Anglo-Catholic Theology* serve as a forum in which to bring out an edition of his *Works* that would supersede that of Alford. In the reaction to the denial in *Tract 90* of the Protestant character of the Thirty-Nine Articles and amidst the xenophobic response to Irish immigration, Jessopp acquired his interest in Donne during his undergraduate years at St John's College, Cambridge, in the mid-forties. At this time two new editions of Foxe's *Book of Martyrs* were in circulation, the Parker Society had begun republishing the works of the English Reformers, and the Oxford Movement, having ushered a number of its leading figures into the 'Roman' church, had become still more suspect to the establishment. Donne, whom Jessopp designated 'the greatest preacher that England has ever produced',[43] was a useful ally in the project of reasserting that obedience to the interests of the state and protests against 'popery' were essential to the nature of the English church.

In accord with the reassertion of anti-papist sentiments within many strands of English Protestantism, in his introduction to the *Essays in Divinity* Jessopp rewrote Walton's account of how Donne had chosen his mature religion. He expanded it with material drawn chiefly from the letters, making the polemic utterly explicit. Jessopp's narrative suggested that the course of the individual life at once recapitulated the course of England's religious history and epitomized the decisive triumph of the reformed religion. He presented Donne's choice of religion as a crisis of conscience for a young man caught between two loyalties. He depicted Catholicism as the out-moded belief that Donne's mother, 'a woman of some celebrity for her fanatical devotion to the Romish religion', had sought to impose upon him. That Donne had had to experience 'painful religious difficulties' around his nineteenth year was chiefly owing to his 'mother's prejudices' and 'zeal for her own creed', which was 'stern and tenacious.' In accord with her 'gloomy' religion, she had been unwilling to 'risk' allowing her sons to be exposed to 'the men of new learning' and had hired as their tutor someone 'ill-affected towards the principles of the Reformation', a 'Jesuit' or 'a Romish priest.' (It was typical for nineteenth-century English writers to know virtually nothing about the Jesuits' historic contributions to art and learning, even as they repeated the idea that Jesuits had been 'subtle' and 'cunning' in their seditious machinations. They were unsympathetic, moreover, to the Jesuits' international perspective.) For his part, Donne had

---

[43] Jessopp, 'Some Notice of the Author and His Writings', p. lxxii. Quotations in the paragraph that follows come from pp. xi–xii and xv–xvii.

been a loving son, leaving on record in the letter that Tomlins had quoted 'an affectionate testimony' to the 'constant superintendence and scrupulous discharge' of his mother's 'maternal responsibility.' Emphasizing the pressures exercised on Donne by the '*Recusant* faction ... in his very home', where he must have been in 'daily intercourse' with 'Romish disputants ... who would spare no exertions' upon him, Jessopp built his story up to a dramatic, and long delayed, climax. Proclaiming that 'the chances of his uniting himself with the Reformers rather than with the Ultramontanists [were] small indeed', Jessopp nonetheless gloried in reporting that 'the piercing logic' and 'commanding intellect' of Donne had seen through the false subtleties of his teachers: 'applying himself to that controversy with zeal, labour and severe application, apparently *for some years*, he came to the conclusion at length' to which, in the eyes of Jessopp, Newman (and alas! too many others) should have come: 'that the Church of Rome had no claim on his obedience, and indeed that here in England it was a schismatical body.'

The presentation of Donne's religious history in Jessopp's Notice thus helped to feed widespread suspicions of 'popery in its social aspect', as the title of R. P. Blakeney's popular book of the early 1850s had it. Subtitled *A Complete Exposure of the Immorality and Intolerance of Romanism*, Blakeney's opening chapter thanked God that Protestant England had survived the revolutions of 1848 and warned of the present 'extreme peril' to Great Britain due to her failure to take seriously the '*great crisis*' precipitated by the 'immense power' of Rome throughout Europe and from 'treason' in 'our ranks' at home. The book synthesized the anti-Catholic rhetoric that had revived after Catholic Emancipation, and renewed the old charges that Catholics encourage 'dissimulation, equivocation, and outright dishonesty', engage in 'vicious persecution' whenever they can, and oppose not only the Bible but knowledge more generally. This account of Catholicism raised again the spectre of underground intrigues fomented by furtive Jesuits and directed against the established church and the Crown. Having rehearsed the uses of disguise and equivocation made by Robert Parsons and Edmund Campion in Elizabethan times, Blakeney urged that 'we have reason to believe that such Jesuits are now in disguise, accomplishing their purposes.'[44] *Popery in its Social Aspect*, like Donne's *Ignatius His Conclave*, associated the Jesuits with Machiavelli and with Lucifer. It also urged that it was 'highly probable, that Jesuitism is at the bottom of chartism, republicanism, and anti-state churchism.' By contrast with this popular bigotry, Jessopp's anti-Catholicism seemed relatively enlightened, not least because he borrowed from Donne himself

---

[44] R[ichard] P[aul] Blakeney, *Popery in its Social Aspect* (Edinburgh: George M'Gibbon, [*c*.1854]), 1–6; 161–7. For a useful account of Blakeney's work, see Wolffe, 120–1.

the nationalistic strategy exploited so effectively in *Pseudo-Martyr*: Jessopp distinguished between two parties of Elizabethan Catholics. There were those whose sincere faith acknowledged that 'the providence of God had placed over them' the lawful English monarch and those whose 'blind submission' to men who 'gloried in crushing every feeling of individual responsibility' ensured that their 'faith' was 'but a name' (pp. xxx–xxxi). Jessopp characterized *Pseudo-Martyr* as 'gentle and calm' in tone 'with a tender avoiding of all that might irritate.' The books to which it was an answer were by contrast said to be full of 'frauds, inquisitorial intolerance, controversial guile.' Donne's Catholic background meant that he knew 'devotional books' that were marked by 'hideous profanity', 'abominations', 'puerile trifling', and 'wicked tricks' (p. xxxiv) and that he could refute them with the unique authority that was recognized, in 1610, when 'the University of Oxford … conferred upon him the degree of M.A.' (p. xxxvi).

In the 1870s, when Jessopp discovered evidence of the piety and learning of Donne's Jesuit uncles and wrote in tribute to the courageous sufferings of the Elizabethan Catholic missioners,[45] he had quite abandoned the perspective that had informed this earlier characterization of the 'Romish party.' By the time he wrote the two mature biographical portraits of Donne that appeared in 1888 and 1897, he had himself become what he long admired in his subject, an erudite clergyman who sought to put his scholarly habits to just and socially beneficial uses. What was missing in these later narratives, however, was a probing account of Donne's verse, as Jessopp himself acknowledged when he finally handed over his materials to Gosse. The essay that Jessopp contributed to *The Nineteenth Century* on 'Letters and Letter-Writers' suggests an important basis of this limitation. 'Literature begins in verse', he wrote, 'for verse is the earliest of all composition' and a merely preliminary 'stage' through which both the individual writer and a whole society must pass before attaining to a 'high level of civilisation and culture' when 'men and women begin to write familiar letters to one another.'[46] For Jessopp, as for Walton, the bulk of Donne's poetry belonged to his youth, the prose letters and religious writing to his maturity; and there remained for him an inexplicable gap between the two.

THE BOSTON EDITION OF DONNE'S POEMS

Still another index of the near pre-eminence of the letters among Donne's writings in the middle decades of the century was the appearance, in the

---

[45] See *One Generation*, 130, 216–17.   [46] Jessopp, 'Letters', 217.

same year as Jessopp's edition of the *Essays in Divinity*, of the only complete edition of Donne's poetry ever to open with the Epistles to Several Personages. Known in England as the Boston edition and designated 'M' in the Variorum, *The Poetical Works of Doctor John Donne* was also the first complete edition published outside Britain. Although its editor was not identified, this edition is now known to have been the work of James Russell Lowell. Seldom the object of critical attention, its nature has been misunderstood even by those whom we would expect to know the most about it. Herbert Grierson, who rightly recognized that it printed 'an eclectic text', erroneously dated it to 1850 and was unable to discern the important continuities between it and the Grolier Club edition.[47] Even Charles Eliot Norton, although he worked closely with two copies in which Lowell had written annotations over the course of thirty-six years, did not thoroughly examine the editorial principles on which his friend had organized the volume and 'corrected' Donne's text.

Lowell's 1855 edition was one of the last volumes to appear in the series of the British Poets published by Little, Brown, and Company under the general editorship of Professor F. J. Child of Harvard.[48] Early in the 1850s Child had entered into an agreement with the publishers to create this collection. Its announced purpose was to make readily available to American readers, in small but handsome volumes, 'all that is of permanent value in English poetry, from Chaucer to Wordsworth.' The proprietors considered as the principal rival to their edition the 'Thesaurus' of English poetry collected by Chalmers (1810) and published in 'twenty-one ponderous octavos.' They sought to differentiate their project on a number of counts: they would omit much 'obsolete and worthless poetry' and include what was 'really excellent'; they would print the 'whole works of the most distinguished authors' and would include '[s]everal volumes of fugitive and anonymous poetry'; they would take '[p]ains ... to secure a correct text' and would offer 'biographical, historical, and critical notices' and provide 'glossaries where such assistance' was deemed necessary. Once the volumes began appearing in 1853, the series garnered rave notices in newspapers from Louisville to Buffalo and in periodicals like the *Southern Literary Messenger* and the *Yankee Blade*. Reviewers embraced the assumption that Americans needed ready access to this body of literature. The judgment of the *Binghampton Republic* was typically reassuring: 'The most

---

[47] *The Poetical Works of Dr. John Donne, with a Memoir* (Boston, MA: Little, Brown, 1855); Herbert J. C. Grierson, 'The Text of Donne's Poems', in *The Poems of John Donne*, 2 vols. (Oxford: Clarendon, 1912), ii, p. lxxv. Evidence supporting many assertions in the paragraphs that follow may be found in my article, 'No Edition Is an Island: The Place of the Nineteenth-Century American Editions within the History of Editing Donne's Poems', *TEXT*, 14 (2002), 169–207.

[48] The edition was brought out simultaneously by James S. Dickerson in New York, and by J. B. Lippincott in Philadelphia.

complete as well as the most desirable collection of the works of the English poets' available.[49]

Lowell was personally responsible for the inclusion of Donne in Child's edition. The sorts of readers he envisaged for his edition had different concerns from those for whom Alford and Jessopp had been working. By the early 1850s Donne already had an established place in the minds of the leading figures in New England literary culture: Ralph Waldo Emerson, Henry Wadsworth Longfellow, Margaret Fuller, Oliver Wendell Holmes, and others held Donne in high regard. Their interest in him as a writer did not depend upon familiarity with Walton's *Lives*, which did not enjoy in North America anything like the popularity it had in Britain. Emerson, born in 1803, first discovered Donne in 1815. Reading Johnson's *Lives of the Poets*, he encountered several quotations in the *Life of Cowley*. In a letter to his older brother, the twelve-year-old copied out a passage from the Valentine Day's epithalamion (lines 85–8)—

> Here lies a she-sun and a he-moon there
> She gives the best light to his sphere
> Or each is both and all and so
> They unto one another nothing owe

—and remarked, 'I should like to see the Poem it was taken from.'[50] His serious reading of Donne's poetry seems to have been delayed, however. By 1828, Emerson had come to regard the literature of the Elizabethan period and the earlier seventeenth century as 'the great splendour of English poetry', but Donne was not yet in his books. He proclaimed 'an affectionate admiration' for the 'pervading etherial poesy' and 'ravishing verse' of Herbert, Shakespeare, Marvell, Herrick, Milton, and Ben Jonson that he had 'for nothing else.' By 1830, when he borrowed from the Boston Athenæum a copy of Donne's *Five Sermons Vpon Special Occasions* (1626), he had also developed a wide knowledge of seventeenth-century sermon literature; and he had decided to look into Donne because his intensive readings in Coleridge so frequently brought Donne's name into his ken. Although he made a note in his journal to secure a copy of 'Donne's Sermons',[51] in the event it was a copy of the 1719 *Poems on Several Occasions* that he came to own and mark and prize.

---

[49] These quotations are drawn from a 'Prospectus of a New Edition of the English Poets now in course of publication by Little, Brown, & Company' (1854). I cite them from a copy bound into *The Poetical Works of John Milton* (Boston, MA: Little, Brown, 1853), which is held in the O'Neill Library at Boston College.

[50] Letter of 2 and 3 June 1815, to William Emerson, in *The Letters of Ralph Waldo Emerson*, ed. Ralph L. Rusk (New York: Columbia Univ. Press), i.10. The lines are quoted as they appear in this edition.

[51] Quotations of Emerson's journal entries are from *The Journals and Miscellaneous Notebooks of Ralph Waldo Emerson*, ed. William H. Gilman et al., 16 vols. (Cambridge, MA: Belknap Press of Harvard Univ. Press, 1960–82), iii. 148, 180–1.

By the 1840s Emerson was peppering his journals with references to Donne, and in his lectures he was making Donne's name one he loved to conjure with. He seems not to have tired of paraphrasing, from one of the verse letters to the Countess of Bedford, 'For Virtue's whole sum is to know & dare.' He shared Margaret Fuller's high regard for 'The Ecstasy.' He cited it as his chief illustration of that rare sort of poem 'written some hundred years ago' that amazes by revealing 'the fortitude or selfreliance' of someone who so 'dared ... to trust his rare perception, as to write it elaborately out.'[52] He came to value Donne less for beauty than for superior philosophical insight, which he found revealed above all in the well-known passage from 'The Second Anniversary':

> her pure and eloquent blood
> Spoke in her cheeks, and so distinctly wrought,
> That one might almost say, her body thought.

'Passion beholds its object as a perfect unit,' Emerson wrote. 'The soul is wholly embodied, and the body is wholly ensouled.' He had admired for many years the poetry by Donne that he later printed in his anthology, *Parnassus* (1874): the whole of 'The Ecstasy', 'The Undertaking', and 'A Hymn to Christ', excerpts from 'The Second Anniversary', the Somerset epithalamion, 'Hymn to God, My God, in My Sickness', and 'To Mr. R. W.'. He had quoted from these passages in his lectures. On the basis of these and other passages, Emerson included Donne with Plato, Shakespeare, Goethe, and a tiny handful of other writers whose minds do not so much 'speak about things' (he was paraphrasing Schelling) as they 'speak the things themselves.'[53] His greatest admiration for Donne as a man, then, was based on the boldness he heard in the voice, which reveals an 'imaginative and analogy-loving soul', like Giordano Bruno or Henry Vaughan. Donne's writing qualified him to be numbered with Milton and Shakespeare and Wordsworth as one of the few 'English Poets who have contributed' to human life something of biblical moment, 'sentences of guidance & consolation which are still glowing & effective.'[54]

Emerson's estimate of Donne's enduring actions was, in a relevant sense, biographical. When he referred to 'Donne' in his journals and lectures, he was thinking about a vital body of writing—sermons and poems alike—in which a bold, distinctive, and living voice addressed readers across the centuries. In

---

[52] *Journals*, xi (1848–51), 94, 322; cf. ix (1843–7), 367; xi. 210.

[53] 'Love', in *Essays. With a Preface by Thomas Carlyle* (London: J. Fraser, 1841), 184; *Journals*, xi. 273–4.

[54] 'Quotation and Originality', in *Letters and Social Aims* (Boston: Houghton Mifflin, 1875), 195; *Journals*, ix. 367.

1840, he cited passages from Donne's Elegies to illustrate a general principle that he would later urge in an essay on Goethe:

It makes a great difference as to the force of any sentence whether there be a man behind it or no. In ... newspaper paragraphs I can discern no form, only some skulking Will o' the Wisp of an irresponsible editor; oftener, some monied corporation. ... But through every clause & part of speech of a right book, I meet the eyes of the most determined of men; his force & his terror inundate every word; the very commas & dashes are alive with him, so that the writing is athletic & nimble, can go far & live long.[55]

Here Emerson's main point shows, against his own long-standing prejudices about the work of editors, why editing Donne matters. At least since 1669 the editors of Donne's poetry had taken it as a principal obligation to render the text intelligible by bringing the spelling and punctuation into conformity with whatever their readers regarded as standard. Every new edition, from the 1719 Tonson in which Emerson read the poetry to the 1839 *Works*, could tell us something about the then current state of standard practices. What's significant is that, collectively, the differences among these editions attest to the instability of the standards and of the 'Donne' that the editors sought to mediate. Each edition contributed to the tangle from which its editor claimed, if only implicitly, to be extricating Donne. While Emerson habitually dismissed 'the restorers of readings' and 'emendators' as belonging to a 'book-learned class, who value books, as such' and know nothing of action and real thinking,[56] Lowell, more than any previous editor, began to discern the causes of the tangles, and to take more effective action to remove them. He glimpsed the dimensions of the problems that had accrued because, one after another, each editor sought to accommodate the texts to a more modern generation. When Lowell saw the first proofs of his edition, he wrote to the printer, to ask whether Mr. Brown could supply 'an old edition of Donne? Either of 1633 or 35?'[57] This request shows that he was poised to launch a critique of the assumption that interventions by editors do not interfere with readers' access to the poet's own voice.

---

[55] *Journals*, vii. 501. Emerson cited passages from 'The Dream', lines 25–6, and 'The Autumnal', lines 1–2. This journal entry was singled out by Raoul Granqvist, *The Reputation of John Donne 1779–1873* (Stockholm: Almqvist and Wiksell, 1975), 164. Many references to Donne in the writings of Emerson and Thoreau are ably discussed by Granqvist, to whose industry in compiling them I am in debt.

[56] 'The American Scholar' (1837), in *The Complete Works of Ralph Waldo Emerson*, i: *Nature Addresses and Lectures*, ed. Edward Waldo Emerson (Boston: Houghton, Mifflin, 1904), 89.

[57] The letter is quoted in *A Bibliography of the First Editions in Book Form of the Writings of James Russell Lowell*, ed. Jacob Chester Chamberlain and Luther S. Livingston (New York: [Privately Printed], 1914), 44. For a detailed study of this aspect of the Boston edition, see 'No Edition Is an Island', 176–80.

Surprisingly given that Lowell's displayed far more variants than any previous edition, when he was preparing it in 1854 and 1855, he had few resources to hand. Besides the Tonson edition, he had access to the three editions that descended from it. Bell, Anderson, and Chalmers all presented a text ultimately derived from the only Restoration edition of Donne's *Poems* (1669). For the eighteenth-century editors, the 1669 edition had considerable prestige both because its canon of poems seemed the most complete and because it set the precedent for what they all successively took to be their most important work, as each sought to outdo the last in modernizing spelling and punctuation. After the Tonson edition, no editor had paid attention to editions or manuscripts from the seventeenth century. Then both Alford and Lowell, in ways quite different from one another, made use of early editions; like their predecessors, however, they also modernized what they regarded as accidentals. Lowell, working in North America, where he was unable to imagine consulting manuscripts and unable to examine all seven seventeenth-century editions, was able finally to make use of a 1635 edition. He also made a surprising use of Alford: for all the poems found in that edition, he consulted it to gain access to the verbal text of 1633. We know this because Lowell identifies no variants as having appeared in the 1633 edition for any poem that had not been printed by Alford.

The paucity of resources available to Lowell makes his de facto achievement the more remarkable. His edition, while it too belongs to the family that derives the text ultimately from 1669, represents the first extensive effort to criticize that tradition by comparing readings printed in the earliest editions. After the Boston edition was published, Lowell continued to develop this critique, writing into the margins of his own copy hundreds of further emendations of punctuation and spelling. He also added slightly more than one hundred further verbal variants—all of them taken, strikingly, either from the 1635 edition or from 1633, an actual copy of which he was finally able to obtain in the 1880s. Lowell's annotations show an increasing fascination with the discrepancies among the editions he knew and a growing propensity to favor readings from the *editio princeps*. It was not until after his death, however, that the process by which the Grolier Club edition came to print Lowell's 'revisions' of Donne's text culminated in the editorial policy whereby the earliest printed version of a poem in a complete edition of Donne's poetry was systematically chosen as the copy-text for a modern edition.[58] Lowell initiated and developed his critique of the modern editorial tradition without ever making a radical break from it, and apparently without ever entertaining the idea, which he

---

[58] For the *Anniversaries* and other poems that had appeared in print before 1633, the Grolier Club edition nonetheless drew on 1633 for its copy-text.

saw badly executed in Grosart's edition of 1872–3, of using manuscripts for copy-texts. Nor does he seem ever to have seriously considered listing variants that appear in manuscripts.

While Lowell's interest in Donne was more intense than that of Emerson and Longfellow and Margaret Fuller and led him already in the 1850s to make a more extensive collation of editions than anyone had previously attempted, like theirs it entailed special admiration for the sincerity of many of Donne's love-verses. In the year that his Donne edition appeared, and just before he was named to succeed Longfellow as Smith Professor of Belles Lettres and Modern Languages at Harvard, Lowell gave in Boston a series of lectures on poetry. It drew large crowds, and included a lecture on poetic diction in which he proposed that Donne had been 'a large poetic soul', who appeared on the scene 'all new and radiant', writing with an 'original force' that transcended the old laws of poetry. Lowell singled out 'A Valediction Forbidding Mourning' as a proof of the proposition that 'everything, when you find a true metaphorical sense becomes elevated.' As if in answer to Johnson's charges that metaphysical poetry was insincere, he praised Dr Donne's having 'conjured the deepest sentiment out of a pair of carpenter's compasses' and proclaimed the poem 'truly sacred.' 'The meaning of it is so pure and holy and profound', he urged, 'that I can fancy that it was written under the immediate inspiration of St. Joseph, the patron saint of the Joiners' Craft.' The suggestion here that the poem had been composed early, when Donne was still under the spell of his Catholic upbringing, issued then into a contradiction of what Walton had said about the circumstances of its composition. 'The poem', Lowell concluded, 'was addressed to his future wife on their being separated for a time.'[59] At this point in his life, Walton was not yet numbered among Lowell's favorite writers. Relying on the abbreviated sketch in Tonson, Lowell knew nothing of the claim that Donne had written the poem for his pregnant wife before departing for the Continent.

While Emerson's life-long reading and Lowell's early reading of Donne were not carried out under the spell of Walton's narrative, their interests were nonetheless in other ways inevitably continuous with those of the studious biographical age. Whereas the 1633 *Poems* began with 'The Progress of the Soul' and 1635 with the newly constituted group designated 'Songs and Sonets', Lowell's edition began, as all the editions after 1669 had, with a life of the author, in this case the abridgment taken over from Tonson. The first

---

[59] Parts of Lowell's lecture titled 'Poetic diction' are preserved in manuscript bMS Am 765 (905), in the Houghton Library; the quotations here are from 6, 3, 4–5, respectively, and are made by permission of the Houghton Library. A detailed summary of the lecture, based on this manuscript, appears in *Lectures on the English Poets* (Cleveland, OH: Rowfant Club, 1897), 167–79.

poems Lowell printed were 'The Storm' and 'The Calm', at the head of the 'Epistles to Several Personages.' He may have placed the Verse Letters first because he could tell, from internal evidence, that many of them belong to the early part of Donne's writing career. Readers who came to these poems having just been informed that 'the more airy part of [Donne's] poetical compositions' were mostly written 'before his twentieth year' and were 'the innocent amusement and diversion of his youth' (pp. xviii–xix) may have found them surprising. Lowell's arrangement encouraged them to hear from the outset Donne speaking in his own voice to his familiars and intimates: he sought to show who Donne's correspondents had been and how he talked with fellow poets and the patrons of poets. Besides Christopher Brooke, there had been Sir Henry Goodyere, to whom some of the most well-known prose letters were addressed. There had been Henry Wotton, ambassador to Venice (as the heading of one of the poems pointed out), an early advocate for the poetry of young John Milton and another of Walton's biographical subjects. There had been Edward Herbert, afterwards Lord Herbert of Cherbury, and his accomplished mother, Magdalen Herbert, whose extraordinary friendship with Donne Walton celebrated in his *Life of George Herbert*. And there had been other women of discerning taste, the Countess of Huntingdon and especially the Countess of Bedford. Donne's Verse Letters illustrated a witty, urbane, sophisticated capacity for discourse that inextricably mixed the playful and the reverent. Often they showed how he had held his balance along that very fine line required in poems that entail flattery. To read these verses first, as an introduction to Donne's poetry, was to have implicit hermeneutical guidelines for making one's way into the rest. Poems like these did not encourage readers to take, say, 'The Flea' or even 'The Good Morrow' as a transparently autobiographical utterance. This is to say that Lowell's edition aspired to be placed in the tradition in which Donne's writings were read primarily as artistic performances, rather than as materials to be mined by biographers. Nor were Lowell's aims like those of Alford and Jessopp, who were seeking to make Donne's works available to lovers of old divinity. The readers Lowell had in mind were not much concerned with locating Donne in relation to the history and politics of the established church, which was of course precisely not established in the United States; they were people likely to value Donne as a 'thinker.'

Two years after the Boston edition appeared, an anonymous reviewer of the whole *British Poets* series for the *North American Review* singled it out for climactic consideration because it 'introduced for the first time to our Cisatlantic public' a writer to whom 'we are inclined to attach a very high value.' In accord with the general tendency of mid-nineteenth-century readers on the eastern side of the Atlantic, however, this 'high value' owed almost nothing to

Donne's having written poetry. 'Donne's graver verse and his religious poems, which are the greater part of the whole', the reviewer said, 'display much more of poetic feeling than of taste. They are deformed by pedantry, crowded with puerile conceits, and often … vitiated by the carrying out a metaphor to weariness.' What the reviewer valued was the fact that the inclusion of Donne's poems in the series gave wider currency to 'a name familiarly known through his Life by Walton, who beheld in him at once the mirror of courtesy, the paragon of learning, and the perfection of sainthood.' He judged Donne's prose to be 'more poetical than his verse' and took occasion, although none of the prose appeared in Lowell's edition, to insert into the review a long quotation (from the Easter sermon of 1627) on the grounds that 'Of all the earlier English divines, there is not one who drops pearls and diamonds from so full a hand' as Donne.[60] The reviewer said nothing about those features of the edition that are most striking when one considers the history of editing Donne's poetry and did not take an interest in the figure of Donne as Lowell's choice and arrangement of materials depicted him.

In various and subtle ways the Boston edition accommodated the poems to readers with biographical interests. The fact that Lowell did not write his own introductory biographical sketch was not owing to the volume's being one of the last in the series to be published; a new biographical sketch would have been out of keeping with the general practice for older poets. Other volumes of seventeenth-century poets that Lowell oversaw printed John Mitford's 'Life of Dryden' and a 'Notice' of Marvell that had originally appeared in the *Edinburgh Review*. Still, because Lowell did write biographical introductions for the poetry of Wordsworth and Keats, it is possible to appreciate some grounds for the unusual way in which he organized Donne's poems.

While grouping by genres was traditional, the arrangement whereby the volume began with the Verse Letters, followed by the Funeral Elegies and Divine Poems was unprecedented. This made it more like Alford's edition—where the groups were printed as Holy Sonnets, Epistles, Funeral Elegies, Sacred Pieces, Miscellaneous Pieces, Poems not in the Edition of 1633—than any other. In fact, Lowell, who owned a copy of *The School of the Heart*, tended to give Alford a good deal of credit. After the Divine Poems he went on to print 'The Progress of the Soul.' Then he followed the order of the five genres that appeared immediately after the abridged *Life* by Walton in the 1719 edition: 'Miscellaneous Poems' (the Songs and Sonnets), Epigrams, Elegies (that is, love elegies), Epithalamions, and Satires. Finally, Lowell printed the Latin poems. This unique arrangement created an edition that, if it seemed

---

[60] The review of Child's series appeared anonymously in the *North American Review*, 84/171 (Jan. 1857), 240–53. For the section devoted to Donne, see 250–3.

at first to invite biographical interpretation, served finally to complicate the idea that readers could follow the poet's life-story from youth to maturity by reading through the volume from front to back. Lowell also employed this strategy in the Wordsworth volume, which began with 'Poems Written in Youth', followed by 'Poems Referring to the Period of Childhood', then 'Poems Founded on the Affections' and 'Poems on the Naming of Places', so that a chronological principle of organization gave way to generic and thematic principles. Placing Donne's Epistles to Several Personages first was in keeping with ideas that Lowell expressed in the 'Sketch of Wordsworth's Life' about the potential importance of a poet's letters for interpreting his poetry. Lowell urged 'every student of his works' to consult 'some valuable letters of Wordsworth' from the period before the 1807 volume was published 'for the light they throw upon the principles which governed him in the composition of his poems.' Then he closed his thirty-page essay with a perspective that was to provide a decisive hermeneutical norm: 'We have thus briefly sketched the life of Wordsworth, a life uneventful even for a man of letters. ... The life and growth of his mind, and the influences which shaped it, are to be looked for, even more than is the case with most poets, in his works, for he deliberately recorded them there.'[61]

This was not an easy rule to follow. In the 'Memoir' written by Norton for the Shelley volume in Child's series it can hardly be said to have been upheld. The 'eventfulness' of Shelley's life proved compelling and, since many of its domestic features had already been revealed in other printed sources, there was no omitting its salient details. Norton made a gentlemanly variation on the rule according to which a writer's relevant life is to be found in his writings and justified it by adducing a precedent found in certain notes written by Mrs Shelley that were incorporated into the Little Brown edition. He proposed that their presence in the volume meant that it would 'only be necessary' for him 'to put the reader in possession of such facts as she has omitted either from a natural reserve, or a very pardonable delicacy.'[62] Norton then rehearsed the circumstances of Shelley's expulsion from Oxford; the history of his stormy marriage to Harriet Westbrooke; and accounts of the elopement with Mary Godwin, and of the subsequent suicide of Shelley's wife. In the latter part of the memoir he incorporated various anecdotes quoted from Leigh Hunt,

---

[61] 'Sketch of Wordsworth's Life', *The Poetical Works of William Wordsworth* (Boston: Little, Brown, 1854), i, pp. xxvii n., xxxii.

[62] 'Memoir of Shelley', *The Poetical Works of Percy Bysshe Shelley*, ed. Mrs Shelley (Boston: Little, Brown, 1855), i, p. xvii. The memoir first appeared anonymously, and it has sometimes been thought that it was written by Lowell. In the Table of Contents of later reprints, Norton is identified as its author.

partly included for their value as entertaining prose and partly for what they might reveal of Shelley's character.

The tension between the line that Lowell attempted to hold in introducing Wordsworth's poetry, so much of which was conspicuously autobiographical, and that which Norton crossed when he composed the 'Memoir of Shelley' comes to a focus in the opening paragraph of the 'Life' that Lowell composed for the Keats volume. Here, the degree to which an author's 'real life' ought to be conceived as inscribed in or as having been lived apart from the poetry was acknowledged to be difficult to ascertain. Lowell sought to get round the difficulty by suggesting that really good readers can discern in the writing 'the gait and gesture' that makes the writer an individual. At the same time he proposed that the writer's 'true nature' was often 'hidden below' the surface:

There are few poets whose works contain slighter hints of their personal history than those of Keats; yet there are, perhaps, even fewer, whose real lives, or rather the conditions upon which they lived, are more clearly traceable in what they have written. To write the life of a man was formerly understood to mean the cataloguing and placing of circumstances, of those things which stood about the life and were more or less related to it, but were not the life itself. But Biography from day to day holds dates cheaper and facts dearer. A man's life, (as far as its outward events are concerned,) may be made for him, as clothes are by the tailor, of this cut or that, of finer or coarser material, but the gait and gesture show through, and give to trappings, in themselves characterless, an individuality that belongs to the man himself. It is those essential facts which underlie the life and make the individual man, that are of importance, and it is the cropping out of these upon the surface, that gives us indications by which to judge of the true nature hidden below. Every man has his block given him, and the figure he cuts will depend very much upon the shape of that—upon the knots and twists which existed in it from the beginning. We were designed in the cradle, perhaps earlier, and it is in finding out this design, and shaping ourselves to it, that our years are spent wisely. It is the vain endeavor to make ourselves what we are not that has strewn history with so many broken purposes and lives left in the rough.[63]

As for Donne, however much Lowell may have wished that his essential life could be discerned in his writings, what emerges from considering these introductions to the early nineteenth-century poets is that the canons for writing biography had already shifted decisively, and the shift was certain to affect the interpretation of the older poet's works. Wordsworth's autobiographical poetry had created a new norm against which his younger contemporaries were implicitly judged. This norm was operative in the assumptions that Lowell and Norton granted about what it was necessary to provide for modern readers.

---

[63] 'The Life of Keats', *The Poetical Works of John Keats* (Boston: Little, Brown, 1854), pp. vii–viii. Lowell's initials appear at the end of the 'Life', p. xxxvi.

The new canons were extended to the reading of Donne's poetry as well. Just as the reading of his letters as sources of personal revelation became normative and obscured the degree to which they had been designed artistically, to give readers pleasure, Donne's poems were increasingly read as slightly veiled transcripts of his own experiences and therefore as documents revealing a real life hidden beneath their surfaces. In the latter half of the nineteenth century indications of interest in Donne's poetry were pretty consistently marked by ambiguity about whether and to what extent the poems provided evidence of a secret life incompatible with Walton's portrait. In the face of that ambiguity there was considerable resistance to the project of reviving Donne's poetry, and not a little ambivalence on the part of some of the revivers.

5

'Sensuous Things'

I do not hide from myself that it needs courage (though I do not claim praise for its exercise) to edit and print the Poetry of DR. JOHN DONNE in our day. Nor would I call it literary prudery that shrinks from giving publicity to such sensuous things (to say the least) as indubitably are found therein. Contrariwise the susceptibility that makes one so shrink is healthy and true, and its sharp though unvociferous warning may not safely be stifled. I deplore that Poetry, in every way almost so memorable ... should be stained even to uncleanliness in sorrowfully too many places.

—A. B. Grosart, Preface to *The Complete Poems of John Donne, D.D.* (1872)

By the 1860s the desire to look into Doctor Donne's writings that had been fomented in the English Romantic period had borne some fruit on the western side of the Atlantic. Lowell's modest edition was a handsome enough book, befitting the admiration for Donne that Emerson had helped to deepen. Meanwhile in Britain the revival of interest in Donne was dissipating. The number of new editions of Walton's *Lives* had fallen off. Alford's edition of the *Works* had largely failed in the purposes that its editor envisaged for it and was an embarrassment to him. Barron Field's attempt to get Coleridge's marginalia published in a volume exclusively dedicated to the Songs and Sonnets had proved abortive. Donne was not included in the Aldine edition of British poets; and the Little Brown volume was largely unknown. At least in the poet's own land, the prediction made in the 1820s according to which John Donne would be remembered but no copy of his poems would be extant at the end of the century was heading for fulfillment. It had been more than half a century since Chalmers had printed the poems. There has never been a longer period during which no new edition of Donne's poetry appeared in England.

A lingering undercurrent of interest in Donne's poetry resurfaced when, in 1872–3, the Revd Alexander B. Grosart published his two-volume edition of

The Complete Poems of John Donne, D.D., Dean of St. Paul's.[1] The edition was part of a larger series, and Grosart committed himself to including Donne before he came to hold him in special esteem. The Fuller Worthies' Library (1868–76) was only one of a number of series that he edited with antiquarian zeal and printed privately for subscribers. Named for the seventeenth-century divine, Thomas Fuller, whose witty *History of the Worthies of England* had been reprinted in 1811 and 1840, the Library's thirty-nine volumes included editions of works in prose as well as verse, by Fulke Greville, Lord Brooke, Henry Vaughan, Robert Southwell, Richard Crashaw, Sir Philip Sidney, George Herbert, Andrew Marvell, and others. At first one hundred quarto copies of Donne's poems were printed along with twenty-five folio copies of the proofs. Later another six copies were printed, and then another fifty.[2] Subscription lists were not printed in the Fuller's Worthies' volumes, but we can make some generalizations from the lists printed in copies of Grosart's Chertsey Worthies' Library. The institutional subscribers in Britain included the British Museum, the university libraries, and the Jesuit college at Stonyhurst. Most subscribers were British gentlemen and scholars. The Chertsey lists include Francis Palgrave, George Saintsbury, Algernon Swinburne, and the holders of chairs in the new discipline of English, David Masson at Edinburgh, Henry Morley in London, and Edward Dowden at Trinity College, Dublin. Fewer than ten percent of the original copies went to North American subscribers, which included the Boston Public Library, and the libraries at Harvard and Princeton Universities. With one conspicuous exception all the individual subscribers seem to have been men: the first copy of each edition was reserved for Her Majesty, the Queen.

Given the limited scope of its dissemination, the hyperbolic and self-serving claims that the editor made for shoddy work, and the fact that the volumes did as much to feed as to overcome a widespread resistance to reading Donne's poetry, it is surprising how cavalierly the Fuller Worthies' edition has been credited with culminating the Donne revival. Kathleen Tillotson, A. J. Smith, and Raoul Granqvist all made it the end-point of their accounts of Donne's reception. When a second Critical Heritage volume appeared in 1996 to chart Donne's reputation from the 1870s to the 1920s, the general editor proclaimed that 'Grosart's great edition' was responsible for 'the full

---

[1] *The Complete Poems of John Donne, D.D., Dean of St. Paul's*, ed. Revd Alexander B. Grosart, The Fuller Worthies' Library, 2 vols. ([London: printed for private circulation], 1872–3). References are given within parentheses hereafter.

[2] Although Grosart's Preface explains that the impression was limited to one hundred quartos and twenty-five separately printed proofs in folio (i. 13), some extant copies (e.g., at Wellesley College Library) carry on the title page the information that 156 copies were printed.

emergence of Donne as a widely-known poet.' He also intimated that it exerted 'a powerful influence upon the development of modern poetry.'[3] Tellingly, the Critical Heritage altogether omits the scathing critique of Grosart's work published by Charles Eliot Norton in the 1890s.[4] Norton's study of 'The Text of Donne's Poems' offered the most thoroughgoing assessment of the subject that had ever been made. It revealed in excruciating detail the hollowness of Grosart's pretensions and showed that, from the point of view of editorial accuracy, this edition would be more appropriately termed than Alford's 'a literary *fiasco*.'

Yet in two ways Grosart's edition contributed significantly to conferring on Donne's writings a larger place in accounts of English literary history than they ever had before. It offered an exuberant concatenation of materials. It framed them, first, in ways that entangled Donne's poetry in the contemporary debates about 'sensuous things' that had been newly inflected by the publication in the *Contemporary Review* for 1871 of R. W. Buchanan's article on Rossetti and the 'fleshly school of poetry.'[5] It pressed these materials—above all Donne's poetry—into service in an attempt to supplement and correct Walton's portrait. Walton's breezy account of Donne's youth was increasingly considered an egregious failing because it probed so little into the subject's most formative experiences. While Grosart's work is likely to appear to us an antiquarian endeavor, it is important to advert to its decidedly contemporary concerns. These aspects of the edition will mostly elude users of the *Variorum*, who, noting that Grosart's name appears there with insistent frequency, will not find there a systematic evaluation of his contributions to Donne Studies. In order to gauge the broader cultural effects of the Fuller Worthies' edition, it makes sense therefore to provide an account of Grosart's contributions on three specific fronts: (1) his attempt greatly to augment the canon of

[3] Kathleen Tillotson, 'Donne's Poetry in the Nineteenth Century (1800–1872)', in *Elizabethan and Jacobean Studies Presented to Frank Percy Wilson* (Oxford: Clarendon, 1959), 307–26; Raoul Granqvist, *The Reputation of John Donne 1779–1873*, Studia Universitatis Upsaliensia, 24 (Stockholm: Almqvist and Wiksell, 1975); B. C. Southam, 'General Editor's Preface', *John Donne: The Critical Heritage*, ii, ed. A. J. Smith, completed with introductory and editorial material by Catherine Philips (London: Routledge, 1996), p. v. Tillotson acknowledged, however, that the 'period really notable for a rapid quickening and extension of interest in Donne is the 1890s' (307).

[4] C. E. Norton, 'The Text of Donne's Poems', *Studies and Notes in Philology and Literature*, v: *Child Memorial Volume* (Boston: Ginn, 1896), 1–19.

[5] Buchanan wrote the article under the pseudonym 'Thomas Maitland' for the *Contemporary Review* (18 (1871), 334–50) in the year following Alford's resignation as editor. It was answered by Rossetti in 'The Stealthy School of Criticism', *Athenæum* (16 Dec. 1871), 792–4. Buchanan replied in turn and published *The Fleshly School of Poetry and Other Phenomena of the Day* (London: Strahan) in the same year that Grosart's preface was published.

Donne's poems; (2) his use of manuscript materials as copy-texts; and (3) his extensive glossing of words and phrases in the poems. In all three spheres Grosart wrought major discontinuities in the history of editing the poetry, and in all three he sometimes created a havoc that he struggled mightily to mitigate and unsuccessfully to control. We can take these up in the order in which those who consult the *Variorum* are likely to encounter them, although this precisely reverses the logical order in which they have just been enumerated.

COMMENTARY, TEXT, AND CANON IN GROSART'S EDITION

At first blush the *Variorum* would seem to confirm the extravagant claims that have been made for the Fuller Worthies' edition. Already in the first published volume it was clear that for many of Donne's poems, for instance, the 'Elegy on the Untimely Death of ... Prince Henry' and the 'Obsequies upon the Lord Harrington', Grosart was the first person to give the date of composition. Grosart's name appears, moreover, with extraordinary frequency among the Notes and Glosses, illustrating that it was he who set in motion critical discussion of dozens of poems. Besides reporting on these conspicuous interventions, the *Variorum* sometimes more subtly acknowledges other innovations. For instance, while the early editors printed the 'Elegy upon the Death of Mrs. Bulstrode' with the love Elegies, by printing the poem in Volume 6, the editors of the *Variorum* have endorsed Grosart's unprecedented decision to group it with Donne's funeral poems.

At the same time, the accumulating evidence gives readers grounds for skepticism in the face of claims for Grosart's achievements. On the title page of his first volume, Grosart proclaimed that Donne's poems are now 'for the first time fully collected and collated with the original and early editions and mss.' Yet the *Variorum*'s lists of verbal variants in the various printed editions provide ample data with which we could augment Norton's critique of Grosart's pedantry and incompetence. The lists show that the editor was erratic and impressionistic in what he took from his source materials. He made reading Donne's poetry more difficult because, instead of clearing out what he referred to as the 'swarming errors and bewilderments of previous editions' (i, p. xii), he introduced hundreds of new ones. There were two principal reasons for this. One was his readiness to accept careless transcriptions, which he compounded by his own carelessness as a transcriber: his version of 'Going to Bed', for instance, instead of printing 'As souls unbodied, bodies uncloth'd must be' (line 34), reads 'As fowles unbodyed boydes [*sic*] uncloth'd must bee.'[6] And in 'The Ecstasy', instead of the lines,

> Where, like a pillow on a bed,
>   A Pregnant banke swell'd up, to rest
> The violets reclining head,
>   Sat we two, one anothers best,

Grosart prints lines that ask readers to conjure an image less consonant with the lovers' intimacy:

> Where like a pillowe on a bedd,
>   A pregnant bancke swell'd upp to rest
> The violet's declininge head
>   Sate we, on one other's brest.

The other, less conspicuous, reason that Grosart introduced many new errors was that he made uninformed choices of manuscript versions for his copy-texts. Among those who knew something about Donne's texts, the seventeenth-century editions already had a bad name; Grosart assumed that old manuscripts would yield something better. Time has certainly vindicated this assumption, and Grosart stands as the editor of Donne who began to reveal the importance of developing valid principles for the choice of a copy-text. The fundamental problem with his procedure was one that, residually, continued to bedevil even the Oxford editions of the 1960s and 1970s: Grosart consulted only a fraction of the extant manuscripts. He arbitrarily attached 'great weight' (i, 3; cf. ii, p. lv) to the inferior manuscript he called 'Stephens' (designated H7 in the *Variorum*) and relied on it oftener than any other.[7] In the 1890s Norton obtained this manuscript, and in 'The Text of Donne's Poems' he demonstrated in detail its consistent inferiority to the edition of 1633.

Criticism of Grosart's incompetence as a textual editor, which has been noticed by readers of his other editions as well, needs to be balanced by a recognition that his antiquarian exuberance made available plenty of previously obscure materials. Pierre Legouis, in an otherwise censuring remark about the 'glaring faults' of the Fuller Worthies' edition of Marvell, praised the industry with which the editor had gone about providing fresh matter

---

[6] This and the following example were among those supplied by Norton in 'The Text of Donne's Poems'; see 3 n. 9.

[7] Grosart's front matter (ii, p. lv) says that at the time he published the Donne volumes the Stephens ms. was in the possession of F. W. Cosens. W. Carew Hazlitt subsequently claimed that *he* had lent Grosart the manuscript. See *Collections and Notes 1867–1876* (London: Reeves and Turner, 1876), 131. This ms., now at Harvard's Houghton Library (English MS 966.6), is designated Δ23 by Peter Beal.

for consideration. Grosart, 'inebriated with Carlylean enthusiasm, could not', Legouis remarked, 'give a sober biography or even portrait of Marvell, but he at least took care to neglect no aspect of his hero.'[8] While this is not quite true of Grosart's work on Donne, his edition did make the poems look quite different from anything anyone had ever seen.

Besides offering claims about the editor's unprecedented collations, Grosart's title page declares that Donne's canon has been 'enlarged with hitherto unprinted and inedited poems from mss.' It also suggests, rightly, that the volumes come complete with an extensive scholarly apparatus: Grosart printed far more textual variants and verbal glosses than any previous editor and provided a good deal of historical information. His first volume contains a six-page preface justifying the undertaking in the face of anticipated objections against an uncastrated edition. The preface also explains that a 'Study of the Life and Writings of Donne' is reserved to volume ii, so that readers will have the whole poetic record with which to evaluate 'the highest claims that have been advanced in his name' (i, p. xi). The editor insists that the 'moral and spiritual study of an intellect so remarkable' as Donne's, 'and of an after-life so white and beautiful' as his, 'is of profoundest suggestiveness' (i, p. x). In the second volume an 'Essay on the Life and Writings' occupies some forty pages, making it by far the longest introduction that had ever accompanied the poetry. It makes great claims for Donne's eminence as an 'Imaginator.' It attempts not only to tease out what is suggestive but also to account for what is graphically sensual in the poems. The essay is then followed by a nine-page 'Bibliographical and Critical Postscript' that describes every previous edition with the exception of Anderson (1793), Chalmers (1810), and Sanford (1819). At the back of the volume there is an eight-page Glossarial Index, listing hundreds of words that the editor clarifies in their places. In the quarto copies, Grosart also displays an engraving of Isaac Oliver's miniature of Donne, a copy of Frank Holl's 'reproduction of an (alleged) Vandyck', a photo-facsimile of the Marshall portrait, and facsimiles of the carving of Donne at St Paul's, of Donne's seals, and of his autograph. The edition is dedicated to Robert Browning, 'the poet of the century for thinkers', with whom Grosart shares his ambivalence about the whole enterprise: the dedication proclaims that the editor knows how much Donne's poetry, 'with every abatement, is valued and assimilated' by Browning.

---

[8] Pierre Legouis, *Andrew Marvell: Poet, Puritan, Patriot*, 2nd edn. (Oxford: Clarendon, 1968), 238. See also Charles Larson, 'Alexander Grosart's Donne and Marvell: "Glorious Old Fellows" in the Nineteenth Century', in *Reinventing the Middle Ages and the Renaissance: Constructions of the Medieval and Early Modern Periods*, ed. William F. Gentrup (Turnhout: Brepols, 1998), 187–99.

The inclusive canon of Grosart's two large volumes is especially striking, both for its size and for the nature of many of the poems incorporated into a 'complete' edition for the first time. Grosart printed far more poems as Donne's than any previous editor had. In fact, he opened the second volume by announcing that he was confident that no further discoveries would much 'modify our verdict' on Donne 'as Man, Poet, or Preacher' (ii, p. ix). Most of the additional poems have been rejected by all subsequent editors, and notably by Grierson, who made a far more extensive study of issues of text and canon. Previously published materials that appeared for the first (and many of them for the last) time included the following: nearly everything printed on thirty-one pages by Sir John Simeon in 1856–7 under the heading 'Unpublished Poems of Donne', two poems first printed by F. G. Waldron in 1802 and dated by him 1625, 'Ten Sonnets to Philomel' from Davison's *Poetical Rhapsody* of 1602, and various other previously 'unprinted and inedited poems from mss.'[9] Among the previously unprinted poems there was one called 'Dr. Donne's Farewell to Ye World.' Its authorship had long been disputed. Grosart took it to be genuinely Donne's because its dismissing of human ambition fit with Walton's portrait of holy dying. As the speaker comes at last to heaven, he proclaims, 'Here will I sit, & sigh my hot youth's folly, | And learne to 'affect a holy malancholy' (ii. 249).

That there had been plenty of 'hot youth's folly' to repent was suggested to subscribers of the Fuller Worthies' series first because, even when he disapproved of them, Grosart had had the 'courage' to print poems that are indubitably Donne's. These included all the English epigrams, which he prefaced by declaring that 'One would very willingly have gone without them' (ii. 266). Of 'To His Mistress Going to Bed', Grosart remarked that he 'should willingly have left [it] unprinted' but for 'unanimous' advice from friends 'that an expurgated edition of Donne would be of no value to students of our Literature and Manners' (i. 99). No doubt his ambivalence was intensified by his misguided sense of obligation to include poems that he took over from Simeon and that qualify as bearers of 'sensuous things': a poem in praise of black beauty that culminates in a fantasy of (illicit) consummation; 'An Elegie to Mrs. Boulstred', which contemplates 'break[ing] the hymen of my

---

[9] Sir John Simeon (ed.), 'Unpublished Poems of Donne', *Bibliographical and Historical Miscellanies*, Philobiblon Society (London: Printed by Charles Wittingham), 3 (1856–7); F. G. Waldron (ed.), *The Shakespearean Miscellany* (London: Knight and Compton, 1802), 'Miscellaneous Poetry', 1–5. Grosart had excluded the 'Ten Sonnets to Philomel' from his Fuller Worthies' edition of Sir John Davies's *Works* (1869). In the *Athenaeum* for 29 January 1876 (161–2), Brinsley Nicholson argued against Grosart's ascription of them to Donne. His arguments in favor of Davies's authorship convinced Grosart, who 'reclaim[ed]' the sonnets in a subsequent edition of Davies's *Poems* (London: Chatto and Windus, 1876), 99 n.

Muse | For one poore hower's love' and presents poetry as a way to 'spill'
one's 'fortune'; and 'Love and Reason', in which the speaker contrasts a desire
ungoverned by Reason with one that works like the sun to 'actuate, produce,
ripen, and free | From grossness, those good seeds which in us lie.' Grosart,
when he printed this last poem, declared that 'it cannot have been written *by*,
though probably it was addressed *to*', Donne (i. 239–42). He seems to have
specially in mind the double prayer at the end: 'Restore this lover to himself
again' and 'Give him a healthy and discerning taste.'

In addition to the poems taken from Simeon, Grosart included two other
elegies from the Stephens ms. that he printed 'for the first time.' One of these
begins 'Trew love fynds wytt' and was subsequently classed by Grierson among
the dubia. Headed by Grosart 'Love and Wit', it offers a cynical commentary
on sexual mores at court. A second elegy, headed by Grosart 'A Love-Monster',
rivals 'Farewell to Love' for what Barron Field called 'indelicate obscurity.' The
speaker recalls 'Sporting with Calda ... and many of them more', and notices
on his swollen body riddling 'signes' that he is about to bring forth a 'Cæsarian
bratt' to 'be cut out' by a barber's 'knyfe.' Grosart's commentary registers his
inability to provide 'a satisfactory solution of the subject of this poem', even
as it speculates, enlisting a popular euphemism ('a Winchester goose') and
technical language ('paraphimosis') that Donne must have been suffering the
effects of a venereal disease (i. 251). Since the great majority of poems that
Grosart sought to add to Donne's canon concerned love and sex, he provided
himself many opportunities to write about the vagaries of human sexuality at
the same time that he deplored licentious speech and breaches of chastity.

SOME CONTEXTS FOR EDITORIAL 'COURAGE'

For all his ambivalence about publishing Donne's poems, there are reasons
to be surprised by Grosart's pre-emptive insistence that it took 'courage.'
Coleridge and Alford had both called for a new edition, and in 1853 *The
Literary World* published Coleridge's observation that 'all the copies' that he
had 'ever seen of Donne's Poems are grievously misprinted.' The Little Brown
edition, far from satisfying the need, made this even more apparent. By the
1860s some requirements for a new edition were discussed in the pages of
Notes and Queries.

The earliest items referring to Donne in *Notes and Queries* (founded 1849)
evince no anxiety about Donne's implication with 'sensuous things.' In fact,
they tend to show that the correspondents and the editor were unacquainted
with what was available to be known. In 1852 a reader of Walton, following

up on the information that Donne had left behind 'the resultance of 1400 authors' and some six score sermons, wrote in to ask the location of the manuscripts. The editor replied to only part of the query, citing the existence of the three seventeenth-century sermon editions and making no reference at all to Alford. Other correspondents asked about, or reported on, Donne's will and seal and the portrait taken in his grave clothes, about his Welsh stock, his mother's death, and the coincidence of this descendent of Thomas More's having married a woman with the More surname. Some attention to Donne's poems was initiated in 1863 when the editor listed six seventeenth-century editions and pronounced the 1669 'unquestionably the most complete.' In this year two correspondents—Grosart writing as 'A.B.G.' and the Revd T. R. O'Flahertie signing himself as 'Cpl' (he lived at Capel, near Dorking)—began making queries and offering information, some of it bearing on the poetry. In 1868 the bibliographer W. Carew Hazlitt proposed that a 'good edition of Donne may be worth a place in the *Library of Old Authors*.' He called for 'some competent person' to undertake the work '*con amore*' and pointed out that it would 'require collation' of all the old copies with one another and 'with any existing MSS., notably with Harl. MS. 5110, which' (as J. Payne Collier had pointed out more than fifty years earlier) purports to contain '*Jhon* [sic] *Dunne his Satires, Anno Domini* 1593.'[10] By this time A.B.G. was already at work on the task.

Of course ambivalence about Donne's poetry was not unique to Grosart. The article in *Lowe's* for 1846 had dwelt upon signs in the poetry of perverse Roman Catholic attitudes towards love. In particular the author singled out the endorsement of celibacy as a mark of 'that false shame which Romanism had attached to the contemplation of the sexual relations.' Even as he praised 'A Valediction Forbidding Mourning', 'The Good Morrow', 'The Ecstasy', and the Bishop Valentine epithalamion as instances of poetry written in a golden time when the Reformation had liberated 'the rejoicing poet' from the false worship formerly enforced 'by the harlot, Rome', he lamented that as the seventeenth century went along the liberty of English Christians had 'been deadened or destroyed by the poisonous taint of Romanism' once again.[11] Ambivalence of a related sort was implied when the editor of *Notes and Queries* cited Walton's remarks that the poems had been 'loosely—God knows, too loosely—scattered in his youth' and that Donne had 'wished [they] had been abortive, or so short-lived that his own eyes had witnessed [their] funeral[s].'

---

[10] See *N&Q*, 3rd ser., 3 (1863), 308–9; ibid. 4th ser., 2 (1868), 483–4; cf. Collier, *The Poetical Decameron, or Ten Conversations on English Poets and Poetry, Particularly of the Reigns of Elizabeth and James I*, 2 vols. (Edinburgh: Archibald Constable, 1820), i. 158–9.

[11] 'Gallery of Poets. No. 1—John Donne', *Lowe's Edinburgh Magazine*, 1 (1846), 228–9. Granqvist discusses ambivalence, 119–22.

This ambivalence was shared by O'Flahertie. In these years he was making queries about Donne's language and about the editorial work carried out by John Donne, Junior; asking about the identities of persons whom Donne had addressed in his verse letters; attempting to trace recently sold copies of the seventeenth-century editions; providing information about Donne's relations with Constantine Huygens and inquiring about the translation of Donne's poems into Dutch; and revealing, in 1868, that he himself had been collecting materials about Donne's life and was preparing a new edition. Two years later, in response to the announcement that Grosart was to include Donne's poetry in the Fuller Worthies' Library, he wrote with information about early editions of the *Anniversaries* and remarked that the *Sheaf of Epigrams* (1652), purporting to contain translations of Donne's Latin epigrams, 'is in great part a collection of filth, which the reverend translator had not the decency to leave under the veil of its original language.' O'Flahertie's confession that he could not find the 'time or courage' to carry out a revision of Walton and an edition of Donne's poems stands as a crucial part of the background to the opening paragraph of Grosart's preface of 1872. So does the tractate published in 1856–7 for the Philobiblon Society by Simeon, MP for the Isle of Wight and something of a Donne collector.[12]

While Simeon proposed that Donne 'may have been deficient in some of the highest characteristics of the poetic mind', he maintained that the poems he was printing 'deserve attention for the keenness of [Donne's] wit, and the exuberance of his fancy,—qualities in which he is perhaps without a rival.'[13] Among the more innocuous poems there were some love sonnets and the poem, 'Absence, hear thou this protestation', which in the last decade of the nineteenth century and the first decade of the twentieth would be printed in revisions of Palgrave's *Golden Treasury*. Yet Simeon's collection also contained a *carpe diem* lyric in which a woman is counseled against 'selfe-love' and a number of love elegies that might qualify as being 'stained even to uncleanliness.' Since 1912 only two of the poems that he printed, 'Love's War' and 'The Liar', have been accepted as part of the Donne canon. In the late nineteenth century, however, Grosart had put his stamp of approval on the whole lot, and readers of his edition generally assumed that they were genuine.

---

[12] See *N&Q*, 3rd ser., 3 (1863), 308–9; ibid. 4th ser., 5 (1870), 565; ibid. 2 (1868), 614. When Simeon's library was auctioned by Sotheby's in 1871, it contained seven items ascribed to Donne. For comparison, the number of items by some other seventeenth- and eighteenth-century writers was as follows: Shakespeare (9), Milton (2), Herrick (1), George Herbert (0), Cowley (0), Marvell (1), Katherine Philips (1), Gray (2), Cowper (2). There was one Walton item, a volume with notes by Sir J. Hawkins, published in 1792 and containing both the *Compleat Angler* and the *Lives*. See *Catalogue of the Valuable and Very Choice Library of the Late Sir John Simeon, Bart., M.P.* (London: Dryden Press, 1871).

[13] Simeon (ed.), 'Unpublished Poems of Donne', 9, 10.

What Grosart's protestation of the need for courage did not take into account was the Little, Brown edition. It had appeared in 1855 and was reprinted at least three times between 1857 and 1866. In his bibliographical essay Grosart wrongly gave the date of this 'Boston' edition as 1864. Clearly, he had a copy of it to hand. Comparisons of variant readings listed in the *Variorum* show that in creating his text he sometimes followed its precedents without acknowledgment. Explicitly, he dismissed its relevance to his project. Had it been known that the volume was edited by Lowell, Grosart would have had to take it more seriously. Lowell was highly respected and widely read in England. In his edition of Southwell, Grosart expressed for him his 'innermost love.'[14] In his second volume Grosart quoted from *Among my Books* Lowell's tribute to Donne's power to 'open vistas for the imagination' and cited his remark concerning 'A bracelet of bright hair about the bone' from 'The Relic', that the 'verse still shines there in the darkness of the tomb, after two centuries, like one of those inextinguishable lamps whose secret is lost' (ii, p. xxxiv).

Lowell was not alone in recognizing Donne's powers of mind, or in recommending the poetry for the astonishing brilliance of his imaginative legacy. Grosart came to think Donne's poetry far above his prose and assigned 'inestimable' value to the Satires in particular (ii, pp. ix, xxviii). He urged that the seventeenth-century commendatory poems had not been unduly extravagant in their praise and declared Donne 'an absolute and unique' and 'incomparable genius' whose poetry is '*thoughtful* in the highest and subtlest region of speculative thought' (ii, pp. xlvii, xliv, xxxiii). 'As an Imaginator it is impossible', Grosart wrote, 'to place Donne too high. The light of his imagination lies goldenly over his thinking' (ii, p. xxxix). 'One characteristic of his thinking', he remarked elsewhere, 'is its sudden out-flashing from the common level' (ii, p. xxxv). He quoted with approval Professor G. L. Craik of Belfast, who argued that while 'Donne's verses look like so many riddles' at first and may seem 'to be written upon the principle of making the meaning as difficult to be found out as possible', they benefit greatly from being approached with the sort of intelligence necessary for reading Shakespeare. An 'insight' that penetrates the surface will discover in Donne's amatory lyrics 'the most exuberant wit' and 'the sunniest ... fancy', Craik wrote, characteristics wholly compatible with 'the truest tenderness and depth of feeling.' Such a reader will find there 'a deep and subtle music' not heard by those accustomed to 'the see-saw style of reading verse.'[15] Similarly, Grosart insisted that to

---

[14] Grosart, Memorial-Introduction, *The Complete Poems of Robert Southwell, S.J.*, The Fuller Worthies' Library ([London: printed for private circulation], 1872), pp. xcv–xcvi.

[15] George L. Craik, *A Compendious History of English Literature*, 2 vols. (New York: Charles Scribner, 1863), i. 579–80. Craik's discussion of Donne was first published in 1845 and was re-issued in London in the year (1861) that *The Golden Treasury* first appeared.

approach Donne's poems one must 'master his language and methods, and with all reverence and humility sit at his feet.' Even as he proposed that readers need to cast 'shaded eyes on poems and lines one must wish he had blotted' (ii, p. xlvii), he did not shrink from making the 'supremest claims' for Donne (ii, p. xxxvii).

Those who have traced the views of the nineteenth-century precursors of Grierson and of T. S. Eliot, while they have often ascribed great importance to Grosart, have generally neglected to report on the less approving estimates of Donne from the 1860s and 1870s. In these decades, even amidst large changes in the criteria by which critics were evaluating poetry, the opinions expressed by Lowell and Grosart were minority views. Much critical writing on Donne sounded like the chorus of virulent disapprobation with which *Men and Women* and *Maud* and *Leaves of Grass* were met when they first appeared in 1855.[16] There were many who had misgivings about a revival of Donne's poetry. Troubled by the 'sensuous things (to say the least)' to be found in the amatory verse, critics in the moralizing tradition of Lord Jeffrey turned attention upon Donne's abuse of the vigor and energy that Coleridge had pinpointed for admiration. H. H. Milman, the first Dean of St Paul's since Donne to have pretensions as a poet, contrasted the 'control and discipline' in Donne's prose with the extravagance of his unruly verse: 'what in those days was esteemed wit ... ran wild in his poetry, and suffocated the graceful and passionate thoughts.' There was a growing tendency to identify Donne with figures in the poems whose 'wildness and extravagance' were 'excusable' because he had written these verses in his youth. Craik maintained that Donne's 'seething ... brain' strove 'to expend itself in all sorts of novel and wayward combinations, just as Shakespeare had made it do in his Romeo and Juliet.' In his view, Donne himself shared with Shakespeare's young lovers the propensity to 'exhaust all the eccentricities of language in their struggle to give expression to that inexpressible passion which had taken captive the[ir] whole heart and being.'[17]

Others, less filled with admiration, repeated Dr Johnson's charges against the metaphysical poets. Those who knew Donne's poetry largely by way of Pope's translations of the Satires typically referred to his harsh numbers and

[16] See John Woolford, 'Periodicals and the Practice of Literary Criticism, 1855–64', in *The Victorian Periodical Press: Samplings and Soundings*, ed. Joanne Shattock and Michael Wolff (Leicester: Leicester Univ. Press; Toronto: Univ. of Toronto Press, 1982), 109–42.

[17] Henry Hart Milman, *Annals of S. Paul's Cathedral* (London: John Murray, 1868), 329; Craik, *Compendious History*, i. 579–80. Cf. Craik's *Sketches of the History of Literature and Learning in England*, 4 vols. (London: Charles Knight, 1845), iii. 168–70. A similar view was found in J. C. M. Bellew's *Poets' Corner: A Manual for Students in English Poetry* (London: Routledge and Sons, 1868), 188–9.

rugged versification and insisted that his cold conceits and display of learning rendered his poems 'obscure' and 'unnatural.' 'As a writer', Thomas Arnold pronounced of Donne, 'the great popularity which he enjoyed in his own day has long since given way before the repulsive harshness and involved obscurity of his style.'[18] Some claimed that Donne had been a child prodigy but squandered his considerable talents on useless book-learning and trivial, dissolute poetic exercises. The condemnations were international in range and damaging in their scope. The Scots clergyman George Gilfillan, who edited a handsome library edition of British poets that included Herbert, Milton, Young, and Cowper, excluded Donne, whose poetry he regarded as a mixture of 'spilt treasure' and 'ingenious nonsense'; 'even the worst passages', he maintained, 'discover a great, though trammelled and tasteless mind.'[19]

Among those who proposed that Donne was decadent, the American essayist and reviewer Edwin Percy Whipple proved especially merciless. In lectures delivered for the Lowell Institute and published in the *Atlantic Monthly*, he proposed that Donne's 'insatiable intellectual curiosity' was his besetting sin from youth well into middle age. Donne had foolishly wasted a whole year of his life making 'an elaborate examination of the points in dispute between the Romanists and the Reformers.' Lamentable 'habits of intellectual self-indulgence' lasted long after his marriage. For thirty years his 'incessant study' masked a constitutional 'indisposition to practical labor.' Walton naïvely mistook this moral indolence for 'humility.' Donne had the 'misfortune', Whipple remarked, 'to know thoroughly the works of fourteen hundred writers, most of them necessarily worthless.' All this 'thought-suffering learning' made his sermons a bore, just as it had ruined his attempts at poetry. The 'amatory poems' are 'characterized by a cold, hard, labored, intelletualized sensuality' that had 'no excuse of passion for its violations of decency.' It is no wonder therefore that at last Donne experienced 'that worst

---

[18] Thomas Arnold, *Chaucer to Wordsworth. A Short History of English Literature from the Earliest Times to the Present Day* (London: Thomas Murby, [1868]), 98. For a summary that is especially helpful on the eighteenth-century views of this subject, see Arthur H. Nethercot, 'The Reputation of John Donne as Metrist', *Sewanee Review*, 30 (1922), 463–74. For influential nineteenth-century views on 'the relation between the poet's peculiar mode of expression and the matter expressed', see [Coventry Patmore], 'English Metrical Critics', *North British Review*, 27 (1857), 130. On 'metrical cogitation', see David Masson, *The Life of John Milton ...* , i: *1608–1639* (Cambridge and London: Macmillan; Boston: Gould and Lincoln, 1859), 447.

[19] George Gilfillan, *Specimens with Memoirs of the Less-Known British Poets*, 3 vols. (Edinburgh: James Nichol, 1860), i. 203; cf. John W. Hales, 'John Donne', in *The English Poets: Selections with Critical Introductions by Various Writers*, ed. Thomas Humphrey Ward, 4 vols. (London: Macmillan, 1880; repr., New York: Macmillan, 1924), i. 558–60.

of intellectual diseases, mental disgust', from which he spent most of his final years trying to recover.[20]

While George Craik and Anna Jameson distinguished between the harshness of the Satires and the music of Donne's lyrics, Whipple instanced the erotic poems wherein Donne 'found he could wittily justify what was vicious.'[21] His censorious judgments were not atypical. In these years there was a good bit of resistance to reviving Donne on the grounds that the love poetry was indecent. The bibliographer Thomas Corser, even as he claimed he was looking forward to the appearance of Grosart's edition, explained his antipathy to Donne by complaining about the salacious aspects of the verse. It is understandable, he suggested, that Donne, who 'lived at a period when great licentiousness was tolerated', should have written some licentious poems, especially since he would surely have suppressed such verses had he lived into more enlightened times.[22] In Corser's view, by the early eighteenth century, civilized society had already progressed to a degree of refinement that made Tonson's printing such poetry an error of judgment. In light of conceptions about the progress of civilization towards greater delicacy, refinement, and 'health', Grosart's claim that it took courage to edit Donne makes a kind of sense.

The ambivalence voiced in Grosart's preface about 'sensuous things' is of a piece with expressions of ambivalence about sensuality found in other kinds of discourse from the period, from medical literature to art history to religious polemics.[23] It was referable not simply to matters of human sexuality but, like 'The Canonization' and other poems by Donne, referable as well to the vexed relations between art and religion. Grosart understood quite clearly that, because Walton's portrait of Dr Donne made him virtually a saint of the English church, the printing of his licentious poetry was a different case from that of Chaucer or Skelton or Carew. To the unpopular policy with which he reluctantly agreed to comply, that the 'pruriencies' of older writers ought to be reprinted 'without mutilation or castration', there was added therefore a

[20] Whipple's lectures were gathered into *The Literature of the Age of Elizabeth* (Boston, MA: Fields, Osgood, 1869), quoted here from 230–8. Similar views were put to more conspicuously didactic purposes by Esther J. Trimble in *A Hand-book of English and American Literature* (Philadelphia: Eldredge and Brother, 1883), 76, a book designed 'For the Use of Schools and Academies.'

[21] Whipple, *Literature of the Age of Elizabeth*, 232. Cf. Craik, *Compendious History*, i. 579–80; [Anna Jameson], *The Loves of the Poets* (London: Henry Colburn, 1829), ii. 95–6.

[22] Thomas Corser, *Collectanea Anglo-Poetica: or, a Bibliographical and Descriptive Catalogue of a Portion of a Collection of Early English Poetry*, Part V, published by the Chetham Society, 91 (1873), 227.

[23] For another example of how Foucault 'accustomed' twentieth-century readers to tracing a 'history of sexuality' by attending to 'religious confessions', 'medical discourse', and 'architecture', see Peter Stallybrass, 'Editing as Cultural Formation: The Sexing of Shakespeare's Sonnets', *MLQ*, 54 (1993), 102.

second, more damning and more interesting notion, which Grosart came fully to accept: that Donne had been a libertine.

The acceptance came gradually, between the appearance of volume i and volume ii. It transformed the editor's whole sense of his project. In the preface to the first volume Grosart had put his finger on what he took to be the central contradiction he was going to have to negotiate. He acknowledged that it is shocking to discover in 'lily's chalice ... a slug crawling' (i, pp. x–xi). At first he sought to deal with the presence of licentious materials by pronouncing in advance of the reader's encounter with them that poems in which Doctor Donne seems implicated in unworthy behaviors are purely fictional: to this end he quoted Herrick's claim, 'Jocond his Muse was; *but his Life was chast*' (i, p. ix). While preparing the Lyrics, Epigrams, and Divine Poems for inclusion in the second volume, however, Grosart became persuaded that Donne had been guilty of actual 'immoralities' (ii, p. xvii). It became the principal goal of his Essay therefore to account for the salacious materials that he was now convinced made it 'impossible to deny' that the poet himself had 'sinned to the uttermost' (ii, p. xvii). To explain how Donne's youth could have been 'not in theory or imagination merely ... profligate and "gay" in the saddest meaning of the words' (ii, p. xvii), he proposed the two crucial 'facts' on which an understanding of Donne's poetry must be based: first, that the religious poetry had been written when he was still a Roman Catholic and, second, that the 'Sheaf of Miscellany Epigrams' was inauthentic. On these twin pillars Grosart sought to erect a revision of the *Life of Donne* that would spell out some implications of Walton's observation that when Donne went into holy orders the English church had gained 'a second St. *Austine*.' He was emboldened in this course by a contemporary of Alford's at Trinity College, Cambridge, the Archbishop of Dublin, who had developed the comparison with the author of *The Confessions*:

there was in Donne the same tumultuous youth, the same entanglement in youthful lusts, the same conflict with these, and the same final deliverance from them; and then the same passionate and personal grasp of the central truths of Christianity, linking itself as this did with all that he had suffered, and all that he had sinned, and all through which, by God's grace, he had victoriously struggled.

This was to go well beyond what Isaac Disraeli had asserted in the 1840s when he wrote that 'Donne, who closed his life as a St. Austin, had opened it as a Catullus.'[24]

---

[24] Grosart (ed.), *Complete Poems of John Donne*, ii, pp. xvii–xviii, quoting from Richard Trench's *Household Book of English Poetry* (London: Macmillan, 1868), 303–4; Isaac Disraeli, *Amenities of Literature* (1841); quoted from a new edn., ed. B[enjamin] Disraeli, 2 vols. (Boston: William Veazie, 1864), ii. 352. Grosart's view was partly anticipated by Leigh Hunt, who in a

In his preface Grosart had listed seven reasons for including Donne among his Worthies. Among them were the following: the fact that the edition was intended for studious purposes and would be available only by a 'private circulation'; a scholarly obligation to be true to the facts of the historical record; and an awareness that 'only through his Poetry' is Donne known 'in the fulness of his faculties.' In this way Grosart touched off a peculiar sort of interest in Donne's poems. He could scarcely have called more attention to the licentious verses than by beginning his whole enterprise by providing an elaborate, and evasive, defense of their publication. What was most significant about the Fuller Worthies' edition, then, is that by bestowing sustained attention on the text of Donne's poems, even though he did much of his work badly, Grosart managed to bring the poetry into a closer and more troubled relation with Donne's life-narrative than any reader since the seventeenth century had been able to contemplate. For all its scholarly dress, Grosart's was a 'biographical' edition in senses of the word that George Eliot deplored and that Norton would seek to expose as being at odds with responsible editing. Grosart expressed hesitance to print Donne's poetry not because he agreed in general with Leigh Hunt that an editor ought not to reprint the pruriencies of older writers. Rather, he was anxious about the effects that disseminating poetry 'stained ... to uncleanliness' (i, p. ix) might have specifically on the hallowed portrait bequeathed to English literature by Walton. As an attempt to incorporate the poetry in a retelling of Donne's life, the apparatus he created for his edition offers extensive evidence of how scholarly discourse could be enlisted to manage Victorian anxieties about 'sensuous things.'

'OBSCURITY'

No example of Victorian resistance to reviving Donne's poetry has been more notorious than the exclusion of all poems by Donne from the great anthology that enforced standards of delicacy and refinement, *The Golden Treasury*, first published in 1861. Palgrave had read through Chalmers's *Works of the English Poets from Chaucer to Cowper* twice, and the exclusion was principled and quite deliberate. He regarded Donne's poems as too coarse for young persons to encounter. Moreover, the precipitous decline in the number of Donne's readers from the mid-seventeenth century to the mid-nineteenth

Supplement to his *London Journal* (No. 7, p. xlix [1835]) remarked that Donne 'had in his youth led a gay imprudent life, which left him poor'; cited from *The Town: Its Memorable Characters and Events*, new edn. (London: Gibbings, 1893), 258.

counted against Palgrave's confidence, as he ultimately put it in his preface to the first edition, in 'the vague general verdict of popular Fame.'[25] The 'far-sought allusions and conceits' and 'strange contorted phrasings' that largely characterized 'English poetry from Surrey to Herbert and Crashaw' seemed altogether characteristic of the poetry of Donne. Even Tennyson's admiration for 'A Valediction Forbidding Mourning' (which may have developed after 1860) was not enough to promote any of Donne's poems beyond the category of 'near admission.' As a poetry for thinkers much of which was 'chiefly amorous', Donne's was 'obscure' in at least three senses. At once uncouth and difficult and little known, his poetry continued through the nineteenth century to be condemned in the terms that had been favored in the eighteenth: it was said to be 'harsh', 'rugged', and 'coarse.' Yet by 1861 the traditional criteria for evaluating poetry were becoming unstable, and the exclusion of Donne from *The Golden Treasury* is by no means the only index of the place of Donne's poetry within Victorian literary history. When, on 27 September 1855, a literary gathering that included Tennyson and the Rossettis met at the Browning residence in Dorset Street and the host read from 'Fra Lippo Lippi', he could scarcely have chosen a better poem with which to challenge the reigning orthodoxy about the nature and purpose of poetry in the very period when Palgrave was choosing poems for his anthology. He was also making way for a substantial re-evaluation of Donne.

Grosart's dedication of his edition to Browning is only one of a number of acknowledgments during the period that there were affinities between the two poets. Browning had begun reading Donne in the mid-1820s, shortly after the article in the *Retrospective Review* had called attention to the love poems. He valued Donne's love of ironic play and himself wrote poetry that was, as Joseph Duncan aptly epitomized its conspicuous affinities with Donne's, 'metrically rugged and intellectually complex.' He shared his interest in Donne with Elizabeth Browning and sustained it throughout his life. Beyond similarities between many poems that the two men wrote, there were rough parallels between the socially disruptive marriages they made and in their relations with their irate fathers-in-law, subjects on which the Brownings' friend Anna Jameson had written with great sympathy for Anne More and John Donne. 'A Grammarian's Funeral' alluded to the most frequently quoted of Donne's letters when it referred to the speaker's dead master as 'soul-hydroptic with a sacred thirst' for learning; more broadly, it recapitulated the grounds for debate about the value of Donne's learning in which Whipple would powerfully

---

[25] See Granqvist, *Reputation*, 134–7; Francis Palgrave (ed.), *The Golden Treasury of the Best Songs and Lyrical Poems in the English Language* (Cambridge and London: Macmillan, 1861), p. xii.

intervene to condemn 'incessant study' as 'self-indulgence.' 'Childe Roland to the Dark Tower Came' borrowed the opening simile from 'A Valediction Forbidding Mourning' and pressed the image of friends gathered round the death bed to a use analogous to what readers could find in the *Anniversaries* or 'A Nocturnal upon St. Lucy's Day': a bold confrontation with nothingness. Browning's many allusions and tributes to Donne in his letters and poems, especially in 'The Two Poets of Croisic', have been noted, and the case for Donne's influence has been aptly developed.[26] What needs emphasizing is that the intelligent and appreciative criticism eventually evoked by 'Fra Lippo Lippi' and other poems by Browning contributed significantly to the transformation of Donne from a saintly preacher of the past into a love poet who spoke powerfully in the present.

   In the face of assumptions that required poetry to be euphonious, lucid, moral, and properly ambitious, the poems in *Men and Women* were at first condemned by criteria similar to those that had been long invoked against Donne's. Browning's poems were said to be 'rough' and 'harsh', full of 'vanity and self-seeking', prone to representing human weaknesses, and overly concerned with 'the value and significance of flesh.' They were, moreover, routinely said to be 'difficult to follow', 'deliberately unintelligible', and 'obscure.' By contrast, when *Dramatis Personae* appeared nine years later, although it printed many poems reminiscent of those in the volume of 1855, Browning's new poetry met with almost universal approbation. John Woolford has ascribed this reversal to major changes in Victorian literary culture, having to do with the conception of poetry and of the roles to be exercised by poets and critics alike.[27] Instead of proud displays by critics who set themselves up as morally superior to the poet and sought to condemn his deviance, reviews of Browning from the 1860s were reflective and analytical and showed the reviewers to be almost wholly on the poet's side, acting as his interpreters and advocates. Among the changes in critical assumptions and method, probably none was more important for the appreciation of poems by Donne and by Browning than the growing tendency among critics to work through what was meant when it was charged that poetry was 'obscure.' Already in 1856, in an early juxtaposition of the two poets, a reviewer of Browning's poetry

---

[26] Joseph Duncan's article, 'The Intellectual Kinship of Browning and Donne' appeared originally in *SP*, 50 (1953) and in revised form as chapter 3 in *The Revival of Metaphysical Poetry: The History of a Style, 1800 to the Present* (Minneapolis, MN: Univ. of Minnesota Press, 1959); see 53. Cf. Tillotson, 'Donne's Poetry', 324–6; ultimately, her study was aimed at describing 'the whole nineteenth-century context of Browning's interest in his "revered and magisterial Donne".' The phrases that Grosart used to characterize Browning appear entirely in capital letters on the dedication page (i, p. v).

[27] For the contemporary reception of Browning's poetry, see Woolford, 'Periodicals', 117–20 and the relevant endnotes. Quoted words and phrases in this paragraph are from Woolford.

for *Putnam's Monthly Magazine* began by comparing Browning with Cowley and Donne on the grounds that his poems make 'very hard reading.' The comparison immediately gave way to a contrast: 'the earlier poets' were said to be 'obscurists' whose sentiments were as conceited as their style, whereas 'Browning must be ranked with the modern school for his profound reality and humanity and faithful reliance upon nature.' Implied here were the grounds that would eventually be invoked to defend Donne's poetry from charges of obscurity as well. Another reviewer of Browning enlisted terms that help to make sense of the fact that Donne's first editors introduced his poems with 'Metempsychosis' and 'The Flea': 'the reader of Mr Browning must learn first of all that he is one of that class of writers whose finest thoughts must be often read "between the lines".'[28]

To make good the claims for the author of *Men and Women*, the reviewer in *Putnam's* insisted that Browning was 'the most purely dramatic genius in English literature since the great dramatic days' (372). Browning's 'occasional obscurity', the reviewer proposed, comes from his having written as a dramatist; his poems require readers studiously to use their imaginations to discern the ways in which the poet writes 'as a critic of all the scenes his various poems describe.' 'The man Browning is not to be found in his poems, except inferentially, like Shakespeare in his dramas' (372). Present in his poems 'as a kind of abstract moral and historical critic' (374), Browning was said to have written in 'The Heretic's Tragedy' something 'as morally effective as a whole volley of sermons, or strings of resolutions of an anti-papal league' (373). Many readers who were inclined to dismiss Browning's poetry as obscure were nonetheless attracted to the fact that it exposed sexual and political corruption, and the reviewer suggested a connection between Browning's polemics and his having been inspired by love and by a 'singular apprehension of womanly experience' (378). The true love between Browning and his wife was thought to contribute to the poet's ability to reveal in many of his poems the unhealthy sexual politics of Catholic Italy. 'No other English poet', the reviewer proposed, 'has given expression to so many and different moods of love' (376). In his poems, 'so often dismissed as rough and uncouth', there is to be found 'the most pervasive music' (378). This was virtually what Jameson had asserted about Donne's love for his wife and the conjugal poetry it inspired.

The critical emphasis upon a reader's ability to imagine how the poet abstracted himself from the voices he used was matched in other reviews

---

[28] 'Robert Browning', *Putnam's Monthly Magazine*, 7 (Apr. 1856), 372; subsequent references appear within parentheses; Moncure Conway, 'Robert Browning', *Victoria Magazine*, 2 (1864), 304; quoted by Woolford, 'Periodicals', 126. Cf. Algernon Charles Swinburne, *George Chapman: A Critical Essay* (London: Chatto and Windus, 1875), 15–18.

of *Men and Women* that stand as exceptions to Woolford's generalization. William Morris acknowledged that Browning's poetry was generally thought to be characterized by 'carelessness, and [a] consequent roughness in rhythm, and obscurity in language and thought', and defended it by observing that much good writing—he instanced *Hamlet*—seems 'obscure' upon first reading and benefits from continuing acquaintance. Similarly, George Eliot, writing anonymously for the *Westminster Review*, called into question several criteria invoked by Palgrave. She contrasted Browning's poetry with the sort of material sought out by persons who are attracted to 'melodious commonplace[s]' and for whom reading 'poems is often a substitute for thought: fine-sounding conventional phrases and the sing-song of verse demand no co-operation.' She celebrated instead a poetry that 'repels not only the ignorant but the idle.' Tweaking those who read with 'drowsy passivity', she praised Browning because he 'sets our thoughts at work rather than our emotions' and 'requires the reader to trace by his own mental activity the underground stream of thought that jets out in elliptical and pithy verse.' She compared the 'majestic obscurity' of Browning to that of Aristotle and contrasted it with 'the obscurity of the stars', which is simply a function of 'the feebleness of men's vision.' Within a generation many readers came to understand these contrasts. Swinburne elaborated an important distinction between poets who are obscure only when readers fail to read them 'in the fit frame of mind' and ones who are obscure at every sitting. The latter, whose thinking is merely 'random', he compared to smoke, the former to lightning, and remarked that critics of Browning might be excused when they 'err through excess of light.'[29] He might have invoked Donne's Satire III, where 'mysteries' are said to be 'like the Sunne, dazzling, yet plaine to all eyes.'

By the 1860s, then, a widening appreciation of Browning's dramatic mono-logues created an atmosphere in which there were alternatives to the idea that Donne's lyrics were transparently autobiographical. Donne's 'obscurity' came increasingly to be understood as a mark of his having been a profound thinker, whose writing demands 'unbroken attention' to its language.[30] Already in 1846 the article in *Lowe's* had remarked that Donne's 'profundity of thought' works 'against his popularity.' Writing to introduce the poems to workingmen a few

[29] Morris's unsigned review appeared in the *Oxford and Cambridge Magazine*, 1/3 (Mar. 1856), 162–72, quoted from 172; George's Eliot's unsigned review appeared in *The Westminster Review*, 65 (Jan. 1856), 290–6; quoted from 290–1; Swinburne, *George Chapman*, 15–20, quoted from 17, 19, 20.

[30] See *Typical Selections from the Best English Authors* (Oxford: Clarendon, 1869), 32. Among references to Donne's 'obscurity', see *Select Poetry Chiefly Sacred of the Reign of King James the First*, ed. Edward Farr (Cambridge: Deighton; London: John W. Parker, 1847), p. xii; *The Sacred Poets of England and America*, ed. Rufus W. Griswold (New York: D. Appleton, 1859), 50; Thomas Arnold, *Short History*, 97.

years later, John Alfred Langford promised pleasures to those willing to read 'A Valediction Forbidding Mourning' 'more than once ... to seize its hidden meaning.'[31] In writing various notes and queries about Donne, O'Flahertie often called attention to obscurities to be cleared up and delivered helpful glosses himself.

Grosart's interpretations show that he had not assimilated what Browning's poetry might have taught him. He frequently offered dubious speculations when, instead of referring Donne's language to books, he sought to refer it to an imagined reconstruction of his life. Before turning to consider the twin 'facts' on which he erected his presentation of Donne, it is worth pointing out that his editing of the lyrics contributed both to his conviction that Donne had committed grave sexual sins and to his belief in the ideal nature of Donne's marriage. He accepted Walton's claim that 'A Valediction Forbidding Mourning' had been written for Donne's wife; and to this he added that the song 'Sweetest love I do not go' belongs to the same occasion. He insisted that 'A Valediction of the Book' (which he printed as 'A Valediction to his Book') was 'doubtless addressed to the poet's wife' and speculated that it 'probably formed the concluding poem of the missing edition of his poems' (ii. 189). Even when he was willing to credit the idea that a poem could be read as a dramatic monologue, he did so not because it enabled him to explore ways in which it involved parody and satire but in order to protect certain aspects of Donne's image. On the basis of a reference to the speaker's 'gowte' and 'gray haires' in 'The Canonization', he claimed that the poem was written 'in the person of another' (ii. 170). This enabled him to reject the possibility that a sexually charged love modeled on the death and resurrection of Christ could have been referable to Donne's relations with his wife:

> Call 'us what you will, we are made such by loue;
>> Call her one, me another flye;
>> We 'are tapers too, and at our owne cost dye;
>> And we in us find th' eagle and the dove;
>>> The phœnix-riddle hath more wytt
>>> By us; we two being one, are yt:
>>> So to one neutral thinge both sexes fytt.
> We dye, and rise the same, and proue
> Mysterious by this loue.[32]

---

[31] 'Gallery of Poets', 230; Langford, 'An Evening with Donne', in *The Working Man's Friend and Family Instructor*, Supplementary no. (Dec. 1850), 20; repr. in *The Literature of Working Men* (London: John Cassell, n.d.).

[32] While the Variorum text of the poem has not yet been prepared, it may be noted that in this one stanza quoted here from Grosart's edition (ii. 169) there are more than a dozen variations each from the texts printed respectively in the editions of Shawcross and of Patrides.

Like virtually every other reader, Grosart resisted seeing that Walton, without intending to, had made it possible to read 'The Canonization' as an autobiographical defense of the marriage. No writing on the poem from the nineteenth century gives any indication that readers were prepared appreciatively to notice ways in which it evinces, through the workings of its central conceit, an understanding of sex and the body which belongs to an incarnational theology utterly characteristic of Italian painting and of preaching at the papal court in the period before the Reformation. As the full title of Leo Steinberg's study of *The Sexuality of Christ in Renaissance Art and in Modern Oblivion* suggests, it was virtually unknown how pervasive the *ostentatio genitalium* was in Renaissance paintings of Christ, and very few people have understood its theological underpinnings. Steinberg presents ample evidence that ambivalence about showing Christ's genitals had already set in during the fifteenth century among those who copied Filippino Lippi's *Madonna and Child with Two Angels* (now in the Uffizi). Given Browning's avid interest in the Filippino Lippi, Fra (Phil)lippo Lippi, and other painters of the Quattrocento, it is significant that Steinberg's attempt to rescue from modern oblivion a knowledge of paintings that affirmed Christ's sexuality virtually begins with two illustrations from another painter in whom Browning took an active interest, Andrea del Sarto. To illustrate his argument, Steinberg refers to a number of paintings by the Lippis, including the *Mystic Marriage of St Catherine*, where the saint is represented as kneeling before the infant Jesus on his mother's lap, his naked genitals (at the center of the painting) the object of her gaze—and the viewer's.[33]

FRA LIPPO LIPPI

When the Fuller Worthies' edition of Donne appeared, the contexts for thinking about 'sensuous things' in poetry and in painting were in flux. Love poetry was more important to the Victorians than it had been to the Romantics, indeed more important than it had been since the seventeenth century. From *Men and Women* onward the sensuous detail in Browning's poetry had been encouraging imaginative exploration of erotic experience.[34] For his poetic

[33] Leo Steinberg, *The Sexuality of Christ in Renaissance Art and in Modern Oblivion*, 2nd edn. revised and expanded (1983; Chicago: Univ. of Chicago Press, 1996), 4, 18, 37, 122, 190; see also Figs. 26, 147.

[34] Isobel Armstrong, 'Browning and Victorian Poetry of Sexual Love', in Isobel Armstrong (ed.), *Robert Browning*, Writers and Their Background (London: Bell, 1974; Athens, OH: Ohio Univ. Press, 1975), 267–98.

portraits of Fra Lippo Lippi and Andrea del Sarto, Browning revised Giorgio Vasari's *Lives of the Artists* (1550) in ways pertinent to understanding how Donne's life-history was rewritten in the Victorian period. In terms analogous to Walton's portrayal of Donne's marriage as 'the remarkable error of his life', Vasari had told the story of Andrea del Sarto's giving up the patronage of François I to marry Lucrezia di Baccio del Fede. Browning, instead of dwelling on the faults of the French king and of Andrea's wife, retold the story to lay the blame for the painter's decline more squarely on the painter himself.[35] Both Andrea's painting and his marriage were spoiled by a prudent 'faultlessness' that made him an opposite number of Walton's impetuous Donne.

The narrative underlying 'Fra Lippo Lippi' sets in motion a different sort of contrast with Donne's life-narrative. This poem glorified a painter's trans- gressiveness. No other poem from the volume of 1855 so thoroughly engaged the predominant cultural ambivalence about 'sensuous things.' Browning not only made Lippi serve as a mouthpiece for his own aesthetic views but his treatment of Lippi's paintings, as J. B. Bullen has observed, made them seem to be possessed of a disturbing, often ambiguous, psychologically penetrating realism.' Browning's poem on Lippi represents, in fact, his major intervention in contemporary debates about Quattrocento painting. These debates had serious implications for understanding both the history of art and the complex relations between art and religion. Bullen shows that Lippi in particular had been a site of interpretative conflict. He 'had always been a puzzle for historians of art', because the realism in his paintings 'was insistent to the point of obtru- siveness' and even Victorians of a decidedly liberal bent regarded Lippi's own '*amours*' as scandalous.[36] In short, the life of the fifteenth-century monk who became a painter was the obverse of the life of the seventeenth-century poet who became a divine. Those who took an interest in both Lippi and Donne were required, when they wrote about both of them (as Anna Jameson and Walter Savage Landor did) to work through a pervasive cultural ambivalence about sensuality—and about Catholicism.

Recent work on Browning's painter poems has shown that from the mid- 1840s when the Brownings took up residence in Italy they were already cultivating an active interest in Lippi and in the larger debates about art history. In 'Fra Lippo Lippi' Browning drew upon Landor, the only English writer to have written sympathetically of Lippi, to respond to Jameson and to the contribution to *Murray's Handbook of Northern Italy* made by the elder

---

[35] See Joseph Bristow, *Robert Browning* (London: Harvester Wheatsheaf; New York: St. Martin's Press, 1991), 103–5. Bristow (esp. 96) has emphasized that Browning used a free hand with his sources, in order to create suitable dramatic vehicles to mediate his views on art.

[36] J. B. Bullen, *The Myth of the Renaissance in Nineteenth-Century Writing* (Oxford: Clarendon Press; New York: Oxford Univ. Press, 1994), 205, 198.

Francis Palgrave, who castigated the 'wretchedly profligate' monastic painter for a life that stood in marked contrast to the continence practiced by earlier Italian painters.[37] Like Browning's friend, John Ruskin, both Palgrave and Jameson had a low opinion of the Renaissance. Accordingly, they attempted to work out ways of adapting to English uses the influential thesis of the French Catholic, A. F. Rio, who proposed that the spiritual glories of early Renaissance painting had been eclipsed in the more materialistic period of the Medicis. Rio's Catholicism was of a sort altogether different from that of the painters studied by Steinberg and the preachers at the papal court, whose principal theme, as John O'Malley has shown, was to develop the implications of the Incarnation into a thoroughgoing affirmation of the human body and 'the dignity of man.'[38] For his part, Rio saw Lippi as an important figure in sowing the decadence into which he proposed that Quattrocento painting fell as it became increasingly devoted to pagan subjects and voluptuous sensations. Jameson, without ever mentioning Rio (whom she knew personally and read), posited a 'great schism in modern art.'[39] This would erase Rio's idea that a fall from medieval Catholic spirituality had led not only to inferior art but to Protestantism as well. She characterized the schism simply as a clash between two schools: one tended to assume that beauty is a means to achieve spiritual goals, while the other regarded beauty as an end in itself, to be pursued for its own sake. Jameson associated Lippi, the 'libertine monk' of 'extraordinary genius' whose 'talent was degraded by his immorality', with the latter school. She acknowledged that he 'was one of the earliest ... who painted with some feeling for the truth of nature.' Yet she condemned him for having '[i]n the representation of sacred incidents' been 'sometimes fantastic and sometimes vulgar.' Beyond this she remarked that 'he was the first who desecrated such objects by introducing portraits of women who happened to be the objects of his preference of the moment.' In view of her remarks about Lippi, what she wrote about Donne, who in 'The Canonization' seemed to represent himself and his beloved as martyrs who 'die' for love and as icons for veneration, is the more remarkable.

Jameson's chapter on Donne comes precisely in the part of *The Loves of the Poets* in which she treats 'conjugal poetry.' She makes no mention of 'The Canonization'—or of any other poems in which Donne represented sexual and erotic passions even more boldly than Lippi had. Urging that Donne's

---

[37] See ibid. 199–203, citing *Murray's Handbook of Northern Italy* (London, 1842), 443.

[38] John W. O'Malley, *Praise and Blame in Renaissance Rome: Rhetoric, Doctrine, and Reform in the Sacred Orators of the Papal Court, c.1450–1521* (Durham, NC: Duke Univ. Press, 1979).

[39] Mrs [Anna] Jameson, *Memoirs of the Early Italian Painters and the Progress of Painting in Italy*, 2 vols. (London: Charles Knight, 1845), i. 110. All the subsequent citations in this paragraph come from i. 113–14.

'matrimonial history' is 'as true and touching a piece of romance as ever was taken from the page of real life', her account is nonetheless filled with ambivalence about 'faults' that are 'glaring' and 'intolerable.' She cites with approval an anonymous critic (it was Brian Waller Proctor) who has written that ' "there is scarce a writer in our language who has so thoroughly mixed up the good and the bad together." ' It then becomes the work of her chapter to attempt a separation. Unlike her later treatment of Lippi, which associates bad living and bad art, Jameson singles out particular works—Donne's elegies 'His Parting from Her' and 'On His Mistress' ('By our first strange and fatal interview'), and 'A Valediction Forbidding Mourning'—as instances of good poetry, which is 'the result of truth, of passion, of a strong mind, and a brilliant wit.' No specific instances of Donne's bad poetry are enumerated. His faults are said to be a result not of 'dissipation' but of 'perverse taste, and total want of harmony', 'cold and obscure conceits', 'pedantry', and 'coarseness.' This left readers to infer that Donne wrote badly when he wrote without conjugal inspiration. Even as this portrait reverses Walton's charge that the marriage was the 'remarkable error' of Donne's life, it leaves firmly in place a disinclination to look into the grounds on which Sir George More objected to Donne—and into the poetry that was 'loosely—God knows too loosely—scattered.' In Jameson's view, it was Donne's marriage, and not his conversion to Protestantism or his taking of holy orders, that constituted his decisive conversion.[40]

When Landor composed an imaginary conversation about Donne, he depicted the marriage as only slightly less decisive. The conversation takes place shortly before Walton wrote his life of Dr Donne. Landor sends Walton and Charles Cotton to Ashbourne, 'the prettiest town in England', to secure from the Dean's former curate, William Oldways, some verses that Donne wrote 'when he was a stripling or little better.'[41] Oldways provides the perspective that Walton will make his own: if Donne were alive, he says, 'he would not wish [his youthful poems] to see the light' (ii. 536). This is not because the verses are licentious but because they were inspired by a woman other than the poet's wife. Oldways identifies her as one 'Mistress Margaret Hayes' (ii. 538). Older than Donne, red-headed, and more circumspect than he, she refused his marital advances.

Landor's Walton, doing research for his first major composition, is broadminded and accepting of the fact that Donne had experienced love before he met Anne More. He expresses full confidence that 'lines' by Donne said by

---

[40] Jameson, *Loves of the Poets*, ii. 94–6.
[41] Walter Savage Landor, *Imaginary Conversations of Literary Men and Statesmen*, 2nd ser., ii (London: James Duncan, 1829), 526. Subsequent citations are given in the text.

Oldways to be 'running so totally on the amorous' are evidence of 'the kindest and most generous affection' that ought not to be suppressed or ignored. '[W]e have seen Donne's sting', he says; 'in justice to him, let us now have a sample of his honey .... I have many things to say in Donne's favour: let me add to them, by your assistance, that he not only loved well and truly, as was proved in his marriage, tho' like a good angler he changed his fly, and did not at all seasons cast his rod over the same water; but that his heart opened early to the genial affections' (ii. 537). After this show of sympathy with Donne's youthful expense of spirit, however, Walton gets 'second thoughts' about whether he will 'insert' the verses, noble though they may be, 'in my biography' (ii. 545). When he offers an explanation for suppressing them, it is not a matter of mutilating or castrating an old author on the grounds that 'pruriencies' ought not to be published. It is a resolve to erect Donne's married life as a high ideal: 'In the whole story of his marriage with the daughter of George More, there is something so sacredly romantic, so full of that which bursts from the tenderest heart and from the purest, that I would admitt no other light or landscape to the portraiture. For if there is aught, precedent or subsequent, that offends our view of an admirable character, or intercepts or lessens it, we may surely cast it down and suppress it' (ii. 545–6).

The significance of this fictional rewriting of Donne's biography, so that what Walton called the remarkable error of Donne's life becomes the chief grounds of his sanctity, is best appreciated by contrasting this imaginary conversation with another that Landor composed. In a conversation depicting Lippi and Pope Eugenius the Fourth, the setting is the confessional, and 'the subject of discourse' is 'crime in all its hideous forms!'[42] The presuppositions here are pretty much those articulated in *Popery in its Social Aspect*, when, describing the workings of confession, Blakeney ascribes immense power to Catholic priests. Dwelling on the idea that the institution of confession made the mind of every priest 'the receptacle of all filth' (171), Blakeney promoted the idea that priests 'give ear to matrimonial secrets' and 'draw aside even the curtains of the marriage bed'; that they discuss privately with women 'subjects which the wife would not mention to her husband,—which the daughter would blush to repeat even to her mother' (170). He urged that priests, already monstrously 'bound by an unnatural law of celibacy', were certain to be corrupted by repeatedly listening to 'confessions of voluptuousness, and sin, and guilt in every form' (170) and asserted that, having thus been corrupted

---

[42] Chapter XIX: 'The Influence and Power of the Confessional', in *Popery in its Social Aspect: Being A Complete Exposure of the Immorality and Intolerance of Romanism* (Edinburgh: M'Gibbon; London: Protestant Educational Institute, (c.1854)), 169. Subsequent citations are given in the text.

themselves, they became instruments of a thoroughly corrupt system that 'exercise[d] great control' in both the domestic and political spheres (176). The confessional was at once 'a widespread conspiracy against the liberties of nations' and, above all, 'a system of impurity' that used 'the mask of religion' to sink 'both priest and penitent deeper in the pit of moral pollution' (178).

At the start of Landor's fiction Lippi admits what he has never before owned in that forum to any other confessor: that 'love of the world and its vanities' induced him to cast off the habit of a monk.[43] The Pope takes advantage of this confidence to attempt to extract from him a detailed account of what his feelings have been amidst his sexual escapades. Lippi defers giving details, recounting instead his abduction by pirates and giving information about the life of his captor. At last, however, he acknowledges his attachment to 'a certain young person, by name Lucrezia', with whom he has conceived offspring. When the pope offers to dispense Lippi from his vow of chastity, to make them 'man and wife' and to make their children legitimate, the renegade monk balks: 'It is man and wife the first fortnight', he cries, 'but wife and man ever after. The two figures change places: the unit is the decimal, and the decimal is the unit.' The conversation climaxes with Lippi at last telling how he painted Lucrezia when she was a fifteen-year-old novice at the convent of Saint Margarita and then seduced her. Whereas Landor's Donne had felt true amorous stirrings in the company of a woman who refused him and then he went on to make an honorable if costly marriage to 'a person of higher condition than himself', Landor's Lippi eschews marriage as a threat to male independence, and he assumes that the pope will appreciate the wisdom of his remaining in an illicit relationship.

If the story of Donne's marriage as retold by Jameson and as revised by Landor seemed congenial to Robert Browning, Jameson's references to Lippi's 'immorality' and Landor's account of his brazen behaviour evoked from the husband of Elizabeth Barrett substantial revisions. Although Browning did not create a full-scale narrative about the course of Donne's life, his treatment of the 'sensuous things' in Lippi's painting had implications for the Victorian project of revising Walton's portrait. Browning was attracted to Lippi as a representative figure, as David DeLaura has shown, precisely because of his transgressive life.[44] Browning knew of Rio's thesis by the mid-1840s and never accepted it. Contemptuous of monastic asceticism as a dodge of those who will not dare in life, his thinking about early modern art largely coincided

[43] 'Fra Filippo Lippi and Pope Eugenius the Fourth', *The Works of Walter Savage Landor*, 2 vols. (London: E. Moxon, 1846), ii. 81; subsequent quotations come from 89.
[44] David J. DeLaura, 'The Context of Browning's Painter Poems: Aesthetics, Polemics, Historics', *PMLA*, 95 (1980), 367–88.

with that of Vasari, who ignored continuities between the Renaissance and the Middle Ages. Moreover, Browning repeatedly took occasion in his poetry to paint Renaissance Catholics in terms that had been familiar in England at least since Jacobean dramatists had made Italy a locus of sexual perversity and corrupt political power. Whereas Jameson, the elder Palgrave, and even Ruskin were not much invested in the aspect of Rio's thesis that sought to account for a discontinuity in art by referring to it as a rupture between Catholicism and Protestantism, in 'Pictor Ignotus', 'The Bishop Orders his Tomb at St. Praxed's', and 'Fra Lippo Lippi', Browning made his poetry a vehicle for anti-Catholic discourses that were circulating in the years following the restoration of the Roman Catholic hierarchy in England.

DeLaura's insights into Browning's ambivalence clarify what was at stake in Grosart's presentation of the sensuous things in Donne's poetry. On the one hand, 'Fra Lippo Lippi' offered a critique of what Browning found timid in Jameson's account of art history, the tendency she shared with Rio and Ruskin to separate the spheres of body and soul. Without in any way crediting the Catholic theology that underwrote Lippi's representations of the human body, Browning attempted to make Lippi a spokesman for an aesthetic that affirmed body and soul together. At the same time his poem manifested a hostility towards Catholics quite out of keeping with his cultivated broad-mindedness. Browning could not understand how the Roman Catholic church accepted a 'frankly sensual treatment of religious subjects'; and in addition he distrusted the intellectual component of Rio's thesis.[45] His poem exposes what he considered the 'effeminacy' of Catholics by making the prior at once prudish and hypocritical: although he is having an affair with his 'niece', the prior criticizes Lippi's insistent representations of 'arms, legs and bodies' in his paintings and insists

> Your business is not to catch men with show,
> With homage to the perishable clay,
> But lift them over it, ignore it all,
> Make them forget there's such a thing as flesh.
> Your business is to paint the souls of men.

This provocation elicits from Browning's Lippi both the rejoinder in defense of 'simple beauty' as 'the best thing God invents' and a robust affirmation of 'The value and significance of flesh' as the locus of meaning in a 'world' that 'means intensely, and means good.'[46] This was the world that had been

[45] Barbara Melchiori, 'Browning in Italy', in Armstrong (ed.), *Robert Browning*, 181–2; cf. DeLaura, 'Context of Browning's Painter Poems', 372.

[46] Quoted from *The Complete Works of Robert Browning*, gen. ed. Roma A. King, Jr, et al. (Athens, OH: Ohio Univ. Press, 1981), v. 188–93.

corrupted by the Catholic clergy, above all through 'the immoral and unchaste influence' of that 'receptacle of all ... filth', the confessional.

Like Browning's Lippi, Donne as he is presented in Grosart's Essay had been an 'impetuous', 'full-blooded', vigorous young man who bridled against unnatural restraints imposed upon him by the purveyors of a corrupt religion. In Grosart's hands Donne's poetry was made to tell an elaborate story about an 'emancipated youth [who] was driven to ultra-boldness of assertion concerning the relations of the sexes and intercourse' when he rejected his strict Catholic upbringing (ii, p. xvii). In this way Grosart sought to make sense of so many 'sensuous things (to say the least)' in the materials he was making available.

THE FULLER WORTHIES' EDITION AS A REVISION OF WALTON'S NARRATIVE

Although Grosart claimed at the outset of his second volume to take an interest chiefly in 'those elements' of Donne's life that he had 'worked into his Poetry' and to prescind from considering matters best left to Dr Jessopp (ii, p. ix), his edition was an integral part of a large-scale attempt radically to reinterpret the significance of Donne's love for Anne More and to make him an authority on married love. Walton had located Donne's embrace of Protestantism early and presented it as a natural result of his subject's learned tendencies. He judged the marriage to have been 'the remarkable error' of Donne's life because it had ruined his chances for a brilliant career. Ultimately he had depicted Donne's taking of holy orders, after long and numerous delays, as the turning point of his life, the conversion of all to good, the making of the man he himself had known. Grosart sought to alter the center of gravity in the inherited narrative by giving far more attention to Donne's early life and by finding in his youthful poems evidence of a more decisive conversion. Accordingly, he made much more of Donne's having been bred a Catholic than Walton had. His essay emphasizes 'two considerable biographical facts' that fly in the face of virtually all prior writing on Donne and claims for them the support of Grosart's learned friend, Brinsley Nicholson. These 'facts', which Grosart sought to establish with many pages of evidence and argumentation, are (1) that the religious poetry was not written in Donne's maturity as the 1635 edition seems to imply, for '*the principal "Divine Poems" belong not to the close but to the commencement of his poetic period, and while he was still a Roman Catholic*' (ii, p. x), and (2) that '*the poems "translated" by Dr. Jasper Mayne, and published in 1652, hitherto used as biographic, are unauthentic, and so too, necessarily, the "Sheaf of Epigrams" to which they belong*' (ii, pp. xviii–xix).

Although in theory the Divine Poems might have had a special place as the work of Doctor Donne, they were in fact little read.[47] The *Variorum* has begun to show that, compared with other genres in which Donne wrote, little was written on them in the nineteenth century. Certainly, they were not so controversial as they might have been. The sonnets 'Show me dear Christ' and 'O to vex me' lay undiscovered in the Westmoreland manuscript. No one was commenting upon—at least not in print—'What if this present', with its comparison between wooing Christ crucified and wooing 'profane' mistresses. Most readers probably took it more or less for granted, without looking into the matter too closely, that the Divine Poems offered evidence of the piety for which Walton had recommended their author.

To support the startling claim that the 'principal' Divine Poems had been written in Donne's youth, Grosart discussed in detail the Catholic elements to be found in three poems, the third of which ('On the blessed Virgin Marie') is now known not to be Donne's. He said nothing about 'Good Friday, 1613. Riding Westward', 'A Hymn to Christ at the Author's Last Going into Germany', 'A Hymn to God the Father', or 'A Hymn to God My God, in My Sickness', which Walton had claimed was written in the poet's last illness. Nor did he discuss the dates when the Holy Sonnets were likely composed. Besides accounting for the marked residue of Catholic doctrine and imagery in many of the Divine Poems, the first 'fact' on which Grosart bases his presentation of Donne had other advantages: by placing 'A Litany' and 'The Cross' before Donne's conversion to Protestantism, he was able to suggest that the criticisms of monarchy in the former and the challenges to 'misgrounded law' in the latter were aspects of a Catholic's response to persecution.

Grosart was remarkably sympathetic to Catholics who had suffered during the Elizabethan persecutions. In the Memorial-Introduction to his edition of Southwell, he displayed his intimate acquaintance with the literature of persecuted Elizabethan Catholics and gave evidence of an uncharacteristic familiarity with contemporary writing by Catholics on Elizabethan history. He expressed great admiration for the 'magnificent and truly apostolic example of burning love, compassion, [and] faith' of Ignatius Loyola. He quoted with approval from letters by Southwell in which the young Jesuit patiently described the 'fears and dangers' faced by Catholic recusants, and he suggested that he had seen hundreds of other letters like them. He wrote about the 'White' Reign of Terror in sixteenth-century England that in some ways

---

[47] Granqvist (*Reputation*, 125–9) documents an increased attention to the Divine Poems from mid-century onward. Yet these poems were by no means widely known.

anticipated the 'Red' Reign of Terror in eighteenth-century France. Then, having narrated from various sources an account of Southwell's death, he did not hesitate to call it 'judicial MURDER', to affirm his 'common human nature and Christianity' with a noble martyr, and to remark that 'I should blush for my Protestantism, if I did not hold in honour, yea reverence, his stainless and beautiful memory, all the more that he was on the "losing side", none the less that beliefs and forms and observances that were dear to him are errors, and more, to me.'[48] This informed tribute to Southwell adds interest to the second of the twin pillars of 'fact' on which Grosart erected his interpretation of the life and writings of the author of *Pseudo-Martyr*.

The circumstances surrounding the death of Henry Donne were not yet known to Victorian students of history, or to readers of his older brother's works. In 1874, the Jesuit historian John Morris would publish a piece on 'The Martyrdom' in 1593 of William Harrington. Morris would refer to the fact that this young priest was 'apprehended ... in the chamber of one Mr. Harry Dunne, a young gentleman of the Inns of Court' and report that the young man subsequently admitted to the authorities that he had made his confession to Harrington.[49] Although the article appeared in a Catholic periodical and was not seen by many Protestants, the general situation of Elizabethan Catholics was coming more to light. In his edition of Southwell, Grosart referred to Morris as 'my good friend' and, in fly-leaves added as supplements to the edition, quoted from two recent books by Morris, *The Troubles of our Catholic Forefathers, related by themselves* and *The Condition of Catholics under James I*. Still, for all Grosart's familiarity with the reasons that Southwell and other young men went into Catholic exile in places like Douai, he firmly repressed contemplating the possibility that the foreign travels on which Donne had embarked at some unspecified time could have been occasioned by his family's desire to provide him with a Catholic education. The most powerful instance of this repression was his programmatic denial of authenticity to the poems ascribed to Mayne.

In preparing his edition Grosart had searched in vain for a copy of the Latin originals on which the translations in 'A Sheaf of Miscellany Epigrams' were supposedly based. Although this contributed to his surmise that the English poems were 'unauthentic', as there are no known copies of many old books, it cannot have been decisive. More tellingly, Grosart suspected the poems because they seemed to show that before his fifteenth birthday Donne had been a soldier on the Continent. Grosart acknowledged that the

---

[48] Grosart, *The Complete Poems of Robert Southwell*, pp. xlii–lxvi.
[49] See J[ohn] M[orris], 'The Martyrdom of William Harrington', *The Month*, 20 (1874), 411–23.

Marshall portrait exhibited Donne in military costume, with a sword. Yet he insisted that 'the theory that Donne went abroad previous to 1596 is wholly contrary to two passages in Walton's Life' that place Donne in those years at the two universities and then at the Inns of Court (ii, pp. xxii–xxiii). Grosart's inclusion of many other licentious poems shows, however, that the indecency of many of the translated Latin epigrams cannot have been the crucial reason for his eventual decision to banish them from the canon. Unwilling as he had been to accept O'Flahertie's designation of them as 'filth', he did register his relief at being able to omit some and his 'satisfaction' (ii. 266) at being able to omit them all. Yet clearly he accepted as Donne's many other poems marked by 'abominations' that he deemed 'ineradicable.' Above all, Grosart regarded the poems with suspicion because, as Jessopp had pointed out, numbers 53–7 show a decided sympathy for and even participation in the army of 'the Prince of Aurange', whereas Grosart was convinced that Donne was a sincere Roman Catholic well into the 1590s.

The basis for banishing 'A Sheaf of Miscellany Epigrams' from the canon is often hinted at in the sustained and spirited discussion that took place in the pages of the *Athenæum* later in 1873. The *Variorum* (viii. 472–80) provides details of the debate about their authenticity and shows that Grosart's arguments carried the day. What it does not show is the intricate basis on which the case against these poems was woven into the major rewriting of Donne's biography being carried out. In the entire discussion about authenticity all the participants, and especially Grosart, seem to have been unwilling to contemplate the possibility that the translator, or some editor, had adapted the poems (whether in the 1630s or even as late as 1652) to make them seem more contemporary. This is the more surprising in that Pope's 'translations' of Donne's satires were well known, and were often shown (e.g., by Grosart, ii, pp. xxix–xxx) to have entailed adaptations to eighteenth-century politics. Not until Dennis Flynn proposed, more than a hundred years later, that many poems among the 'Sheaf of Epigrams' refer to the Spanish siege of Antwerp in 1584–5 were readers likely to contemplate an alternative.[50] Flynn proposed that it is likely that, if the poems are based on authentic Latin originals, Mayne translated them in ways that erased evidence of Donne's political involvement in a Catholic cause. What has gone unexplored is what Grosart was better positioned than any other nineteenth-century reader to discern: that while some poems may have been translated to cover over Donne's youthful Catholicism, others may have been doctored to make Donne seem early and reliably Protestant—a proper enemy of the Spanish. For all Grosart's

[50] Dennis Flynn, 'Jasper Mayne's Translation of Donne's Latin Epigrams', *JDJ*, 3 (1984), 121–30.

openness to knowing about the Elizabethan persecution of Catholics, he was no different from hundreds of other readers of Walton who did not think it extraordinary that Walton had either failed to look into or declined to provide details about Donne's religious upbringing. Eager as he was to fill in Donne's lost youth by reading the poetry as evidence of Donne's youthful sinfulness, Grosart was curiously unwilling to question Walton's having placed Donne at Oxford and Cambridge in the 1580s.

Grosart protested that when he wrote about Donne, he did not write 'as a Protestant or a clergyman (Nonconformist), but as a literary judicial critic' (ii, p. xv). Yet his sustained interest in the poet's having been bred as a Catholic was unusual. It was, moreover, profoundly related to a subtle and pervasive aspect of his ambivalence about Donne's sensuality. The narrative that he constructed in his preface relies upon evangelical assumptions about the course of a true Christian's life that enabled him to contextualize the deplorable sensuality he found in Donne's poetry. He posited a period of dissipation as an integral part of the authorized pattern found in spiritual autobiographies and made familiar in popular fiction. Having dismissed from the canon poems that seemed to indicate Donne's early involvement in an international Protestant cause, and having assigned the bulk of the religious poetry to a period of sincere if misguided Catholicism, he proposed that in the 1590s Donne entered a second major phase of his life. Donne rejected the religion of his youth and, as 'a rebound from his Roman-Catholic teaching and restraints', he 'plunged into the immoralities of the period' and 'sinned to the uttermost' (ii, pp. xvi–xvii). It was at this time that he wrote the satires, elegies, and numerous licentious poems that were rightly to be deplored.

Grosart confided that the reading he had done while preparing editions of Crashaw and Southwell showed him that Catholic literature is marked by 'a morbid disowning and condemnation of the relations of the sexes, a profoundly untrue way of discussing marriage and family-ties, [and] a perplexing readiness to intrude into the veiled mysteries' of the flesh and even of the Incarnation (ii, p. xvi). There was no need for him to say anything about the readily available interpretative categories that made such perversions easily discernible to evangelical Protestants. His presentation of Donne's dissipation as something that happened to him presupposed familiarity with the paradigmatic evangelical narrative in which God's 'grace and mercy' propels a true Christian through periods of works-righteousness and desperate sinfulness before delivering him at last. Grosart's fascination, moreover, with the sensuality of Donne's poetry entailed a disposition to credit popular stereotypes about Catholic attitudes towards the body and sex. Even as he proposed 'sorrowfully' to condemn Donne's youthful sins and to alert readers to the 'thrills of contrition, stingings of accusation, wails over abiding stains and wounds, and passionate weeping' (ii, p. xvii) to be heard in Donne's poems and letters and sermons, Grosart was able to rely upon the likelihood that readers would understand that Donne's life epitomized both the need for the Reformation and the benefits to be derived from it.

Where Walton had plotted Donne's youth as a rational progress to enlightened Protestantism, Grosart drew heavily upon evangelical characterizations of popery to chart a more complicated journey. His remarks about 'an indelicate delicacy' and 'false shame' in the Catholic understanding of sex and his judgment that Donne's youthful Catholicism had exposed him to ideas of sex that 'are nasty in the extreme' (ii, p. xvi) seem moderate and even judicious compared to the hysterical claims common in contemporary anti-Catholic rhetoric. Yet familiarity with the conventions of that rhetoric reveals that Grosart sought to make Donne's story more authentically evangelical than Walton's version showed it to have been.

Grosart's proposal that Donne had rebelled against Catholic views of sex seemed plausible in light of the long-standing tradition of condemning 'the immoral and unchaste influence of the confessional.' Considered in the context of Victorian cultural logic about the long-term effects of youthful dissipation,[51] Donne's erotic poems—by Grosart's time increasingly read as transcripts of the poet's own escapades—were becoming the stuff for a cautionary tale. In a society where 'spend' was popular slang for 'ejaculate', Donne's youthful verses were said to demonstrate a prodigal expense of spirit.[52] The misogynistic poems of a writer known to have been a great visitor of ladies in his Lincoln's Inn days might now be seen to bear out the notion that 'self-excitation', as one medical expert put it, 'sometimes makes of the young man a woman pursuer, but probably more often a woman hater'.[53] When these ideas were woven together with the knowledge that Donne had married precipitously (thus showing his lack of self-control), that he had fathered a large number of children, and that Anne More had at last died after giving birth, readers who were developing a prejudice against large families had a new explanation for Donne's having been a ne'er-do-well through the long years at Mitcham and after. Donne had not been repaid for his youthful dissipation by sexual impotence, as predicted by writers of manuals for young men. To many Victorian readers, however, the failure of his great expectations in the years following his marriage seemed an appropriate punishment, his going into the

---

[51] Cf. Masson's presentation of Milton's youth as a contradiction to 'the "wild oats" theory', in *Life*, i. 240.

[52] Edward Dowden, 'The Poetry of John Donne', *Fortnightly Review*, new ser., 47 (1890), 791.

[53] See Horatio Robinson Storer, *Is It I? A Book for Every Man* (Boston: Lee and Shepard, 1867), 57.

church a fitting redemption, and his success as a preacher the crowning reward for his penitence.

Against the possibility of reading Donne's story in this way, Grosart told of a man who had been redeemed not by a rational inquiry into the controversy between the papist and reformed religions, nor by taking orders in the church, but by the love of a good woman. Donne's wedding, far from having been the remarkable error of his life, was his conversion. His marriage was his salvation. To illustrate the third and climactic phase of the life Grosart 'enlarged' the canon with poems that had not been printed in any previous edition of Donne's poetry, and he urged that several of the best love poems owed their beauty to the poet's genuine love for his wife.

To balance his revelation of Donne's brushes with sexual perversion, Grosart sought to illustrate that Donne had gone on to become a good Christian husband whose genuine love poetry gave expression to lawful love. At the head of the Lyrics, for instance, before the Songs and Sonnets, he printed the *Ten Sonnets to Philomel*, which are strikingly different from the poems that follow. For one thing they actually are sonnets; for another, they are pretty conventional love poems. Unable to offer evidence that they had been written for Anne More, Grosart simply remarked that 'One likes to think that these Sonnets were addressed to Donne's future Wife. The date (1602) of publication seems to admit of it. They sound tender and true .... Whoever she was, she had a sweet voice, and attracted the Poet thereby' (ii. 155). In any event, before a reader encountered 'The Flea', these poems were there to suggest the poet's susceptibility to a love that was 'true' in the sense that it was ordered and regulated. Similarly, in printing the Elegies in Volume 1, Grosart, although for most of them he followed the order from the 1635 edition, printed first the endearing poem that had often been printed as 'On his Mistress' but which, with some justification from a seventeenth-century manuscript, was sometimes headed as Grosart printed it, 'Refusal to Allow His Young Wife to Accompany Him Abroad as a Page.' In his Essay Grosart endorsed this interpretation just as he did Walton's claim that 'A Valediction Forbidding Mourning' had been written for the poet's wife, and he presented both poems along with 'The Anniversary', 'another commemoration of his Wife', as consummate examples of the poet's surpassing 'imaginative faculty' (ii, pp. xxxix–xli). It was increasingly common in this period to assign lyrics to Donne's relationship with his wife. Grosart recommended J. C. M. Bellew's opinion that the 'superb conclusion' of 'The Anniversary' —

> Let us live nobly, and live and add again
> Years and years unto years, till we attain
> To write threescore: this is the second of our reign.

—'is one of the finest and grandest expressions of conjugal affection that adorn our English literature.'[54]

Grosart's satisfaction that Donne had ultimately repented his hot youth's folly is registered finally by the way in which he concluded his edition: he chose a long poem in couplets that had been ascribed to Donne in Waldron's *Collection of Miscellaneous Poetry*, where it was dated 1625, and created for it the heading 'Lament for His Wife.' Like the *Sonnets to Philomel*, this poem helped to create the impression that the relations between Anne More and her husband had been altogether more respectable than those between Donne and the women who inhabited his licentious pieces. At this time not only was Donne's Latin epitaph for his wife unknown, but the Westmoreland manuscript still lay undiscovered and the sonnet 'Since she whom I lov'd' would not be brought to light until the 1890s. To compare the poem with other poems by Donne in which a survivor expresses grief at the loss of a dear woman—the *Anniversaries* or 'A Nocturnal upon St. Lucy's Day', which no one in the nineteenth century took to refer to the death of Anne—is to glimpse how tame Grosart sought to make Doctor Donne finally appear. Near the end of the poem the survivor comes to his beloved's tomb with wistful thoughts:

> O had that hollow vault where thou dost lye
> An eccho in it, my stronge phantasy
> Would winne me soone to thinke her wordes were thine,
> And I would howerly come, and to thy shrine
> Talke, as I often did to talke with thee,
> And frame my wordes, that thou shouldst answer me
> As when thou livedst. I'd sigh and say I lov'd,
> And thou shouldst doe so too, till we had mov'd,
> With our complaints, to teares each marble cell
> Of those dead neighbours which about thee dwell.
> And when the holy Father came to say
> His orisons, wee'd aske him if the day
> Of miracles were past, or whether he
> Knowes any one whose fayth and pietie
> Could raise the dead; but he would answere, None
> Can bring thee back to life: though many one
> Our cursed dayes afford, that dare to thrust
> Their hands prophane, to raise the sacred dust
> Of holy saintes out of their beds of rest.

---

[54] Bellew, *Poets' Corner*, 194, as quoted by Grosart (ed.), *Complete Poems of John Donne*, ii, p. xli.

> Abhorred crimes! Oh may there none molest
> Thy quiet peace, but in thy arke remaine
> Untoucht, as those the old one did containe;
> Till He that can reward thy greatest worth
> Shall send the peacefull Dove to fetch thee forth!

(ii. 349–50)

For the boldness of poems such as 'The Canonization' and 'The Relic', where the doctrine of resurrection is made to hint that for the redeemed bodily erotic experience may be renewed on the other side of death, Grosart sought finally to substitute this placid lament that would illustrate Donne's 'keen and life-long grief' (ii. 347).

BEYOND AMBIVALENCE: J. B. LIGHTFOOT AND WILLIAM MINTO

Although the Fuller Worthies' edition made Donne's poetry newly available to a small group of readers, there is some evidence that, in England, Donne was still likelier to be remembered as a preacher than as a poet. Richard Peterson has documented in fascinating detail the quiet campaign to restore the effigy of Dean Donne standing atop an urn memorably described in Walton's *Life*. In the year that Grosart's second volume appeared, this white marble monument, which had been neglected in the crypt of St Paul's since the Great Fire of 1666, was refurbished and placed against the south choir aisle in the present cathedral, where it may be seen today.[55] The story of its restoration found its way into a sermon preached in 1877 at St James's Church, Westminster, by one of the leading preachers of the day, himself a canon of St Paul's, the great New Testament and patristic scholar J. B. Lightfoot, Lady Margaret Professor of Divinity at Cambridge. Lightfoot was invited by the Rector of St James, John Edward Kempe, to inaugurate a series of sermons that would celebrate the greatest preachers in the history of the English church. The printed collection gave Donne pride of place, explaining that his case represented a challenging extreme: the editor observed that the published materials were 'not meant as a contribution to English hagiology' and that the invited preachers had not 'overlooked or extenuated' the many 'faults and defects' to be found in the sermons of their predecessors.[56]

---

[55] Richard S. Peterson, 'New Evidence on Donne's Monument: I', *JDJ*, 20 (2001), 1–51.

[56] John Edward Kempe, Introduction, *The Classic Preachers of the English Church: Lectures Delivered at St. James's Church in 1877* (London: John Murray, 1877), p. xviii.

For his part, Lightfoot took the occasion of preaching on Donne to create an unprecedented synthesis in the broad ecclesiastical tradition within which Alford and Grosart had edited the prose and verse. Relying on their editions, he presented Donne as 'the poet-preacher' and quoted extensively from the sermons, acknowledging that Donne's style was regularly marked by extravagance and affectation of the sorts found also in the poetry. At the same time he aimed to look beyond these faults to the often startling ideas expressed by 'the most animated of the great Anglican preachers' (15), who had found in the experience of preaching the same 'holy delight' that he ascribed to the early fathers of the church (20). Lightfoot quoted, for instance, Coleridge's favorite passage about how 'Death ... makes us all equal when it comes.' Yet he also cited as the 'most terrible passage' in all Donne's sermons, one in which we are invited to imagine what it would be like to fall *out* of 'the hands of the living God ... into a bottomless pit':

That of that providence of God, that studies the life of every weed and worm and ant and spider and toad and viper, there should never, never any beam flow out upon me; that that God who looked upon me when I was nothing, and called me when I was not, as though I had been, out of the womb and depth of darkness, will not look upon me now, when, though a miserable and a banished and a damned creature, yet I am His creature still, and contribute something to His glory, even in my damnation; that that God who hath often looked upon me in my foulest uncleanness and when I had shut out the eye of the day, the sun, and the eye of the night, the taper, and the eyes of all the world, with curtains and windows and doors, did yet see me, and see me in mercy, by making me see that He saw me, and sometimes brought me a present remorse and (for that time) to a forebearing of that sin, should so turn Himself from me to His glorious saints and angels, as that no saint nor angel nor Jesus Christ Himself should ever pray Him to look towards me ... [57]

What is striking about Lightfoot's own sermon is that he quite simply credited the claim that the poems show that Donne had 'sinned to the uttermost' and then, by quoting passages in which Donne himself prays memorably for mercy, went on deftly to develop the evangelical paradigm by which Grosart had sought to make sense of Donne's life.

Lightfoot's sermon was masterfully constructed. Its first epigraph is a text from the Gospel of Luke (7:42) that highlights the idea that forgiveness is above all for great sinners: 'Tell me therefore which of them will love him most.' Then as the discourse unfolds Lightfoot develops a hint from Walton's elegy and compares Donne to Mary Magdelene, with whom Luke's sinful

[57] Lightfoot (*The Classic Preachers*, 16–19) quotes from Alford's edn, i. 241, and iii. 386. Subsequent quotations from Lightfoot's sermon are identified by page numbers in parentheses.

woman had traditionally been identified; and he makes explicit the hints from Grosart whereby Donne's life had been a version of grace abounding to the chief of sinners. In this way he makes sense of the idea that Donne's 'romantic career ... is more poetical than his poetry' (11). Attempting to account for Donne's having been regarded as 'the most powerful preacher of his day' (13) and above all for 'the thraldom in which', as eyewitnesses had attested, Donne had 'held his audience' (20), Lightfoot not only quotes 'pithy sayings' and passages of imaginative boldness and great beauty; he urges that 'the secret of [Donne's] power as a preacher ... was the contrition and the thanksgiving of the penitent acting upon the sensibility of the poet' (11). All through his sermons there is 'an energy, a glow, an impetuosity, a force as of a torrent' (14); and '[n]o contrition was more intense than his' (22). Undergirding these assertions is the conviction that the poetry shows the grounds for Donne's having come to feel great remorse: 'his shame is written across his extant poems in letters of fire. In some of these', though Lightfoot did not quote any,

there are profligacies which it were vain to excuse as purely imaginative efforts of the poet, or unworthy condescensions to the base tastes of the age. We are driven to the conclusion that they reflect – at least to some extent – the sensuality of the man himself. Of such an offence I can offer no palliation. I know no crime more unpardonable in itself, or more fatal in its consequences, than this of prostituting the highest gifts of genius to a propaganda of vice and shame, this of poisoning the wells of a nation's literature and spreading moral death through generations yet unborn.   (7–8)

This was a far stronger condemnation, and a much more personal condemnation, than any lodged by Gilfillan or Taine or Whipple, and one that took much more seriously the long-term implications of the poet's having been, though 'Donne was not in many cases responsible for the *publication* of his poems' (8 n.), a writer. 'Donne's penitence was intense; he did all he could to retrieve the consequences of his sin. But he could not undo his work, could not blot out the printed page' (8). What saved him (if not all his unwitting readers) was his marriage: 'whatever may have been the sins of his youth and early manhood, his married life shows him a changed man' (8). Lightfoot was quite explicit about seeing Donne's marriage as the moral experience by which he appropriated the theological truth he had embraced intellectually when he converted to Protestantism. Marriage 'taught him to feel and to absorb into himself ... the doctrine of Christ's atoning grace' (10). It was the experience of true love that brought home to him the full horror of the sordid life he had once led. And as the recognition of one's sinfulness is for Lightfoot the timeless *sine qua non* from which a truly Christian life must proceed, Donne's having made this his principal theme qualifies him as 'the most modern of our older Anglican divines' and makes him worthy 'to be reckoned the first of our Classic preachers' (21). Here at last was the reading of Donne's sermons for which Alford, who had died in 1871, had long hoped in vain. What had made it possible (and made it seem timely) was Grosart's edition of the poetry, where the editor had not overcome a massive ambivalence about Doctor Donne's manifest sensuality. Lightfoot accomplished what Grosart had not been able to pull off: he proposed a fully integrated account of Donne's life and work. It was based on a mature faith to match the one Donne had ultimately voiced in 'A Hymn to God, my God, in my sickness' where Lightfoot found 'the broad lesson of his life and teaching' (26):

> So in *His* purple wrapped, receive me, Lord;
> By these *His* thorns give me His other crown;
> And as to others' souls I preached Thy Word,
> Be this my text, my sermon to mine own:
> *Therefore, that He may raise, the Lord throws down.*

Three years later a lesson of an altogether different sort was drawn from Donne's life and career in the groundbreaking article written by William Minto for *The Nineteenth Century*. Minto sought to account for how Donne's poetry had been (like his monument) buried in obscurity. What joins Minto's account of Donne as a poetic failure to Lightfoot's celebration of 'the first of our Classic preachers' was the degree to which both men managed to point the reading of Donne beyond the deep ambivalence that had been characteristic of mid-Victorian discourses.

Minto's essay moved Donne into a new sphere of interest. When Lightfoot preached his sermon in 1877, Minto, who had already written two highly regarded books on literary history, was editing the radical paper, *The Examiner*, attempting to forward the journalistic goals of its founder, Leigh Hunt, and of contributors like Hazlitt and Lamb, Shelley and Haydon. He was also contributing articles on literary figures (including Byron, Chaucer, Dickens, and Fielding) to the ninth edition of the *Encyclopedia Britannica*, for which he would go on to write highly influential entries on J. S. Mill and Wordsworth. In January 1879 when he was writing on Britain's involvement in Asian politics for the *Daily News* and the *Pall Mall Gazette*, he published his first essay, on 'the Eastern question', in *The Nineteenth Century*. This was a relatively new journal, only in its fourth year of publication. It was edited by James Knowles, who along with his friend Tennyson had been a founding member of the Metaphysical Society. He had also succeeded Alford as editor of *The Contemporary Review*. When Knowles founded *The Nineteenth Century*, he got leading intellectuals to contribute signed articles on topics of current interest. Among the regular contributors in these years were Gladstone and

Cardinal Manning, Ruskin, Huxley, J. A. Froude, and Matthew Arnold. The appearance therefore of Minto's study of 'John' Donne in this forum went a good distance in making what had been an ecclesiastical and literary subject of interest to a larger public than those for which Alford and Grosart and Lightfoot had labored when they edited and wrote about the works of 'Dr' Donne.

That Minto should have written on Donne's poetry is in some respects surprising. At the University of Aberdeen, where he took the MA in 1865, he had accomplished something unprecedented: he took honors in three subjects, classics, mathematics, and philosophy. After that he studied divinity, abortively, then went to Merton College, Oxford, which he left without taking a degree. What happened to his religious faith in these years is not altogether clear, although presumably his views in the 1870s were included in the description of the staff of *The Examiner* written by his protegé, who confided, 'We are atheist and republican.' In his maturity Minto seems studiously to have avoided in lectures and conversation every theological topic, making the more remarkable the sympathy he showed for Donne's religion.[58] If Minto's theological interests waned early, his literary knowledge deepened during a later period at Aberdeen when he served as assistant to Alexander Bain, holder of the dual chair that combined logic and English and to which Minto would himself be summoned in 1880. It was not the piece on Donne that made the academic reputation by which he was invited to take up the chair. Rather, Minto's *Manual of English Prose Literature, Biographical and Critical* (1872), his *Characteristics of English Poets from Chaucer to Shirley* (1874), and a monograph on Defoe (1879) were decisive. The *Manual*, which was widely used as a textbook in England and the United States into the twentieth century, acknowledged that Donne had been the founder of the metaphysical school of poets. It praised the 'force of intellect' in his sermons and urged that, while they offer 'a delicious feast' for 'an intellectual epicure', they are quite beyond the comprehension of an ordinary congregation.[59] The book on poetry made no mention of Donne at all, even as it gave extended discussion to the poetry of many lesser figures. The estimate of Donne offered in the article for *The Nineteenth Century* was utterly consistent with the judgments

---

[58] Cited here from a letter of 26 Oct. 1874, by Edmund Gosse to George Brandes; quoted by Ann Thwaite, *Edmund Gosse: A Literary Landscape, 1849–1928* (Chicago: Univ. of Chicago Press, 1984), 529 n. For Minto's reticence on theological topics, see the remarks of P. Chalmers Mitchell, in William Knight's Introduction to Minto's posthumously published *The Literature of the Georgian Era* (1894; New York: Harper and Brothers, 1895), p. xl.

[59] William Minto, *A Manual of English Prose Literature, Biographical and Critical Designed Mainly to Show Characteristics of Style* (1872; rev. edn. Edinburgh: Blackwood and Sons, 1881), 253.

found in these books. When, in the early 1880s, Minto revised *Characteristics* extensively he nonetheless added nothing about a poet who 'belongs to the class of failures in literature', as he had concluded in his article, 'failures, that is to say, for the purpose of making an enduring mark.' In verse as in prose Donne performed 'for the delight and amusement of a small circle', an 'intellectual or artistic aristocracy', and for this reason he can never have more than 'a limited popularity' (863).

Among contributions to the nineteenth-century revival of interest in Donne's poetry none has been more undeservedly neglected than Minto's. He anticipated many of the most productive perspectives for reading Donne—formalist, new historicist, and reader response—that were exploited in the twentieth century. Yet nearly everyone who wrote on the Donne revival in the mid-twentieth century considered Minto's criticism beyond their purview; and even Joseph Duncan, in his admirable study of *The Revival of Metaphysical Poetry*,[60] misrepresented Minto's argument, which turns on what he had learned about Elizabethan poetry while writing *Characteristics of English Poets* and about Donne's poetry from examining Grosart's edition with close scrutiny. Unlike readers who were principally concerned with the implications of the poetry for understanding Donne's place in ecclesiastical history, Minto considered Donne squarely within the period when he was writing most of his poems, an era incomparable in the history of English literature inasmuch as at no other time 'did so much intellect go to the making of verses.'[61] Having read the major interpreters of Donne before him—Jonson and Carew and the other writers of commendatory verses in the 1630s, Walton and Samuel Johnson, De Quincey and Coleridge, and Taine; having thought through, with an independence of mind unprecedented in critics before him, the issues that these writers had raised; and having read Donne's poetry with close attention to the social contexts in which it was written—Minto began his treatment of Donne with a consideration of readers' responses to the poetry. He wrote, in fact, a defense of Donne against the theory that Taine had developed out of Johnson, according to which metaphysical poetry represented a degeneration of the glories of Elizabethan dramatic literature. Minto based his argument on an important distinction in terms of which no one else had been thinking about Donne: between poetry of the court, circulating in manuscript among an elite, and poetry of the stage, written for public consumption. Drawing on what Ben Jonson had said about Donne's best verses, Minto pointed out that Donne wrote much of his poetry 'before the dramatic masterpieces of

---

[60] Duncan, *Revival*, 122.

[61] *Characteristics of English Poets from Chaucer to Shirley* (1874; 2nd edn., Edinburgh: William Blackwood and Sons, 1885),182.

Shakespeare were produced' (848) and that he had made it available only to a small coterie, in which 'more veiled and intricate forms of utterance' were required than on the stage (847).

Beyond observing that Donne was not simply a decadent follower of the Bard, Minto developed the Coleridgean notion that Donne was 'of like essence' with Shakespeare. Arguing that the poetry of the court and the poetry of the stage cross-fertilized one another, Minto quoted from 'The Indifferent' and 'Woman's Constancy', the two poems on which Coleridge had written his most wide-ranging comments. He also quoted 'The Funeral', enlisting all three to illustrate Donne's ability to shift 'between jest and earnest' in the same poem. Dr Johnson, he maintained, had missed this essential quality of Donne's verse, because he was unsympathetic to 'impassioned mysticism and the subtle fancies born of it.' Coleridge had for a long time missed it too. As he explained in his marginal note on 'The Canonization', as long as he persisted in looking for 'grand lines and fine stanzas', he failed to see the relation of the parts to the whole. Long before it became a critical doctrine in the twentieth century, Minto pointed out that 'there is no poet whose images are more closely interwoven with some central thought' than Donne (857). Unable or unwilling to see this, Johnson had quoted 'fragments torn from their context', with the result that Donne's poetry, known only in quotable bits, seemed 'grossly absurd and unnatural' (857) to critics who have no sympathy for the poet and who, 'like travellers, too often see only what they look for' (847).

Minto's conviction that writing is 'always ... conditioned by its readers' (847) led him to offer an account of Donne's life substantially different than could be found in Walton, whom he mentioned only casually, or in Grosart, whom he did not name although he took his quotations from his edition. Aware as others were that Walton had suppressed almost all mention of Donne's erotic verses, Minto proposed an interpretation of the early poetry that helped to explain its evident lack of conventional refinement. He recognized its profound relation to classical poetry and implicitly to Ovid and Tibullus, whose poems stand behind the Elegies in particular. The central paradox of Donne is not, Minto urged, 'that in the evening of his life he should have become or rather been made one of the pillars of the English Church.' Rather the real anomaly is that an 'ardent bookworm ... should have entered the lists with the erotic poets of the Court, and by the ascendancy of his wit have founded a new school' (853). What Minto regarded as needing to be accounted for, then, was that a poet who had made so extraordinarily positive an impression on his contemporaries should have fallen into almost complete obscurity. Minto ignored the concerns of those who were scandalized by the licentious poems of Doctor Donne. At the same time the readers for whom

Minto was writing were numbered in the last of three groups whom he classified when he wrote that 'for one person that reads De Quincey's essay on Rhetoric or Coleridge's priceless fragments of criticism, twenty read Johnson's *Lives of the Poets*' (846).

For these readers Minto rehearsed the salient features of Donne's biography, even crediting the idea that Donne had passed through a 'slough of despond' (850), yet pointing the whole discussion towards explaining why Donne had failed to make a lasting impression as a writer. The superficial facts of Donne's life provoke an inquiry, Minto observed, into whether he was more Talleyrand than Augustine. While Minto came down against the former alternative, he clearly admired the fact that Donne had 'questioned and canvassed everything with all the daring of an intellectual athlete, till he was ready to believe nothing, ready at least to maintain with brilliant rhetoric the converse of any proposition that was generally accepted in the world' (854). An 'invincible repugnance to the commonplace' (862) was at once the central characteristic of Donne's mind and a cause of his long-term failure as a writer. Instead of following the well-traveled path, in his groundbreaking satires, his facetious love poetry, and the *Metempsychosis* Donne 'sallies into the pure empyrean of hyperbole' (859). 'His poetry was really a sort of new departure in the trifling style' (848). This had gone altogether unappreciated in the eighteenth century, and in the standard accounts of literary history 'Donne has suffered not a little from the perversity of critics who have insisted upon giving too serious a meaning to his fantasies' (856). At the same time Minto singled out one species of fantasy that Donne himself took seriously and for which he would be increasingly prized from the 1890s onward: his treatment, in many letters and poems, of a kind of ecstasy between two friends or lovers, or between himself and 'the great soul of the universe' (857). Before Minto no one had been proposing to read Donne's poetry in all these ways.

That Minto was implicitly accounting for the omission of Donne from *The Golden Treasury* is suggested by the way in which his article begins and ends, with a disdain for the commonplace and a prizing of what can be appreciated only by 'the studious few.' In some respects, Minto felt a profound affinity with Donne, and some of the characteristics that he praised in him were mentioned in the chorus of tributes to Minto published shortly after his death in 1893 at the age of 48. Minto was remembered as both a critic and a teacher. In the former capacity his knowledge was 'not derived from secondary sources' and 'his criticism was invariably at first hand' and included appreciation of 'out-of-the-way authors.' By the same token he was remembered for having taken pleasure in discovering and encouraging young writers, out of a 'pure love of literature.'[62] What Minto had said of Donne, moreover—that his contemporaries valued him not only for what he accomplished but for what they expected him to be capable of doing—was repeatedly said of Minto, who at the time of his death was planning a book that would incorporate his writings on Donne and Wordsworth.

It is of interest how wrong Minto was, at least for the best part of the next hundred years, about the prospects for Donne ever being appreciated. Probably he had been self-consciously provocative. His own interest in Donne had been initiated by that protégé whom he had discovered and made his sub-editor at *The Examiner*, Edmund Gosse. Minto had been best man at Gosse's wedding, and while they were working daily together Gosse had contributed to the *Britannica* a rather wooden entry on Donne. Years later when Gosse published *The Life and Letters of John Donne* (1899), he traced his ambition to write a new biographical study of Donne back to 1880. In this way he indirectly paid tribute to the piece in *The Nineteenth Century*, which had revealed to him the project he himself sought to embrace with the help of Jessopp's research. A more profound and gracious tribute to Minto came from his one-time teaching assistant and eventual successor in the English chair at Aberdeen: Herbert J. C. Grierson acknowledged that his mentor's article had stimulated his interest in Donne, which later bore fruit in the edition of 1912 and the anthology of 1921.[63] Minto's article had a good deal to do with the eventual incorporation of Donne into the curricula in the nascent Departments of English literature. It was well known in New England and often cited there during the 1890s, as critical attention to Donne and the academic study of his works gained an unprecedented prominence at Harvard. Minto's article had much less influence in England, however, where in the last two decades of the nineteenth century the figure of Donne became increasingly important within the large collaborative project designed to produce genuinely scientific biographies of all historically significant Englishmen. Donne was of interest to the general editor of the *Dictionary of National Biography* and to a number of his contributors partly because he had been a writer but also, more tellingly, because he had been written about. Before proceeding to the chapters that treat the ways in which Donne came to be taken more seriously as a writer than as the hero of biographical narratives, the chapter to follow will chart

[62] See Knight's Biographical Introduction to *The Literature of the Georgian Era*, p. xv; see also, the University of Aberdeen's *Alma Mater* for 4 Mar. 1893, n. p. The issue was titled 'In Memoriam William Minto.'

[63] Edmund Gosse, *The Life and Letters of John Donne, Dean of St. Paul's*, 2 vols. (1899; repr., Gloucester, MA: Peter Smith, 1959), i, p. vii; Grierson is quoted in a letter to Duncan, *Revival*, 217 n.

the course of Donne biography in the last two decades of the century. The biographers who sought to provide an alternative to Walton's hagiographical portrait found it utterly necessary to look into Donne's writings. While they were unsympathetic to the idea that Donne was an authoritative love poet, they all contributed to the redefinition whereby he came to be known as a writer.

6

Donne in the Hands of Biographers

Whoever can write anything which shall give a true and sufficient idea of John Donne, such an idea as will make the general reader of poetry understand why he is regarded as a poet of surpassing genius, may deem himself no longer an apprentice in the art of criticism. Donne is the most baffling of the minor poets; Whipple and Lowell, Gosse and Dowden, and a number of lesser men, have tried their hands, and yet no lover of Donne feels that anything adequate has been said, and those who know the poet still remain an elect number.

—*The Dial* (1896)

After the appearance of the Fuller Worthies' edition, interest in developing an integrated account of Walton's preacher and Grosart's poetic 'Imaginator' intensified. As rare as copies of Grosart's two volumes were, Donne's poetry was more available in Britain than it had been for half a century, and the canon had been greatly expanded. Because we know that nearly all the poems added by Grosart have not been accepted as genuine, we underestimate the short-term significance of this expanded canon: late Victorian readers were taken in by Grosart's claims. Some, regarding a historic person's domestic life as too insubstantial to matter in the important work of writing the biography of the nation, dismissed the augmented body of love poetry as irrelevant to understanding Donne's significance. Chief here was Augustus Jessopp, who contributed the entry on Donne to *The Dictionary of National Biography*. Others felt excitement, however, at the prospect of drawing on long hidden materials, as Edward Dowden sought to do, to develop 'a true and sufficient idea of John Donne.'[1] Both groups were agreed that the popular account by Walton warranted serious revision.

---

[1] The epigraph comes from a review of the Muses' Library edition of *Poems of John Donne*, ed. E. K. Chambers (London: Lawrence and Bullen; George Routledge and Son; New York: Charles Scribner's Sons; E. P. Dutton, 1896), *The Dial* (Chicago), 20 (1896), 280. In addition to materials that have been discussed in Chapters 4 and 5 above, the reviewer was referring to Dowden's

Walton's *Lives* stood at once as an enduring inspiration to a studious biographical age and as an impediment to the emergence of the scientific writing that was to culminate its efforts in the *DNB*. Acknowledged as a pioneer in the writing of English biography, Walton was nonetheless said to have produced work that was unscientific: he treated dates casually and handled documents cavalierly, and he failed to provide a satisfying account of Donne's poetry. Beyond this, some judged that his chief deficiency lay in his organization of materials according to a narrative pattern that belonged to an outmoded stage of culture.

Serious reappraisal of Donne's life began in the entry that appeared in the *DNB* in 1888.[2] It continued in the sketch of *John Donne, Sometime Dean of St. Paul's* that Jessopp contributed nine years later to a series called 'Leaders of Religion.' It seemed to culminate in *The Life and Letters*, in which Edmund Gosse drew on the poems to supplement and ultimately, as he thought, to undermine Walton's portrait. Yet, curiously, Gosse's work revealed the dogged persistence of Walton's providential pattern and prompted the principal editor of the *DNB* to take matters into his own hands. That Leslie Stephen wrote an extensive essay on Donne, one that offered a far more secular interpretation of the life and writings than had ever been proposed, is indicative of Donne's signal importance to the large general project of writing the nation's biography.

Work by David Agimoni and Jeffrey von Arx on Victorian biographical writing as an ideological force helps to clarify the degree to which late Victorian studies of Donne were themselves productive discursive events, each aimed in its way at closing discussions to which some gaps in Walton's account seemed to give rise. Agimoni has examined how freethinking historians sought to build up, individual biography by individual biography, a master-narrative that would demonstrate the progressive principles by which the nation had developed. These historians sought to show how England had left behind what

---

essay, 'The Poetry of John Donne', which first appeared in *The Fortnightly Review*, new ser., 47 (1890), 791–808, and to Gosse's essay, 'The Poetry of John Donne', which first appeared in *The New Review*, 9 (1893), 236–47. Both essays were reprinted, and Gosse's was notably expanded in *The Jacobean Poets* (London: J. Murray; New York: Charles Scribner's Sons, 1894).

2 In her appraisal of 'Walton's Legacy' in the nineteenth century, Jessica Martin locates the beginning of a spirit critical to Walton on scientific grounds in the edition of the *Lives* edited by William Dowling and published in London in 1857; see *Walton's Lives: Conformist Commemorations and the Rise of Biography* (Oxford and New York: Oxford Univ. Press, 2001), 310. Clearly, however, the 1852 edition of Donne's *Life* by Tomlins antedated Dowling's work. The starting point in this chapter is Jessopp's concern not merely to annotate and supplement Walton but to rewrite his narrative. Martin traces some ways in which a 'scientific' approach dominated biographical writing about Donne well into the middle of the twentieth century (310–15). She sees it as having reached its apex in David Novarr's book, *The Making of Walton's Lives* (Ithaca, NY: Cornell Univ. Press, 1958).

were considered, in Auguste Comte's scheme of history, earlier theological and metaphysical stages of development. Stephen's investment in this cultural work helps to account for the energy that he finally channeled into an interpretation of Donne's person and career. Stephen shared with John Morley, Frederic Harrison, and other liberal intellectuals a disposition to write an individual life as a microcosm of the national biographical story. He also shared with them the experience of being 'deeply troubled by the residual authority of religious organisations.'[3] In the context of late Victorian reassessments of national history, Donne proved an especially fascinating case both because he had anticipated an enlightened liberation from traditional authority and because he had finally taken a retrograde path, veering away, when he went into the church, from what many intellectuals wanted to believe was the inevitable course that England's future would take. It is this context, the emerging disciplinary hegemony of 'history', that tends to define the principal ways in which Donne was discussed in the last years of the nineteenth century in England. In the United States (as the chapters to follow will show) the new discipline of 'English' provided a less politically charged arena in which Donne came to be read and studied.

THE DICTIONARY OF NATIONAL BIOGRAPHY

In December 1882, having resigned as editor of the *Cornhill Magazine*, Stephen announced in the *Athenaeum* that the publisher George Smith had secured his services to oversee a new *Biographia Britannica*, and he asked for help from 'the most competent living authorities.' In the months that followed, as he assigned articles on various persons whose surnames began with the letters A and B, he began to rely heavily upon '[t]hat remarkable person, Dr Grosart', as he referred to him with irony in a letter to Gosse. Grosart's extensive editorial labors had earned him a reputation as a leading expert on seventeenth-century divines; at first Stephen gave him a large number of assignments. Nonetheless, Grosart took offense when others were assigned lives that he wished to write. His presumptuousness was only the beginning of large-scale problems for the *Dictionary*. Stephen confided to Gosse his frustration at the verbal abuse 'that old fool Grosart' kept heaping upon him for rejecting the 'theory of his vested

---

[3] David Amigoni, *Victorian Biography: Intellectuals and the Ordering of Discourse* (London: Harvester Wheatsheaf; New York: St. Martin's, 1993), 145. Cf. Jeffrey Paul von Arx, *Progress and Pessimism: Religion, Politics, and History in Late Nineteenth Century Britain* (Cambridge, MA: Harvard Univ. Press, 1985).

right in people.'⁴ What compounded Stephen's frustration, however, was a discovery made late in 1884 by Smith and by the subeditor, Sidney Lee: several of Grosart's submissions silently incorporated copyrighted material that he had published in the *Encyclopædia Britannica*.

The discovery caused Stephen great embarrassment. It also delayed the appearance of the first volume of the *Dictionary*. In one of his semi-annual letters to his friend Charles Eliot Norton, Stephen explained that 'An accursed Doctor of Divinity, one Grosart (his D. Dship gives an extra flavour to my execrations) has been cheating me. He actually sent me & nothing but a lucky accident saved me from publishing, articles taken word for word from others which he had contributed to the Encyclopaedia. Having found out this villainy,' Stephen added, 'I next discovered that he had been systematically manufacturing sham references.' Although permission was secured from the *Britannica* to republish the material with acknowledgment, and more than a hundred articles credited to Grosart appeared in early volumes of the *Dictionary*, the dimensions of the problem were great. Stephen felt he had to check through all Grosart's submissions. He spent a great deal of time on the demoralizing task of 'looking into Grosart's wickednesses.'⁵ Amidst much unpleasantness Grosart was dropped as a contributor before the project reached the letter D.

For the article on Donne Stephen might have turned to Gosse. 'I have made more enemies in these two years', Stephen wrote to him, 'than in ten of editing the Cornhill', the worst being Grosart, who 'would send me to the stake, if he could.'⁶ Stephen had already given Gosse a number of articles, including Thomas Lovell Beddoes, through whose papers Gosse had worked with Robert Browning in 1883. (It was on the basis of his intimacy with the more celebrated poet, whose death in 1889 qualified him for inclusion in the first supplement to the *Dictionary*, that Gosse was later assigned the article on Browning.) Gosse had written the entry on Donne for the ninth *Britannica*. He had, moreover, isolated the writing of a literary biography of Donne as 'perhaps the most imposing task left to the student of Elizabethan and Jacobean literature' and had resolved to undertake it himself.⁷ Yet it was Jessopp to whom Stephen gave the Donne commission.

---

⁴ *Selected Letters of Leslie Stephen*, ed. John W. Bicknell, 2 vols. (Basingstoke: Macmillan; Columbus, OH: Ohio State Univ. Press, 1996), ii. 305; also, Stephen's letter of 29 Sept. 1883 to Gosse, cited by Gillian Fenwick, *Leslie Stephen's Life in Letters: A Bibliographical Study* (Aldershot, Hants: Scolar Press; Brookfield, VT: Ashgate Publishing, 1993), 234.
⁵ Stephen, *Selected Letters*, ii. 316, 318.   ⁶ Ibid. ii. 325.
⁷ See Edmund Gosse, *The Life and Letters of John Donne Dean of St. Paul's*, 2 vols. (London: William Heinemann; New York: Dodd, Mead, 1899), i, p. vii. Subsequent references are given in the text.

Having retired after serving for twenty years as headmaster of King Edward VI's School, Norwich, Jessopp was now an Oxford D.D. and a well-to-do country parson with leisure for scholarship. He was contributing articles to *The Nineteenth Century*, he had become as knowledgeable as anyone in England about the lives of the ancient Catholic nobility in the later sixteenth century, and his book *One Generation of a Norfolk House* (1878) had established his reputation as a gifted historian. Stephen entrusted him with the important entries on Queen Elizabeth and William Cecil, Lord Burghley. He must have seemed just the man to remove Donne from the ethereal sphere of hagiography and to place him squarely in Elizabethan and Jacobean history.

As a historian Jessopp was prepared to present Donne in terms that fit with Stephen's conception of the *DNB*. In fact, his predilection for a prose Donne, whom he regarded as the greatest preacher in England's history, proved to be important. From the outset of the *DNB* project, there was a decided bias that favored the inclusion of literary figures and that ensured detailed treatment for writers. Smith's early communications with Stephen show that they were seeking to emulate the prestigious French model, the full title of which suggests the priority it gave to writers: *Biographie universelle, ancienne et moderne, ou Histoire, par l'ordre alphabétique, de la vie publique et privée de tous les hommes qui se sont fait remarquer par leurs écrits, leur actions, leur talents, leures vertus ou leur crimes.* For the projected British counterpart, not only was being a writer a decisive criterion for selection, but the readily accessible catalogue at the British Museum was Stephen's practical starting place for making lists of proposed subjects.[8] Concerned to present the history of modern literature in its relation to society, Stephen himself undertook a large number of the principal men of letters from the time of Milton. Among the poets, he wrote on Dryden, Pope, Gray, Cowper, Burns, Wordsworth, Coleridge, and Byron; among the novelists, Defoe, Richardson, Fielding, Jane Austen, Scott, the Brontës, Dickens, Thackeray, and George Eliot; among the essayists, Swift, Gibbon, Johnson, Boswell, De Quincey, Macaulay, Hallam, and Carlyle. He wrote as well on philosophers, social critics, and economists: Hobbes and Locke, Berkeley, Hume, Hartley, Adam Smith, Reid, the Mills, Malthus, and others. Having previously published the *History of English Thought in the Eighteenth Century*, he also wrote on many divines. Donne belonged to an earlier period than these figures, however. Stephen recognized in him an especially complex case, one that called for the specialized knowledge that Jessopp had been acquiring through forty years.

[8] See H. C. G. Matthew, *Leslie Stephen and the New Dictionary of National Biography*, The Leslie Stephen Lecture, 25 October 1995 (Cambridge: Cambridge Univ. Press, 1997), 2 n., 14.

In compiling a monumental history of all the most significant Britons 'from the earliest times to the present day', Stephen wanted articles that would show how history had unfolded along lines that could be predicted on the basis of 'liberal, progressive, and secular' principles. Von Arx reminds us that if the 'argument that biography derives its significance from a firm grounding in history is self-evident to us', this is a tribute to Stephen's insistence that the project be conducted according to a scientific methodology that was to leave little room for contributors to offer speculative literary criticism or to register their personal opinions.[9] In the defense of the *Dictionary* that Stephen published in the *National Review* in 1896, he explained the larger cultural significance he envisaged for it, by which intellectuals familiar with the scientific study of history were to make clear the progressive principles embedded in the normative literary tradition. The biographical entries had to conform to certain strict principles of method and format, and 'the life of a divine, for example, should be given to one who has studied the theology or ecclesiastical history of the day, and who therefore knows the significance conferred upon a particular action or expression of opinion by time and place.' Moreover, the biographer 'must content himself with a pithy indication' of his subject's 'historical position in the development of the time; give a sufficient summary to show how the doctrine is to be classed in its relation to the main currents of thought; and indicate the way in which it has since been judged by competent writers, and what is the view now taken by experts.'[10] In commissioning the various articles, Stephen sent potential contributors a model entry on Joseph Addison, which, if it was not about a divine, was about a man whose education had equipped him to participate in the large story that the *Dictionary* was to illustrate piece by piece: the gradual secularization of knowledge and of cultural authority.

There are good reasons why a satisfying account of Donne as 'a poet of surpassing genius' was not going to appear in this forum. 'A *DNB* article is', as the editor of the new *Oxford DNB* has characterized the work of his predecessors, 'a biographical memoir with a distinctive grammar and format.'[11] The model essay epitomized what Stephen was looking for from expert contributors. It announced that Addison was an 'essayist, poet, and

---

[9] Von Arx, *Progress and Pessimism*, 60.

[10] Stephen, 'National Biography', *National Review*, 27 (1896), 51–65; reprinted in *Studies of a Biographer* (London: Duckworth, 1898), i. 25–6; cf. von Arx, *Progress and Pessimism*, 58–60.

[11] Matthew, *Leslie Stephen*, 24. For more detailed discussion of the ways in which Stephen codified the conventions of modern autobiographical writing, see Trev Lynn Broughton, *Men of Letters, Writing Lives: Masculinity and Literary Auto/Biography in the Late Victorian Period* (London: Routledge, 1999), 43–6.

statesman.' It traced his family background, his classical education, and his travels. When it called attention to his accomplishments as a Latin poet, it emphasized that his poetical reputation not only earned him a place among 'professional authors' but launched his political career, for in the early eighteenth century 'political patronage was beginning to descend upon the literary class.' While insisting that Addison's writings reveal his 'true power', the paradigm gave many details about how his 'high character, modesty, and sweetness of temper' helped to ensure that he was well connected. Its central emphasis, however, was the great influence of the *Tatler* and the *Spectator* as forerunners of the high journalism: by achieving 'the widest popularity', these papers spread abroad many significant ideas and set a standard for later periodical writers. In short, Addison was a pre-eminent example of the man of letters who had helped to wrest away for English literature the sort of authority that had long been subject to clerical monopoly.

Stephen's own articles, besides giving details about his subjects' public careers and political loyalties, typically described their education and traced their intellectual development. The article on Addison pointed out, for instance, that his 'academical position' at Oxford 'might suggest the intention of taking orders.' Stephen acknowledged that this intention seems to be confirmed in one of Addison's poems. He discounted, however, Thomas Tickell's claim that Addison was 'deterred' from a clerical career 'by his modesty.' Instead he proffered that securing political patronage simply made it unnecessary for him to go into the church. At the same time, Stephen observed that Addison had placed his 'classical acquirements' at the service of 'the culture of his age', which scorned 'Gothic obscurity' and looked with 'contempt' upon popery and 'catholic observances.'

This essay also set the standard for how articles were to be concluded. It gave some details of Addison's life with his wife and daughter. Then, because he had been a writer, it provided a descriptive bibliography enumerating his published contributions to society, his best pieces of poetry (as it were). Gillian Fenwick has studied the astonishingly short shrift that the *DNB* gave to women, both in its choice of subjects and in its handling of family life. Building on her work, Colin Matthew has summed up one important basis for its bias against domesticity:

[T]he division between 'private' and 'public' life reached its zenith at the time that the *DNB* was being written. It was in the late nineteenth century that the 'double standard', in Keith Thomas's phrase, was most clearly defined. A sharp distinction was drawn between the 'public' and 'private' aspects of a male life and this affected the handling of sex ('private') and domesticity in *DNB* articles. Women were literally an appendage to men in most articles. They were mentioned only at the end, following the death of the subject, ... like a vampirish adjunct.[12]

If this criticism sounds rather like something Virginia Woolf might have registered, it is important to recognize the full extent of her father's bias, which ultimately accounts for the Donne entry's having been given to Jessopp rather than to Gosse. In the months when Stephen was preparing the first volumes of the *Dictionary*, he was appointed the first Clark lecturer at Cambridge. The frame of mind in which he went about preparing and delivering his twenty-four lectures on English literature is revealed in his letter of 13 April 1884 to Norton. 'The Cambridge lectures', Stephen wrote shortly after finishing them,

were in a sense, a success; that is I had a large class ... consisting chiefly of young women from the ladies' colleges. The female student is at present an innocent animal, who wants to improve her mind and takes ornamental lectures seriously; not understanding with her brother students, that the object of study is to get a good place in an examination & that lecturers are a vanity & a distraction. In this matter I confess that I sympathize with the male; & grew half inclined to laugh in the faces of my respectful & intelligent hearers. Moreover I felt keenly the absurdity of repeating the weary old criticism upon Pope & Addison, and wondered increasingly that anyone should care to hear me read articles wh. I should regard as too trite for a magazine. They could have got it all up in half the time in two or three books. ... I am pretty well resolved to draw my neck out of this halter; and am left with the rather unpleasant reflection that I have wasted a good deal of work. The only per contra is the £300 due to me. Moral: it is a mistake to take work for one's left hand whilst the right is full. The lectures were well spoken of, I believe; but they were not worth making into a book—so enough of that.

The lecturer's enterprise is conceived according to various binaries—left hand versus right, women versus men students, literary study versus practical getting on in the world, writing for magazines versus making books—that serve in the many *DNB* articles to figure imaginative literature as a lesser, feminine domain that threatens to draw men away from serious pursuits.[13] Donne could be designated at the outset of his *DNB* entry a poet as well as a *divine* as long as there were no pretentious interpretations of his poems. What was called for was plain information.

---

[12] Gillian Fenwick, *Women in the Dictionary of National Biography* (Aldershot, Hants: Scolar Press; Brookfield, VT: Ashgate Publishing, 1994); Matthew, *Leslie Stephen*, 16.

[13] Stephen, *Selected Letters*, ii. 309–10. On the ways in which biography served as 'the genre through which Victorian literary patriarchy ... attempted to reproduce itself', see Broughton, 'Froude: The "Painful Appendix"', *Carlyle Studies Annual: Carlyle at 200. Lectures I* (Normal, IL: Illinois State Univ. Department of English, 1995), 66. For understanding the designation of Donne as 'poet and divine', see Stephen's 'Proposed Method for the *Dictionary of National Biography*', published in Appendix I of *Selected Letters*, ii. 546.

THE WORK OF AUGUSTUS JESSOPP

There were relatively few directives enshrined in Stephen's paradigmatic article on Addison that the writer of an entry on Donne would have found it difficult to follow. Jessopp provided a good deal of information about Donne's family life and education. He kept the focus on its public significance. Unlike Walton, he told how closely the government's 'relentless persecution' had touched Donne's Catholic family.[14] Predictably, he quoted the famous passage from *Pseudo-Martyr* (1610) in which Donne claims that 'No family (which is not of far larger extent and greater branches) hath endured and suffered more in their persons and fortunes for obeying the teachers of Roman doctrine.' Jessopp lodged this quotation, however, in a cryptic surmise that Donne must have articulated this idea as early as 1599 (more about this momentarily). He also observed that there is no evidence to confirm Walton's speculation that Donne had studied at Cambridge, and he pointed out that it was Donne's early education by Jesuits that best equipped him to become a writer. In briefly retelling the famous story of the clandestine wedding, he treated the marriage chiefly as an impediment to Donne's career, observing that the lovers 'developed ... a passionate attachment which neither had the resolution to resist.' He made no attempt to connect Anne More with Donne's verse. In providing information about their children, Jessopp sought to detail the dishonesty and notorious dissipation of John Donne the younger. In fact, he wrote a brief *DNB* entry on him, reporting that the surviving papers of the younger Donne had proved to be 'full of the most shocking indecencies.' Jessopp also revealed that John Donne, Junior, had once whipped 'a little boy of eight years' for startling a horse, with the result that the 'poor fellow languished' for three weeks and then died, though the culprit, who was in holy orders, was acquitted at his trial for manslaughter. The general purport of this entry was to exonerate the father. Anything in the published record that might make the former Dean of St Paul's seem vile was owing to an ungrateful, probably atheistical, son whose temerity in going into the church was matched by the venality with which he sought to exploit his father's good reputation by publishing materials never meant for the press. Upon receiving drafts of the two Donne articles in February 1888, Stephen was pleased and wrote back, remarking about 'John the beast' that he had not

---

[14] The Donne entry appeared in volume xv of the *Dictionary*, first published in 1888, 223–34. In quoting from the *DNB*, I have omitted reference to volume and page numbers, since these vary widely between the original and the reprints, whereas all the passages I have quoted are unvaried.

previously been 'acquainted with his character which seems to have been charming.'[15]

The submission on the elder Donne clearly demonstrated that Jessopp was the pre-eminent authority on him. Because he knew how sermon literature was implicated in seventeenth-century history, he was able to characterize the preacher's contributions to public life and to present him as a writer of enduring significance. As the first biographer to make substantial use of the sermons to trace Donne's career, Jessopp took seriously that they had been prepared for publication. He understood Donne's careful preparations precisely as public acts, which showed his concern both to leave a record for posterity and to exert a continuing influence. This helps to make sense of the fact that Stephen allocated Jessopp more than twenty columns for the entry (even more space than was given to Ben Jonson), whereas the entries on most other seventeenth-century poets and divines were much briefer. While the article on Milton (written by Stephen) occupies thirty-four columns, for instance, the entry on George Herbert is allotted only eight, the one on Robert Herrick four. Jeremy Taylor occupies something over thirteen columns, and Lancelot Andrewes eight. Walton, largely on the basis of the extraordinary popularity of *The Compleat Angler*, merits nearly nine.

At the end of the Donne entry Jessopp devoted five columns to displaying the most thorough bibliographical account of the works that had ever been assembled. The earlier columns emphasized that Donne regularly preached to the great and the influential: the benchers at Lincoln's Inn, who heard 'the noblest examples of pulpit oratory which the seventeenth century has bequeathed to posterity'; the admiring Princess Elizabeth at Heidelberg; the discerning Dutch at the Hague, where the States-General awarded him with a gold medal struck in commemoration of the Synod of Dort; the members of the Virginia Company, who heard before it was published 'the first missionary sermon printed in the English language'; and the citizens of London, whose coming to hear him at St Paul's, St Dunstan's, and Paul's Cross showed that his 'popularity was always on the increase' and attested to the fact that 'he rose to every occasion, and surprised [even] his friends.' Above all Jessopp dwelt on the preaching at Whitehall, where Donne had often appeared before King James and preached 'the first sermon which Charles I heard after his accession.' Jessopp said little about the theology, the spiritual vision, and even the hermeneutical practices that informed these sermons. He simply observed that the sermons were extraordinarily popular, both as live performances and

---

[15] Leslie Stephen's letter of 13 Feb. 1888 to Dr Jessopp is in the Garber Collection at Case Western Reserve University, Cleveland, OH, (ALS, 4 p), and is quoted by permission of the University Library. My thanks to N. Sue Hanson for help with transcription.

in their printed afterlife. The entry gives a reader little basis for understanding how they could have been attractive.

Limited in its conception of Donne as it is, Jessopp's portrait is subtle and powerful. It reveals something that its writer and its editor had in common: a concern to promote independent thinking, exemplary public behavior, and action according to one's conscience. The first third of the article hearkens repeatedly upon conscience, ascribing to Donne's forebears brave sufferings for 'their convictions' and a willingness to go into exile 'for conscience' sake.' It does not hesitate to condemn Henry VIII, who 'barbarously murdered' Sir Thomas More 'for refusing to assent to the royal supremacy in matters spiritual.' It explains that Donne had gone early to Oxford because the government of Henry's daughter had 'made compulsory' a 'crucial test of loyalty' meant to exclude Catholics from taking degrees. It silently revises Walton's assertion that Donne rationally scrutinized the contradictory claims of the Church of Rome and the Church of England; instead it dwells on the likelihood that as a young man Donne was 'distressed in mind' because of the cruel treatment accorded to his brother by government authorities.

Jessopp's highlighting of conscience is consistent with the fact that *Pseudo-Martyr*, which he had long regarded as a 'great' work, has a prominent place in the article. It is presented as a turning point in Donne's life, both because it was suggested by and probably remunerated by the King and because it ratified the policy enunciated even earlier by James that Donne was to 'receive church preferment or none at all.' Jessopp reported that his own wide reading in contemporary polemics had turned up conspicuous similarities between *Pseudo-Martyr* and *Biathanatos* on the one hand and works written by Thomas Morton on the other. This showed that the prelate who had first offered Donne a church living 'owed to Donne's learning very much more than it was advisable, or at that time necessary, to acknowledge in print.' This discovery also confirmed that it was by virtue of Donne's intimate acquaintance with Catholic literature that he was able to exercise an unparalleled and enduring authority as an opponent of popery.

Jessopp's archival researches yielded new information about the paths on which Donne trod as he made his approach to conformity with the established church and later to a position as its official minister. His account left two questions unanswered, however: (1) how, and with what motivation, was Donne's change of religious allegiance made? and (2) what was the basis of the scruples that kept Donne for so long from taking holy orders? With respect to the first question Jessopp brought readers to the very brink of the inference that it was from terror that Donne had conformed. Just after narrating the story of Henry Donne and quoting the passage from *Pseudo-Martyr* about the family's suffering, the article modulates, in the course of seeking to account for

Donne's serious study of disputes 'between the Roman and Anglican divines', into an uncharacteristic speculation:

The fate of his only brother might well account for the direction which his studies took; but when Robert, earl of Essex, set out on the Cadiz voyage in June 1596, and an extraordinary gathering of young volunteers joined the celebrated expedition, Donne was one of those who took part in it.

Here, without fully articulating the idea to which the first clause brings us to the threshold (that Donne feared for his life and sought a rationalization for changing his religious allegiance), the semicolon cuts off the thought before it fully forms. Jessopp then invites us into a partner clause that disallows the inference that Donne's character was fearful or timid. In fact, Donne's courage is made to explain the risk he took when a 'passionate attachment' to a young girl led to an action that 'spoilt' his 'career.' The quoted passage in which Donne fairly brags about his family's sufferings, which Jessopp placed at the end of his account of Henry Donne's death by 'gaol fever' in 1593, is made the occasion for the remark that 'Well might Donne, six years after this event', have said what he said in *Pseudo-Martyr*. That this suggests a courtship in the Lord Keeper's home that moved along potentially tragic lines—'She loved me for the dangers I had passed, | And I loved her that she did pity them'—is confirmed by the more elaborate story Jessopp told a few years later in his book:

The young lady developed rapidly, and in her budding womanhood she had constantly at her side the poet secretary, just ten years her senior, in the bloom and beauty of his youth, the peerless universal genius, whom to look at and to listen to was to love. What else could follow but that between the two an absorbing passion should spring up? which soon got the mastery of both one and the other, till considerations of prudence, even of duty, exercised over them no restraining force.[16]

Jessopp's view of the imprudence of the wedding had, in fact, a thoroughgoing significance for his interpretation of Donne's life. His book not only rehearsed the familiar story of Sir George More's anger upon discovering the marriage. It emphasized the legal seriousness of the offense for which Donne lost his position and was sent to prison in an age 'when a daughter's hand was assumed to be almost absolutely at the disposal of her father': the clandestine wedding had been both a sin against the canon law and a 'civil offense against the Common Law.'[17] The seriousness with which Jessopp regarded Donne's law-breaking and his prison record lies behind his interpretation in the *DNB* of Donne's long-standing reluctance to take holy orders.

---

[16] Augustus Jessopp, *John Donne Sometime Dean of St. Paul's A.D. 1621–1631* (London: Methuen, 1897), 20–1.
[17] Ibid. 23.

In recounting Morton's offer of 'the valuable living of Long Marston in Yorkshire', Jessopp reports that 'Donne could not get over his conscientious scruples to enter the ministry.' He says nothing about the content of those scruples, perhaps leaving readers familiar with Grosart's edition, or Lightfoot's sermon on the poet-preacher, discreetly to recall that before his marriage Donne had known something of sexual adventure. What is more likely, however, is that readers would draw upon Jessopp's own article, with its attention to the scrupulous consciences that had inspired many members of Donne's family to bear exile and other forms of suffering, to infer that Donne fully recognized the gravity of his illegal wedding. Donne's consciousness of his transgression, and of the shame that his prison record continued to bring on him, not only rendered him willing but made him in a sense eager to live as a 'needy man with a scanty fortune and no ostensible means of livelihood.' His very lack of a position enhanced his authority to write against Catholics who were resisting the oath of allegiance, since he manifestly had not betrayed his co-religionists for worldly gain.

Beyond this, readers were left to infer, Donne's tender conscience must also have been formed out of his experience with the brutal extremes to which the established church had been willing to go in order to enforce conformity: intimate knowledge of the persecution made him reluctant to become one of its public officials. Jessopp's studies had showed him that 'for at least twenty years of Elizabeth's reign torture of the most revolting kind was habitually employed upon wretched men and women,' including members of Donne's family. In his *DNB* article on Lord Burghley he told of the company of 'spies and informers' Cecil had kept in his pay and used 'without scruple' as 'detective police', whose job it was by various means of 'torture and other barbarities' to get information about suspected papists. And in his article on the Queen herself he augmented the picture, reporting with regret that 'there is no sign that Elizabeth ever felt one throb of pity' for a popish recusant 'or ever hesitated to sign a warrant for execution or to deliver over a miserable wretch to be dealt with by the "rack master".'[18] Jessopp's Donne, when at last he embraced holy orders, had not only paid his penalty by having lived so long without a place. He had convinced himself that the Jacobean church was a more fit vehicle of divine government than the Elizabethan church had been. In this respect the Donne entry in the *DNB*, with its focus on issues of conscience, played its part in demonstrating the theory of moral progress that was the central theme in Stephen's overall account of English history.

Jessopp's concern to place Donne squarely in intellectual and moral history also helps to explain his long-standing reluctance to explore any claims for

---

[18] Jessopp's entry on Queen Elizabeth first appeared in the *DNB* in 1889.

Donne 'as a poet of surpassing genius.' His *DNB* article mentions many of the poems, almost always in an effort to illustrate Donne's connections with great and influential persons. Jessopp calls attention to the 'epistles in verse addressed to the Countess of Bedford, the Countess of Huntingdon, the Countess of Salisbury, and the two daughters of Robert, lord Rich', and to the funeral elegies written in honor of the Marquis of Hamilton and members of Lady Bedford's circle. He also credits the claim that Donne sent his 'Divine Poems' and 'Holy Sonnets' to Lady Magdalen Herbert. In reporting on the course of Donne's relations with Sir Robert Drury he gives details about the printing of the Anniversaries; and in rehearsing something of Donne's 'obligations to Somerset, which were very great', he acknowledges that Donne wrote an epithalamium on the occasion of his scandalous marriage. Jessopp also duly mentions the hymn quoted by Walton and said by him to have been 'set to music and sung by the choir of St. Paul's.' He says absolutely nothing, however, about the fact that Donne wrote love poetry. In fact, in the bibliographical portion of the entry, Jessopp's list of early editions fails to include 1635, which first gathered the Songs and Sonnets into a group and moved them to the front of the collection.

In suppressing mention of Donne's erotic verse, Jessopp's biographical acts exacerbated the problem of developing an integrated account of the life and writings. In the nineties, as the Grolier Club and Muses' Library editions of the poems were published and the love poetry came to be widely discussed, a growing conviction that Walton had been a poor reader of the poetry was powerfully articulated. In his introduction to a new edition of the *Lives* Vernon Blackburn urged that 'The first very curious and interesting matter to note' about Walton's account

is the deliberate—I had almost written the sinful—suppression of Donne's secular career. Donne, the literary artist, the poet of high-sounding phrase, scarcely exists in these prattling pages. ... The early years of poetic inspiration are to this unscrupulous biographer a matter for gloomy silence. ... The reader, therefore, is prepared to find a 'penitential' rather than a poetic Donne.[19]

This criticism also touched Jessopp, who assumed that Donne was quintessentially a divine, and who, for all his patient labors to get the dates and chronology right, shaped his account in a manner that finally did not disturb the principal contours of Walton's narrative. Far more than Walton, Jessopp was unable to make sense of much of Donne's poetic activity. Like Blackburn, he seems to have projected naïveté onto his predecessor, without attending

[19] Introduction to Walton's *Lives of Doctor Donne*, etc., English Classics, ed. W. E. Henley (London: Methuen, 1895), pp. xv, xiii, respectively. Cf. also Charles Hill Dick, Introduction to Walton's *Lives*, the Scott Library (London: Walter Scott, [1899]), pp. vii–xi.

to what seemed discreetly implied in the remark that 'none was so like' St Augustine 'before his Conversion: none so like St *Ambrose* after it: ... his youth had the infirmities of the one, his age had the excellencies of the other.'[20] The Preface to Jessopp's book of 1897 voices his recognition of what others thought needed to be done, however, and acknowledges that he was not prepared to do it. Although Jessopp had once had the ambition to edit the complete works, he owned at last,

I have never been able to feel much enthusiasm for Donne as a poet; and it is as a poet that Donne's fame has chiefly come down to us. Who was I that I should undertake to deal with the life of the man whose poetry I had not the power of appreciating at its worth? There must be some deficiency, some obliquity, in my own mind. It was only slowly and reluctantly that I was brought to see that such a work as I had hoped to do, only Mr. Edmund Gosse was fitted to undertake. There is no man in England who has written so exquisitely on Donne as he, or shown such subtle sympathy with his poetic genius. It is to him, accordingly, that I resign that delightful and honourable task which I once hoped to accomplish myself. It is from him that any adequate and elaborate biography is to be looked for.[21]

After making this admission, Jessopp embraced two expedients: he published his modest sketch of Donne as a divine and he entered into plans for collaboration with Gosse, who was persuaded to renew his earlier resolve to write a 'life and letters.' Meanwhile, by failing to integrate an account of the love poetry into a religious interpretation of Donne's life, Jessopp had lent further credence to the charge that Walton had been engaged in a kind of hagiography that precluded scientific accuracy.

To the factual data that had been provided in the *DNB* article Jessopp's book of 1897 added little. The biographer elaborated his interpretations and made explicit his ratification of Walton's construction of a providential pattern. He singled out among the most revealing aspects of Donne's life his capacity for friendship, which was illustrated by copious citations from the letters, and his conscientious passage over the many steps to the altar he had traversed. Ultimately, the book was toothless. Here was the foremost authority in the world on Donne's life, who knew more about the family history than anyone else had since the poet's own lifetime. Yet he had nothing to say about the intriguing reference to 'my fathers soul' in the Holy Sonnet, 'If faithful souls be alike glorifi'd.' Courageously equipped with detailed knowledge about the vagaries of Elizabethan ecclesiastical history, Jessopp uttered not a word about Satire III or the elegy sometimes called 'Recusancy.' Deeply acquainted with Donne's scriptural knowledge, he did nothing to

---

[20] *The Lives of Dr. John Donne*, etc., 4th edn (London, 1675), 38.
[21] Jessopp, *John Donne Sometime Dean*, pp. viii–ix.

illuminate the biblical grounds on which the sonnet 'Batter my heart' deploys its shocking metaphors. Nor did Jessopp acknowledge the existence of poems that conspicuously engage traditionally Catholic materials. In fact, the book failed to treat dozens of poems in which Donne was drawing upon the wide reading in ecclesiastical literature about which Jessopp had diligently informed himself in order to make his case for the importance of *Pseudo-Martyr* and *Biathanatos*. Although Jessopp duly quoted the letter to Sir Robert Carr in which Donne had remarked that as a poet 'I did best when I had least truth for my subjects,' he altogether failed to probe the implications of this provocative assertion.

THE ABORTIVE COLLABORATION

There is scarcely any more dramatic evidence for the general displacement of the Jacobean preacher to whom he had devoted his studies for more than forty years than Jessopp's sad acknowledgment that 'it is as a poet that Donne's fame has chiefly come down to us.' At the same time there was something wonderfully generous about Jessopp's willingness to collaborate with Gosse. The article on Donne that Gosse had written for the *Britannica* was merely pedestrian. By the time Jessopp agreed to collaborate with him, however, Gosse had been working on the poetry for more than a decade. In the mid-1880s, he had put his imagination to work on Minto's discussion of how manuscript poetry had circulated. He drew a dynamic picture of eager Cambridge students passing round unpublished poems during the very years when their author was Dean of St Paul's. This picture of Donne's popularity among the younger generation of poets was printed in *From Shakespeare to Pope* and was complemented a few years later in *Gossip in a Library*, where a chapter on *Death's Duel* explored the basis for Dr Donne's popularity as a preacher. In 1893, Gosse wrote an extended article on Donne's poetry for the *New Review*, and it was reprinted in *Littell's Living Age*. The following year he expanded it for incorporation into his book on *The Jacobean Poets*. It is this piece that made Jessopp supremely aware of his own incompetence to write about the poetry. Gosse was able to represent Donne's poems as a new, anti-Spenserian departure in literary history and to discuss them in relation to those of Ovid and Tibullus, of Browning and Robert Bridges and the French symbolists, and to make claims for the surpassing interest of the amatory lyrics. Although Gosse tended to denigrate the verse letters, the article enhanced Jessopp's hopes for a collaboration, both because Gosse cited with approval the phrase from the *DNB* article in which Jessopp referred to Donne's 'unusual and indefinable witchery' and especially because Gosse seemed eager to subordinate everything he had to say about the poems to the biographical project in which Jessopp was known to be engaged. Rejecting Grosart's claim that the religious verse had been written in Donne's youth, Gosse proposed that the Holy Sonnets had been written late, after Anne's death. He urged that they throw 'very interesting' light 'on Donne's prolonged sympathy with the Roman Church, over which his [other] biographers have been wont to slur'; and he commenced the work of extracting from the Divine Poems a history of Donne's religious opinions. At the same time he deferred to 'future biographers' full discussion of matters that 'are worthy of their closest attention in developing the intricate anomalies of his character.'[22]

The proposed collaboration between Jessopp and Gosse never materialized, however. In the preface to *The Life and Letters of John Donne, Dean of St. Paul's* Gosse praised Jessopp's 'excellent article' in the *DNB* and told how his own belief that 'Donne is quintessentially a poet' had finally precluded their working together. Ultimately, Gosse got Jessopp to hand over the materials that he had gathered. Thanking Jessopp for this 'unexampled generosity', Gosse proceeded to incorporate the fruits of a vast amount of archival research, much of it devoted to ordering and annotating Donne's letters. It was to the poems that he turned, however, to get at what the letters could not provide, the basis for an account of Donne's early manhood. While Jessopp had seen in the fact that the manuscript poems were 'read out in clubs and coteries' evidence of their having been mere 'trifles', Gosse found that their popularity helped to explain the extraordinary number of imitations that Donne's poems had spawned. Jessopp, for all his apparent naïveté about literary history, nonetheless called attention to a significant difference between what the Victorians had come to expect of love poetry and what readers had sought in the seventeenth century. 'Poetry in those days', Jessopp wrote, 'was not generally accepted as the legitimate language in which the soul might pour forth its nobler thoughts—its longings, its holier sorrows and regrets.' Gosse turned this observation into evidence that Donne had been extraordinarily 'modern', way ahead of his time, and that his verses in fact did contain not only 'nobler thoughts' and 'longings' but the secret record of the poet's lost youth that it was now his responsibility to uncover.[23]

The first three chapters of *The Life and Letters* evince the failed collaboration about as dramatically as it is possible to imagine. Chapter 1 inducts Jessopp fully

---

[22] Gosse's article, 'The Poetry of John Donne', is quoted from the reprint in *Littell's Living Age*, 5th ser., 84 (1893), 435, 432, 433, respectively.

[23] Gosse, *Life and Letters*, i, p. xi; Jessopp, *John Donne Sometime Dean*, 19, 89. Cf. Gosse, 'The Poetry', 435.

into the work of providing a biography that uncovers secrets: acknowledging that we have no information about Donne's experience as a small child, it tells the stories of Donne's staunch Catholic ancestors and relatives that Jessopp had patiently and sometimes courageously uncovered. Chapter 2 then treats the period in the early 1590s when Donne began writing. Here Gosse trots out his strong suit, which had persuaded Jessopp to withdraw. Surveying the late sixteenth-century European literary scene, he places Donne's earliest poems in the broad international context established by Isaac Casaubon's lectures on Persius's satires and in the specifically English context in which they made a mark that distinguished Donne among the sudden vogue for satire in which Hall and Marston and Lodge also participated. More strikingly still, emphasizing Donne's taking up the writing of satire in 1593, when Spenser was in his 'heydey' and lyric, dramatic and pastoral verse in their 'luxuriant blossoming', Gosse sounds a theme that Jessopp was unequipped to imagine: 'from the very first Donne was a rebel against the poetic canons and tendencies of the age' (i. 28–9). Chapter 3 then treats the love poems as just those transcripts of Donne's own personal experience that constitute the most startling revelations Gosse's method has to offer. This section, treating a period from which there seemed to be no surviving correspondence, turned many poems into the virtual equivalent of personal letters. Gosse strung together various erotic poems to create a narrative documenting the course of an affair with a married woman alleged to have taken place in 1596. This work made an utter break with Jessopp's assumptions about the nature of poetic materials and about the nature of biography itself. Years later, in an article on 'biography' for the *Encyclopædia Britannica*, Gosse generalized from the approach he had taken not only with Donne but in his books on Gray and Ralegh, Congreve and Coventry Patmore. A biography, he insisted, must concentrate on the individual. 'Broad views are entirely out of place in biography, and there is perhaps no greater mistake than to attempt what is called the "Life and Times" of a man.' Gosse preferred what he might have called a deep view. In writing the life of Donne, he joined the ranks of that growing number of professionals who were now ascribing ultimate explanatory power to a model of psychology according to which a person's secret life, especially a person's secret sexual life, was to provide the ground for a genuinely satisfying explanation of their public behavior. Gosse's third chapter implicated his Donne volumes in this framework and at last dragged Gosse himself, when Norton reviewed *The Life and Letters*, into the controversial discussion about the practice of biography that, from the 1880s onward, kept coming to a focus in obsessive debates about James Anthony Froude's editorial labors on the papers of Jane and Thomas Carlyle. Lest mention of the Carlyle controversy in which both Stephen and Norton were 'embroiled' for more than twenty years get us ahead of ourselves[24], however, we should first linger over some features of Gosse's own life that help to clarify what was at stake for him in writing on Donne.

THE PLACE OF DONNE'S *LIFE AND LETTERS* IN GOSSE'S CAREER

Gosse's attitudes towards Donne were deeply ambivalent, and he alternated between a resolve to undertake the biography and reluctance to believe that he could pull it off. As a former Clark lecturer who had aspirations to academic respectability, Gosse put himself on trial when he finally carried through the knotty project of editing the letters and presented his findings 'with a thousand apprehensions' (i, p. xii). Thinking about *The Life and Letters* within the perspective of his whole career, it is instructive to notice that Gosse's dramatic revelations of (alleged) dirty secrets in Donne's life—an affair with a married woman, deviling for Somerset, taking holy orders without having an apt spiritual disposition—were offered by a man who spent much of his life (Gosse did not die until 1928) trying to keep his own secret out of sight. Gosse was extremely well connected, and most of his acquaintances seem to have been willing to overlook the carelessness of his scholarship. That he came to enjoy a high reputation as a biographer is attested by the fact that when the eleventh edition of the *Encyclopædia Britannica* was in preparation, it was he who was asked to contribute the article on the subject of 'Biography.' In fact, when the new edition appeared in 1910–11, there was also an entry devoted to Gosse himself, in which readers were informed that he had been made 'chief literary advisor' to the *Encyclopædia* in testimony 'to the high position held by him in the contemporary world of letters.' This unsigned article made no mention of the devastating revelations of Gosse's incompetence that in 1886 had set in motion a scandal that reached the popular press; nor were there any hints of the reputation for inaccuracy that clung to him thereafter, so that at Oxford for instance it was commonly said of someone who produced a howler that he had 'made a Gosse of himself.'[25]

---

[24] As Broughton (*Men of Letters*) points out in a compelling discussion of various grounds on which the whole 'embroilment' mattered, it was Stephen's biographer, F. W. Maitland, who chose this word to describe 'the way many late Victorian intellectuals felt implicated in the whole mess'; see esp. 90.

[25] *Encyclopaedia Britannica*, 11th edn (Cambridge: Cambridge Univ. Press, 1910–11), iii. 953; see also, Evan Charteris, *The Life and Letters of Sir Edmund Gosse* (New York: Harper and Brothers, 1931), 194.

Not having had a university education, Gosse was always eager for academic respectability. As early as 1883 he put himself forward for the newly founded Clark lectureship. The position was awarded to Stephen, whose embarrassment at this he put into a letter to Gosse, suggesting that he probably would not retain the post for long and would do what he could to ensure that his admired friend would succeed him.[26] Meanwhile, Gosse took his aspiring academic show on the road. He lectured at the Lowell Institute in Boston and at the new Johns Hopkins University. He turned down a chair at Yale and, returning to England, did indeed succeed Stephen as Clark lecturer. After Cambridge University Press turned his lectures into a book, Gosse had the humiliating experience at the hands of John Churton Collins that turned out to be 'the central episode' of his literary career.[27] It also profoundly affected the course of his biographical work on Donne, by which he sought to vindicate his reputation.

Gosse's writing on Donne, for all its stylistic verve, its frequent high drama, and its pretensions to scholarly accuracy, belongs to the school previously presided over by Grosart, from whom Gosse borrowed freely and often uncritically. Without acknowledging Grosart as the source of an eccentric theory about the dating of Donne's religious poetry, Gosse's early *Britannica* article asserted that many of the Divine Poems were written in the poet's youth when he was still a sincere Catholic. It also gave wider dissemination to Grosart's surmise that on the rebound from popish ascetical practices Donne had plunged into excesses of another sort. It accepted as genuine the ten sonnets to Philomel and confidently proclaimed that the miscellaneous elegies and lyrics also date from 'early manhood.' Above all, it recapitulated the ambivalence that had marked Grosart's enterprise: 'It is singularly difficult to pronounce a judicious opinion on the writings of Donne,' Gosse wrote, and he went on to offer that mixture of conventional and personal opinion that for the *DNB* Stephen instructed his contributors scrupulously to avoid:

The first impression of an unbiassed reader who dips into the poems of Donne is unfavourable. He is repulsed by the intolerably harsh and crabbed versification, by the recondite choice of theme and expression, and by the oddity of the thought. In time, however, he perceives that behind the fantastic garb of language there is an earnest and vigorous mind, an imagination that harbours fire within its cloudy folds, and an insight into the mysteries of spiritual life which is often startling. Donne excels in brief flashes of wit and beauty, and in sudden daring phrases that have the full perfume of poetry.

[26] Stephen, *Selected Letters*, ii. 301–2.
[27] Ann Thwaite, *Edmund Gosse: A Literary Landscape, 1849–1928* (Chicago: Univ. of Chicago Press, 1984), 277.

A similarly unresolved estimate appeared in Gosse's first monograph on English writers, *Seventeenth Century Studies*, where he acknowledged that he was unable to deal 'adequately' with 'the inscrutable Dean of St. Paul's', who is 'so great and yet so mean' and 'combine[s] within one brain all the virtues and all the vices of the imaginative intellect.'[28]

Ten years later Gosse's article on Donne's poetry for *The New Review* suggested some mitigation of this ambivalence. It concentrated to a great extent on prosody. Yet it also hinted at the course that its author's subsequent work would take when it declared the 'amatory lyrics' the 'most interesting' of the poems. After pronouncing 'The Flea' a 'gross and offensive piece of extravagance', Gosse remarked that ' "The Good-Morrow" ... strikes a very different note.' He then went on to set a detective's problem to which he would present *The Life and Letters* as the solution:

As a rule, these poems are extremely personal, confidential, and vivid; the stamp of life is on them. None the less, while confessing with extraordinary frankness and clearness the passion of the writer, they are so reserved in detail, so immersed and engulfed in secrecy, that no definite conjecture can be hazarded as to the person, or persons, or the class of persons, to whom they were addressed. One or two were evidently inspired by Donne's wife, others most emphatically were not, and by their lawless, though not gross, sensuality remind us of the still more outspoken, 'Elegies.' In spite of the alembicated verbiage, the tortuousness and artificiality of the thought, sincerity burns in every stanza, and the most exquisite images lie side by side with monstrous conceits and ugly pedantries.[29]

In Gosse's book of 1897, *A Short History of Modern English Literature*, there at last came clear the antipathy towards Donne that rendered collaboration with Jessopp impossible. When he presented the lyrics as 'the essence of Donne', he condemned their lack of 'classical shape' and designated the poet as 'the father of all that is exasperating, affected, and "metaphysical" in English poetry.'[30] He also compared the deleterious influence of Donne to that of Carlyle.

That Gosse quite disliked Donne might have precluded his writing a comprehensive biographical memoir. A constellation of circumstances made the task too opportune to pass by. Raoul Granqvist and Clement Wyke have shown that he embraced this 'most imposing task left to the student of Elizabethan and Jacobean literature' in an attempt to shake off the reputation that had bedeviled him ever since Collins exposed the extent of factual error

[28] E.W.G., 'Donne, John', *Encyclopaedia Britannica*, 9th edn (Boston: Little, Brown, 1877), ii. 364–5; *Seventeenth Century Studies* (London: Kegan Paul, Trench, 1883), p. ix.

[29] Gosse, 'The Poetry', 433.

[30] See Edmund Gosse, *A Short History of Modern English Literature* (1897; repr., London: William Heinemann; New York: D. Appleton, 1898), 122–3.

in his most scholarly book.[31] Collins had examined *From Shakespeare to Pope* in his ambitious article for the *Quarterly Review* on 'English Literature at the Universities', the major purport of which was to urge that the study of English literature be instituted and conducted on the highest standards. Illustrating in painstaking and painful detail dozens of errors in Gosse's book, the article insisted that Cambridge University Press should not have given it its imprimatur. *From Shakespeare to Pope* was filled with inaccuracies, especially in the matter of dates; and even where Gosse had got his facts right, he frequently boasted with 'officious egotism' of the discoveries he had made, whereas Collins showed many of these were common knowledge.[32] Humiliated, Gosse wrote to Thomas Hardy that 'the *Quarterly Review* has felled, flayed, eviscerated, pulverized and blown to the winds poor Me in thirty pages of good round abuse.' Although he sought to defend himself in letters to the *Times* and the *Athenæum*, Gosse naturally enough wished to slink from public sight, having been called, as he informed Hardy, a 'charlatan' and 'imposter' and having been shown in several places to have been writing out of 'gross ignorance.' The scandal provided copy for many newspapers and periodicals over the course of several weeks.[33] Collins's larger concern with educational reform was generally ignored, and Cambridge elected Gosse to a second term. The demonstration of the Clark lecturer's dilettantism likely contributed, however, to the delay in instituting an English curriculum. Against the background of scandal and suspicion that clung to his scholarship, Gosse continued to cultivate literary friendships, and he managed to keep on writing. By the late nineties, having suddenly to hand (by what must have seemed to him extraordinary good luck) the fruits of Jessopp's half-century of research, Gosse could not resist an opportunity to reverse the setback he had suffered more than a decade earlier. He set out once again to provide the

---

[31] The idea that Gosse deserves considerable credit as a contributor to the Donne revival has been called into question. See Clement H. Wyke, 'Edmund Gosse as Biographer and Critic of Donne: His Fallible Role in the Poet's Rediscovery', *Texas Studies in Literature and Language*, 17 (1975–6), 805–19; Raoul Granqvist, 'Edmund Gosse: The Reluctant Critic of John Donne', *Neuphilologische Mitteilungen*, 87 (1986), 262–71, and 'The Reception of Edmund Gosse's *Life of John Donne*', *English Studies*, 67 (1986), 525–38.

[32] See Phillip Mallett, 'Edmund Gosse', in *The Dictionary of Literary Biography*, cxliv: *Nineteenth-Century British Literary Biographers* (Detroit: Bruccoli Clark Layman, 1994), 139.

[33] Gosse's letter to Hardy is dated 17 Oct.; see Charteris, 198–9. Gosse wrote to the *Times* on 19 Oct., and his letter is quoted by Thwaite, *Edmund Gosse*, 286–7. His self-defense appeared in the *Athenæum* on 23 Oct., and its modesty did much to confirm the surmise that many wished to make, according to which Collins must have been harboring some personal malice. The Houghton Library at Harvard holds (shelf-mark: *EC85.G6951.888l [B]) a rare volume ascribed to Gosse and titled *Reply to the Quarterly Review*. It contains hand-written letters by Gosse and his wife and copies of several defenses, mostly but not exclusively by Gosse himself, that were published in Oct. and Nov. 1886.

definitive study of Donne for which an unprecedented number of readers was now waiting.

The *Life and Letters* contributed significantly to a better understanding of Donne. Especially important was its dissemination of poems, letters, and other materials from the valuable manuscript that since Donne's lifetime had been in the library of the Earls of Westmoreland and that Gosse acquired in the early 1890s. As the most widely reviewed work on Donne that had ever been published, Gosse's biography aroused further interest and provoked new study. It warranted reprinting sixty years after it first appeared, and R. C. Bald professed to hold in esteem Gosse's 'many and great' contributions to the study of Donne.[34] Yet, as Dennis Flynn has observed, most of what is valuable in the two volumes likely derives from Jessopp. Gosse was so prolific a writer and so busy cultivating his relations with the literati that he had little time, much less any inclination, to do the sort of archival research necessary to order and annotate the tangled mass of Donne's letters.[35] Nor did he avail himself of the opportunity to have Jessopp check the volumes before they went to press; it would have been all too obvious how much of his former collaborator's work had been made to look as if it were Gosse's own.

What was distinctly not Jessopp's in the *Life and Letters* was the conviction that the key to devising an adequate account lay in the love poems and Holy Sonnets. Gosse regarded these poems as offering unparalleled access to his subject's private, individual experience. He claimed that his biographical researches had included repeated scrutiny of the erotic poems, which had required him to surmount 'dangers.' He acknowledged, only to dismiss them, that there were perils involved in 'conjectural reconstruction.' The amatory verses of Spenser and Drayton were said to be beyond the capacities of the 'most ingenious reader' because they provide too 'shadowy and nebulous [a] basis [for] any superstructure of conjectural biography' (i. 61). The fact that Donne's love verses were not printed in his lifetime, however, made them a special case. The 'curious alternations of cautious reserve and bold confession' in the poems proved they were 'sincere' and confirmed Gosse's surmise that there was something 'which could not be confessed' (i. 78). There are 'few cases in literary history', he alleged, where the 'method' of conjectural reconstruction is 'more legitimate than here' (i. 62). Although Donne's life between 1592 and 1602 'is shrouded in a mist' (i. 55) and his movements are 'tantalisingly concealed' behind 'smoke and twilight' (i. 59), his poems have 'so convincing' an 'accent … that it is impossible not to believe' they

[34] R. C. Bald, *John Donne: A Life* (Oxford and New York: Oxford Univ. Press, 1970), 18.
[35] Flynn's observation was offered as an integral part of his reflections on writing Donne's biography, delivered in his presidential address to the John Donne Society in 1999.

contain 'the accurate record of a genuine emotional event' (i. 62). What the biographer needs, Gosse explained at the outset, is 'some intrepidity and a great deal of patience' to make the letters 'tell a consecutive and intelligible tale' (i, pp. vii–viii). By the time he reached Chapter 3, he had added to the prose letters the lyric poems: 'It will be our business in the present biography', he remarked, 'to break up this inchoate mass of verses, and to redistribute it as carefully as possible, so as to let it illustrate the life of its author' (i. 60–1).

Eager to reveal Donne's darkest secrets, Gosse proceeded like an alchemist, trying by repeated readings to turn up new discoveries. He charged all other biographers since Walton with 'attempting to conceal those tenebrous and fiery evidences' (i. 63) of Donne's youth, when 'a magnificent rebel', 'one of the most headstrong and ingenious intellects of the century', was 'concentrating itself on the evolution of its own *vita sexualis*' (i. 69). In the hands of a trained biographer, Gosse insisted, 'there is hardly a piece of his genuine verse which, cryptic though it may seem, cannot be prevailed upon to deliver up some secret of his life and character' (i. 62). Famously, Gosse turned up from the lyrics and elegies a secret history of Donne's sexual awakening. Less famously, he extracted from the Holy Sonnets 'the accent' of someone 'who has discovered the truth so late, and has such a sense of the passage of time and of the nearness of his dissolution, that he hardly dares to hope that he may yet work for God' (ii. 106–7).

Lest he be mistaken for a betrayer of professional secrets, Gosse presented his work as a sort of joint enterprise into which the reader was invited to enter: 'careful study' of Donne's case, 'after twenty readings' had led to a breaking of 'the first obscure crust' and the revelation of 'a condition of mind and even a sequence of events so personal, that we hardly dare to take our legitimate advantage from it' (i. 61–2). Inasmuch as it was Donne's own imprudence in leaving behind intimately revealing verses, it is allowable 'to reconstruct the story', as there is almost no 'danger of a mistake' that might misrepresent the truth (i. 67). Although Donne had come to consider his youthful verses as 'scandalous or trivial', he had not been able to 'bring himself to destroy them.' 'We feel that no outrage on his memory was performed in the act of their posthumous publication,' Gosse concludes, for 'he had expected all along to be ultimately pushed up the slopes of Helicon, faintly resisting' (i. 60). Gosse readily embraced Grosart's justification for seeking secret truths on the grounds that his interest was scholarly and not merely prurient and that the revelation of secrets was likely to produce healthy moral lessons. 'To pretend that Donne was a saint in his youth', Gosse urged, 'is to nullify the very process of divine grace in the evolution of a complex soul, in the reduction of a magnificent rebel to a still more brilliant and powerful servant' (i. 63). Son of a zoologist that he was, Gosse nonetheless presented his own work as scientific only up to a point. When he came to conclude his account, he once again renewed the language of mystery: Donne was 'surely the most undulating, the most diverse of human beings.'

Splendid and obscure he was, in the extreme versatility and passion, the profundity, the saintliness, the mystery of his inscrutable character. No one, in the history of English literature, as it seems to me, is so difficult to realise, so impossible to measure, in the vast curves of his extraordinary and contradictory features. Of his life, of his experiences, of his opinions, we know more now than it has been vouchsafed to us to know of any other of the great Elizabethan and Jacobean galaxy of writers, and yet how little we fathom his contradictions, how little we can account for his impulses and his limitations. Even those of us who have for years made his least adventures the subject of close and eager investigation must admit at last that he eludes us. (ii. 290)

Along with this invitation for the reader to render him praise and thanks, Gosse expressed again his abiding ambivalence about his subject.

Not long after the book was published, Richard Garnett praised it as being 'both entirely sympathetic and entirely scientific', so that it 'commands our full assent.' An anonymous writer in *Book Reviews* claimed that 'Mr. Gosse has made every factor in Donne's life comprehensible and even inevitable' and praised for their 'special excellence' the chapters in which he had made biography out of Donne's lyrical poems.[36] Not all reviews were so positive. In criticizing *The Life and Letters* reviewers isolated three features of Gosse's portrait in particular: one reviewer pointed out that Gosse's vicious treatment of Donne's relations with Somerset was based on his having confused John with the jurist Sir Daniel Donne (Dun); many questioned whether the poems show that Donne actually carried on an affair with a married woman in 1596; and several expressed skepticism about the claim that the preacher had experienced a belated religious conversion after the death of his wife in 1617. Writing to the *Athenæum* about the 'novel theory as to Donne's late "conversion"', H. C. Beeching exposed the dubious grounds on which Gosse had dated certain letters in which he claimed to find evidence of Donne's lack of spiritual ardor in the early years of his priesthood. He also pointed out that we might expect the sermons of any newly ordained man of middle age to carry signs that he was still learning his craft.[37]

---

[36] Richard Garnett, 'Mr. Gosse's Life of Donne', *The Bookman*, 10 (1899), 583; *Book Reviews*, 7 (1899), 483.

[37] Beeching wrote three letters to the *Athenæum*, all of which were published under the heading 'The Life of Donne': 3761 (25 Nov. 1899), 723; 3762 (2 Dec. 1899), 760; and 3764 (16 Dec. 1899), 836. Along with the last of Beeching's contributions, the *Athenæum* published a letter from Arthur Vincent revealing that a document supporting the Lady Frances Howard's nullity suit ascribed by Gosse (and Jessopp before him) to John Donne was actually written by Sir Daniel Dun, 'one of the commissioners who tried the case' (836).

THE MOMENT OF DONNE'S CONVERSION

From Gosse's point of view, there was a compelling logic in his theory of a late conversion: it made sense of Donne's failure to mark a clear difference between the Roman Catholic and Anglican periods of his life. Where Walton had written approvingly of Donne's having 'betrothed himself to no religion that might give him any other denomination than a Christian', Gosse took the Christianity of Donne's youth to be an empty category. He presented Donne in the years when he was working for Bishop Morton as a cynical Catholic who had put himself out for hire. At the same time Gosse repeatedly took opportunities to call attention to evidence that even in his maturity Donne remained deeply indebted to his Catholic upbringing. He made a good deal of the fact that the three sonnets unique to the Westmoreland manuscript had never been printed. He suggested that there had been a conspiracy on the part of the editors of the 1633 and 1635 editions to suppress them 'because of the leaning which they betrayed to certain Romish doctrines' (ii. 109). Readers who consulted Gosse's Appendix C, where he included these poems, would find there Donne's representation of his sexual rivalry with the deity, his playful depiction of the cuckolding of God, and his frank admission of the 'contraries' within him that held him back from whole-hearted commitment. If these details were not convenient for Gosse's theory that the sonnets had been written after Donne's conversion, at least what was offensive in them could be laid at the door of popish religion.

Gosse's hatred for popery was of long standing and was thoroughgoing. Smelling out 'popery' was just the sort of thing that he had been trained to do from his earliest years, when his father, Philip Gosse, taught him how much 'the so-called Church of England' had in common with 'the so-called Church of Rome.' In *Father and Son*, the son contrasts the moment in which he is writing, which is 'loose and indifferent' and regards enthusiastic expressions of contempt for Catholics as 'illiberal', with the olden days in which the Brethren with whom he was raised made 'flaming denunciations of the Papacy.' 'I have no longer the slightest wish myself to denounce the Roman communion,' Gosse writes, 'but if it is to be done, I have an idea that the latter-day Protestants do not know how to do it.' He then castigates liberals who 'make concessions and allowances' and 'put on gloves to touch the accursed thing.'[38] No such

---

[38] Edmund Gosse's *Father and Son: A Study of Two Temperaments* was first published anonymously in 1907. It is quoted throughout from the 3rd American edn, subtitled *Biographical Recollections* and published in Gosse's own name (New York: Charles Scribner's Sons, 1908), 98.

charge could be brought against his portrait of Donne's early manhood when in his 'enslavement to the flesh' (ii. 109) he had been busy reaping what his popish upbringing had sowed. Gosse ferreted out in graphic detail what 'some of the most sensual poetry written in the history of English literature' (i. 69–70) revealed about the activities of a man whose conscience had been 'entirely emancipated' and whose 'religious sense was occupied exclusively with the scholastic skeleton of dogma' (i. 67). The 'early writings' are 'full of the pagan riot of the senses, and far indeed from any trace of the pietist or the precision' (i. 27); they show that for many years Donne lived 'without the outward decencies and rudimentary principles of piety' (ii. 100). Only late in his life was Donne delivered from the vice in which he had wallowed. Gosse took as a key piece of evidence the sonnet that begins 'Since she whom I loved hath paid her last debt' and propounded the theory that after Anne More's soul had been 'early into heav'n ravishéd' Donne at last 'became "converted" in the intense and incandescent sense' of the term (ii. 99). To get the poem to support this theory, he cut short his quotation before the lines in which the poet speaks of his beloved as having been an occasion of grace while she lived: 'Here the admiring her my mind did whet | To seek Thee, God.' For Gosse, Donne had been saved by the God who took away his wife and assigned him the widower's lot.

Jessopp had observed that after his wife's death Donne threw himself into preaching. Gosse took up this idea and found evidence in the poetry to reveal that a religious transformation had taken place: 'he dedicated himself anew to God with a peculiar violence of devotion' (ii. 99). Not just a new chapter but a whole new life had opened up, the one that Walton had witnessed, although as devout members of the Church of England Walton and Jessopp were unable to make plain its workings. Gosse acknowledged that readers would evaluate evidence of the transformation according to their differing 'tempers', but assumed that virtually anyone could appreciate that the paradigm of a life split dramatically in two by an evangelical conversion would explain Donne's first forty years much better than Walton had. 'Those who are in the habit of observing the religious life of others with attention', Gosse writes at the opening of his chapter on the years 1617–1621 (apparently without irony and certainly attempting to distance his penetrating gaze from Walton's 'rose-coloured' spectacles),

are familiar, in whatever temper they may regard it, with the spiritual phenomenon which is known as 'conversion.' It is not a matter of conviction or works, though the first may produce and the second result from it; nor is it in any degree universal among those who are eminent for piety and unction. It may come to the most and to the least instructed; it is a state of soul, a psychological condition abruptly reached by some, and not reached at all by many. Some pass into it who afterwards pass out again into indifferentism; some never experience the sudden advent of it, although their fidelity to the faith persists unshaken.   (ii. 99)

Gosse himself had long since ceased to consider himself a Christian when he wrote this. When he first took an interest in Donne in the 1870s, he was bravely proclaiming himself an atheist,[39] though not to his father, who, as he would record in *Father and Son*,

always insisted on the necessity of conversion. There must be a new birth and being, a fresh creation in God. This crisis he was accustomed to regard as manifesting itself in a sudden and definite upheaval. There might have been prolonged practical piety, deep and true contrition for sin, but these, although the natural and suitable prologue to conversion, were not conversion itself. People hung on at the confines of regeneration, often for a very long time. ... Such persons were in a gracious state, but they were not in a state of grace. If they should suddenly die, they would pass away in an unconverted condition.[40]

In the treatment of Donne's religious experience in *The Life and Letters*, Gosse generously (as he thought) resorted to the dogmatic categories his father had provided. These conspicuously included the belief that religious conversion 'manifests itself in a sudden and definite upheaval' and then resolves itself 'on some day, at some hour and minute.' Gosse, as one who had been accustomed from his youth among the Brethren in Devonshire carefully to observe 'the religious life of others', was thereby equipped to discern that Donne, even after he had taken holy orders, remained unconverted. 'And, without question' Donne's own awareness of this 'was at the base of the long vacillation and delay in adopting the ... entirely inevitable profession of priest' (ii. 101). Here at last was the answer to the question that Jessopp's *DNB* article had raised about the nature of the scruples that for so long kept Donne out of the church. To Gosse's mind Donne's long resistance to an evangelical conversion also explained the frigidly intellectual nature of so much of his verse. Once he had this answer, Gosse also had a structure for his narrative that would differentiate his interpretation from Walton's. Adapting from Grosart the paradigm according to which grace abounds to a sinner, Gosse relocated the time, if not altogether the source, of Donne's conversion: it took place not by virtue of his marrying a good woman but by virtue of his having lost her.

The first eleven chapters of *The Life and Letters* are thus made to serve as an elaborate confession of the sinful past. Gosse, whom his father had designed for the ministry and taught to ask 'leading questions' of candidates for baptism,[41] served as Donne's interpreter, reconstructing from his words the requisite

---

[39] See Thwaite, *Edmund Gosse*, chap. 5.
[40] Gosse, *Father and Son*, 191.   [41] See ibid. 193.

rehearsal of sins: how he had been mired in popery and licentiousness, what his venal motives had been in the years after his marriage and how they had led him to display a desperate obsequiousness to the head of the established church and his corrupt ministers, and what hypocritical shows of religious piety he had made as a newly ordained minister. Gosse's Donne had proceeded into a sacred calling without having that experimental knowledge and feeling of faith that were prerequisites for an authentic Christian ministry. As a self-appointed confidant to Donne, Gosse forgave him, as it were, in view of a sudden and extraordinary occurrence that could be pinpointed, on the basis of a reading of the religious sonnets, to the winter of 1617.

What is remarkable about Gosse's novel theory is the slender, dubious, and ultimately circular evidence that he presents to support it. 'The immediate result of Donne's recovery from the depression caused by his wife's death, and of his subsequent ecstasy of spiritual life, was the composition of two cycles of sonnets' (ii. 104). After presenting *La Corona* as indicative of 'Donne's new attitude to religion' and claiming that its seven poems must be nearly identical with the six said in the title of the verse letter 'To E. of D.' to have been included with it,[42] Gosse illustrates the poet's new religious 'unction' by turning to the Holy Sonnets. Here he finds that the poet has left behind abundant evidence that he had passed through the requisite crisis; at last 'the voice of personal emotion is more clearly audible than anywhere else in the religious poetry' (ii. 106). In presenting these poems as evidence of Donne's belated conversion, Gosse simply assumed that each one transparently records the poet's own experience. He also took for granted that all nineteen sonnets found in the Westmoreland manuscript were written at the same time. This meant that his discovery that one of them must have been composed after Anne's death solved for all of them the question when they were written. This surmise rivaled for naïveté the theory according to which the lyric poems prove Donne's involvement in a messy extramarital affair.

LESLIE STEPHEN

It was Gosse's theory of Donne's religious conversion, however, that prompted the leading biographer in the English-speaking world to declare his hand.

---

[42] In claiming that *La Corona* belonged to the period just after Donne's conversion, Gosse took a hint from Chambers's presentation of 'To E. of D.' in the Muses' Library edition. In order to secure the poems for this late date, Gosse went through an elaborate set of moves to identify the addressee as Lord Hay, Viscount Doncaster. On the vexed history of trying to identify the recipient and the specific poems, see Dennis Flynn, ' "Awry and Squint": The Dating of Donne's Holy Sonnets', *JDJ*, 7 (1988), 35–46.

Jessopp's entries in the *DNB* had piqued Stephen's interest in Donne. If Jessopp's book of 1897 added little, from Stephen's point of view it was nonetheless significant in having demonstrated that Walton's portrait of Donne's religious nature could not be made to disappear simply by doing some scholarly research. A thoroughgoing reinterpretation was needed, and for a time there had been reason to assume that Gosse would provide it. When, instead of demolishing Walton's interpretation, Gosse enlisted Nonconformity's evangelical paradigm and located the religious turning point in Donne's life a few years later than Walton had, Stephen decided that he would bring the truth to light himself. In his essay on Donne for the *National Review* he substituted for Walton's 'ardent panegyric' a genuinely secular interpretation. 'For explanation' of Donne's life, Stephen declared with his familiar mixture of faint praise and cutting irony,

one has hitherto been referred to the admirable Izaak Walton. His life of Donne is said to be the masterpiece of English biography. ... If, indeed, the book is to be read as we read *The Vicar of Wakefield*—as a prose idyl—a charming narrative in which we have as little to do with the reality of Donne as with the reality of Dr. Primrose, I can only subscribe to the judgment of my betters. But there are two objections to the life if taken as a record of facts. The first is that the framework of fact is of the flimsiest; and the second that the portraiture has a palpably 'subjective' element.   (38)

Stephen might have gone on to discuss Gosse's *Life and Letters*, had he not so clearly recognized that he would have had to say virtually the same things about it. When he revised his essay and incorporated it into *Studies of a Biographer*, Norton read it and upbraided him for not taking occasion to expose Gosse's 'false pretenses, his misinterpretations, his worse than schoolboy mistakes.' Stephen replied that he had known all along that Norton was going to complain that he had gone too easy on Gosse. 'The simple truth is', he confided, 'that Gosse is a personal friend—though not in a high rank among friends. ... The poor man gets so many kicks & suffers from them so acutely that I resolved to hold my tongue as to his defects.' In fact, Stephen was holding his tongue even here. In writing for the *DNB* he had often, as for instance in the article on Gray, relied on Gosse's scholarship only to discover later his errors.[43]

Norton's disappointment notwithstanding, Stephen's essay made as powerful a critique of Gosse's interpretation as it did of Walton's. In order to make his own estimate of Donne, Stephen relied upon Gosse for the raw materials.

[43] Leslie Stephen, 'John Donne', *National Review*, 34 (1899), 595–613; parenthetical references given in the text pertain to the revised version in *Studies of a Biographer*, 2nd ser., iii. 36–82 (New York: G. P. Putnam's Sons; London: Duckworth, 1902); Stephen, *Selected Letters*, ii. 533; Norton is quoted in the endnote, 534. Charteris (190–1) gives details of some errors in the *DNB* for which Gosse was responsible.

He also did some reading in Donne's works, and although he admitted that he had not got very far in the sermons, he offered some of the shrewdest commentary on the rhetoric and style of Donne's prose since De Quincey. He had no truck with Gosse's interpretations of Donne's poems and acknowledged that, like Jessopp, he did not hold the poetry in high esteem: 'I rarely get to the end, even of the shortest [poem], without being repelled by some strange discord in form or in substance which sets my teeth on edge' (37). Yet he saw more clearly than any previous critic what Donne was doing with his displays of 'metaphysical' learning. Thirsting for all kinds of knowledge, Donne had for a time lost himself in 'omnivorous studies of divinity and philosophy' and he 'had studied the application of the art [of logic] to casuistry', so that what now strike readers as 'unaccountable conceits are simply applications' to the writing of verse of the 'still dominant scholastic philosophy' taught in the universities (48–50). Unprepared as Stephen was to deal with Donne's experiments in form and prosody, he aimed to do what he did best: to place the poems in intellectual history, gently questioning whether 'Mr. Gosse does not attribute to Donne too much of deliberate and conscious literary revolt' (45). Stephen handled Jessopp's pretensions for Donne in a similar manner, questioning whether *Pseudo-Martyr* amounted to anything more than 'mere by-play' in an ephemeral dispute between Romanists and Anglicans (60–1). Stephen's exasperation with Walton's hagiographical portrait, with Jessopp's claims for Donne's learned contributions to Anglican polemics, and with Gosse's narrative about a rake who eventually got religion shows up only occasionally as impatience with Donne himself. Stephen knew quite well the grounds on which he might identify himself with Donne, and he knew where he differed from him.

While Donne had gone late into the church to which his family had steadfastly remained outsiders, as a young man Stephen had taken deacon's orders in that church and been ordained a priest as a precondition for the academic career to which he aspired. In the early 1860s, however, when he was a fellow and chaplain at Trinity Hall, he gave up his faith. He later described the event as 'not discovering that my creed was false, but that I had never really believed it.'[44] Stephen remained for some time in Cambridge, working for academic reform, and then finally resigned from the church, an action that, given Trinity's regulations, required him to leave the university. He was then in his early thirties, a man without a position. He was, moreover, barred from a political career (for example, standing for Parliament) by virtue of his being a clergyman. At last his brother helped him to find work as a writer, and he readily discovered that high journalism offered a platform from which

---

[44] Leslie Stephen, 'Some Early Impressions', *National Review*, 42 (1903), 214.

he could exercise his reforming energies. Stephen's many articles and reviews on religious topics show that already in the 1860s and 1870s he had taken up as his new life's work the project of transferring cultural authority from the church and the university to freethinking intellectuals and writers.

During his years as a journalist, Stephen witnessed with increasing anxiety the revival of various religious forces in England that seemed to him a threat to social progress. Von Arx has demonstrated that the conservatism characteristic of his jeremiads in the 1880s and 1890s, which so often expressed itself in the language of 'pessimism' that Stephen also enlists in the essay on Donne, was already latent in the early journal articles. These were written in the years after the restoration of the Catholic hierarchy and amidst the new Ritualism of the High Church, and often, as in the essay titled 'Matthew Arnold and the Church of England', expressly against the claims of the Broad Church to offer England's best hope for national unity.[45] Suspicious of alliances among diverse religious groups who were refusing to dwell on their old differences, and of a toleration based not on skepticism but on a respect for others who had also worked hard to develop a mature faith, Stephen tried valiantly in the face of large-scale changes in religion to hold resurgent religious groups responsible for positions to which their forebears had historically been committed and that he regarded as socially harmful. Meanwhile, he styled himself and other freethinkers as above the fray. This ploy became increasingly difficult to sustain, however, and Stephen's transfer of energy to writing on intellectual history and then to editing the *Dictionary* enabled him at least to maintain a semblance of detachment. As a historian he could work against religious ideas and movements by presenting them as retrograde and by showing that society had developed beyond the stages during which it was generally assumed that they had some validity.

Donne was a trouble to Stephen because his religious attitudes were maddeningly conciliatory and accommodating. The very thing that had made his sermons attractive to Walton—'that their main character [was] not controversial but holy', to borrow the words of George Herbert—qualified Donne in the later nineteenth century to be considered a pillar of a tolerant and potentially comprehensive *via media*. As Beeching pointed out, Donne sought to soften the 'fierce controversial style' of preachers in his day. He deprecated the casual abuse by which polemicists invoked the term 'heresy' when they encountered differences from their own opinions. While he was prepared to expose the fallacy of pseudo-martyrdom and the 'pretensions

---

[45] See von Arx, chap. 2, 'Leslie Stephen: Inventing the Progressive Tradition.' For bibliographical details about the relevant articles, see 215 n. 'Matthew Arnold and the Church of England' appeared in *Fraser's Magazine*, new ser., ii (1870), 414–31.

of Calvinistic omniscience', 'with a fine religious tact' he steered a middle course and refused 'to be deterred by any shibboleths from welcoming truth' in whatever corner he found it.[46]

Nonetheless, Donne was of interest to Stephen because his life narrative partly anticipated the larger story that intellectual history had to tell. The opening sentence of Stephen's account proclaims Donne 'intermittently fascinating.' Its first paragraphs launch a more interesting textual erotics than one finds in Grosart or Gosse when, developing a more sophisticated form of ambivalence, Stephen goes on to confess that he is 'attracted as much as repelled' by Donne himself (37). In a spirit similar to that in which Gosse had finally owned that his subject was unknowable and in which Garnett denominated Donne a 'perpetual puzzle', Stephen announced that the basis of his fascination with a man who had been 'involved in the great religious struggles' of his time was that 'events conspired to make life one long problem in casuistry for Donne himself' (40). Donne seemed to have broken free from the religious 'chain' tied round him in his youth by a band of zealots. He had liberated himself from 'intellectual fetters' (42–3) and 'his early prejudices drop[ped] off' (64). Donne, too, had known what it was to be excluded from the universities on religious grounds, and what it was to be without a position and to have one's prospects severely curtailed. He, too, had turned to political writing and in his *Biathanatos* and other works had anticipated 'some recent pessimists' (62).

What most puzzled Stephen about Donne was that, having once achieved 'by the force of reason' a 'neutral position' on questions of religion (42–3), he then went backwards, into the church. The 'palpably "subjective" element' in Walton's account was the act of ascribing this to the workings of providence. Gosse, at least, had understood that what had been 'inevitable' in Donne's life's story was not, as Walton naïvely thought, that his embrace of a sacred calling coincided with his sanctification according to a divinely appointed pattern. It was simply the command of a secular King, who as far as Gosse was concerned was emphatically not the head of any genuine church. Even as Gosse had answered, in shrill tones, 'A thousand times, no!' to the question whether Donne had been 'insincere and ungodly' when he accepted 'the profession of the Church' (ii. 99), he detailed the venal motives mixed into Donne's decision. For his part, Stephen saw Donne as 'a man full of scruples', adding that they were 'intellectual' as well as 'moral', and he proposed that had Donne accepted Morton's offer even his friends would have understood that the act was cowardly and that his 'main motive was of the worldly kind.'

---

[46] H. C. Beeching, 'The Spirit of the English Church, as Exhibited in the Literature of the Seventeenth Century', *Religio Laici* (London: Smith, Elder, 1902), 72, 64, 63, respectively.

Ultimately, Donne's 'whole career was forced upon him, not carved out by his own taste', which sometimes led him to drift and often, as in the 'blunder' of his marriage (63), impelled him to act on the basis of his 'thirst for pleasure' (59–60). Although there was 'a strain of the Hamlet in Donne' and the treatise on self-murder shows that he was willing to explore 'the finest imaginable case of casuistry', in the years before his ordination 'this most complex and perplexing character' was ultimately 'confused' and 'distracted' (63–4).

When Stephen revised his essay, he added a long section in which he firmly denied that Donne underwent 'a transformation of character' (66). In accord with the sorts of argument he had repeatedly made against active religious groups in his own time (that their Christianity, far from being admirable, entailed morally reprehensible positions such as the doctrines of the atonement and of eternal rewards and punishments), he granted Donne whatever 'sincerity' his religious apologists wished to claim for him. He then insisted with respect to sincerity that its genuine character 'does not prove that it did not include some elements rather repulsive than admirable' (67). 'A man, I fancy, may most sincerely believe all the thirty-nine articles, and be deeply religious, and yet be a bigot and a sour and selfish fanatic, content to save his own soul and to resign himself, complacently or savagely, to the damnation of his fellow creatures' (66). Stephen gathered up all the evidence he could to make the case against saintliness. Donne accepted preferments and 'comfortable addition[s] to his income, involving no increase of duty' (67). He transacted the marriage of his eldest daughter 'in a purely commercial spirit' (68). He used his massive learning to hold congregations in his spell and, by the 'weight of [the] many great names' he invoked, to warn 'the ignorant … not to presume' to have opinions of their own (72). He fawned before the monarch, who 'for him is scarcely short of an earthly god', and hypocritically praised James's disgracefully profligate court, though 'nobody knew better than Donne what was the moral purity of the favourites' (73).

Disdainful of clergymen as he had become, it did not occur to Stephen that when Donne preached before James on Proverbs 22:11 ('He that loveth pureness of heart, for the grace of his lips the king shall be his friend'), he could scarcely have chosen 'a better text', as Beeching deftly observed, with which to put a startling challenge 'without risk of treason.'[47] The most effective feature of Stephen's essay was his profound denial of sympathy to a figure whom

---

[47] Beeching was moved by the Donne article in the *National Review* to contribute to Stephen's old organ, the *Cornhill*, an 'apology' for 'Izaak Walton's Life of Donne', 3rd ser., 8 (1900), 249–68; quoted here from 267. Beeching's telling criticisms prompted the principal expansions found in the version Stephen published in *Studies of a Biographer*.

he consistently damned with faint praise. Whereas Gosse had been willing, when he introduced his theory of an evangelical conversion, to allow that readers of various 'tempers' on questions respecting religion would draw their own conclusions from his demonstration of Donne's transformation, Stephen addressed a knowing reader who would share his skepticism about religious conversion. He wrote to score points against those who wished to place a positive construction on Donne's sincerity. As his ironic assimilation of 'the masterpiece of English biography' to Goldsmith's vulgar 'prose idyl' shows, Stephen's treatment of Donne was marked by a consistently condescending tone. The rhetorical strategy he enlisted substituted for Walton's implied reader, whose 'ingenuous' character betrays naïve credulity, a sophisticated fellowship of freethinkers, who recognize that religious interpretations are at best the functional equivalent of those illusions knowingly indulged by readers of fiction. In this way Stephen sought to make readers who would credit a theological perspective feel their exclusion from the brave new world of intellectual respectability, in which suspensions of disbelief were temporary and made condescendingly. Yet as he condemned Walton's hagiography, Stephen may have protested too much. His denial of religiously conscientious experience to Donne was congruent with his consistent denial to biographers, and to himself as an autobiographer manqué, of 'narratives of inward events, conversions or spiritual crises' on the grounds that, as Trev Broughton has shown, accounts of agonizing inner experiences are abnormal and unmanly.[48] Still, Stephen's assiduously secular treatment of Donne shows that he could not resist turning the old categories on those who still lived by them. Tangled in his own ways in the business of observing the religious life of others with attention, Stephen sought to wish away the religious perspective not only of Walton but finally of Donne himself. As a judge operating in the ultimate court of letters, he pronounced that for all Donne's talent and energy he had 'become obsolete because he belonged so completely to the dying epoch' (80).

To the revised version of his essay Stephen also added a new conclusion that held out hope that Donne would eventually be freed from the clutches of those who bestow 'eulogies' upon his religion. He identified Donne's 'conviction that man's nature is corrupt, and that the great majority will be damned' with the modern 'pessimism' for which he himself was a spokesman, and sought to score a final point, urging how unlike Donne's 'misanthropical sentiments' and 'melancholy' were to 'the amiable and optimistic view of the universe which seems to be generally taken as religious by modern preachers' (81–2). In this way Stephen hedged his bets and even proved prophetic. If the vogue

---

[48] See Broughton, *Men of Letters*, 6, 16–17.

for Donne turned out to be lasting, his essay would also have lasting value, because it demonstrated that the cultural authority attached to Donne's name was so ambiguous that it could as readily be enlisted to undermine as to support the forces that the preacher had been made to serve.

CHARLES ELIOT NORTON AND AN ANTI-BIOGRAPHICAL CRITICISM

Given how much Norton and Stephen shared in their concern to establish the cultural authority of men of letters, it is striking that the grounds of Norton's objections to Gosse were quite different from those which had to do with Donne's religion. As a life-long New Englander and the son of a Unitarian clergyman, Norton came from a tradition of established dissent. From Stephen's perspective this was no oxymoron but a manifest contradiction in terms. Norton belonged to a university that had never been tied to the Roman or Anglican communions and that had, in fact, been founded to train ministers in an ecclesiastical politics that precisely rejected the claims of those churches. Moreover, although Norton was known to be agnostic, President Charles W. Eliot of Harvard had courted him and had persuaded the Overseers to reverse the requirement by which only Christians were hired onto the faculty. In short, Norton lived and worked in a climate where he could afford to be less aggressive than Stephen about the secular premises on which he went about his work.

Norton was also a puritan in some relevant senses of the term. His precision and fastidiousness equipped him especially well to undertake the editing of Donne's poems, on which he exercised greater care than any previous editor. At the same time, in the face of what Stephen called the 'frank disregard of decency' (47) in much of Donne's poetry, Norton displayed more ambivalence than his English friend. His norms for editorial precision were made abundantly clear in 'The Text of Donne's Poems', when he illustrated in detail Grosart's 'pedantry', 'carelessness', and 'lack of intelligence.'[49] To most readers who encountered this study it must not have been immediately apparent why Norton thought a demonstration of Grosart's incompetence necessary. The Fuller Worthies' edition was nearly twenty-five years old, and the Muses' Library and Grolier Club editions were obviously superior to it.

---

[49] Charles Eliot Norton, 'The Text of Donne's Poems', in *Studies and Notes in Philology and Literature*, v: *Child Memorial Volume* (Boston: Ginn, 1896), 3.

Yet Norton's vilifying attack can be explained partly on the grounds that once he took up responsibility for completing James Russell Lowell's edition for the Grolier Club he had discovered how consistently negligent Grosart had been. And there was the more personal consideration: whereas Stephen had had to act with polite discretion in dropping Grosart as a contributor to the *Dictionary*, as a distant and anonymous reviewer Norton felt free to give his friend's enemy his due. Other grounds for Norton's extended demonstration of Grosart's editorial blundering can be recognized, moreover, when we consider the dynamics of nineteenth-century discourse that ostensibly evades sex. The quarrel that Norton had with Grosart and ultimately with Gosse belongs within the context of a late Victorian culture that was not so much refusing to recognize sex as it was finding ways of talking about it as a powerful and decisive secret, a secret to be shared by a group of initiates.[50]

If like other Victorian admirers of Donne Norton felt a deep ambivalence in the face of the poet's sensuality, the similarities between his and Grosart's expressions of it hide deeply felt differences. Grosart's preface played upon the potentially prurient interests of his intended readers, virtually inviting them to look for the poems that the editor 'deplored.' Norton, who affirmed Ben Jonson's estimate of Donne as 'the first poet in the world in some things', was genuinely dismayed that this poet had ever written pieces such as 'The Flea' and 'The Indifferent.' In the preface to the Grolier edition he remarked that 'few, capable of such high reaches as he, sink lower than he at times descends' (i, p. xvii). Norton freely acknowledged that he was troubled by the prospect that a writer of so sublime a poem as 'The Autumnal' may have had the sorts of experiences represented in other elegies. He deeply regretted that the 'robes of Donne's sacred muse get sadly smirched by contact with his verses of the stews' (i. 225). Elsewhere, commenting on 'A Valediction Forbidding Mourning', he sought to dismiss what he considered Donne's less worthy love poems by distancing them from their author. Extensive revisions in the manuscript copy of Norton's notes for his edition show that he labored over the wording of this comment until he arrived at what was printed: 'It would be well could we believe that others of his love poems were less the utterance of his personal sentiment than exercises of his dramaturgic fancy employing itself on experiences and emotions not his own' (i. 221). Ten years later, when he brought out the first edition of Donne's love lyrics ever published as a volume in its own right, his preface called attention to Donne's licentiousness in a way that functions quite differently from Grosart's prefatorial invitation to peruse

---

[50] See Michel Foucault, *The History of Sexuality*, i: *An Introduction*, trans. Robert Hurley (New York: Vintage Books, 1980), esp. 51–73.

his volumes: Norton observed that he had simply omitted some poems, which he did not name.[51] It is too easy to dismiss this simply as bowdlerizing. Unlike Grosart, whose preface shows that he considered censoring Donne, Norton never thought to cut from the Grolier Club edition any poem genuinely written by him. His edition of *The Love Poems* shows that he was ultimately concerned to extricate Donne's best poetry from the sorts of contexts in which Grosart and Gosse had established for it when they insisted on reading Donne biographically, that is, chiefly for what his writings might reveal about his erotic experiences. Norton sought to promote the reading of Donne within a wider horizon, not a 'life and times' nor a national biography but a broad cultural history. When he came in the early nineties to the work of editing Donne, he had spent much of his career developing an account of this history.

Norton's interest in the proper editing of Donne had a great deal to do with his conceptions about art history and with his political analysis of what the United States needed at the end of the nineteenth century. This helps to explain what otherwise remains anomalous, the extraordinarily negative criticisms that he also wrote in response to the work of Gosse. When *The Life and Letters* appeared, Norton wrote a lambasting review that needs to be understood in light of his opinions on the relation between the artist and the public. Based on hundreds of careful annotations that Norton had made in his personal copies of the volumes, the review appeared anonymously, in two substantial installments, in the periodical with which he was most closely connected, *The Nation*.[52] It began with praise for Jessopp's *DNB* article as the first 'trustworthy' account of Donne's life ever written and went on to refer to 'the delightful so-called "Life" by Walton.' The tone here was reminiscent of Stephen's telling condescension: even as Walton's work is dismissed for its historical inaccuracies, it is said to be 'one of the most exquisite pieces of biography in the language.' As for Gosse's book, after calling attention to the 'chorus' of praise (112) with which it was being greeted in England, Norton proceeded to demonstrate that its author had not read Donne's satires and lyrics 'with even ordinary attention or intelligence.' He illustrated this with reference to Gosse's discussion of some half-dozen poems. His remarks on the handling of Satire III in particular are indicative of the fact that Norton was less anxious than Stephen about Gosse's dubious theories about Donne's religious history. He pointed out that Gosse portrayed the poem as 'a diatribe against the extravagance and hypocrisy of the Religious Man' (112), whereas its 'main

---

[51] Charles Eliot Norton, Preface, *The Love Poems of John Donne* (Boston: Houghton Mifflin, 1905), p. v.

[52] [Charles Eliot Norton], 'Gosse's Life of Donne', *The Nation*, 70 (1900), 111–13, 133–5. Cf. Granqvist, 'The Reception', 536–7. The volumes in which Norton wrote his annotations are in the Houghton Library at Harvard, shelf mark *EC.D7187.W899gb.

conception' is 'that religious truth was not to be found complete in the creed of any one church' and that this 'was one of Donne's abiding convictions, as appears alike in certain of his letters and of his sermons.' Gosse's hypothesis concerning Donne's eventful liaison with a married woman was designated by Norton 'a pure chimera' based upon consistent 'inability to interpret correctly Donne's plainest' poetry (113). The second installment of the review then included a long discussion of *Ignatius his Conclave* and offered an even more detailed demonstration of Gosse's incompetence in dealing with Donne's prose. Finally, Norton took up what might have been Gosse's really significant contribution to an understanding of Donne, his printing of the letters, only to offer the *coup de grâce*: the letters are so badly annotated that 'from page to page the reader goes stumbling along over Mr. Gosse's errors.' In words that Norton borrowed from Donne himself, 'the book is full of falsifications in word and sense, and of falsehoods in matter of fact, and of inconsequent and unscholarlike arguings' (135). What Norton did not say, but what he understood quite well, was how thoroughly intense was Gosse's dislike for his subject, about whom he had elsewhere written that 'No one has injured English writing more than Donne, not even Carlyle.'[53] Norton cannot have been pleased by that unflattering comparison of Donne to his personal friend of many years.

Norton's attacks on the incompetence of Grosart and Gosse were on the whole justifiable, and time has vindicated his criticisms. The insistence on careful scholarship was warranted and necessary; it set an important standard and made a lasting contribution to the Donne revival. Yet the energy that Norton put into these attacks suggests his sense that a great deal was at stake in interpreting Donne.

Norton's interest in editing Donne has been thought to have arisen out of a sense of obligation to his friend Lowell. The idea that he took up the work rather grudgingly as a cumbersome duty derives from an incomplete appreciation of what was at stake in a passage from a letter to Mrs Alexander Carlyle, in which Norton remarks that at first he had thought that 'it would be a slight task' but found 'that a minute comparison of all the editions of the poems in the seventeenth century was desirable, in order that the various readings might be given in foot-notes, and that an introduction and explanatory notes were also required.'[54] These remarks need to be seen in the

---

[53] Gosse, *A Short History*, 123.

[54] Kermit Vanderbilt, *Charles Eliot Norton: Apostle of Culture in a Democracy* (Cambridge, MA: Belknap Press of Harvard Univ. Press, 1959), 174. Compare *Letters of Charles Eliot Norton* with biographical comment by his daughter Sara Norton and M. A. De Wolfe Howe, 2 vols. (Boston: Houghton Mifflin, 1913), ii. 200–1. See in particular Norton's letter of 4 Mar. 1895, ii. 224–5.

context of a long and detailed correspondence concerning the duties of an editor towards distinguished men of letters. Norton and Mrs Carlyle had a common understanding of what considerations would make 'an introduction and explanatory notes' a requirement for an edition of Donne's poetry.

In the niece of his good friend Thomas Carlyle, Mary Aitken Carlyle, Norton could expect a sympathetic reader. She respected not only his conscientious editorial work but his discretion. Mary had been the companion of Carlyle's old age; and after his friend's death Norton had become increasingly involved in the family's personal affairs. When Froude published Carlyle's *Reminiscences* in 1881 and the volume set 'All London … talking' (as Benjamin Jowett put it), it offended the family and created a problem for Stephen, who wrote to Norton for advice on how to handle the matter in the *DNB* entry he was preparing on Carlyle. Like Carlyle and like Donne, Stephen was a widower. Averse as he was to entering the fray, he nonetheless found the history of Carlyle's domestic life compelling, at least as a potential foil for his own. He was swept up into the controversy, moreover, by virtue of its implications for the writing of biography and judged that Froude (as Donne would also prove to be) was 'an unsolved problem' who 'alternately attracted and repelled him.'[55] Meanwhile, Froude's edition of the *Reminiscences* positively outraged Norton. He found the publication of Carlyle's personal remarks about his wife, against the author's explicit written wishes, a tasteless invasion of privacy. Understanding that, as Broughton has summed up the situation, Froude's expose 'raised fundamental questions about the authority of individual men—as celebrities, as husbands, and as men of letters—to determine the boundaries of their own privacy', Norton launched a vituperative attack on Froude's editorial practices. Writing in the *New Princeton Review* for 1886, he accused Froude of treacherously betraying his friendship with Carlyle by making public personal papers that the author had considered intimate, even sacred. As if to clinch his case, Norton listed numerous editorial blunders that Froude had made: mistakes in transcription, punctuation, and capitalization; omission of words and phrases; etc. In the following year when Norton brought out his own edition of Carlyle's

James Turner has pointed out (private correspondence) that not too much should be made of Norton's attempt, as early as 1848, to purchase the copy of Donne's *Poems* (1669) that had belonged to Charles Lamb and in which Coleridge had written his marginalia. In the late 1840s Norton was buying old books in large numbers, both for his father and for himself. Given Coleridge's influence on the American Transcendentalists and the interest that Norton had in Coleridge, on whom he wrote one of his earliest articles, the principal appeal of the Donne volume in 1848 was likely that it contained Coleridge's marginalia. See Turner's *The Liberal Education of Charles Eliot Norton* (Baltimore, MD: Johns Hopkins Univ. Press, 1999), 58–60.

[55] See Broughton, *Men of Letters*, 90–4; cf. also 62. For Jowett's remark, see William S. Lilly, 'New Light on the Carlyle Controversy', *Fortnightly Review*, 79 (1903), 1001; Frederic W. Maitland, *The Life and Letters of Leslie Stephen* (London: Duckworth, 1906), 375.

Reminiscences with Mary Aitken's encouragement, he repeated the charges. He succeeded in undermining the praise that had been afforded Froude in England. In a letter of 28 August 1886, however, his friend John Ruskin chided him for his 'niggling and naggling article on Froude's misprints.' When in the following decade Norton published his attacks on Grosart and Gosse, he was not just 'niggling and naggling.' He was demonstrating his belief that great writers deserve to be treated with a sustained concern for accuracy.[56]

Although he lodged his most profound objections to the work of Froude and Grosart and Gosse within demonstrations of their editorial blunders, the basis for Norton's attacks was his concern to protect the privacy of the great writers, particularly from a prurient interest in their sexual life. He also sought to rule out the implication, as Broughton has argued, that literary genius and marital happiness are necessarily at odds with one another. In 1903, after the 'Carlyle controversy' had been raging for more than twenty years, Alexander Carlyle made it clear what had led the family to remonstrate. In *The Nemesis of Froude* he proposed that the editorial work on the papers relating to Carlyle's relations with his wife had been guided at virtually every step by a faulty assumption: Froude had credited an unscrupulous rumor that Carlyle had been impotent. He edited the papers to show that Mrs Carlyle had been bitterly disappointed in the marriage and had often contemplated divorce or suicide because her husband had not been able to give her children. Carlyle's survivors regarded all this as the work of a 'prurient imagination' bent on leaving a 'deplorable ... stain on English literature.' In the face of Froude's innuendoes, Alexander insisted that Carlyle's writings are 'characterised by splendid virility, and [show] that he was every inch a man.'[57]

For his part, Norton was much too discreet to refer directly to the charge of impotency. He had seen that Froude had made Carlyle seem unspeakably

---

[56] Broughton, *Men of Letters*, 89; see also her chapter 5, ' "Revelations on Ticklish Topics": Impotence, Biography, and Froude–Carlyle'; *The Correspondence of John Ruskin and Charles Eliot Norton*, ed. John Lewis Bradley and Ian Ousby (Cambridge: Cambridge Univ. Press, 1987), 494–5. The letters were first edited and published by Norton himself, who explained in his preface that because he held 'with those who believe that there are sanctities in love and life to be kept in privacy inviolate', he had omitted materials that were 'too personal, too intimate' for publication; see Turner, 301–5.

The wider impact of Norton's attack may be glimpsed in the case of Gamaliel Bradford. In 'The Poetry of Donne' (*Andover Review* 18/106 [1892], 350–67), Bradford had lavished a good deal of praise on Grosart's edition. But in his personal copy of the article (viz. 357–8), shelf mark *AC9.B7276.Zzx in the Houghton Library at Harvard, the lines of praise have been crossed out. When Bradford republished the essay in his book, *A Naturalist of Souls: Studies in Psychography* (New York: Dodd, Mead, 1917) virtually the only changes he made in the piece (25–59) were the suppression of all references to Grosart. (He did not take the trouble, nonetheless, to alter his Donne citations to accord with a better edition.)

[57] Alexander Carlyle and Sir James Crichton-Browne, *The Nemesis of Froude: A Rejoinder to James Anthony Froude's 'My Relations with Carlyle'* (New York: John Lane, 1903), 68–9.

cruel to his wife. He brought out his own edition of the *Reminiscences* with a view to setting the record straight. Although Norton thought his acrimonious attacks against Grosart and Gosse's work on Donne, made in the name of scholarly accuracy, were similarly designed to safeguard Donne from prurient curiosity, still we need to acknowledge that Donne had been dead for more than two and a half centuries. What Norton was protecting was an idea of 'Donne' that in the late nineteenth century had become sacred to the coterie of well-bred men of letters that had gathered around Lowell, a circle from which the likes of Grosart and Gosse were ever to be excluded.

The 'Carlyle controversy' served to intensify objections that Norton, like Stephen, had long had to biographers prying into the personal lives of their subjects, and thereafter he objected repeatedly and vociferously to the growing tendency among modern writers to document 'the surface details of ordinary life' and to indulge 'curiosity about personal lives and biological drives.' He counted among the worst offenders the 'feminine lyricists', whose highly personal poems showed they were lacking the 'keen sense of self-respect' and 'that reticence which comes of large experience and high breeding.' Beyond this, he strongly disapproved of the growing tendency, in an egalitarian society with mass publishing, to consider the 'intimate affairs of men ... public property.' In editing Longfellow's poetry, Norton singled out the misfortune that dogged the modern writer, intrusive interest in his domestic life from vulgar readers, 'who assumed that the notoriety of his works justified the treatment of their author as a public character.' When Lowell died and he was urged to write a biography, Norton took occasion to remark, 'we are losing the sense of the sacredness of the privacy of life.'[58]

In an article paying tribute to Lowell, Norton explicitly denied the public access to any secrets of their friendship: 'I cannot take my readers, however worthy of confidence they may be, within the inner circle of intimacy' (847). He defended this reticence with a quotation from a lecture Lowell had given on Chapman:

Is it love of knowledge or of gossip that renders these private concerns so interesting to us, and makes us willing to intrude on the awful seclusion of the dead ... ? ... Of course in whatever the man himself has made a part of the record we are entitled to find what intimations we can of his genuine self, of the real man, veiled under the draperies of convention and circumstance. (847)

---

[58] Charles Eliot Norton, 'Feminine Poetry', *The Nation*, 22/556 (Feb. 1876), 132; Vanderbilt, *Charles Eliot Norton*, 165–7; Charles Eliot Norton, *Henry Wadsworth Longfellow; a Sketch of his Life, ... together with Longfellow's Chief Autobiographical Poems* (Boston: Houghton Mifflin, 1906), 37; idem, 'James Russell Lowell', *Harper's New Monthly Magazine*, 86/516 (May 1893), 846–7. Subsequent references to the article on Lowell are given in the text. Cf. also Norton's letter of 1891 to J. B. Harrison, *Letters*, ii. 206.

Norton went on to argue that the only biographical information readers needed was in the poetic 'record.' Lowell, he insisted, had 'nothing ... which he needed to conceal' (847), and all that was to be known of his life was contained in his poems 'with a fulness and frankness which make them one of the most complete records in literature of the life of a young poet' (849). This was not to forbid biographical interest but to delimit it within a protected sphere of masculine discretion, in accord with an attitude toward books that Norton ascribed to Lowell: 'They represented their writers to him.' It was as if the very men whose books he owned dwelt in Lowell's study: 'it was Dante, Shakespeare, Calderon, Donne, Walton, who were his familiars, and not merely their works with which he was acquainted' (854). Lowell's own poems, Norton maintained, give utterance not to 'merely personal sentiment, but to the dumb emotions and the convictions of a people' (849). The sentiment was expanded in Norton's edition of Lowell's letters, with an unmistakable allusion to Froude and Carlyle:

But portions of every man's life are essentially private, and knowledge of them belongs by right only to those intimates whom he himself may see fit to trust with his entire confidence. Vulgar curiosity is, indeed, always alert to spy into these sanctities, and is too often gratified, as in some memorable and mournful instances in recent years, by the infidelities of untrustworthy friends.[59]

When Norton came to present Donne's love poetry to the American public, he also presented Walton as a true friend to Donne. In accord with the arrangement of authors on Lowell's bookshelves, he emphasized that virtually all that one needs to know can be found in Walton's *Life*.[60] He said nothing about Donne's personal life, and he sought to ward off interest in it. Against the growing tendency to read the erotic poems biographically, Norton quoted again Walton's claim that Donne 'wished they had been abortive or so short lived that his own eyes had witnessed their funerals.'[61] To safeguard Donne's 'genuine self' he erased the licentious poems from the part of 'the record [in which] we are entitled' to search for 'the real man.' Committed to a belief in the moral function of literature, in his edition of *The Love Poems* he sought the better to recommend his favorite Donne poems—'The Ecstacy', 'The Anniversary', 'Lecture upon the Shadow', and 'A Valediction Forbidding Mourning'—by suppressing licentious verses that he was certain Donne had

---

[59] Charles Eliot Norton, 'Editorial Note', *The Letters of James Russell Lowell*, ed. Charles Eliot Norton, 2 vols. (New York: Harper and Brothers, 1893), i, p. iii.

[60] In his introduction to the two-volume Grolier Club edition (*The Poems of John Donne from the Text of the Edition of 1633*, rev. James Russell Lowell [New York, 1895]), Norton acknowledged, however, the recent contribution to the *DNB* by Jessopp (i, p. xix).

[61] Preface, *The Love Poems of John Donne*, p. v; cf. the Introduction to the Grolier Club edition, i, p. xx; and 'The Text of Donne's Poems', 5.

regretted and disowned. Unlike the Grolier Club edition, this volume would give a due impression of the essential Donne, whose life (by Walton) and works proved that he had been at once a good husband and a man of letters.

Having come to write on Donne late in life, Norton fitted the poetry, both the exquisite and the licentious, into the theory of the history of Western art that he had developed many years previously. It was a theory that in its broad outlines was shared by Ruskin and Carlyle, a perspective that saw the medieval period as a time of enormous vitality and creativity. This thinking was of a piece with a widespread yearning among a cultural elite in late nineteenth-century England and New England to recapture 'the "real life" of the premodern craftsman, soldier, or saint.' Some of these 'antimodern' vitalists, who have been studied by Jackson Lears, comprised a group who idealized the late Middle Ages as an 'epoch pervaded by *eros*—by perpetual excitement born of boundless desire.' Theirs was a theory, moreover, that fed and was fed by the Dante revival in which Norton played a prominent part. Norton tended to downplay interest in the erotic aspects of the era and looked chiefly to thirteenth-century Italy as a locus of what Lears denominates 'authentic experience' and 'intense spiritual ecstacy.'[62] In the commentary accompanying his translation of *La Vita Nuova*, he sought to account for Dante's remarkable achievement by placing him at a particularly opportune moment in cultural history. Under the spell of the widespread belief that social history can be understood on the model of the story of growth and maturation in an individual life, Norton wrote of thirteenth-century Italy that

after a long period of childhood, [Italy] was now becoming possessed of the powers of maturity. Society ... was once more rapidly advancing. Throughout Italy there was a morning freshness, and the thrill and exhilaration of conscious activity. Her imagination was roused by the revival of ancient and now new learning, by the stories of travellers, by the gains of commerce, by the excitements of religion and the alarms of superstition. She was boastful, jealous, quarrelsome, lavish, magnificent, full of fickleness,—exhibiting on all sides the exuberance, the magnanimity, the folly of youth.[63]

The rudiments of Norton's version of this theory dated back to an extended European sojourn. In the mid-1870s, when he returned to America and took up the post of Professor of Fine Arts at Harvard, he elaborated his theory in lectures that he repeated and adapted for more than twenty years. His most influential course concentrated on ancient Athens in its golden age and on the flowering of Gothic style in Venice and Florence. He generally ended

---

[62] T. J. Jackson Lears, *No Place of Grace: Antimodernism and the Transformation of American Culture 1880–1920* (New York: Pantheon, 1981), 5–6, 159.

[63] *The New Life of Dante: An Essay, with Translations* (Cambridge, MA: Riverside, 1859), 7–8.

his account of the history of art with the Renaissance. The governing idea was crystallized in his book of 1880, *Historical Studies of Church-Building in the Middle Ages*, in which Norton depicted the Gothic cathedral as an 'ideal referent', 'an expression of popular will in society and government' embodying 'sincerity in art, purity in religion.'[64] The sincerity and passion of this 'real life' had been compromised, in his view, during the Italian Renaissance, when '[o]riginal thought was discouraged', and 'pseudo-classicism' began to 'stifle fresh and independent works of mind.' Norton traced the origins of the 'spirit of dependence on the past' to 'deep-lying moral deficiencies' and complained that in 'poetry, in scholarship, in painting, sculpture, and architecture, men' allowed the 'masters of the ancient world [to be] made the despots of the modern.' While it would be wrong to credit the idea that as far as Norton was concerned 'there was no significant art after the year 1600,'[65] his adherence to a theory of art history that had descended from Rio through Anna Jameson and Ruskin meant that for him Donne would have to be considered a special case.

When Norton took up Lowell's editorial work, he found that he could fit Donne into his canon because the Renaissance had reached England belatedly. The English poet shared with Dante originality and freshness, a sense of life lived with spiritual intensity at a high pitch of sincere emotion. Brought up in the traditions of medieval Catholicism, Donne seemed to Norton to evince in his youthful poetry an extraordinary spiritual energy worthy to be compared with that of the makers of Italian Gothic cathedrals. Donne had the good fortune to live in a similarly golden era, for the Elizabethan Age in England had been a period of enlightenment and reformed religion. The period is described in terms not only reminiscent of Norton's characterization of thirteenth-century Italy but relevant as well to his hopes for America:

The growth and consciousness of national power and the jealous pride of national independence in England ... had quickened the imagination of her people. The vast discoveries of the world combined with the new learning to animate the intelligence alike of men of affairs and of men of thought with fresh and stimulating inspiration. The tremendous debate of the Reformation, with the social and material changes to which it led, called forth constant discussion of the deepest problems, not as mere abstract subjects of controversy, but as bearing directly on the lives and fortunes

[64] Vanderbilt, *Charles Eliot Norton*, 125–6, 56, respectively. On Norton's role in establishing the prestige of High Culture, see Lawrence W. Levine, *Highbrow/Lowbrow: The Emergence of Cultural Hierarchy in America* (Cambridge, MA: Harvard Univ. Press, 1988), 176–7.

[65] Charles Eliot Norton, *Notes of Travel and Study in Italy* (1859; Boston: Ticknor and Fields, 1860), 305, 304, respectively; Vanderbilt, *Charles Eliot Norton*, 126. In *The Liberal Education*, (94, 149, 154–5), James Turner presents evidence of his interest in paintings by Turner, the Pre-Raphaelites, Reynolds, and others, which invalidates Vanderbilt's claim.

of the disputants. The debate was at fire heat with passion. The conditions of the world, moreover, afforded unwonted variety of opportunity for the display of strong individualities, yet society was gaining the settled order and the established form requisite for the higher development of intellectual life.[66]

Like Dante, Donne had an 'unbounded zeal' for learning. Yet he had the bad luck to have been influenced by the Italian Renaissance. With Lord Herbert of Cherbury, Donne was one of 'the striking illustrations which the England of 1600 affords of the force which this Italian spirit still exerted after its native source had run almost dry.'[67] Donne's poetry, like Michelangelo's art, showed signs of the moral deterioration ushered in by greater luxury and political despotism, which cheapened taste. It seems likely that Norton had in mind some of Donne's poems when he told his classes that the choice of ignoble subject matter in art corrupted the sense of beauty. 'There are poems in the body of English poetry which are full of merit in their mere form,' he remarked rather cryptically, 'but so foul that one regrets to have come across them.'[68] Unfortunately for Donne, he was 'a child of [the] spirit' of the Renaissance.

He shared in its exaltations and debasements, in its confusion of the sensual and the supersensual, in its love of physical and its adoration of spiritual beauty, in its poetic fervor, its ardor for experience and for learning, its rapid changes of mood, its subjection to the things of the flesh, its ascetic aspiration for things of the spirit. [In the time in which Donne lived there] was a mingling of the purest and most vivifying air with a poisonous malaria. ... [The Renaissance] had refined manners, it had corrupted the moral sense; it had quickened life, it had spread mortal contagion. A nature so susceptible as Donne's was subject to its full effect.[69]

Where for Norton the world of Dante had been 'boastful, jealous, quarrelsome, ... full of fickleness', guilty only of youthful folly, the world of Donne was older and darker. It was degenerating in the ways that Norton considered parallel to the situation of *fin de siècle* America. This was the vision that would be adapted to significantly different ends by his cousin's grandson, whose account of literary history in his essay on 'The Metaphysical Poets' turned on the idea that 'something ... happened to the mind of England between the time of Donne or Lord Herbert of Cherbury and the time of Tennyson and Browning.' T. S. Eliot, who had been an undergraduate at Harvard during the last years of Norton's life, went on to elaborate his theory of 'a dissociation of sensibility' in terms reminiscent of his older relation's account of art history. He presented Donne and his contemporaries as the heirs of

---

[66] Norton, Introduction, Grolier Club edition, i, p. xxi.   [67] Ibid. xxii.

[68] 'Lectures on the History of Ancient Art', taken and compiled by Harry F. Brown, Lecture IV, 6 Oct. 1888, 16; quoted by Vanderbilt, *Charles Eliot Norton*, 177.

[69] Norton, Introduction, Grolier Club edition, i, p. xxii.

Dante and the thirteenth-century Italian poets. Similarly, in 'Tradition and the Individual Talent', he protested against vulgar curiosity about writers' private lives when he proposed the theory of the 'impersonal' artist, who has 'not a "personality" to express, but a particular medium, ... in which impressions and experiences combine in peculiar and unexpected ways.'[70]

There was something curiously disingenuous about the way in which Eliot, when he came back to Harvard in 1932 to deliver the first Charles Eliot Norton lectures, sought to place his own work in relation to that of his distant relative and predecessor. After opening with a quotation from Norton on the presidential politics of 1876, Eliot announced that the 'present lectures will have no concern with politics.' He went on to offer what might have seemed merely conventional praise for the man in whose memory the lectures had been funded. He then proceeded to single out for praise that 'Norton always preserved his privacy' and stood for the separation of public and private spheres and that he understood 'the permanent importance of literature' as a means of fending off barbarism.[71] If today Eliot's theory of the impersonal artist is widely regarded as a cover for his troubled sexual history,[72] this does not cancel out the fact that it once had considerable value for advancing the understanding of Donne's poetry. The failed collaboration between Jessopp and Gosse left as its legacy the fissure between a youthful roué and a grave and learned doctor of the English church. It was by concentrating on the medium rather than the personality of the artist that Donne's poems were freed from the biographical matrix that had provided the grounds on which interest in them had revived in England. The vogue for Donne that arose in the 1890s was superseded in the twentieth century by a sustained critical scrutiny that led to Donne's establishment as a major poet. The prominence of Norton as a precursor for this critical scrutiny rightly suggests that the position Donne came to occupy in literary studies owed a good deal to the early incorporation of his writings into the English curriculum at Harvard, where there was not the same necessity that there was in England to puzzle over Donne as an enigmatic presence within the larger project of writing the national biography.

[70] T. S. Eliot, *Selected Essays* (London: Faber and Faber, 1932), 287, 20, respectively.

[71] T. S. Eliot, *The Use of Poetry and the Use of Criticism* (1933; repr. New York: Barnes and Noble, 1959), 13–15.

[72] See, e.g., Cynthia Ozick, 'A Critic at Large: T. S. Eliot at 101', *The New Yorker*, 65/40 (20 Nov. 1989), 119–44, 149–54.

7

Donne at Harvard

It is, I know, a tercentenary 1631–1931; but for my own experience within the terms of this paper, our time is roughly 1906–1931 ... . Professor Briggs used to read, with great persuasiveness and charm, verses of Donne to the Freshmen at Harvard assembled in what was called, as I remember, 'English A.' I confess that I have now forgotten what Professor Briggs told us about the poet; but I know that whatever he said, his own words and his quotations were enough to attract to private reading at least one Freshman who had already absorbed some of the Elizabethan dramatists, but who had not yet approached the metaphysicals. I can from that point trace uncertainly the progress of my own relations with Donne, but I cannot account for his general emergence towards tercentenary fame.

—T. S. Eliot, 'Donne in Our Time' (1931)

The tercentenary anniversary of Donne's death was celebrated during the year before T. S. Eliot inaugurated the Charles Eliot Norton Lectures at Harvard. Having been invited to contribute to a collection of essays to mark the occasion, Eliot took the opportunity to write a valediction to Donne without mourning. He began by paying tribute to the teacher who had introduced him to 'the metaphysicals' during his freshman year at the College and then, with a modesty false or true, went on to downplay his own role in the massive rewriting of English literary history that had taken place during the decade after the publication in 1921 of Grierson's anthology of metaphysical poetry. The title of his contribution, 'Donne in Our Time', perhaps undercut the celebratory purposes of the volume with a pun: Eliot's essay proposed that the vogue for Donne was probably over and that readers would be moving on, as he had, to reading other poets. In fact, through the rest of his life Eliot continued to distance himself from Donne. In the essay 'To Criticize the Critic', he repeated his dissatisfaction with having been 'credited with starting the vogue for Donne and other metaphysical poets'; and he insisted that he 'did not discover' them.[1]

Whatever Eliot's personal and professional reasons for attempting to break the connection that others routinely made between him and Donne, the telling point in the tribute that he paid to Dean Briggs is that Donne's place in English literature was already taken for granted in the English curriculum when Eliot matriculated in 1906. There were four interrelated factors that contributed to the unprecedented prominence conferred upon Donne at Harvard:

1. A living tradition in New England of considering Donne a major writer, dating back to Emerson, Thoreau, and Margaret Fuller, and spread abroad by James Russell Lowell, a tradition that was quite independent of the anxieties about Donne's place in the national history with which the reading of his poetry was coloured in England;

2. The editing of Donne's poetry by Lowell for F. J. Child's British Poets series, and later by Lowell, Lowell's daughter, and Charles Eliot Norton for the Grolier Club;

3. The collection by Norton of a significant body of artifacts relating to Donne, including seventeenth-century manuscripts and editions;

4. The charismatic presence of Le Baron Russell Briggs, who, during the period when Eliot was at Harvard, was Dean of the Faculty of Arts and Sciences, Boylston Professor of Rhetoric, and the teacher of more freshmen than any other member of the English Department. Briggs did not invent or discover Donne any more than Eliot did. What he did was to bring the poet squarely into the curriculum, making Harvard the first place in the world where Donne's writings were considered a substantial academic subject in their own right.

The interrelations among these four factors make Harvard unique in the history of studying Donne. They go a good distance towards explaining the confidence with which, above all in the essays on 'The Metaphysical Poets' and 'Tradition and the Individual Talent', Eliot disseminated a revised version of English literary history in which Donne was assigned a central role.

The theory whereby good poetry manifests a 'unified sensibility' was deeply rooted in New England literary culture, where Donne had long been admired

---

[1] T. S. Eliot, *To Criticize the Critic, and Other Writings* (London: Faber and Faber; New York: Farrar, Straus and Giroux, 1965), 21. Eliot's essay, 'Donne in Our Time', was published in Theodore Spencer (ed.), *A Garland for John Donne: 1631–1931* (Cambridge, MA: Harvard Univ. Press, 1931 repr., Gloucester, MA: Peter Smith, 1958), 1–19.

for displaying it. In Eliot's review of Grierson's anthology, as he proposed to locate a moment when poets began to dissociate thought from emotion, he gave a new inflection to this traditional criterion. He also intervened (as we shall see in due course) in what had been a local debate about the course of literary history that had been playing out in the English curriculum during the years he had spent at Harvard. This is not to deny that what Eliot denominated a 'dissociation of sensibility' can be connected with his reading of Remy de Gourmont's *Probleme du Style*, or with the work that he did for his dissertation on the philosophy of F. M. Bradley, or with the humanism of Irving Babbitt, whom (with Briggs) he remembered as his most influential teacher.[2] It is, however, to acknowledge that pedagogical and material considerations can be as determinative as exotic French theory and prestigious ideology of the perspectives from which reading takes place. In order to understand the ways in which Eliot contributed to the transformation of Donne from a biographical subject into a writer who was recognized as having played a significant part in English literary history, we need to ask about the 'metaphysical' poet whom Tom Eliot met in Dean Briggs's class, What was he like and what were people seeing in his poetry? What were the conditions that made it possible in 1906 for a college student to encounter the poetry of Donne in his freshman English course? Moreover, how was it that, a quarter of a century later, the influential figure that Eliot had become was able to take for granted that there had been nothing unusual about his having first read that poetry in an academic context? This chapter explores the interrelations among the four factors that established the relevant conditions of possibility.

DONNE IN GREATER BOSTON

By the late nineteenth century in and around Boston artists, writers, publishers, and avid readers of poetry valued Donne's verse with an unparalleled degree of admiration. In the gay nineties Donne's name was woven into the cover-design of *Poet-Lore*, a journal newly relocated to Cambridge and 'devoted to the appreciation of the poets and to comparative literature.' It glowed there with the names of a hundred other writers, in the company Hafiz and Racine, Sappho and Kalidasa and Isaiah, Wordsworth and Aeschylus. When the new Public Library opened in Copley Square, Donne was among the five hundred writers and artists whose names were chiseled in large characters

---

[2] See Herbert Howarth's *Notes on Some Figures Behind T. S. Eliot* (Boston: Houghton Mifflin, 1964), 127–35.

onto the outside walls. Much of the enthusiasm for Donne flowed through Norton. He began complementing the substantial Dante holdings in his personal library with a growing collection of early books and manuscripts relating to Donne. Increasingly, he was sought out by those who admired the poet's verse. Annie Fields hosted him in her Charles Street salon. Her partner, Sarah Orne Jewett, made a gift to him of a 1649 edition of the *Poems*. Gamaliel Bradford, who had written a 'psychographical' study of Donne, called on him at his home, Shady Hill. Louise Imogen Guiney, who worked as a postmistress and was a poet herself, secured his help in creating a memorial for Keats in Hampstead; she also joined him in editing a translation of Dante. Her friend, Thomas Whittemore, who was to become an international connoisseur of art and friend to the great collector, Isabella Stuart Gardner, came to study art history with him at Harvard, where Francis Child, George Herbert Palmer, and Dean Briggs were his colleagues. Norton was the most important, but not the only, academic who had a hand in cultivating Donne as the 'fashionable' poet in the literary culture of Boston in the nineties.[3]

Traces of the attention afforded to Donne can be found in records of private reading by New Englanders of various backgrounds, religious orientations, and social classes. Interest was disseminated through public lectures, printed essays, and popular anthologies. Its chief fount was Emerson and its ambassador Lowell. Its subtlest exponent, however, was Thoreau, whose abiding interest in Donne's poetry has not been much probed. His notebooks and other writings, including *Walden*, show how early and how deeply Donne came to be lodged within New England literary culture.

Emerson, like Thoreau and T. S. Eliot after him, first encountered Donne's poetry in his student days. While he was at Boston Latin, Harvard's principal feeder school, he chanced on snippets from the poetry in the course of his early independent reading. The letter into which he copied lines from the Valentine's Day epithalamion was addressed to his older brother, who was already at the College. Over the next dozen years Emerson came to the conclusion that the seventeenth century was the age of 'the great splendour of English poetry.' Yet Donne came relatively late into his pantheon, after Herbert and Marvell. He marked his copy of the Tonson edition extensively, and he drew on the marked passages both in his lectures and in making his influential anthology, *Parnassus*, first published in 1874. He seems never to have tired of quoting the lines from the Second Anniversary that he took to epitomize the poet's sensibility:

---

[3] See Raoul Granqvist, 'A "Fashionable Poet" in New England in the 1890s: A Study of the Reception of John Donne', *JDJ*, 4 (1985), 337–49.

> her pure and eloquent blood
> Spoke in her cheeks, and so distinctly wrought,
> That one might almost say, her body thought.[4]

In his own poetry Emerson often employed geometrical metaphors for exploring or characterizing spiritual realities, as Donne had. His transcendentalist philosophy readily accommodated a love of correspondences, especially those between Nature and the human mind. Not surprisingly, therefore, he was the American poet most frequently compared to the metaphysicals, whose writings he repeatedly praised.[5]

By 1869, when Annie Fields recorded her impressions of a lecture by Emerson on the seventeenth-century poets, Donne was a writer with whom literate Bostonians were readily familiar. It was in this year that E. P. Whipple, fellow founding member with Emerson of the Saturday Club, brought out the book in which he vilified Donne for the indolence and irresponsibility entailed in his wide theological reading. Some months earlier Whipple had been publishing in the *Atlantic Monthly*, the journal edited by Mrs Fields's husband (and unofficially by her), the lectures on Elizabethan literature on which his book would be based. Annie Fields's enthusiasm for Donne seems to have been undaunted by her brushes with Whipple's strictures against the 'ludicrous complexity' of Donne's mind and the 'moral laziness' represented in his 'thirty years of incessant study.'[6] In the nineties she was still happily reading Donne with Jewett, who when the couple set up house together in Charles Street brought along her well-worn copy of a 1639 edition of *Poems by J. D.* In nineteenth-century Boston the reading of Donne's poetry cut across boundaries of age and sex and sexual orientation.

HENRY DAVID THOREAU

Because Emerson stimulated the interest in Donne around Boston and because Thoreau was closely associated with him, it has been assumed that the younger man's interest in Donne was derivative. Yet Thoreau's incorporation of

---

[4] Quoted here from *Parnassus*, ed. Ralph Waldo Emerson (Boston: James K. Osgood, 1875), 273.

[5] See Norman A. Brittin, 'Emerson and the Metaphysical Poets', *American Literature*, 8 (1936), 1–21; Joseph Duncan, *The Revival of Metaphysical Poetry, The History of a Style, 1800 to the Present* (Minneapolis, MN: Univ. of Minnesota Press, 1959), 72–7.

[6] Whipple's lectures on literature from the age of Elizabeth, which had been given for the Lowell Institute in 1859, were published between Feb. 1867 and Dec. 1868. He treated Donne in one called 'Minor Elizabethan Poets', *Atlantic Monthly*, 22/129 (July 1868), 29, 31.

Donne's poetry into *Walden* evinces a distinctly independent reading. When in 1837, the year that he graduated from Harvard, Thoreau took Emerson as his mentor, he had already read a good deal of older English literature.[7] Emerson encouraged him to continue this reading and shared with him his large collection of excerpts. In the autumn of that year Thoreau began keeping a journal of his own, and he prefaced it with three mottoes all drawn from seventeenth-century writers. Over the next several years he copied thousands of lines of older poetry into notebooks. Among these were about one hundred lines of Donne's verse, discrete 'nuggets' of the sort that Emerson habitually transcribed in his journals but chosen independently of Emerson. Only one of the Donne poems that would be included in *Parnassus*, 'The Undertaking', appears among Thoreau's journal entries; it is possible that it was he who called Emerson's attention to the passage about forgetting 'the he and she.'

The fascination with Donne as a 'sturdy' thinker displayed in Thoreau's journals was rooted in the most distinctive new interest that he acquired during his years as an undergraduate. English literature was scarcely an integral part of the Harvard curriculum in the 1830s; as elsewhere, the classical languages were at the heart of the required studies. Study of the modern European languages, however, had become a significant curricular activity. Prompted by Longfellow, the Smith Professor, Thoreau read Goethe's *Wilhelm Meister's Apprenticeship* in the translation by Carlyle. Under the tutelage of Edward Channing, the Boylston Professor of Rhetoric and Oratory, he was required to read and declaim English poetry; and he began to write about literature in English. In April 1836, he submitted for his forensics course an essay on the 'Advantages and Disadvantages of Foreign Influence in American Literature', and later that year he wrote an essay on the speeches in Book II of *Paradise Lost*. It was in this same year that Channing, in an unprecedented move, began hosting voluntary discussions of the early English poets.[8] Whether Thoreau participated in these meetings or not, he was caught up in the increasingly literary education that Channing aimed to foster. The library charging records show that as a sophomore and junior, Thoreau was reading Goldsmith and Chaucer. As a senior he was looking into Johnson and Hazlitt on the English

---

[7] See Robert Sattelmeyer, *Thoreau's Reading: A Study in Intellectual History with Bibliographical Catalogue* (Princeton, NJ: Princeton Univ. Press, 1988), 12–15.

[8] Kenneth Walter Cameron, *Thoreau's Harvard Years: Materials Introductory to New Explorations* (Hartford, CT: Transcendental Books, 1966), Part II, 14, 12, respectively. The ms. of the essay on Milton is in the Houghton Library: MS Am 278.5.5*. On the discussions of English poets led by Channing, see Sattelmeyer, *Thoreau's Reading*, 12–13. On Channing's practices, see Franklin E. Court, 'The Early Impact of Scottish Literary Teaching in North America', in Robert Crawford (ed.), *The Scottish Invention of English Literature* (Cambridge: Cambridge Univ. Press, 1998), 152–4.

poets and Burke on the sublime. He also borrowed copies of Cowper's *Works* and Gray's *Poems*, and he steeped himself in Milton, the prose as well as the poetry. He was already making use, moreover, of Chalmers's massive collection of the British poets.[9] He left college convinced that he was going to become a poet himself. Other Transcendentalists may have gone to the seventeenth century because Coleridge and Lamb had recommended its writers, or in an attempt to come to terms with the legacy of Puritanism, or in hopes of finding workable political strategies.[10] Thoreau regarded the task of collecting nuggets out of older poetry as a necessary part of a writer's apprenticeship.

During the first five years after his graduation, Thoreau's opportunities to read older literature were only sporadic. At times he had the liberty of Emerson's library. A decisive moment came in late autumn 1841 when Emerson arranged for him to spend two weeks in Cambridge, precisely so that he could make concerted use of Harvard's library in the newly built Gore Hall. When Thoreau first walked in and saw the books, he lost heart. '[L]ooking over the dry and dusty volumes of the English poets,' he wrote upon scanning dozens of title pages and renewing his acquaintance with Chalmers, 'I cannot believe that those fresh and fair creations I had imagined are contained in them. English poetry from Gower down, collected into one alcove—and so from the library window compared with the commonest nature, seems very mean. Poetry cannot breathe in the scholar's atmosphere.' Nonetheless, though he felt 'oppressed by an inevitable sadness', he returned to *The Canterbury Tales* and resolved to 'appreciate Chaucer' by coming 'down to him the natural way through the very meagre pastures of saxon and ante-Chaucerian poetry.'[11] At some point in his early twenties, as he confides in *Walden*, he embarked on an ambitious attempt to make his way through all twenty-one volumes of Chalmers 'without skipping.'[12] Between 1841 and 1843 he filled several blank books with nuggets of British poetry, augmenting in the autumn of 1843 what he had begun at Harvard by making visits to New York libraries. The notebooks are dense with passages from Carew and Donne, Herrick and Lovelace, poets who offered examples of what Thoreau considered effective writing.

[9] The library charging records are housed in the Harvard University Archives, UA III.50.15.60. See the volumes for 1834 through 1837.

[10] Robin Grey, *The Complicity of Imagination: The American Renaissance, Contests of Authority, and Seventeenth-Century English Culture* (Cambridge: Cambridge Univ. Press, 1997).

[11] Thoreau's entry for 30 Nov. 1841, in *Journal*, i: *1837–1844*, gen. ed. John C. Broderick (Princeton, NJ: Princeton Univ. Press, 1981), 337–9.

[12] Library charging records for 1841–2. Thoreau's reference to attempting to read through Chalmers 'without skipping' is in the chapter called 'Former Inhabitants; and Winter Visitors', *Walden*, ed. J. Lyndon Shanley (Princeton, NJ: Princeton Univ. Press, 1971), 259. Parenthetical references are to this edition.

During the two years that Thoreau spent at Walden (1845–7) his interest in poetry was largely directed to these nuggets. In the book that he wrote there, *A Week on the Concord and Merrimack Rivers*, he incorporated several extracts from Donne, including as a motto for the 'Friday' chapter lines from 'The First Anniversary': 'Summer's robe grows | Dusky, and like an oft-dyed garment shows.'[13] By the 1850s, he was reading mostly contemporary poetry. Still, his interest in Donne endured. He had copied over from one journal into another the more extended commentary on 'Doctor Donne', in which he designated the verse letters 'perhaps best' among Donne's poems. Nearly half the lines he had quoted from Donne in the journals were derived from the Epistles. They show that he regarded Donne as a source of the sort of practical wisdom that he would attempt to infuse into *Walden*.

Although Thoreau shared his idiosyncratic extracts with only a few other persons, the ones he took from Donne are congruent with the ways of reading that Channing and Emerson encouraged. They help us understand the sort of readership for which Lowell prepared an edition that was to lead off with the letters. Many of the Donne nuggets concern the vexed and yet profound relations between abstract virtue and material embodiment. Probably the earliest extract was a passage spoken by Allophanes in the Eclogue prefacing the Somerset epithalamion:

> angels, though on Earth employ'd they be,
> Are still in Heav'n; so is he still at home
> That doth abroad to honest actions come.

Elsewhere Thoreau quoted from 'The Dream',

> Thou are so true, that thoughts of thee suffice
> To make dreams truth

from 'Love's Progress',

> Although we see celestial bodies move
> Above the earth, the earth we till and love—

and from 'To the Countess of Huntingdon',

> Why love among the virtues is not known,
> Is, that love is them all contract in one.

His excerpts belong to a kind of wisdom literature, composed within and for a group of persons who relish friendship as a principal means of cultivating virtue. The theme of friendship is explicit in the first of eight extracts from

---

[13] *The Selected Works of Thoreau*, Cambridge Edition, ed. Walter Harding (Boston: Houghton Mifflin, 1975), 211.

'The Storm' and 'The Calm', the poems with which Lowell's edition would open. Thoreau excerpted Donne more extensively than other poets, above all because Donne's verses so often contain memorable dicta and striking phrases ('a point and one | Are much entirer than a million').[14]

Except for 'The Undertaking', which he transcribed in its entirety, the longest excerpt comes from the verse letter, 'To Sir Edward Herbert, at Juliers.' Edward (later, Lord Herbert of Cherbury) was a significant counter in Transcendentalist literary culture. Margaret Fuller read his life and translated his Latin poems, and she wrote a fictional dialogue between Edward and his younger brother, George, in which she seems to have figured herself as the elder brother and Emerson as the author of *The Temple*. She found in the natural philosophy of Lord Herbert what Thoreau found in the pastoralism of Walton's *Compleat Angler*, a basis for wide toleration and a grounds for responsible personal agency.[15] Thoreau's attention to the verse letter to Herbert confirms Robin Grey's thesis that the Transcendentalists valued seventeenth-century writers because they offered models for effective personal action. As Donne depicts Edward Herbert, he is the epitome of efficacious activity, one who shows the way to conduct the principal 'business' of life, 'to rectify | Nature, to what she was.' Thoreau incorporated his excerpt from the poem into *Walden* (1854), but without citing its title or giving the name of its author. He placed it in the climactic section of 'Higher Laws', the very chapter in which he offers a penetrating discussion of the union of thought and feeling. 'I have been thrilled to think that I owed a mental perception to the commonly gross sense of taste' (218). Urging that human beings, both individually and collectively, should pass through a stage of hunting and fishing if they are to rise to 'a life in conformity to higher principles' (216) such as vegetarianism and unself-conscious chastity, Thoreau proposes that 'Nature is hard to be overcome, but she must be overcome' (221). Donne's praise of Herbert as one who has 'due place assigned | To his beasts and disaforested his mind' endorses the main point: Thoreau claims to have within himself one 'instinct toward a higher' life and 'another toward a primitive rank and savage one' and to 'reverence them both' (210). Donne's lines also make a pivot into the next chapter, 'Brute Neighbors', where they reverberate through an exploration of the behavior of animals, all of whom Thoreau regards as potentially relevant to human self-understanding, since all animals in the world are 'beasts of

---

[14] From 'Obsequies to the Lord Harrington', lines 68–9. Thoreau's extracts from Donne are quoted from the edition from which he took them, viz., *The Works of the English Poets*, ed. Alexander Chalmers (London, 1810), v. See *Thoreau's Literary Notebook in The Library of Congress: Facsimile Text*, ed. Kenneth Walter Cameron (Hartford, CT: Transcendental Books, 1964), 320–5.

[15] See Grey, *The Complicity of Imagination*, 88–106.

burden' carrying 'some portion of our thoughts' (225). Donne's lines praising Herbert as one of the happy few who 'can use his horse, goat wolf, and ev'ry beast | And is not ass himself to all the rest' also serve to associate animals with the potentially destructive forces within Nature that are not to be eradicated but, in carefully demarcated places (like Thoreau's hut and garden), to be held at bay, while the human capacity for godlike discipline civilizes a space. It is an index of Thoreau's transformative reading of Donne that he commandeered these verses, making them a pivot into his climactic discussion of sexual purity. The metaphors of the 'disaforested mind' and the fenced out animals modulate in Thoreau's account into praise for the person who makes of his body a temple: 'the spirit can for the time pervade and control every member and function of the body, and transmute what in form is the grossest sensuality into purity and devotion' (219). 'What is chastity?' Thoreau asks. 'How shall a man know if he is chaste? He shall not know it. We have heard of this virtue, but we know not what it is' (220).

The chapters of *Walden* where Thoreau directly quotes Donne entail a sufficiently thoroughgoing appropriation of the poetry to call for re-evaluation of the standard lore about Lowell's well-known essay on Thoreau. Although that essay, first published in 1865, has been characterized as vengeance for Thoreau's scathing letter to Lowell about the censoring of 'Chesuncook' in the *Atlantic Monthly*, ultimately Lowell bestowed high praise on his contemporary. The essay concludes by presenting Thoreau as a 'master' who 'had caught his English at its living source, among the poets and prose-writers of its best days.' Thoreau's 'literature', Lowell wrote, 'was extensive and recondite; his quotations are always nuggets of the purest ore: there are sentences of his as perfect as anything in the language.' At the close, Lowell explicitly associates Thoreau with Donne, of whom he had elsewhere written that he 'wrote more profound verses than any other English poet save one only, [and] never wrote a profounder verse than "Who knows his virtue's name and place, hath none".'[16] Whatever they may have thought of one another personally, in their reading of Donne Lowell and Thoreau were of one mind. That their orientation towards Donne's verse endured is evinced in the commonplace book begun as a Harvard freshman by George Lyman Kittredge, who was to become his university's world-renowned Shakespearean. In December 1879, Kittredge inscribed as his epigraph on the first page inside the cover, a passage from Satire IV, 'Not alone | My loneness is.' The pages that follow contain

---

[16] 'Thoreau' (1865), *The Complete Works of James Russell Lowell, Literary Essays*, i (Boston: Fireside Edition, 1899), 80–1; Lowell's review of Julius H. Ward's *The Life and Letters of James Gates Percvial* for the *North American Review* (1866) is quoted here from *Literary Criticism of James Russell Lowell*, ed. Herbert F. Smith (Lincoln, NE: Univ. of Nebraska Press, 1969), 149.

several quotations from the verse letters and from the satires, which he notes that he read 'two and three times.'[17]

GAMALIEL BRADFORD AND THE PRACTICE OF PSYCHOGRAPHY

Half a century after Thoreau, another young man who had recently left Harvard began to keep a literary journal; it too would grow to prodigious size and would contain many references to Donne's writings. The writer was a direct lineal descendant of Governor Bradford of the Plymouth Colony. Gamaliel Bradford VI (1863–1932) enrolled at Harvard College in 1883 during the period when Child was presiding over an unprecedented proliferation of courses on English literature. Curricular developments at Harvard had only an indirect impact on Bradford, however. For reasons of health, he left the college early and continued his education privately. His own promiscuous reading gave him material for journal entries. By the time he was in his mid-sixties, Bradford estimated that his journal had grown to 1.4 million words. (That is, it was longer than Emerson's but shorter than Thoreau's.) Extracts representing about one-seventh of the whole were published in 1933, in one substantial volume. Given Donne's prestige at that moment, it is unsurprising that the book's editor included the striking entry for 13 March 1896. Written four years after Bradford had published a study of Donne's poetry and within weeks of the appearance of the Muses' Library edition, the entry reads as follows:

Today should be chiefly noticeable for my purchase of Donne's *Poems* which I have long desired. A great, a marvellous man, one of the most vigorous, energetic, original writers in English or any other language, outdoing by far even Shakespeare in extravagance and excess of figurative expression, difficulty, and concentration, but I sometimes think outdoing even Shakespeare in supreme imaginative beauty, worth all the Popes and Goldsmiths and Grays that ever lived rolled into one, though I love those men too. Yet how little time I get to read any of them, when I ought to know Goldsmith and Donne both by heart! Ought, do I say? Foolish remnant of a Puritan conscience, why do I chatter about 'ought', instead of revelling in the ecstasy of all these pleasures as they come?[18]

---

[17] Commonplace Book of George Lyman Kittredge, Curriculum Collection, HUC 8878.315, Harvard University Archives.

[18] *The Journal of Gamaliel Bradford*, ed. Van Wyck Brooks (Boston: Houghton Mifflin, 1933), 83; for further biographical information and the estimate of the relative size of the journal, see the Preface, pp. vii–xiii; cf. also Dale Warren, 'Gamaliel Bradford: A Personal Sketch', *South Atlantic Quarterly*, 32 (1933), 9–18.

When Bradford wrote this entry he may still have been thinking of himself as the literary heir of Emerson. He had been encouraged in this aspiration by his uncle, with whom he often travelled, Emerson's old friend, George P. Bradford. One of the early entries in the journal shows that Gamaliel himself worked for a time in the study at the Manse, where Emerson had written *Nature*. In 1896 he was halfway through what would be nearly thirty years of composing dramas, novels, and poems, in hopes of making his name. Donne was to him, as to others who lived with the twin legacies of puritanism and Unitarianism, an object of fascination as well as a source of pleasure. 'The word which stamps itself on every line of his works, on every trait of his nature', Bradford wrote in his essay of 1892, 'is intensity, that restless, hungry energy of mind, which will not let a man shut his eyes while there is a corner of thought unprobed, unlightened. Vigour of intellect, fervour of emotion,—these are what give Donne his high position as a man and as a poet.'[19] The New England tradition of valuing Donne for what would come to be called a 'unified sensibility' facilitated his seeing in Donne's poems the fusion of physical and spiritual 'hunger' that had attracted Thoreau. One need not claim that *Walden* contributed anything directly to the vogue for Donne in the nineties to notice that it was also in this decade that Thoreau's book first achieved wide popularity.

By the time of his death in 1932 Bradford was known as the Dean of American biographers. All told he wrote biographical sketches of some one hundred and fourteen men and women, ranging from Xenophon, Catherine the Great, and Lenin, to Henry Clay, Henry Adams, and Henry Ford. He wrote on Casanova and on Thomas à Kempis. Among poets, his subjects included Whitman and Emily Dickinson, Cowper and Keats. The premise of the 1892 article on Donne for a local New England journal was that, although the poet was still largely unknown to the wider reading public, his poetry was becoming more widely read and revealed a peculiar psychology. Bradford's approach to introducing him owed something to the emerging field of psychoanalysis and more to the new canons of biography formulated by Saint-Beuve. It was nonetheless quite different from Lytton Strachey's revolt against Carlyle and the Victorian love of hero-worship. Its emphasis fell decidedly on the poet's personality. This was a new departure in the history of Donne biography in that Bradford assumed that any and every piece of Donne's writing was of potential value for the access it offers to its writer's 'soul.' Years later, when

---

[19] Gamaliel Bradford, 'The Poetry of Donne', *Andover Review*, 18/106 (1892), 351–2. When Bradford incorporated the article into *A Naturalist of Souls: Studies in Psychography* (New York: Dodd, Mead, 1917), he revised it only superficially. The changes he made may be seen in the Houghton Library copy, shelf number *AC9.B7276.Zzx. Parenthetical references reflect the pagination in the *Andover Review*.

he incorporated the essay into *A Naturalist of Souls*, he presented it as one of his earliest forays into 'psychography', or 'soul-writing.' The term had been made current in England by George Saintsbury, and Bradford claimed it as his own.[20]

By making Donne's psyche his principal focus, Bradford sought to create a synthesis of the facts that could be known from Walton's narrative and the inferences that could be drawn from reading between the poet's lines. He did not assume that the poems offer transcripts of narratable experience. Instead he sought, in ways more anticipatory of, say, Georges Poulet and the Geneva critics of the mid-twentieth century than of Gosse, to find in the record evidence of recurring mental preoccupations. In speaking of Donne's 'intensity' and 'hungry energy' and 'restlessness' Bradford gave names to qualities to which other readers had been attracted and for which Donne was increasingly being compared to Hamlet.[21] Bradford attempted to relocate the 'peculiar qualities of passion and intensity' (355) from the works to the mind that had produced them. This climaxed in a claim that Donne's great 'poetical gift' was identical with 'the essence of his moral character' (356). Bradford found the poetry subtle, strange, and uncouth; and he reckoned that readers inevitably find it difficult because it is the record of honest 'effort' and 'struggle' (356–7). He proposed that Donne's writings require of readers no less moral courage and expenditure of energy; and they promise that Donne 'must remain pre-eminently great to those who will labour with him' (367). This greatness, while Bradford thought that it may be glimpsed above all in the lyrics, was said to be a quality of the 'soul' revealed in all Donne's writings, 'which, not ignorant of the wretchedness of this world, is yet forever ravished with the love and worship of the eternal' (367).

Donne's religious vision had not been the subject of much attention in New England literary culture. Emerson had been more sympathetic to the Platonic than to the Christian aspects of his poetry. Thoreau drove forward the tendency to value Donne for a philosophical wisdom that in no way depends upon the claims of revelation. His extracts contain only two lines from the Divine Poems, and these have to do with ethics rather than religion. Whipple's lectures, moreover, encouraged people to regard Donne's theological learning as so much rubbish. The concluding sentiment of Bradford's article, reminiscent as it was of the sonnet 'Batter my heart', augurs a new willingness to look at Donne's religious poems. While Walton had presented them as tokens of the Dean's mature piety, and Grosart countered that they were mostly products

---

[20] On Bradford's use of the term 'psychography', see Matthew Joseph Maikoski, 'Gamaliel Bradford: Psychographer', Ph.D. dissertation, University of Pittsburgh, 1954, 96–8; for commentary on the article about Donne, see 22–3.

[21] See Duncan, *The Revival of Metaphysical Poetry*, 117.

of youthful Roman Catholicism, Bradford found them to be of a piece with Donne's writing quite generally, revealing a vision of human life as all 'struggle and war' (367). It was this vision that warranted pyschographical study. It is of some interest, therefore, that the leading psychologist at Harvard, like other erstwhile members of 'the Metaphysical Club', did not deign to write anything on Donne. William James knew something of Donne, of course. He might have discussed Donne's religious struggles and 'sickness of soul' in his Gifford Lectures, which became *The Varieties of Religious Experience*. But Donne's peculiar religious history eluded all his paradigms, and he seems to not have known what to do with him.[22]

LOUISE IMOGEN GUINEY

While Bradford was urging that all Donne's poetry reveals the massive moral struggle of a great talent, a more comprehensive and sympathetic appreciation of Donne's religious vision was taking shape in the imagination of Louise Imogen Guiney. The daughter of a civil war general, Guiney was born in 1861 and educated at Elmhurst Academy, a convent school in Rhode Island, where she acquired an impressive grounding in music, literature, history, and French. She also began there to make the name for herself as a writer that through the 1880s and 1890s increasingly accompanied the several books of poems and essays that she brought out with leading publishing houses in Boston and New York. (Bradford considered her a possible subject for one of his psychographies, but despaired of gaining access to the materials that would make such a study possible.[23]) In virtue of her social and religious background, Louise Guiney seems an unlikely participant in the admiration for Donne that spread through greater Boston in the nineties. Yet she bears thinking about because in 1894 she published a shrewd study of the friendship between Donne and Magdalen Herbert and because she seems to have been the first person ever to publish an article on the poet in a Catholic periodical.

While it is difficult to know the details of Louise Guiney's literary studies at Elmhurst between 1872 and 1879, it is clear that she encountered there an ambivalence towards English literature common among American Catholics. Latin—the language of the liturgy, of theology, and of ecclesiastical

---

[22] For a study of the pragmatist milieu of which James was a part, see Louis Menand, *The Metaphysical Club* (New York: Farrar, Straus and Giroux, 2001); in a letter of 8 Aug. 1907 to James (Houghton Library, shelf mark: bMS Am 1092 [626–634]), Norton referred to Donne in terms that presuppose the recipient's long-standing familiarity with his poetry.
[23] See Bradford's *Journal*, 353.

diplomacy—continued to have a central importance within Catholicism. Yet in the last three decades of the nineteenth century Catholic schools gave increasingly larger scope to English literature; and in greater Boston the fact that so many Catholics were of Irish extraction heightened what were in any event perceived by Catholic educators to be inherently difficult political and pedagogical problems with the study of this subject. The nature of these problems may be glimpsed in the opening pages of a textbook compiled by the Jesuit Edward Connolly for the use of advanced students in Catholic schools. Connolly's *English Reader* (1877) consisted largely of excerpts from classic English literature 'which the fathers and grandfathers of the present generation were fond of learning by heart in their school-days.'[24] It began, nevertheless, with a Prelude made up of four passages from Cardinal Newman's *Idea of a University*. Connolly invoked Newman in order to defend the practice whereby young Catholics would be reading literature composed almost entirely by Protestants. His decision to introduce the book in this way reminds us of the anomalous position in which American Catholics found themselves: as part of an international community based chiefly in counties where the Romance languages predominated, they were suspect not only to American Protestants but to Roman ecclesiastics. Because the language of instruction in their schools derived from England, the process of acquiring literacy, and of learning to write effectively, entailed fundamental differences from what obtained among native speakers of French and Italian and Spanish. As Newman put it, whatever the future religious allegiances of English-speakers on a world scale, 'English Literature will ever *have been* Protestant' (19). Newman urged that, pedagogically, it was important to acknowledge the literary power and 'incomparable gifts' even of writers (he instanced Milton and Gibbon) who were hostile to the Catholic church (17–18). He recommended a bold embrace of classic English literature—from Shakespeare and the makers of the Protestant Bible and Prayer-Book to Addison, Swift, and Hume. Students needed to know first hand the English language as it appears in the writers who formed it and endowed it with vigor, made it supple and dexterous, graceful and precise (18–19).

At the same time that Connolly sought to invite students to understand the importance of their subject, he had to reassure them—and the authorities who would give the imprimatur—that these studies would not compromise their faith. His embattled position is evident in another passage that he

---

[24] *The English Reader*, ed. Rev Edward Connolly, S.J. (New York: Benziger Brothers, 1887), 3. Subsequent references appear in parentheses in the text. On connections between the Guiney family and the Jesuits, see Henry G. Fairbanks, *Louise Imogen Guiney* (New York: Twayne, 1973), 115–17.

printed out of Newman: at the head of a chapter titled 'Literary and Critical', where students would encounter excerpts from De Quincey and Hazlitt and Dr Johnson, Connolly gave his selection the provocative heading, 'English Literature is neither Atheistical nor Immoral' (196). Not surprisingly, what many Catholics took away from the sort of approach represented in Connolly's *Reader* was a sense of their inferiority and a defensiveness about belonging to an intellectually impoverished subculture. This was decidedly not the case with Louise Guiney, however. Her Catholic education propelled her into such wide reading and deep learning that administrators at Smith College, until they discovered that she had no formal degree, urged her to apply for a faculty position in their new English Department.

For all the sympathetic engagement with English literature evident in Louise Guiney's essays, it is clear that the Catholic education she received from the Religious of the Sacred Heart, who came from a French foundation with ties to monarchy, deeply informed her tastes. By the 1890s, she was reviewing contemporary poetry submissions for Copeland and Day, publishers of *The Yellow Book*. She was also working to rehabilitate the reputation of Keats.[25] Her greatest literary passion, however, was for seventeenth-century poets, whom she associated with a Church of England that had known what it was to be put on the defensive. She admired the Herberts, she valued Donne the more for his having had close associations with them, and her favorite poet was Henry Vaughan. She visited England as often as her genteel poverty enabled her to, and she developed many friendships there with men of letters. She shared her interest in Donne above all with Gosse, whom she and Fred Holland Day persuaded to preside at the dedication of the Keats memorial in Hampstead. It was to Gosse that she dedicated *A Little English Gallery* and to whom she commended Whittemore, then a youthful member of the English faculty at Tufts College, with the playful asseveration, 'I do not believe Mrs. Gosse and you have ever let over your Sunday threshold a greater lover of one John Donne, D. D.'[26]

Guiney's dedication in the *Gallery* (1894) presented her essays as a 'friendly trespass' upon Gosse's 'fields.' She led off the volume with a carefully researched essay on Mrs Herbert (under the title 'Lady Danvers') from which the future author of *The Life and Letters of John Donne* could have learned something about how to read the poems. Drawing upon information in Walton's *Life* of her son George and in the sermon preached by Donne at her funeral

---

[25] On Guiney's role in the Keats Revival, see Stephen Maxfield Parrish, *Currents of the Nineties in Boston and London: Fred Holland Day, Louise Imogen Guiney, and Their Circle* (New York: Garland, 1987), esp. chap. 2.

[26] Letter of June 1899, in *Letters of Louise Imogen Guiney*, ed. Grace Guiney, with a Preface by Agnes Repplier, 2 vols. (New York: Harper and Brothers, 1926), ii. 1–2.

in 1627, and attending to poems by Donne plausibly connected with her, Guiney composed a sustained meditation on an exceptional woman's place in English literary history. Unsentimental as it is, in the final pages the essay modulates into an account of the career of Lady Danvers's widower. It turns out that John Danvers, notoriously twenty years his wife's junior, left little evidence of his exploits after her death. What Guiney reports on the basis of her research—that Danvers's subsequent marriages show a recurring pattern of living off women's money—is made to throw light on the discretion that Donne had employed in praising his friend's young husband. The final implication is that discretion had been required not only of Donne but of Lady Danvers herself, in order to make the best of a situation in which the two old friends had increasing reason to conclude that she had thrown herself away on a mercenary spendthrift.

This portrait of potential tragedy is carried off with a subtlety and good humor worthy of the protagonists. Guiney generously assumes her readers' ability to recognize that the friendship between Donne and Mrs Herbert, although it involved passions potentially adulterous, was relished by them with the twice-born 'Innocence' to which Donne refers in 'To the Lady Magdalen Herbert, of St. Mary Magdalen.' She presents them through the early years of their friendship as genuinely respectful of Anne Donne and in later years, after Anne's death, as wise enough not to be weighed down with regret about the tie to Danvers. The picture of virtue that emerges is not idealized: the two friends were sufficiently self-disciplined to leave unacted upon what their mutual love and reverence did not quite leave wholly unsaid. Delicately acknowledging that the verse letter beginning 'Mad paper stay' playfully mingles imagery of erotic passion with respect for a woman about to marry another man, Guiney credits the recipient with an intelligence that appreciated the frank acknowledgment of their mutual feelings and that enjoyed Donne's chivalrous projection of a shared future in which they would not stamp out the passion but keep it under control. Adopting for herself the perspective of the 'perplexing eye | Which equally claims love and reverence', Guiney goes on to suggest—in a footnote to a passage that refers to Mrs Herbert's beautiful blond hair—that certain of Donne's erotic poems belong to the sort of relationship in which a man confesses his smoldering passion precisely by way of praising the power of the woman's virtue to help him restrain it. Citing the motto of the Knights of the Garter, *Honi soit qui mal y pense*, she calls attention to the 'bracelet of bright hair about the bone' and shrewdly proposes, for the first time in the published record, that the 'boast' of 'The Relic' and the 'roguery' of 'The Funeral' display a genuinely uncloistered virtue. It was just this sort of virtue, as Thoreau recognized, that is ascribed in another of Donne's verse letters to Mrs Herbert's eldest son; and when Guiney wished to provide a modern example of a chaste and nurturing friendship between a younger man and an older woman, she recalled what Thoreau had quoted out of Chaucer to Mrs Emerson, 'You have helped to keep my life on loft.'[27]

Unlike Norton, with whom she was collaborating at the time she published *A Little English Gallery*, Louise Guiney did not value Donne's love poetry chiefly for those poems that posit an ethereal passion of the sort that Dante had for Beatrice. She recognized all over Donne's poetry a basis for his subtle representation of the relations between body and soul in traditional Catholic notions about the body's potential for resurrection and in the incarnational and sacramental vision of reality of which these notions are an expression. Whether we ever find an unpublished sketch of Donne's life that she is reported to have written, and whether (if we do) it provides detailed discussion of these aspects of the love poetry, still it is fair to say that Louise Guiney felt a kinship with features of Donne's sensibility that often proved a stumbling block to readers brought up in Protestantism. Like Donne, she had noticed that the '*noli me tangere*' spoken by the resurrected Jesus to the Magadalen was not an absolute but a temporary dictum: 'for I am not *yet* ascended to my Father' (John 20: 17; emphasis added).

Possibly much of the earlier sketch on Donne was incorporated into an article published in the Jesuit journal, *The Month*, in 1920, the year of Miss Guiney's death. Titled 'Donne as a Lost Catholic Poet', it took for granted the wider familiarity that Grierson's edition had made possible and recommended to Catholics the Divine Poems in particular. Guiney proposed that Donne was 'one of our greatest apostates' (18), and she wasted not a moment castigating him for having changed his religion. Rather she emphasized his 'unassailably sincere' pursuit of truth, and observed that it 'must be admitted without reservation that Donne seems never to have suffered a throb of remorse, once his decision was taken' (18). For her, Donne was a 'lost Catholic poet' not in the sense that his soul would perish on the shore, but in the sense that Catholics, in their vincible ignorance, did not yet appreciate what Grosart had suspected and Grierson had 'memorably' shown, 'that Donne, wherever his utterance is devotional, shows himself a child (and not a strayed child) of the old Church' (13). Exploring the religious dimensions of the verse, she thus displayed an affinity with Donne based on their common Catholic heritage and on her respect for his religious quest. In this way she prodded Catholics to a more generous catholicity in their tastes and spirituality than had been envisaged by the followers of Cardinal Newman. Connolly's *Reader*, which

---

[27] Louise Imogen Guiney, 'Lady Danvers', in *A Little English Gallery* (New York: Harper and Brothers, 1894), 40 n., 19.

the Jesuits at Holy Cross College in Worcester and at Boston College used to introduce the study of English literature, contained no excerpts from Donne or Herbert or Vaughan.[28]

THE MAKING OF THE GROLIER CLUB EDITION

When Louise Guiney and Fred Holland Day attempted to enlist James Russell Lowell to sponsor an initiative that would erect in Hampstead the first public memorial to John Keats, they found him ill and unsympathetic. After Lowell died in August 1891, they turned to his friend Norton, whom they persuaded to serve as Treasurer of the campaign. Norton was at this time busy about many things. As Lowell's literary executor, he was putting together a new ten-volume edition of Lowell's collected *Writings*. He was also editing five other volumes of Lowell's previously uncollected and unpublished writings. Meanwhile, besides carrying out his teaching duties as Professor of Fine Arts, he was bringing out his own work on Dante, including the three-volume translation of the *Commedia* (1891–2) and a revised version of his translation of *La Vita Nuova* (1892). Moreover, he was working on his collection of literature for children, *The Heart of Oak Books*, which would come out in six volumes in 1894–5. Sometime during this period of intense productivity, probably in 1892, Norton also took over principal responsibility for another project that had been dear to Lowell for three decades. During the final months of his life Lowell had been at work in the company of his daughter, Mabel Burnett, on a revision of the Boston edition of Donne's poetry.

While Emerson had habitually dismissed 'the restorers of readings' and 'emendators' as belonging to a 'book-learned class' who know nothing of action and real thinking,[29] Lowell, during the period when he agreed to serve as the president of the newly founded Modern Language Association, returned to editing Donne. Having served as U.S. minister first to Spain and then to the Court of St James, he was undaunted by attitudes toward editorial work that considered it merely academic. In the 1880s, he recommitted himself to

---

[28] L. I. Guiney, 'Donne as a Lost Catholic Poet', *The Month*, 136 (1920), 13–19; page references appear within parentheses. Among the unpublished works listed in the Descriptive Bibliography by E. M. Tenison in *Louise Imogen Guiney: Her Life and Works, 1861–1920* (London: Macmillan, 1923), 325, is 'a character sketch and a criticism' of John Donne. According to James M. Mahoney (private correspondence, 27 Jan. 1999), the curator of the most extensive collection of Guiney's papers, this essay is not among the materials housed in the Guiney Room at Holy Cross College in Worcester, MA.

[29] 'The American Scholar' (1837), in *The Complete Works of Ralph Waldo Emerson*, i: *Nature Addresses and Lectures*, ed. Edward Waldo Emerson (Boston: Houghton, Mifflin, 1904), 89.

producing for a book-collecting club based in New York a 'correct' text of Donne's poems.

Through most of the twentieth century recognition of the signal importance of the Grolier Club edition was confined pretty much to the consciousness, so long as he lived, of one man. In the front matter for his edition, Herbert Grierson confessed that when he first resolved to edit Donne's poems in 1907, had he known of this edition, he probably would 'not have ventured on the arduous task.'[30] When he came upon the Grolier volume, he had already collated all the seventeenth-century editions. Immediately, he perceived that its editors had demonstrated what his work thus enabled him only to confirm: that among the printed editions, the first (1633) offered 'the best text' on which to base a modern edition. After his belated discovery, and stimulated by Norton's demonstration in 'The Text of Donne's Poems' that a judicious consideration of manuscript evidence could be of help in establishing the text, Grierson realized that in order to make a genuine editorial advance, he would have to examine the manuscripts. Indirectly and decisively those whom Grierson respectfully called 'the Grolier Club editors' influenced the history of reading Donne.

Grierson came to speak of 'the Grolier Club editors' because it was not clear from the front matter in the edition just which of the three persons named there—Lowell and Norton and Mrs Burnett—was responsible for which aspects of the editorial work. Careful inspection of the relevant artifacts preserved in Harvard's Houghton Library shows that the difficulty experienced by Grierson owed a good deal to deliberate actions on the part of Norton. As her father's co-laborer, Mabel Burnett had gradually discovered that the revisions of the Boston edition on which Lowell had been working off and on over thirty-six years were ultimately unsatisfactory. What she and Norton finally preserved of Lowell's work were hundreds of emendations meant to bring the text of Donne's poems into conformity with modern usage in matters of spelling and punctuation. Lowell's choices for the verbal text were silently overridden.

While working in North America in the 1850s, it had probably not occurred to Lowell to attempt to consult manuscript copies of Donne's poems. Even if he had been in England, his notions about how to edit older English literature would not have required it. Still, he sought to learn what had been printed in the first two editions, and he was the first modern editor to use them to

---

[30] *The Poems of John Donne from the Text of the Edition of 1633*, rev. by James Russell Lowell, with the Various Readings of the Others Editions of the Seventeenth Century, and with a Preface, an Introduction, and Notes by Charles Eliot Norton, 2 vols. (New York: Grolier Club, 1895); Herbert J. C. Grierson, 'The Text and Canon of Donne's Poems', *The Poems of John Donne*, 2 vols. (Oxford: Clarendon, 1912), ii, p. cxiii n.

begin a critique of the editorial tradition that descended from 1669. His labors in editing Dryden and Marvell and Donne for Child's British Poets series inspired lengthy and detailed critiques of other editors' work. Reviewing for the *Atlantic Monthly* a series then being published by John Russell Smith in London as the 'Library of Old Authors', Lowell contrasted the vitality of those who read older literature for '[r]areties of style, of thought, [and] of fancy', with the 'archæologic perversity' of antiquarians, who waste vast amounts of energy working on virtually worthless materials. He criticized in painstaking detail volume after volume in Smith's series, and many years later had the effrontery to incorporate his reviews into a long essay in *My Study Windows*. Lowell's petulant criticisms are of continuing interest because in the course of delivering them he articulated what he considered the principal qualifications of an editor of older literature: 'patience and accuracy', 'illimitable reading', and 'philological scholarship.' By the last of these he meant something like a literal love of words, rather than *Wissenschaft*. In particular Lowell criticized editors for deploying 'faulty punctuation', which distorts a writer's intended meaning.[31]

In editing Donne, not only in 1854 but again in 1866, when he spent nearly a month's 'unremitting work' on revisions of his edition (only to learn that the publisher was content with a mere reprint), Lowell gave most of his energy to finding punctuation that would make each line intelligible to modern readers.[32] His idea of producing a 'correct' text therefore tended to accommodate the punctuation to modern practice even as it occasionally restored the verbal text to an earlier reading. To create his text, Lowell drew upon experiences gained in his own 'illimitable reading', and he exercised the 'patience' entailed in comparing various editions. The 'accuracy' for which he was striving was to be achieved by experience and intuition, not by scholarly methodology. He did not assume that a 'correct' text could be found in any extant edition. In fact, Lowell may have sought to print variants at the bottom of the pages as much to enable discerning readers to appreciate the superiority of his taste as to provide data that would encourage readers to contemplate alternate interpretations. That is the conclusion to which Mabel Burnett came when she took over the task of rounding out the work that her father left unfinished.

Lowell's emendations may be seen in two copies of the Boston edition now housed in the Houghton Library. They consist of hundreds of annotations made in pencil, the great majority of which propose alterations of spelling

---

[31] James Russell Lowell, 'Library of Old Authors', *My Study Windows* (Boston: James R. Osgood, 1871), 291, 300, 331.
[32] See Lowell's letter of 15 Aug. 1866 to Norton, bMS Am 765 (96), Houghton Library, Harvard University.

and punctuation. Lowell's proposed emendations of the verbal text also show that at some point he had got hold of a copy of the 1633 edition. He used it to 'correct' a number of readings (especially among the Songs and Sonnets) and to augment the number of variants that he planned to print. When Mabel Burnett sought to extend to unemended poems what she called, in a letter to Norton, 'Papa's way of correcting', she was unable to detect any consistent principle on which he had chosen among various readings. Using a 1654 edition, along with 1633 and 1635, she began making a more thorough collation. This gave her the idea that an editor ought to inform the reader in which edition each poem had first been printed, and she began to study all the seventeenth-century editions.[33] Eventually, she turned responsibility for preparing the edition over to Norton, who reviewed all of Lowell's work and quietly transformed it.

While it was Mabel Burnett who first glimpsed the desirability of compiling a variorum edition, it was Norton who made the practical decisions necessary to get the Grolier Club edition out. From his experience of working with the text of Dante, he was able to grasp what was at stake in editing older materials. In fact, when he took over the work, he was already familiar with the very scholarship on Dante's text that twenty years later Grierson would endorse as a model for his work with Donne. Ultimately, Norton decided to preserve most of Lowell's emendations of the spelling and punctuation. Instead of printing Lowell's eclectic verbal text, he hit on the expedient of making the verbals conform to 1633 (or to the earliest complete seventeenth-century edition in which a given poem had been printed). He may have felt specially justified in implementing this procedure because Lowell had been moving in the direction of accepting more readings from 1633. In any event, on the title page of the edition Norton presented Lowell as the editor and himself as the mere writer of the introduction and annotations. Of the work done by the woman who defined the problem to which his compromise was the answer he made only brief mention in the front matter.

NORTON'S DONNE COLLECTION

Besides the effects that the Grolier Club edition would have on Grierson, who acknowledged them, and on Eliot, who left unexpressed his debts to his older cousin, the editorial work that Norton first took up in a spirit of *pietas*, out

[33] Mabel Burnett, undated letter to Charles Eliot Norton, Norton Papers, bMS Am 1088 (898), Houghton Library, Harvard University.

of his affection for Lowell, had continuing effects on him. It prompted him to make a close study of the Muses' Library edition. It encouraged him to continue collecting and annotating seventeenth-century artifacts connected with Donne. It occasioned his beginning to study manuscript copies of the poetry, and issued into his publishing an article that summed up the state of Donne studies at the end of the nineteenth century. And it led to his publishing, in 1905, the year that the bulk of his Donne collection came to Harvard, the handsome volume he called *The Love Poems of John Donne.*

Fruitful as his studies of Donne proved for Norton personally, not all these projects had an immediate impact. In particular, 'The Text of Donne's Poems' remained largely unnoticed through the twentieth century; even when a second *Critical Heritage* volume was published in 1996, there was no mention of its existence, although Grierson had recognized that it offered the most informed discussion of the value of manuscript evidence available. Norton's writing of this piece was occasioned by the fact that E. K. Chambers's Muses' Library edition appeared '[a]lmost at precisely the same moment' as the Grolier Club edition and without either editor's having known of the other's work.[34] Norton's article offered a patient and sympathetic analysis of Chambers's eclectic text in the relation to three manuscripts, generously praising it as 'the best [edition] that exists', and claiming that it 'requires little more than some additional annotations to be altogether satisfactory and final.'[35] When a new edition of the Muses' Library Donne appeared in 1901, however, Norton's criticisms were ignored, and none of his proposed emendations were incorporated.

The three manuscripts against which Norton compared the Muses' Library edition were called by Grierson N (for Norton), S (for Stephens), and Cy (for Carnaby).[36] Norton acquired all of them within a year of the publication of the Grolier Club edition, and they augmented the growing collection of Donne artifacts he had been assembling ever since he and Mabel Burnett decided that they would consult all the seventeenth-century printed editions. All three manuscripts have been housed in the Houghton lobby since the library opened in the early 1940s.

Today, as one enters the oval lobby of the Houghton, these manuscripts may be seen behind locked glass doors. Sitting beneath Donne's name inscribed high upon the wall, and next to another collection with Milton's name above it,

---

[34] On the simultaneous appearance of the two editions, see Charles Eliot Norton, 'The Text of Donne's Poems', *Studies and Notes in Philology and Literature*, v: *Child Memorial Volume* (Boston: Ginn and Co., 1896), 4; cf. also, Norton's note inside one of his annotated copies of the Grolier edition, *AC85.N8223.895d, Houghton Library.

[35] Norton, 'The Text of Donne's Poems', 5.

[36] In the *Variorum* these editions are designated, respectively, H_4, H_7, and H_3.

Figure 1. The Donne Cabinet, Lobby of the Houghton Library, Harvard University

are gathered on four shelves nearly all the Donne items that Norton collected. (See Figure 1.) On the topmost shelf, there are copies of seventeenth-century editions of *Pseudo-Martyr*, *Conclave Ignati*, the *Devotions*, *Deaths Duel*, and other individual sermons published during Donne's lifetime; on the second shelf, copies of all seven seventeenth-century editions of the *Poems*, and of *Biathanatos*, the prose *Letters*, and Walton's *Lives*; on the third, Lowell's and Norton's personal copies of the Boston and Grolier Club editions, and several books once owned by Donne himself; and on the lowest shelf, copies of the three posthumously published sermon collections, of Donne's last will, of the unpublished manuscript that Barron Field had sent to the Percy Society, and, along with the three manuscripts described in 'The Text of Donne's

Poems', the Utterson, O'Flahertie, and Dobell manuscripts, which were added to the Norton collection. That is, some books and manuscripts were acquired with the proceeds of a fund endowed in Norton's honor. Others came to Harvard through the offices of James Munn (Harvard class of 1912), who saw to it that the library built on its strength in sixteenth- and seventeenth-century literary holdings, of which the Donne collection from Norton and the George Herbert collection from George Herbert Palmer were virtual cornerstones. This is to say that Harvard built a great library only after the deaths of Lowell and Child and Norton, in the early part of the twentieth century, when several special collections were purchased to complement the books and manuscripts assembled by Harvard faculty members. Some of the Donne holdings came to Harvard from the library of Sir Edmund Gosse.[37]

The dimensions of Norton's contribution to the study of Donne through his collection of manuscripts, editions, and related materials have not been fully appreciated. Partly this is owing to the fact that Norton has been known first and foremost as a Dante scholar. The large personal library that he put together at Shady Hill, which in 1905 various friends arranged for Harvard to purchase, contained much more than Donne materials.[38] Once his books were transferred to Gore Hall, they were installed as 'the Norton collection' in glass cases right outside the head librarian's office, and a bust of the man who had collected them was placed nearby. (See Figure 2.) Shortly after Norton's death in 1908, in commemoration of his eighty-first birthday, the library held in its art room a display of Norton's books. Journalists who covered the exhibition remarked on the evidence they gave of Norton's wide scholarship and literary connections. Among numerous presentation copies from Rossetti, Clough, Dickens, Thackeray, and many contemporary writers, and amidst specimens of early printing and illustration, they were surprised to notice how 'remarkable' a Donne collection Norton had assembled.[39]

With another century's hindsight Norton's collection of Donne materials is still more remarkable. When in the 1850s Child had commissioned Lowell to edit Donne for his series, the library's only holding of seventeenth-century

---

[37] See William Bentinck-Smith, *Building a Great Library: The Coolidge Years at Harvard* (Cambridge, MA: Harvard University Library, 1976), 104–44; see also *The Houghton Library* (privately printed for Harvard College, 1942), a copy of which is held in the Harvard University Archives, HUB 1457.5, Box 16.

[38] See James Turner, *The Liberal Education of Charles Eliot Norton* (Baltimore, MD: Johns Hopkins Univ. Press, 1999), 407–8. The purchase price was $15,000. For details of the transaction, see *Annual Reports of the President of Harvard College*, 1904–5, 214–17.

[39] See 'Memorial to Norton: Books of Late Professor Are Exhibited', *Boston Evening Transcript*, Monday, 16 Nov. 1908, and 'Rare Volumes of Charles E. Norton', *Boston Sunday Herald*, 22 Nov. 1908.

Figure 2. The Charles Eliot Norton Collection, with a bust of the collector, Gore Hall Treasure Room, Harvard University, *c.*1908

Donne editions was a copy of the *Essays in Divinity* (1652).[40] In 1866 the library acquired through the Shapleigh Fund, which was increasingly being drawn upon to purchase old books, its first copy of a seventeenth-century edition (1635) of the *Poems*. A quarter century later, when Lowell and Norton were preparing the Grolier Club edition, Harvard still owned fewer than half a dozen seventeenth-century editions of books by Donne. Then suddenly, in 1905, the library acquired from Norton twenty rare items by and about Donne. Before Norton died, the O'Flahertie manuscript and another dozen rare books that he had retained temporarily for his own use made their way into Gore Hall. As it happened, then, two of the five editions of Donne's poems published in the nineteenth century were connected with Harvard. So was the first edition of Donne's love poems ever published as a volume in its own right. Moreover, in the first four years that T. S. Eliot spent in greater Boston, the library of his college acquired the material resources for the serious study of Donne. The collection was unique in North America; and over the next fifteen years it was substantially augmented and appreciated considerably in value. In 1921, George Winship, the librarian of the Harry Elkins Widener Collection, reported that 'no more interesting collection' than Norton's had ever been added to the Harvard Libraries and declared that its 'most distinctive'

---

[40] For a time it was thought that a 1633 edition of the *History of the Septuagint* was also Donne's.

component, of greatest 'permanent value', was 'the collection of first editions of the works of John Donne.'[41]

DONNE'S ENTRY INTO THE CURRICULUM

None of the factors that made Donne prominent in greater Boston—the tradition of taking his writings seriously, the editing of his poems, and the collection of manuscripts and editions—brought his writings into the Harvard curriculum. It was Le Baron Russell Briggs who first began teaching Donne, nearly twenty years before Eliot arrived as a student. A Harvard graduate himself (class of 1875), Briggs tutored Greek at his alma mater and became an instructor in English in 1883, the year that Gamaliel Bradford matriculated. He moved quickly up the ranks. In 1890 he was promoted to Professor of English, and the following year was appointed Dean of Harvard College. In 1902 he became Dean of the Faculty of Arts and Sciences, a position that he continued to hold when, in the following year, he was named President of Radcliffe College for women.

Briggs was a tall, bespectacled man, genial, affable, a favorite with the students for decades. Known as an avid sports fan, he promoted intercollegiate athletics and in particular envisaged a place for the Harvard eleven as a football powerhouse. (His name is commemorated at Harvard today in the Briggs Athletic Center.) When Tom Eliot first encountered him, and was inspired by him to read the poetry of John Donne, he was in the midst of an influential administrative career that did not preclude his teaching hundreds of freshmen every year in large lecture courses on rhetoric and on English literature. He had been widely expected to succeed Charles W. Eliot as President of the University. In the event, President Eliot retained the post for so long that Briggs's time was past.

A good deal can be ascertained about what Briggs told his students about Donne. Starting in 1895 he gave his lecture on Donne to freshmen virtually every year for more than two decades. There are extant sets of student notes on versions of the lecture from 1895, 1900, 1906, and 1909. In addition, there are extensive student notes on Briggs's lectures in Harvard's first course on seventeenth-century literature. Before examining what these notebooks and

---

[41] George Parker Winship, 'The Norton Collection in the Library', *Harvard Alumni Bulletin*, 23 (May 1921), 706–7. Lists of 'Expensive Books purchased, 1887–78 to 1919–20' show that the Norton Fund was used to acquire some seventeen books connected with Donne, a significant portion of the overall expenditure (University Library Records, UA III.50.28.87.3, Harvard University Archives). My thanks to Brian Sullivan for calling these materials to my attention.

other materials available in the curriculum collection of the Harvard Archives can tell us, it is worth noting that the modest tribute to Briggs in 'Donne in Our Time' points obliquely to some telling peculiarities of Eliot's earliest encounters with Donne's poetry.[42]

First, we might reflect upon Eliot's disarming claim that he had 'forgotten what Professor Briggs told us about the poet', except that 'his own words and his quotations were enough to attract to private reading at least one Freshman ... who had not yet approached the metaphysicals.' On 9 January 1906 Francis M. Rackemann was present at a version of the lecture that Eliot would hear a year later, and his classnotes are in the archives. Unfortunately, they are brief and not especially informative. The notes show that early on Briggs explained to the students that the term 'metaphysical', when it is applied to poetry, 'means far fetched and overdone.' More helpfully, they indicate that, while Briggs assigned before other lectures the reading of poems by Jonson, Herrick, and Dryden as they appeared in *Ward's English Poets*, he did not assign any of Donne's poems for reading. He assigned only Walton's *Life of Donne*; and near the outset of his lecture, he proposed that it makes a 'good introduction both to Walton and to Donne.' Briggs told the students about the various genres in which Donne had written, and he emphasized the satires and praised the verse letters as Donne's best poetry.[43] From lecture notes taken in other years we know that this was in keeping with what Briggs ordinarily said. The folder that houses Rackemann's notes contains one real surprise, however: a printed pamphlet with summaries of the lectures from the whole first half of the course, annotated in Rackemann's hand with a view to preparing for the course examination. (These annotations show that, whenever the pamphlet was printed—and it contains no information about who created it and had it printed—it was in circulation at the time

---

[42] Notes by students from Briggs's lecture on Donne in English 28 may be found in the Curriculum Collection of the Harvard University Archives at the following locations: for 1895, James Duncan Phillips, HUC 8894.324.2, 63–5; for 1900, Anonymous, HUC 8899.324.28, 31–3; for 1906, Francis M. Rackemann, HUC 8905.325.28, 66–7; for 1909, Albert Morton Bierstadt, HUC 8908.324.28, 22^v-3^r.

Notes by students from Briggs's lectures on Donne in English 15 may also be found in the Curriculum Collection at the following locations: for 1890, Raymond Calkins, HUC 8889.324.15, 1^v-12^r; for 1892, Fred N[orris] Robinson, HUC 8887.325.77. Two other sets of notes from the 1892 version of the course are located elsewhere: William Lyon Phelps's notes on 'English Literature of the 17th Century' (1892), William Lyon Phelps Papers, Manuscripts and Archives, Yale University Library, MS Group 578, Series III, Box 17, Folder 202, 1–27; and Martin Grove Brumbaugh's notes on the same course, housed in the Vault Collection in the archives of Juniata College, Huntingdon, PA. My thanks to archivist D. F. Durnbaugh for providing a photocopy of Brumbaugh's notes.

[43] Rackemann, HUC 8905.325.28, 66–7; Rackemann lists the required readings for the course on one of several unnumbered pages that follow 75.

Rackemann and Eliot were taking the course.) The summaries may have been prepared by students from previous years or by teaching assistants. What is discontinuous in them from all the extant sets of written notes is this: they make it sound as if Briggs spent considerable time emphasizing Donne's 'decadent' style: 'There is much *smut—unclean phrases*. ... Profound lewdness and the utterly vile is here—lust of the flesh.' Eliot may have had rather less learned motives for looking into the 'metaphysicals' after hearing Briggs's lecture than the vague recollections in 'Donne in Our Time' suggest. The only quotation from Donne's poetry to appear in the pamphlet is 'Mark but this flea, etc.'[44]

Second, we should advert to the fact that, after the passage that serves as the epigraph for this chapter, Eliot goes on to say he next heard of Donne when he went to London. That was in 1911. Whether during his senior year, when Norton's library went on exhibit, he had noted its numerous Donne items we do not know. Still, our inference that he did not encounter Donne again in the curriculum is probably accurate. Eliot's academic record shows that more than half the courses he took as an undergraduate were freshman courses. Besides the one in which he heard Dean Briggs, he enrolled in only one other English course, Advanced Composition. In his third year he did take Comparative Literature 6b, 'The Literary History of England and its Relation to that of the Continent from Chaucer to Elizabeth.' This course may have helped to kindle interests that contributed to the ways in which he eventually sought to locate Donne in literary history. But the course did not take up Donne, who was always grouped in the Harvard curriculum with seventeenth-century writers and was treated as discontinuous with Spenser and the Elizabethans. Moreover, although Eliot also took Comparative Literature 7, 'Tendencies of European Literature in the Renaissance', the instructor's lecture notes show that the course was wholly confined to the fifteenth and sixteenth centuries.[45] Even when Eliot went on to read for an AM in English, he did not take any courses in which it was usual to examine the writings of Donne.

Third, Eliot does not exactly say that he took English A. At the risk of playing the saucy pedant chiding schoolboy inaccuracy we can observe that, although Eliot rightly remembered that this was the designation of the standard freshman course taught by Briggs, he never took it. English A was a composition course and one of the few required courses. At the time of his admission Eliot was given credit for English A on the basis of work he had

[44] Anonymous pamphlet, headed 'English 28', 9–10.

[45] Papers of M. A. Potter, Lecture Notes in Comparative Literature 7 (*c*.1907), HUC 8907.214.70, Harvard University Archives. For Eliot's transcripts, see Harvard University, Student Records, Thomas Stearns Eliot, UA III.15.75.12 and UAV 161.272.5, Harvard University Archives.

done at Milton Academy. This freed him to take English 28, the 'History and Development of English Literature', another large lecture course principally for freshmen. It was taught by five specialists in the various periods. Briggs generally gave six lectures on seventeenth-century literature: one each on Donne, Jonson, Milton, and Dryden, one on other poetry of the period, and one on prose. Characteristically, he began his first lecture by observing that 'Spenser had a little school, but his influence was not wide' and 'Milton's influence was slight in his own time. ... The masters of English poetry up to Milton were Ben Jonson and John Donne.' They 'ruled English poetry until Dryden dispossessed them.'[46] In view of the popularity of English 28, it is fair to conclude that at the start of the twentieth century, although the curriculum contained a half-course devoted exclusively to Milton, a majority of the students who elected courses in English were introduced to the study of literary history by an account that gave equal or greater weight to Donne.

Fourth, it is notable that it seemed to Eliot not in the least extraordinary that an undergraduate might first learn of Donne's poetry in a college English course. From the time he first encountered it in English 28 he took it for granted that Donne's poetry had a well-established place in literary history. When, twenty-five years later, he accepted the invitation to write an essay for the tercentenary, he assumed that readers were more interested in knowing his personal history as a reader than in examining how it was that Dean Briggs had given so much prominence to Donne.

One basis on which Donne's writings had entered the English curriculum is perhaps necessary although certainly not sufficient to explain why it was at Harvard that it happened early: President Eliot's famed elective system. In the 1870s Child was giving elective courses on the history of the language and on Shakespeare. In 1876–7, having parlayed the offer of a chair at the newly founded Johns Hopkins University into a position as Harvard's first Professor of English, he ceded the chair of rhetoric to A. S. Hill and began teaching a range of linguistic and literary subjects.[47] Three years later when 'Collegiate Instruction for Women' commenced at what would become Radcliffe, there were even more elective courses available at Harvard, and Child's younger colleagues began the practice of repeating English electives for women at the so-called 'Harvard Annex.' At first English was a much more popular subject among the women than the men. Between 1876 and 1888 the Harvard English Department had fewer students than Greek, Latin, history, mathematics,

---

[46] Anonymous (1899–1900), HUC 8899.324.28, 31–3; cf. Rackemann, HUC 8905.325.28, 66, and Bierstadt, HUC 8908.324.28, 22ᵛ.

[47] See Jay Heinrichs, 'How Harvard Destroyed Rhetoric', *Harvard Magazine*, 97/6 (July–Aug. 1995), 37–42.

chemistry, or natural history. Among the women, however, English was by far the most popular subject.[48]

In 1887 Harvard announced plans to enlarge the instruction it gave in literature, and in the second half of the 1887–8 academic year Dean Briggs inserted Donne into the curriculum in a decisive manner when he gave Harvard's first course on the seventeenth century. Eighty-one students took the new English 15, which was divided into two parts, poetry and prose. Donne was the anchor of the first part, and Walton the starting point for the second. Briggs began with several lectures on Donne. When he taught the course again the next year, for women as well as for men, he gave five lectures on Donne, at least twice as many classes as he devoted to any other author. He also required three written exercises based on each student's private reading of Donne's poems.[49] This remained the case even in 1891–2, the year in which Briggs became Dean of the College and the last time he gave the course in the form he first conceived it. When, in 1897–8 he was asked to remodel English 15, so that it would cover only the second half of the century, Donne remained the point of departure and continued to have a prominent place in the lectures. J. H. Gardiner, inheriting the remodeled course in 1899–1900, similarly started with two classes on Donne. In subsequent lectures, as he introduced new authors, Gardiner frequently related them back to Donne as their most relevant predecessor.[50]

Besides the foundational place that Donne had in English 28 and in English 15, Donne's writings made their way onto the syllabus in other courses. In 1890 Briggs introduced the 'History and Principles of English Versification' (English 16). It was never as popular as courses on individual authors or on literary periods, and it was given under the designation 'Primarily for Graduates.' Still, we know from the notebook of a student who took the course in 1890–1, that Briggs treated in detail Donne's handling of the heroic couplet. When English 32 was created in 1896–7 to cover in the first half-year 'English Literature of the Elizabethan Period (1557–1599)' and in the second the period that had been cut from the old English 15, Donne was included by George Pierce Baker in the inaugural session of the course that proceeded 'From the

---

[48] What was to be renamed Radcliffe College in 1894 was at this time called the Society for the Collegiate Instruction of Women. Each year a table of enrollment statistics was published by the college in its annual *Report of the Treasurer and Secretary* of the Society; now accessible online via a link on the Harvard University Archives web page.

[49] See Calkins, HUC 8889.324.15, 1^v–9^v.

[50] See Papers of J. H. Gardiner, English Authors I, folder 'English 15. Opening. I. II.', Typescript from L. B. R. Briggs (to Gardiner), 'ENGLISH 15. 1897–98'; also, in the same folder, Gardiner's lecture notes headed 'Donne: Jonson', HUG 1415.24, Harvard University Archives. For a set of student notes on Gardiner's course, see Curriculum Collection, Arthur B. Myrick Notes on English 152, HUC 8899.324.15.

Death of Spenser to the Closing of the Theatres (1599–1642).'51 Gardiner taught the early seventeenth century the following year and presented Donne as its most important author. When the course was handed on to William Allan Neilson in 1901, although only one lecture was afforded to Donne, the lecturer praised his ability to produce a wide range of love poetry, and pronounced him the 'most tantalizing of poets.'52 (This bespeaks the influence of Harvard on Neilson. He had been an undergraduate at Edinburgh; and, as his classnotes show, he had imbibed there Masson's opinion that Donne was a poet of 'Metrical Intellection.') Meanwhile in English 34, a new course on 'English Letter Writers', Charles Townsend Copeland assigned the letters of only three writers who had lived before the eighteenth century, and Donne was one of them.53

What was Donne made to look like in the lectures for these various courses? The picture is not uniform, nor was Donne's position stable. It is worth noting several ways in which Donne was *not* presented. Harvard lecturers typically pointed out that Walton's *Life of Donne* enjoyed far greater popularity in Britain than in the United States, and they did not treat Walton as if he needed correcting. Nor did they encourage students to regard the *Life* as a key to understanding Donne's poems. There is no evidence that Donne's life and writings were made an illustration of the converting power of religion or of marriage. Nor were they read as suggestive of the extreme conditions that might lead a talented person to compromise himself in order to have a career. Occasionally some aspect of his writings, such as the phrase 'masculine persuasive force', may have qualified Donne to be of interest to the purveyors of the rhetoric of masculinity.54 Yet he was not a significant counter in the proliferating discourses of gender or of race.

From student notebooks compiled in English 15 we can infer that Briggs intuited that to begin with several lectures on Donne would enable him to illustrate how he meant to teach English literature in general: to inform students about what there was to read, to tell them about the grounds on

---

51 William Lyon Phelps, notes on English 16, 'Briggs's History and Principles of English Versification, 1890–91', William Lyon Phelps Papers, Manuscripts and Archives, Yale University Library, MS Group 578, Series III, Box 17, Folder 202, 54–5, 60.

52 William Allan Neilson, [Lecture Notes for English 32ª], in [Division] 32. Personal Papers of William Allan Neilson, Series III, Box 19, Folder 339, Smith College Archives. Cf. W. Allan Neilson, 'Lectures on Historical English Literature by Prof. [David] Masson' (1889), ii, 161–2, in [Division] 32. Personal Papers, Series 1, Box 14, Smith College Archives.

53 See Faculties of Arts and Sciences, Department of English 1899–1900, 14, Curriculum Collection, HUC 8899.124.3, Harvard University Archives.

54 See Kim Townsend, *Manhood at Harvard: William James and Others* (New York: Norton, 1996; London: Harvard Univ. Press, 1998), esp. chap. 2. For evidence that Briggs assigned Walton's *Life of Donne* for reading in English 28, see, in the Curriculum Collection, Phillips, HUC 8894.324.2, 60.

which readers had found certain writers interesting or important, and to motivate them to read the works for themselves. Briggs then expected students to formulate their reactions. Even in English 28, the large lecture course in which Donne was covered in a single lecture, he sometimes asked students to write specifically on their reading of Satire III. What he himself had to say about this poem shows that he thought it an apt introduction to Donne: Briggs presented the lines about Truth standing on a high hill that is difficult of access as emblematic of Donne's own poetry, an acquaintance with which sometimes required to be forced.

For Briggs, Donne's importance was above all what Coleridge had recognized when he proposed that reading the satires would be the best preparation a young scholar could have if he wished to enjoy reading Milton. In 'Principles of English Versification', Briggs gave considerable scope to the satires. He organized the course not by chronology or with a view to covering particular authors but according to verse forms. Donne appeared as one of the writers who had discovered the fitness of the heroic couplet for satire. When Briggs introduced him into the course, he did it in a way that enabled him to recommend his poetry more generally: 'Donne did just what he pleased with the language. His wit at times led him to write with harsh audacity. ... In his satires, scarcely anything but the rimes holds the verse together. Otherwise it would sound like prose.'[55] Still, Donne had a limited place in the lectures. Although Briggs sometimes recommended Jacob Schipper's *Englische Metrik*, he seems not to have noticed—no doubt because Schipper organized his study by verse forms and not by authors—that this massive handbook had effectively demonstrated the great variety of verse forms that Donne had employed.[56] Even in the section of course devoted to the sonnet, there was no consideration of Donne, probably because the controversial religious material would have distracted from Briggs's purpose.

The evidence about Briggs's teaching of Donne available from more than a dozen notebooks kept by students, although it cannot be assumed to be strictly reliable, does not preclude our making other generalizations. Briggs was exactly that individual whose 'judgment that a work is great', as John Guillory has proposed, because it was 'made in a certain institutional context', helped to 'insure the ... continual reintroduction' of Donne's poetry 'to generations of readers.'[57] His teaching of Donne was based on personal enthusiasm for

[55] See Phelps's notes on English 16, 'Briggs's History and Principles of English Versification', 54–5.

[56] J[akob] Schipper, *Englische Metrik in historicischer und systematischer Entwickelung dargestellt*, 3 vols. (Bonn: Emil Strauss, 1880–8), ii: *Neuenglische Metrik* (1888).

[57] John Guillory, 'Canon', in *Critical Terms for Literary Study*, ed. Frank Lentricchia and Thomas McLaughlin, 2nd edn (Chicago: Univ. of Chicago Press, 1995), 237.

a writer who, though difficult of access at first, would, he told thousands of students, influence for life readers who took the trouble to acquaint themselves with his works. Before his administrative duties became extensive, Briggs's teaching of Donne was also based on the latest scholarship. He was unusually aware of the history of reading Donne: of the great popularity that Donne had enjoyed within manuscript culture; of the almost complete eclipse of Donne's writing that had taken place in the long eighteenth century and of the repetition of merely conventional dismissals of his poetry through most of the nineteenth; and of the shrewd reading nonetheless represented in writings by Coleridge and De Quincey, and later by Minto and Saintsbury. Briggs's understanding of Donne also owed something to Gosse, who emphasized Donne's impact on other seventeenth-century poets. When Gosse had come to Boston in 1884 to give his series of lectures at the Lowell Institute on 'Poetry at the Death of Shakespeare', the 850 seats in the lecture hall were filled each time he spoke. In the opening lecture he asked the audience to imagine Cambridge University in the 1620s: it was, he said, 'a hotbed of poetry', where the 'exciting, fantastical, hysterical canzonets of the great Dean of St. Paul's were eagerly passed from hand to hand, and were as seed that sprung up in the breasts of dozens of ardent young writers'. Not yet at work on the project in which he would treat Donne as a biographical subject, Gosse presented him as a poets' poet, one who had shown what it means to write principally for other writers. The lectures went on to trace the deadly effect that Donne had had on English writing. Gosse placed Donne at the head of a 'craze for calling heaven and earth to witness the ingenuity of a conceit' and mitigated his charge that Donne's influence 'spread like a canker' through English literature by assigning the blame to his imitators.[58] This was good enough for Briggs, who went on to give sustained attention to Donne in his courses and to make less of Donne's successors.

In lecturing on Donne in the 1880s Briggs quoted from the latest edition of Donne's *Poems*, the Fuller Worthies' edition, which he assumed on the basis of Grosart's own claims to provide the best available text. Briggs was not taken in, however, by the prurient interest in Donne's sexual life that the editor's Preface set in motion, nor by the imperative that Grosart and others felt to find in the poetry secrets about Donne's youth. In English 28, although Briggs typically assigned the *Life of Donne* by Walton at the class before he was to lecture on Donne, the actual lecture that he gave (a version of which Eliot

[58] Edmund Gosse, *Six Lectures Written to be Delivered Before the Lowell Institute In December, 1884* (London: Chiswick Press, Oct. 1884), 'Privately Printed in an Impression of Only Four Copies', Lecture I, 18, 28. The copy in the Houghton Library (*AC85.H8395.Zz884g) is inscribed by the author to William Dean Howells, their 'onlie begetter.'

heard) was an invitation to read Donne's poetry and to attend to its style. The fact that Briggs's treatment of Donne in English 15 began with remarks on the biography did not set Donne apart from other writers in the course, or in most other courses. The series of lectures was organized on the basis of the various genres in which Donne had written. While Briggs, in the tradition that descended from Lowell and Thoreau, had an unusually high regard for the verse letters, it was not because they revealed private details about the author's relationships but because they are busy with thoughts and frequently startle readers. Briggs acknowledged that the effects of Donne's writing on other writers were mostly bad, and he explained this by developing Gosse's point into the more precise claim that Donne's greatest qualities provoked imitation, almost always by persons who were incapable of his boldness of thought.

To Briggs's mind Donne was important for what his poetry could provoke readers to imagine. He recommended on these grounds the Anniversaries and lyrics such as 'The Dream' and 'The Relic', a poem that 'shows more sides of Donne than any other poem of equal length' and is 'the best epitome of Donne.'[59] He seems never to have tired in praising the rugged Third Satire. 'We go to [Donne] for thought', Briggs often said, 'not for song.' If there was a sense of mission in this teaching, and many others besides Eliot remembered that there was, it was because he was convinced that keeping Donne's reputation alive depends upon developing a willingness to join him in feats of imagination that require 'intellectual struggle' and repay it with 'remarkable force.' He challenged students by proposing that 'Donne's verse is the best test to find out your metrical sense—your ear' and by acknowledging that 'Besides the metrical entanglement, there is the thought tangle.' At the same time that he was urging that far more than other poets Donne requires rereading and that, for instance, ' "Good Friday" is well worth hard study,' he flattered his students and promised them pleasure: 'Every great poet has to create the taste necessary to enjoy him.'[60]

By contrast with what others at Harvard had to say about Donne's poetry, Briggs's views were remarkably free of overdetermining theories. There was nothing in his presentation of Donne that smacked of Norton's contempt for post-medieval art, nor of Norton's presentation of Donne as 'a child' of the Renaissance, who 'shared ... in its confusion of the sensual and the

---

[59] Robinson, notes on English 15, n.p.; Phelps, notes on English 15, 24.

[60] Robinson, notes on English 15, n.p.; Phelps, notes on English 15, 23, 7, 19, 27, 9, respectively. The idea in this last quotation comes ultimately from the article on Donne in *Lowe's Edinburgh Magazine*, 1 (1846), 232. It was likely mediated to Briggs through Grosart's quotation of it in his edition, ii, p. xli. Briggs invoked it often; see also, in the Curriculum Collection of the Harvard Archives, Anonymous, HUC 8899.324.28 (1900), 32, and Calkins, HUC 8889.324.15, 3ʳ.

supersensual, in its love of physical and its adoration of spiritual beauty' and who suffered from its corrupted 'moral sense', which while it had 'quickened life' had also 'spread moral contagion.' As Professor of Fine Arts, Norton did not teach Donne. It was Gardiner who imported his views into the English curriculum. If, like Briggs, he regarded Donne as the most important seventeenth-century author, it was only partly on the grounds that the poems challenge readers to use their minds. For Gardiner, Donne was the last great figure of the Renaissance in England, a Titan at a time when there were giants on the earth; and his writings showed the marks of the decadence that crept into England from Italy, so that Donne forever 'stands for all the failing power of the renaissance.'[61] Like Norton, Gardiner was too discreet to cite particular passages that evinced the worst of it. He called attention, however, to discrepancies between Walton's *Life* and Donne's poems, the earliest of which, he claimed, display 'an intensity of voluptuousness that is of the essence of the renaissance' ('Donne. Biography', 2) and which no reader of Walton would ever suppose were written by Dr Donne. Unlike Grosart, Gardiner, who also gave for many years a course on the English Bible as literature, did not feel ambivalent about the contradictions he turned up. He urged that 'when you read [Donne] you cannot help fe[e]ling that he was one of the great men of the earth who had the great experiences' ('Donne. [I]', 10). His course unfolded in an attempt to show that, since the later seventeenth-century, readers had been incapable of understanding a depth of passion comparable to that of Michelangelo and Dante and Shakespeare in his *Anthony and Cleopatra* and that, instead of appreciating the profound thinking that informs Donne's writing, they noticed only the elaborate ingenuity of his figures. Nor did it trouble Gardiner that this passion had 'only incidentally' been poured into verse, and that Donne was a poet 'as it were by avocation' ('Donne. II', 8). Gardiner contrasted him with Ben Jonson and especially with Bacon on the grounds that he was precisely unambitious for himself and his writings and that he never 'pushed his own fortunes' nor wrote verse that would enforce some 'dogma' ('Donne. [I]', 1–2). Donne's having gone into the church was as irrelevant to the essence of his writing as the claim that the Bible contains divine revelation was to its status as great literature.

After the turn of the century Gardiner and Briggs no longer taught English 15 and English 32, and Donne was notably downgraded in the curriculum along with seventeenth-century literature generally. Before 1900 the study of English

---

[61] Norton, Introduction, *Poems of John Donne* (Grolier Club edn), i, p. xxii; Papers of J. H. Gardiner, English Authors I, in folder 'English 32²', Summary', 2, HUG 1415.24, Harvard University Archives. Subsequent quotations are from three sets of lecture notes in the folder headed 'Donne'; short titles and page numbers are given in parentheses.

literature had been such a growth industry that there was plenty of room to study all periods from Chaucer through the nineteenth century, though it is only fair to note that when President Eliot asked a faculty member how his teaching was going, he generally meant, How many students are your courses attracting? By the first decade of the twentieth century the economic principle whereby more up-to-date writing drives out older literature decidedly began to affect the curriculum. This is most conspicuous in the case of course offerings in the summer school, which from the start was a money-making operation. From the summer of 1895 onwards the number of offerings increased almost every year. Composition courses were especially popular, 'English Literature of the Eighteenth Century' was generally offered, and nineteenth-century courses were introduced. In 1897 there were seven students in a course on Chaucer, forty-three in the eighteenth-century course. With the exception of Shakespeare courses, rarely was there any course that treated writing from the sixteenth or seventeenth century.[62]

As for the regular courses in the English Department, the proportion of offerings on nineteenth-century literature and on American literature increased considerably after Child's death in 1896. Moreover, early in the new century Barrett Wendell instituted, as an alternative to English 28, a new course called 'History of English Literature from the Elizabethan times to the present.' This large lecture course not only omitted consideration of Anglo-Saxon and medieval literature, but diminished the scope that the rival course for freshmen headed by Briggs allotted to Donne. Meanwhile half-year courses on Spenser and on Milton continued to be given. In English 32b Donne was displaced into the middle of the pack, pride of place now devolving upon Bacon, who had been the subject of a standard half-course in the days when Child presided over the Department. Donne's letters dropped out of the syllabus altogether in Copeland's English 34. In 1903–4 Wendell, just returned from giving the Clark lectures in Cambridge, taught English 32b and English 15, covering the whole seventeenth century. He took the occasion to persuade himself, as he framed it in the preface to the book he made from his lectures, that the 'main outlines of [his] conception' of the period were valid.[63]

Wendell's views on the sixteenth and seventeenth centuries served as the reigning theory about the course of English literary history through the whole time that T. S. Eliot was at Harvard. In *The Temper of the Seventeenth Century*

---

[62] Here and elsewhere in this chapter, data on enrollments are taken from the *Annual Reports of the Presidents and Treasurers of Harvard College*, published by the college at the end of each academic year and now accessible online via a link on the Harvard University Archives web page.

[63] Barrett Wendell, *The Temper of the Seventeenth Century in English Literature*, Clark Lectures given at Trinity College, Cambridge in the Year 1902–3 (London: Macmillan; New York: Charles Scribner's Sons, 1904), p. vii. Subsequent page references appear within parentheses.

in English Literature Wendell gave altogether about a dozen pages to Donne, which is to say that he published more on him than Briggs or Gardiner or any other member of the English faculty did. The amount of attention he gave Donne owed a good deal to his having been so long at Harvard, where he needed to take Donne more seriously than he would have if he had studied and taught anywhere else. Donne's 'fame, whether we care for him or not', Wendell wrote, 'is proving permanent' (122). In a prelude to his chapter on 'The Disintegration of Lyric Poetry', Wendell made his treatment of Donne an integral, in fact climactic, part of a thesis that he developed out of Gosse, according to which, after the death of Shakespeare, Donne was principally responsible for the 'fall' from the glories of the Elizabethan age 'into the affectations of a mannerism which grew lifeless the moment the master who vitalized it fell asleep' (126). As the great heretic of seventeenth-century letters, Donne had presumed to write 'with utter disregard' for Spenser's salutary appropriation of classical Italian influences and for Jonson's sturdy exposition and practice of 'the permanent poetic principles of the enduring classics of antiquity' (120). The final paragraphs of Wendell's chapter make it clear that all these claims were to be put at the service of a larger theory of recurrence in literary history, which he invoked to castigate his contemporaries for their decadence: assimilating Spenser to Wordsworth, Ben Jonson to Tennyson, and Donne to Browning, he urged that though they were not exactly responsible for the coming poetical 'disintegration', their respective tendencies had portended it (126–7). In 1905–6, the year when Tom Eliot was making his application to Harvard, Wendell's theory made its way into the course descriptions for English 32b and English 15. The course on English literature from 1599 to 1642 was now said to deal 'with those writers who may be regarded as marking the disintegration of English literature during the first half of the Seventeenth Century', while the course covering 1642 to 1700 treated 'those writers who may be regarded as marking the reintegration of English literature during the second half of the Seventeenth Century.'[64] These course descriptions carry the narrative that Eliot would seek to reverse when, in reviewing Grierson's anthology of metaphysical poetry, he expounded the theory of a 'dissociation of sensibility' that took place in the seventeenth century and from which, he insisted, 'we have never recovered.'

[64] *Official Register of Harvard University, Department of English 1905–6*, 2/26 (Cambridge, MA: Harvard University, 30 June 1905), 12.

8

A Subject Not Merely Academic

Donne … must be read, and by every catholic student of English literature
should be regarded with a respect only 'this side idolatry.'

—George Saintsbury, *A History of Elizabethan Literature* (1887)

In the decade before T. S. Eliot matriculated at Harvard, several graduates who
had studied with Dean Briggs brought Donne into the curriculum of other U.S.
colleges. By the time that Eliot heard Briggs's lecture in 1907, however, the study
of Donne at Harvard was on the decline. These developments—the spread of
Donne studies beyond Harvard and the waning of Donne's reputation in the
University where he had been made a substantial academic subject—created
apt conditions for Eliot to display his individual talent a decade later as he began
engaging a neglected literary tradition in which Donne had played a central
part. As Anne Ferry has shrewdly observed, even before Eliot began writing
about Donne, he had imagined a future anthology, an alternative to Palgrave,
in which readers would discover in a poem such as 'Whispers of Immortality'
a long delayed coupling between the dead writers of the seventeenth century
and the living modern verse in which they assert their immortality. By 1923,
when Eliot reviewed the Nonesuch edition of Donne's *Love Poems*, he was
happy to share with others the credit for the 'discovery' of the metaphysicals.
His review pointed out that Donne had been receiving 'close attention from
some of the most interesting younger poets', that he had 'been approved, for
many years, by Mr Edmund Gosse and Professor Le Roy Barron [sic] Briggs',
and that to an incalculable degree the catholic taste of George Saintsbury was
responsible for widespread interest in Jacobean and Caroline poetry.[1]

Eliot understood quite well that the 'close attention' lavished on Donne's
poetry by the likes of Arthur Symons and Rupert Brooke was not merely a
reaction against Victorian stodginess. The ferment among younger poets was

---

[1] Anne Ferry, *Tradition and the Individual Poem: An Inquiry into Anthologies* (Stanford, CA:
Stanford Univ. Press, 2001), 247–50. See also T. S. Eliot, 'John Donne', *Nation and Athenaeum*,
33/10 (9 June 1923), 331–2.

the by-product of cultural investments of teachers and critics and editors who had been made restless by the routine condemnation of poems that, upon inspection, continued to resist attempts to make them lie flat. When it came to crediting Victorian pedagogues and critics for having appreciated a poet whom they wished to regard as 'modern' *avant le lettre*, other self-conscious moderns proved much more grudging. They remembered only that in nineteenth-century Britain the academic tradition had routinely damned Donne's writing.

DONNE IN VICTORIAN ACCOUNTS OF LITERARY HISTORY

There is some evidence that Donne's character came up in early 'English' courses in England. D. J. Palmer's study of *The Rise of English Studies* cites in passing an examination question set at University College, London: 'State what you know concerning the *personal* history of Donne, Cowley, Lee, Butler, and Otway.'[2] This question reflected the priority of Walton's Donne in the 1840s. It was not indicative of the ways in which Donne was typically presented in Victorian literary histories. Handbooks, compendiums, and anthologies that deigned to mention his writing treated it as manifesting a decline from the glories of the Elizabethan era. This was the traditional view that Briggs sought to reverse; and it was the orthodoxy that Wendell restored in the Harvard English curriculum just before Eliot arrived.

Among Victorian accounts of English literary history, Hippolyte Taine's multivolume *Histoire de la Littérature anglaise* (1863), translated into English in the 1870s, stood out for its ambitiousness.[3] The claim for its theoretical sophistication was made by a leading authority in the German university system, Johannes Scherr, who praised his French colleague for having 'so penetrated into the very genius of a foreign nation as to form a completely impartial judgment of its productions.'[4] English-speakers were not convinced. When, in 1900, J. Scott Clark of Northwestern University wrote an introduction for a new edition of the *Histoire* and celebrated it as a 'classic', he observed that Taine's principal weakness as a critic manifested itself in his treatment

[2] D. J. Palmer, *The Rise of English Studies: An Account of the Study of English Language and Literature from its Origins to the Making of the Oxford English School* (London: Oxford Univ. Press, for the Univ. of Hull, 1965), 25–6. The question was set by the philologist, Robert Gordon Latham; the italics appear in the original.

[3] H[ippolyte] Taine, *Histoire de la Littérature Anglaise* (1863), translated as *History of English Literature*, by H. Van Laun (Edinburgh: Edmonston and Douglas, 1871).

[4] Johannes Scherr, *A History of English Literature*, trans. M. V. (London: Sampson, Low, 1882), 2.

of the seventeenth century, when sincere religious differences multiplied dramatically. Taine, unable to 'appreciate the religious conditions that surround his subject', was 'sometimes inaccurate or unjust from a lack of sympathy.'[5]

Taine was known for his interest in the psychology of writers and for his reading literature in terms of race, geography, and the movements of historical process. Where others might have had plenty to say about Donne in these contexts, Taine dismissed his poetry in a few paragraphs. He presented it as the pre-eminent example of a decadent 'affectation' that succeeded the great Elizabethan writers. Donne's 'strained' style and 'absurd comparisons' showed that English writers in the early seventeenth century rose to the same 'height of folly' that the sonneteers of Italy and Spain did once 'the poetic vitality' of 'a unique and wonderful' epoch had worn itself out 'by its very efflorescence.'[6] This was to define Donne squarely by means of a theory that posited cycles of cultural production that moved from inception, through growth and flowering, to decay. The theory enabled Taine to explain how Donne's poetry at once sustained some of 'the energy and thrill of the original inspiration' and nonetheless contributed to a decided falling off from the glorious achievements of 'the pagan Renaissance' in England. The contours of this theory were similar to those in Rio's thesis about Quattrocento painting. The valuations placed on religious phenomena, however, were reversed. Like Rio, Taine posited a passage from ripeness to decadence. While for Rio there had been a fall *from* Christian integrity, for Taine there was a fall *into* Christian fanaticism.

Most British writers on literary history told a still more simplistic story. Without recourse to a theory of cycles of aesthetic growth and decline, they retailed the facts and located Donne beyond the pale. They also assigned him a role in an unfolding story of the national literature. Popular handbooks typically represented Donne as the head of a 'metaphysical school', remarking on the harshness of his verse, the eccentricity of his language, and the unnatural quality of his conceits. All the old familiar charges were repeated: the writing was 'obscure', 'perverse', 'monstrous', 'morbid', 'tasteless.' Textbooks generally traced Donne's decadence to personal circumstances that made him more susceptible than others to infectious foreign influences and dissuaded him from tapping into the stream of undefiled English that flowed from Spenser to Wordsworth. Henry Morley's *Manual of English Literature*, for instance, emphasized the pressure placed on Donne to conform to Roman Catholicism and observed that he spent 'some years' in Italy and Spain.[7] John

---

[5] J. Scott Clark, 'Special Introduction', *History of English Literature*, rev. edn (New York: Colonial Press, 1900), p. vii.

[6] Taine, *History of English Literature*, quoted from rev. English edn (1900), i. 241, 242, 237.

[7] Henry Morley, *A First Sketch of English Literature* (London: Cassell, Petter, and Galpin, [1872/73]) 527–9.

Hales, in a headnote for Ward's *English Poets*, informed readers that Donne's mother was a descendant of Thomas More and remarked that Donne learned perfect Italian and Spanish during his travels abroad.[8] Meanwhile William Spalding's *History of English Literature* explained that the 'corrupt taste' of the early seventeenth century, when even Shakespeare's writing showed signs of infection, had come to England ultimately from Italy.[9] Piecing things together readers could discern by what route the contagion had spread. George Gilfillan made the diagnosis virtually explicit: Donne was 'a great genius ruined by a false system.'[10]

All these accounts were available in textbooks used in North America. By contrast, however, literary histories actually composed in the United States, where Donne's religious history did not carry a special charge, tended to explain his faults in merely personal terms. Both vicious and condescending pictures circulated. They are marked by a certain pragmatism, not to say anti-intellectualism; and they seem to have been pointed especially to student readers. Edwin Whipple needed no theory of literary decadence or malignant foreign influences in order to castigate Donne for the indolence of his life of study and for his aversion to practical labor. Professor Henry Beers of Yale, with less sympathy than Dr Johnson had shown, condemned Donne for having 'ransacked cosmography, astrology, alchemy, optics, the canon law, and the divinity of the schoolmen for ink-horn terms and similes.' 'Donne's figures', he insisted, 'smell of the lamp.'[11]

Over the second half of the century, however, both in Britain and in the United States, it became increasingly difficult to dismiss Donne as the head of a deviant movement that simply wore itself out. By the 1880s some who had been resisting a revival began to feel that they were losing the battle. David Masson, who had treated Donne in the course of a hundred and twenty-odd pages on literary history in his *Life of John Milton*, revised his account extensively. In the 1859 edition Masson insisted that Spenser's poetry be seen as the decisive precedent for Milton and that the 'new variety of literature' initiated by Donne, which exercised 'an influence violently

---

[8] John W. Hales, 'John Donne', *The English Poets. Selections with Critical Introductions*, i: *Chaucer to Donne*, ed. Thomas Humphry Ward (London and New York: Macmillan, 1880), 558–60.

[9] William Spalding, *The History of English Literature* (New York: D. Appleton, 1853), 276.

[10] George Gilfillan, 'John Donne', *Specimens with Memoirs of the Less-Known British Poets*, 3 vols. (Edinburgh: James Nichol, 1860), i. 203.

[11] Henry A. Beers, *An Outline Sketch of English Literature* (New York: Chautauqua Press, 1886), 140. On the early teaching of English literature in the United States, see Franklin E. Court, *The Scottish Connection: The Rise of English Literary Study in Early America* (Syracuse, NY: Syracuse Univ. Press, 2001).

anti-Spenserian', was a false alternative that Milton had wisely rejected: 'in proportion as we regard Spenser's genius as that of poesy in its essence, so we must be glad that the avatar of Donne, as an intermediate power between Spenser and Milton, was so brief and partial.' After the appearance of Grosart's edition and the publication of Minto's piece in *The Nineteenth Century*, the nail that Masson had so easily driven into his vast structure came loose. In his 1881 revision, he quoted approvingly from Grosart. He now proposed that Donne could 'stand to all time' as the supreme 'example of the genius of metrical intellection at its utmost.' This was to concede that as a contemporary of Spenser Donne had been 'a subtle thinker and dialectician', and still to denigrate his verses as 'metrical cogitation.' The claim for 'Spenser's genius' and the charge that Donne's 'influence' was 'violently anti-Spenserian' were silently omitted.[12] Meanwhile, a new volume of literary selections compiled by Rosaline Orme Masson and introduced by her husband afforded Donne fully ten pages. Here, in a book designed to complement the facts and narratives purveyed in textbooks, were substantial excerpts from the satires and *Metempsychosis*, praise for the Second Anniversary, but also a refutation of De Quincey's claim that Donne's rhetoric displays 'majesty' and 'sublimity.' Some categories of praise after all had to be reserved for Milton.[13]

Within a decade a new version of literary history was significantly upgrading Donne's place. As Eliot acknowledged, Saintsbury made the decisive intervention, several years before he succeeded Masson in the English chair at Edinburgh. In the mid-eighties Macmillan and Co. commissioned Saintsbury to write a *History of Elizabethan Literature*. This was to be the second of four volumes in a comprehensive history. Saintsbury's account, far from depicting the seventeenth century as a decline, extended the period of achievement from 1560 to 1660. What he aimed to do with the term 'Elizabethan' is analogous to what Walter Pater had done with 'the Renaissance': he referred it as much to a spirit as to a historical era and deepened its effectiveness as a category of praise. Because Saintsbury's volume was the first in the series actually published, in 1887, the other writers—Stopford Brooke on the earliest period, Gosse on the eighteenth century, and Edward Dowden on modern literature—had to work round his assertion that his volume concerned 'the greatest period.'[14]

[12] David Masson, *The Life of John Milton: Narrated in Connexion with the Political, Ecclesiastical, and Literary History of His Time*, i: *1608–1639* (Cambridge: Macmillan, 1859), 447; rev. edn (1881; rpt., Gloucester, MA: Peter Smith, 1965), 485, 487, 489.

[13] *Three Centuries of English Poetry Being Selections from Chaucer to Herrick*, ed. Rosaline Orme Masson, gen. preface by David Masson (London: Macmillan, 1876), 338–40.

[14] George Saintsbury, *A History of Elizabethan Literature* (London: Macmillan, 1887), p. vii.

Saintsbury's *History of Elizabethan Literature* proved popular on both sides of the Atlantic. The extent of its influence is suggested in the grudging tribute that Ludwig Lewisohn paid to Saintsbury in the 1920s:

How many wretched candidates for collegiate degrees, lower or higher, have not burned the oil of preëxamination midnights in order to pore over a few, at least, of his ten thousand pages; how many teachers of English in innumerable institutions of all varieties and grades of what is euphemistically known as learning have not, innocent of all contact with the original documents, derived their pedagogical material, and thus their bread and butter too, from [his] pages.[15]

Lewisohn gives no hint of the unique quality of Saintsbury's insights into 'metaphysical' poetry. The condescending tribute epitomizes the climate in which modernists liked to believe Donne was their own discovery.

Conditions in the universities and in academic publishing had been quite different when Macmillan's enlisted Saintsbury's participation in their new history of literature, well in advance of the actual incorporation of English studies at Oxford and Cambridge. In the 1880s Saintsbury, then in his early forties, was working in London as a literary journalist. He was also seeking an academic post. (The offer from Edinburgh did not come until 1895.) He had published both a *Primer* and a *History* of French literature. He had written a biography of Dryden (1881) that was much admired for the clarity, balance, and fairness that it demonstrated toward a complex subject.[16] He had been reading English literature of the sixteenth and seventeenth centuries for twenty-five years, and his admiration for it had kept increasing. He wrote about this literature with evident pleasure and concentrated on the works rather than the writers' lives. Relying on others for quotidian matters such as 'dates and biographical facts', he managed to put Donne into his grave five years before 1631. What mattered to him, and increasingly to readers of his book, was the fiery imaginative passion of Donne's poetry.[17]

Saintsbury credited what Ben Jonson and Izaak Walton had said about the early date at which Donne had composed nearly all his verses and therefore took up Donne in a chapter on Spenser and the poets of the 1590s. He emphasized his accomplishments as a satirist and his pre-eminent influence upon poets of the seventeenth century. Donne is, he asserted, 'one of the most historically important of poets' (146). There was no implication here that the influence had been deleterious, no assertion that the effects manifested decadence. Saintsbury freely acknowledged, without ambivalence, just about

---

[15] Ludwig Lewisohn, *Cities and Men* (New York: Harper and Brothers, 1927), 43.

[16] See P. E. Hewison, 'George Saintsbury', *Dictionary of Literary Biography*, cxlix: *Late Nineteenth- and Early Twentieth-Century British Literary Biographers*, ed. Steven Serafin (Detroit: Bruccoli Clark Layman, 1995), 210–18.

[17] Saintsbury, *Elizabethan Literature*, 147. Subsequent citations are given in the text.

everything that others had said against Donne's writing. He asserted that none of the charges cancel out 'the force and originality of Donne's intellect' (150), which show themselves so convincingly that, whichever poems Jonson may have been referring to when he said Donne wrote all his best pieces before he was twenty-five, he aptly described Donne as 'the first poet of the world in some things' (146).

No textbook writer had ever tried to make Jonson's claim good. In fact, no one who had written on Donne—not Coleridge nor the writer in the *Retrospective Review*, not Lewes nor Lowell nor Minto—had made such specific and powerful claims. Saintsbury singled out Donne's 'faculty of suddenly transfiguring common things by a flood of light, and opening up strange visions to the capable imagination' and urged that in this 'Donne is surpassed by no poet of any language, and equalled by few' (146). He named as Donne's 'peculiar poetical quality' his 'fiery imagination shining in dark places', working a 'magical illumination of obscure and shadowy thoughts with the lightning of fancy' (147). These points he illustrated with extracts familiar and unfamiliar, from 'The Relic' and 'The Dream', the *Anatomy of the World*, the fifth satire, and other poems, only to propose that 'a full anthology' was needed. Donne 'must be read', he concluded, paraphrasing Jonson on Shakespeare, 'and by every catholic student of English literature should be regarded with a respect only "this side idolatry", though the respect need not carry with it blindness to his undoubtedly glaring faults' (150).

Saintsbury was not much interested in proposing a theory to explain the origins of Donne's faults. Nor did he attempt to extract a moral. It would be interesting therefore to see what sort of book he would have written if he, rather than Gosse, had undertaken the 'life and letters.' Saintsbury consistently maintained that a literary biographer's interest is the writer's works, not the life apart from the writings. In all his biographies he gave only scant attention to his subjects' youth. In the case of Donne this would have put him sharply at odds with the dominant practice in the nineties. Saintsbury's idea of poetry attended to form and relished beauty. What he valued in Donne depended precisely on what the poet had imagined and could provoke readers to imagine. When he was engaged to write the Introduction for the Muses' Library edition, he provocatively announced: 'The human Donne whom Walton depicts is so exactly the poetical Donne whom we knew, that the effect is uncanny. Generally, or at least very frequently, we find the poet other than his form of verse: here we find him quite astoundingly akin to it.' Having thus reversed the traditional order of things by which Donne's verse had been regarded as an appendage to his life, Saintsbury proceeded to rehearse the requisite biographical facts. Then, comparing Donne to Dante and to Shakespeare, he singled out the 'fire' found in Donne that 'not even in the very greatest poets of all can be ever surpassed or often rivalled.' To the evidence he had first adduced in 1887 he added still stronger claims for the Second Anniversary and the lyrics, which 'show [Donne] in his quiddity and essence.'[18]

Saintsbury's admiration prompted Dowden, widely regarded as the foremost Shakespearean in the world, to examine both the poetry and the sermons. On 7 May 1890 he brought the fruits of this study before the Elizabethan Literary Society at Trinity College, Dublin. He began and ended with references to Shakespeare, first reinterpreting Saintsbury's hijacking of Jonson's praise by acknowledging that there is 'indeed a large expense of spirit in the poems of Donne', and finally proposing, by way of an allusion to *The Tempest*, that Donne awakens in readers 'wonder and love.'[19] In the heart of his lecture Dowden made Donne of interest not so much by comparing him with the Bard as by connecting his imaginative productions with poems by Tennyson and Arnold, Browning and Coventry Patmore. Climactically, he related the Third Satire and the Anniversaries to Tennyson's *In Memoriam*, regarded as a great autobiographical poem. Dowden knew well enough that it is difficult to place most of Donne's poems in precise biographical contexts. He was excited, however, by the prospects for a more accurate biography that had been raised when Jessopp's article appeared in the *DNB*. In his lecture he rehearsed the most charming bits of Donne's love story out of Walton, augmented them with praise for the 'autobiographical' elegy in which the poet sought to dissuade a 'Shakespearean Viola' from accompanying him to foreign lands, and proposed that, whatever the elusive biographical facts, many of the poems 'gain an added interest' when they are read in the light of 'his personal history' (798). Unlike Gosse, who would claim to find in the poems the real history of Donne's sexual passions, Dowden simply recommended the pleasures of a fiction that made Anne More the object of the poet's concern in 'The Good Morrow', 'The Anniversary', and 'Lecture upon the Shadow.'

In writing about the prose and verse letters and on 'The Litany' Dowden felt himself on firmer biographical ground. He dwelt at length on the period after the marriage when Donne experienced 'melancholy', which his hearers were likely to regard 'as a disease of the nineteenth century' (793). He saw as the real turning point in Donne's life his decision not to wallow in gloom, which, whenever he took it, was the root of his decision to become a preacher, 'enticing others', as Walton wrote, 'by a sacred art and courtship to amend their lives' (794). Dowden proposed that, while no single poem provides a

---

[18] Saintsbury, Introduction, *Poems of John Donne*, ed. E. K. Chambers, 2 vols. The Muses' Library (London: Lawrence and Bullen; George Routledge and Sons; New York: Charles Scribner's Sons; E. P. Dutton, 1896), i, pp. xii, xviii, xxviii.

[19] Edward Dowden, 'The Poetry of John Donne', *Fortnightly Review*, new ser., 47 (1890), 791, 807. Subsequent references are given in the text.

key to all of Donne's career, 'The Litany' best reveals how he made his own struggle for balance between the extremes of sensuality and spirituality into a *via media* that he could recommend to others. This was to offer a shrewder, more penetrating entry into Donne's verse than readers could find just about anywhere else. Dowden's lecture was published in *The Fortnightly Review* a month after he delivered it and was reprinted almost immediately in the *Eclectic Review* and in *Littell's Living Age*. In 1895 it reappeared in a collection of his essays.[20] Even more than Minto's 'excellent' piece in *The Nineteenth Century* (808), praised by Dowden for its having discerned the extraordinary promise in the *Metempsychosis*, it created a sense that there was much gold to be mined from Donne's 'quartz and wash-dirt' (791). Not quite single-handedly Dowden touched off the spate of publications that made the 1890s by far the most prolific period of writing about Donne that there had ever been.

While Saintsbury and Dowden were instrumental in the establishment of English studies in Britain, and both men may have sometimes made passing mention of Donne in their classrooms, apparently neither of them actually taught his poetry.[21] Work on the teaching of English in nineteenth-century Britain by Franklin Court and others suggests that no one before Grierson, who lectured on Donne's poems to honours students at Aberdeen in 1907, seriously contemplated sustained academic study of his works.[22] The fact that the most perceptive academic writers on Donne—Minto, Masson, Saintsbury, Dowden, Norton, and Grierson—all taught outside England suggests that his writing, like English literature itself, was made canonical from the margins. It is difficult to know, however, whether the margins extended to the faraway reaches of the Empire. Gauri Viswanathan's valuable study of how English literature served in colonial India as an ideological 'strategy of containment' provides scant information about how particular authors and works were taught and makes no mention of Donne.[23]

[20] *Eclectic Magazine of Foreign Literature, Science, and Art*, 52 (1890), 234–44; *Littell's Living Age*, 186 (1890), 195–205; *New Studies in Literature* (London: Kegan Paul, Trench, and Trübner; Boston: Houghton Mifflin, 1895), 90–120.

[21] On the importance of Dowden and Saintsbury, see the first chapter of Brian Culver's Ph.D. dissertation, ' "My Face in Thine Eye": John Donne's Poetry and The Institution of English Studies, *c*.1850–1950' (New York University, 1998). I am grateful to Dr Culver for making his work available.

[22] Franklin E. Court, *Institutionalizing English Literature: The Culture and Politics of Literary Study, 1750–1900* (Stanford, CA: Stanford Univ. Press, 1992). Compare John Churton Collins, *The Study of English Literature: A Plea for its Recognition and Organization at the Universities* (London: Macmillan, 1891); Herbert J. C. Grierson, Preface, *The Poems of John Donne*, 2 vols. (Oxford: Clarendon, 1912), i, p. iii.

[23] Gauri Viswanathan, *Masks of Conquest: Literary Study and British Rule in India* (New York: Columbia Univ. Press, 1989).

As for North America, Robin Harris's history of English Studies at Toronto and Heather Murray's work on the curriculum in other Canadian universities provide no grounds for supposing that Donne was taught in nineteenth-century Canada.[24] Something similar might almost be said about the situation in the United States. If we attend to the collection of reports from some twenty English departments first published in *The Dial* (Chicago) in 1894, reports that contain an extraordinary amount of information about which writers were being taught, we would deduce that Donne did not figure in the teaching of English literature in America. When the collection was augmented a year later in William Morton Payne's book, *English in American Universities*, amidst hundreds of references to teaching dozens of English authors there was not the least mention of John Donne.[25] Even the Harvard entry does not refer to him. (It was written by Wendell.) When we look beyond Harvard into the archives of other colleges for traces of the earliest teaching of English literature, it turns out that the writer whom Wendell was eager to displace from the prominence that Briggs had conferred on him had shown up incidentally in a few other places. At Brown University, in Providence, Robinson Dunn's lectures on English literature adverted to the publication of *Pseudo-Martyr* by 'a champion of Protestantism' and dismissed the writer's poetry as 'quaint' and unattractive.[26] Occasionally Donne was made a whipping boy in lectures elsewhere. Beers's derogatory account of his 'forced and unnatural style' in his *Outline Sketch of English Literature* (1886), a book designed principally for the middle-class participants in the Chautauqua educational programs, reflects what he told his students in New Haven as well.[27] At Princeton Donne was mentioned in passing, disparagingly, in an 1878 lecture on *Samson Agonistes*.[28] Nonetheless, there is evidence that in a few U.S. colleges Donne already occupied a more than an incidental place in the curriculum.

[24] Robin S. Harris, *English Studies at Toronto: A History*, with a foreword by H. Northrop Frye (Toronto: Univ. of Toronto Press, 1988); Heather Murray, 'English Studies in Canada to 1945: A Bibliographic Essay', *English Studies in Canada*, 17/4 (Dec. 1991), 436–67.

[25] William Morton Payne (ed.), *English in American Universities* (Boston: D. C. Heath, 1895).

[26] Oliver Henry Arnold, 'Prof. Robinson P. Dunn's course of English Literature' (*c.*1863), ii, n.p. Lecture notes taken by students, MS-1M-2, Brown University Archives.

[27] Beers, *Outline Sketch*, 141.

[28] William R. Wilder's notes on 'Lecture Twelfth' for the course on English Literature given by James Ormsbee Murray (1878), in the Lecture Notes Collection AC#-052, University Archives, Department of Rare Books and Special Collections, Princeton University Library. Princeton has relatively rich holdings for documenting the teaching of English literature in the late nineteenth century; its Archives do not contain materials that indicate that Donne was part of the curriculum.

BEYOND HARVARD

A decade before the Oxford English school was founded and three decades before the Cambridge English tripos was established, thanks especially to Dean Briggs, Donne was an object of study in several of the leading American universities. In each case academic interest in Donne as a writer was imported from Harvard and enhanced by attention to what was being written about his poetry by Saintsbury and Dowden. In 1892–3 'Minor Poets of the Sixteenth and Seventeenth Centuries' was offered for the first time at Stanford. 'In this course,' according to the University Register, 'Spenser, Shakspere, and Milton will be treated incidentally.' Although apparently no syllabus or lecture notes from the course survive, there is good reason to suppose that Donne appeared prominently on the syllabus. The course was given by Henry Lathrop, a recent graduate of Harvard who named his oldest son Francis Child. As a senior Lathrop had taken Briggs's course on the seventeenth century. For two years before he went to Stanford he taught at Harvard and worked as Briggs's assistant.

Along the eastern seaboard south of Boston academic interest in Donne gradually grew more intense than it was at Harvard. As early as 1876–7 the newly founded Johns Hopkins University engaged Child as a visiting professor, and he was the first person to offer an English course there. Although he turned down President Gilman's offer of a professorship, he remained a resource for the fledgling English Department. Likely he had a hand in arranging it when Gosse repeated at Hopkins in 1885 the lectures on seventeenth-century poetry that he had delivered in Boston. Child also facilitated Norton's going to Baltimore in 1893–4 to deliver the Percy Turnbull Memorial Lectures. When Norton interrupted work on the Grolier Club edition to lecture on Dante at Hopkins, his host was James Bright, the most influential member of the English faculty. Two years later Bright gave a 'Seminary' course on 'English Poets from Donne to Dryden.' Probably this was the first strictly postgraduate course anywhere in which Donne occupied so prominent a place. It was the first such course for which a student, Clyde Furst, wrote a paper on Donne that he then went on to publish. Furst's seminar paper was not what we might expect of work coming out of a department known for its commitment to philological studies. Prominent among its concerns were the relations between Donne's love poems and his life. Furst published his essay in a periodical that came out in Philadelphia. Three years later he made it the opening chapter in *A Group of Old Authors*, a book made up of writing he had done for his graduate courses.[29]

Philadelphia was a congenial place to publish an essay on Donne in the mid-nineties. The first Ph.D. dissertation ever written on Donne (to be considered in detail momentarily) was completed under Felix Schelling at the University of Pennsylvania in 1893. Within a year or two, even though older literature had little scope in Penn's English curriculum, Donne was an integral part of Schelling's courses on 'The Age of Elizabeth' and on the 'Principles of English Versification.' The writer of the dissertation was Martin Grove Brumbaugh, who had spent the 1891–2 academic year as a special student at Harvard. He took only two courses there, Shakespeare with Child and the seventeenth century with Briggs. When he moved to Philadelphia, he already had it in mind to write his thesis on the poet whom Briggs had made central to the course.

A still more thoroughgoing connection with Briggs was wrought by William Lyon ('Billy') Phelps, who was to become one of America's most celebrated English professors. After graduating from Yale and spending one year there as a graduate student and another teaching at Westminster School in Dobbs Ferry, New York, Phelps gave his third year out of college to reading systematically through English literature on his own. Then, in the autumn of 1890 he enrolled at Harvard, to round out his graduate coursework while he worked on a thesis for Yale. Harvard graduate students were required by Child to study Anglo-Saxon, Old Norse, and other philological subjects. Phelps insisted, however, that he would study only literature, which had been much more scantily available to Yale's undergraduates than it was to Harvard's. It happened that the seventeenth century course was not offered the year he arrived, and Phelps took Briggs's 'History and Principles of Versification' instead. In the following year, having received an AM from Harvard and a Ph.D. from Yale (on the same day in June 1891), he accepted a position as teaching assistant to Wendell. Through a series of exchanges with President Eliot he bargained it into an instructorship. Meanwhile, he gave himself relief from the staggering obligation to mark over eight hundred essays each week by enrolling in Briggs's English 15. (He also worked closely with Briggs and Lathrop as fellow teachers of composition.) After turning down an offer from the new University of Chicago, Phelps left Harvard in 1892 to begin teaching at Yale. Four years later he began to teach his own course on the seventeenth century. Previously,

---

[29] Clyde Bowman Furst, 'The Life and Poetry of Dr. John Donne, Dean of St. Paul's', [Philadelphia] *Citizen*, 2 (1896), 229–37; idem, *A Group of Old Authors* (Philadelphia: George W. Jacobs, 1899), 13–57. Furst's name appears among the list of students in Bright's 'Donne to Dryden' seminary in the Johns Hopkins University *Circular* 15/124 (Mar. 1896), 50.

Beers had taught courses on Elizabethan and Commonwealth literature and on Milton and his contemporaries. Phelps taught Yale's first course on the seventeenth century as a unit. Like Briggs's English 15 on which it was modeled, this course began with Donne and treated poets and prose writers from the whole century. Phelps gave less scope than Briggs had to Jonson, and he shuffled Milton into the middle of the pack. The course became part of Phelps's standard repertoire, along with ones on contemporary drama and on the poetry of Tennyson and Browning.

Despite the decline in Donne's prominence within the English curriculum in the years just before T. S. Eliot arrived, then, the early teaching of Donne by Briggs and other lecturers at Harvard confirms the theory that teachers who put writers onto the syllabus contribute decisively to defining the canon. Although Briggs taught his seventeenth-century course (English 15) only three times at Harvard and once at Radcliffe, he lectured on Donne in English 28 for more than twenty years. That three sets of notes from the 1892 version of English 15 are now located in three separate archives illustrates the influence for which Briggs was legendary and attests to its dissemination.

BILLY PHELPS AND THE SONS OF DONNE AT YALE

The most ample and informative of four extant notebooks that tell us what went on in English 15 was produced by a graduate of Yale. This is not surprising given that Billy Phelps brought an acquired knowledge of seventeenth-century writers with him when he came to Harvard. Three years before he took Briggs's course, he had filled five blank books with notes on English authors. These notes were, as he recorded, 'from outside sources only', which was to say that they were not taken during lectures but were the record of the independent reading that Beers and J. E. Whitney required 'outside' class and on which he had been examined during his studies for the Ph.D. The title-page in the first of Phelps's notebooks indicates that he began his reading 'with the close of the Elizabethan Period.' The very first writer on whom he made notes was Donne.[30]

When Phelps began his independent study of English literature, he based his first set of reading notes on the Fuller Worthies' edition, translating the headings by which Grosart had divided materials in his Memorial-Introduction into '4 ways to study Donne': '1. Satirist. 2. Thinker & Imaginator. 3. Friend.

[30] Phelps's notebook for Briggs's English 15 is among the William Lyon Phelps Papers, Manuscripts and Archives, Yale University Library, Ms. Group 578, Series III, Box 17, Folder 202; the reading notes on Donne are cited in the two notes that follow. Page references for quotations from this notebook are subsequently given within parentheses.

4. Artist.' Phelps noted that 'Donne probably plunged into the Immoralities of his Time', and that 'The Divine Poems belong to the beginning of his poetic period—when he was a Catholic.'[31] Sometime later in the year he went back to Donne again for more in-depth reading. Volume iii of his notebooks contains another twenty-two pages on Donne, beginning with the observation, 'In the metaphysical school, the decay of poetry is as manifest as we have observed it in the drama.' Among these pages there is further evidence of his continuing to read Donne through spectacles provided in traditional handbooks about literary history. There are also signs of dissatisfaction with Grosart's chronology:

The character of Donne must have been full of contradictions. His 'divine poems' express the meditations of a devotee, while his elegies contain some of the most volup-tuous ebullitions of unbridled profligacy. He was also a fierce satirist of public manners and morals, and a deep and thoughtful student. If we had nothing but internal evidence to go on, I should say that his elegies and amatory poetry express the licentiousness of his youth; and that afterward he repented of the follies of his early life, became a Catholic and spent the rest of his days in theological study and pious meditation. He undoubtedly fell into the immoralities of his time, and was as grossly sensual as many of this contemporaries; this is seen not only directly in his amatory poetry, but indirectly in the constant reference he makes to his sins in the Divine Poems.[32]

The hiatus between the initial impressions that Phelps recorded in volume i and the extensive annotations that he wrote into volume iii is likely accounted for by information recounted in his autobiography. Over a period of five or six months he experienced severe eye-trouble. Often he found that he could read for only ten minutes at a time. What is surprising is that he should have started his independent reading in the history of English literature with Donne, and what is telling is that he should have gone back to him. Likely, both developments owe a good deal to the fact that Saintsbury's claims for Donne in *Elizabethan Literature* had begun to have an impact at Yale. In the mid-1880s, when Beers was still routinely dismissing the metaphysical poets in a few sentences, the standard Yale textbook had been Morley's *First Sketch of English Writers*. Morley gave a couple of biographical pages to Donne, stressed the importance of *Pseudo-Martyr*, and quoted the familiar passage out of the Second Anniversary about the 'pure and eloquent blood' that showed in the cheeks of Elizabeth Drury. In 1888, Beers switched texts, to Saintsbury's new book. This was also the moment when he began assigning Donne to be considered in 'portions ... for outside reading and examinations.'

[31] Vol. i of Phelps's reading notes are in the Yale Archives, YRG 47, RU 159, Box 6, Folder 39; quoted here from 7–8.
[32] Vol. iii of Phelps's reading notes are in the Yale Archives, Ms. Group 578, Series III, Box 16, Folder 199. The pages are unnumbered.

These changes are a marker of the metamorphosis that this book has been charting. Beers's uneasy recognition of the flux surrounding the name of 'Donne' is shown in his essay called 'Shakespere's Contemporaries', where he gives a glimpse of the 'learned divine' being displaced by the poet. As Beers attempts to account for the failure of virtually everyone in the Bard's own time to have appreciated 'the almost infinite superiority of his work to that of all his contemporaries', he contrasts the literary culture epitomized in Walton's *Lives* with that of the nineteenth century. He isolates as a decisive difference between the two eras the fact that accomplished writing had become a ground for the sorts of scrutiny and celebrity that generate popular biographies. Formerly, someone 'in high place who was incidentally an author, a great philosopher & statesman like Bacon, a diplomatist [*sic*] & scholar like Sir Henry Wotton, a bishop or a learned divine, like Sanderson, Donne or Herbert, might be thought worthy to have his life recorded. But a mere man of letters—still more a mere playwriter [*sic*]—was not entitled to a biography. Nowadays every writer of fair pretensions has his literary portrait in the magazines.' Not surprisingly, in light of this ambivalent tone, when Beers published his own textbook in 1890, *From Chaucer to Tennyson*, he simply repeated the dismissal of the metaphysicals from his old Chautauqua lectures.[33] And yet by 1892, when Phelps was studying the seventeenth century with Briggs at Harvard, Beers had begun to teach a full-year course on 'The literary history of the half century from 1603 to 1660, with special reference to the decadence of the drama, the development of prose, the "metaphysical poets" and the writings of Milton'; nonetheless, he continued to follow the lead of Taine, his usual preceptor, in placing Donne in the period of decline between Shakespeare and Milton. Meanwhile, his new colleague, Albert S. Cook, was using Taine and Morley as textbooks for his course on the 'History of English Literature.'[34] This gives us a more precise idea of how different a seventeenth century Phelps encountered in the company of Briggs.

When Phelps went to study at Harvard, he was not about to write a Harvard Ph.D. thesis, which at the time would inevitably have concerned some philological topic. Instead, he worked daily on his Yale thesis, on the

---

[33] Henry A. Beers, 'Shakespere's Contemporaries', uncatalogued typescript, Beinecke Library, Yale University, Za Beers 58, 1–2. The typescript contains a draft of an essay published in *The Connecticut Wits, and Other Essays* (New Haven, CT: Yale Univ. Press; London: Humphrey Milford, Oxford Univ. Press, 1920), 239–40. The spelling 'Shakespere' throughout the typescript indicates that the essay likely dates to the late nineteenth century. See also *From Chaucer to Tennyson: English Literature in Eight Chapters with Selections from Thirty Authors* (New York: Chautauqua Press, 1890), 105–7. When new editions of the latter work appeared in 1894 and 1898, Beers made no changes in his discussion of Donne.

[34] Information about courses given here comes from the *Catalogue of the Officers and Students of Yale University* for the relevant years.

eighteenth-century origins of English Romanticism, and meanwhile took the several literature courses that earned him his AM degree. These included, in addition to Briggs's course on versification, Chaucer with Kittredge, Shakespeare with Child, Elizabethan Literature with Wendell, and English drama with George Pierce Baker. Phelps's notes from all these courses attest to the pleasure with which he read. The extensive notes that he made on Donne during Briggs's lectures the following year give a glimpse of how he was envisaging the transition he was about to make to college lecturing. Phelps noted, for instance, that Briggs spoke frequently of the daring force of Donne's imagination and echoed Saintsbury on his 'strange and unearthly power of vision' (3). Briggs also stressed that Donne 'had an unfettered soul' (19), that he was at once 'passionately sensuous [and] passionately intellectual' (22), and that he can be appreciated only by repeated readings. 'It's easy to read D. several times & not know him; not to feel any kinship. His acquaintance must be forced' (19–20). Again and again, Briggs observed that Donne 'sets you thinking' (10), and that 'We go to Donne for thought' (23). These views appear in all the extant sets of notes. Phelps recorded them with greater frequency and care than the others, as if he were trying to take up the challenge.

Other materials in the archives evince the spirit in which Phelps brought Donne into the Yale English curriculum: a collection of programs from an annual spring dinner held at one or other New Haven hotel and variously called 'A Jovial Gathering of the faithful Sons of Donne', 'The Feast of the Metaphysicals', or something similar. These dinners were reminiscent of the saltings that took place in seventeenth-century Cambridge, in which Milton is known to have taken part. They always included a series of toasts, given by faculty and students alike. Already in 1901 this feast celebrated Donne as the poet of the new century; 'old Ben Jonson's days' were said to have ended with the century that had past. Phelps himself served as the toastmaster and various students, typically referring to themselves as 'the Progeny of Donne', picked out favorite passages and recited poetry, often parodies of their own devising. An extended example survives in a ten-page typescript from 1905 headed 'A Session of the Poets.' Here, Apollo ascends Parnassus to judge a contest between the Metaphysicals and 'Bill Wordsworth and his Pals.' 'Eddie Gosse' and 'Billy Phelps' also serve as judges. 'The Dean of Old St. Paul's' is summoned to perform first and told to 'Sit down when you are *Donne*.' He offers a short poem that makes him seem one part the writer of 'The Damp' and one part Falstaff:

> When I'm dead-drunk, and doctors know not why
> And my friends' curiosity
> Will search my pockets to find out the means.

> When will they find *thy* ticket in my jeans. [sic]
>   I think a sudden gleam of hope
>   Will tell them how I got the dope.
> They'll pawn their watches for whate'er they'll get.
> (I think the night will be extremely wet).

Apollo later summons Tennyson, who bows to Gosse before singing 'The Idleness of the King.' What is typical is that the skit makes Donne, Crashaw, and Herrick witty, while rendering Wordsworth, Tennyson, and Browning wooden and boring. With Donne, the program proclaims, 'All is warmth, and light, and good desire.'[35] We can recognize here the same Billy Phelps who thought that reading is first of all for pleasure and who decided to give his university's first course on the modern novel, despite strong objections from the senior faculty. It was he who kept Donne's name in prominence at Yale well into the 1920s—and made it a byword for imaginative pleasure.

On the other hand, it is important not to claim too much for Phelps, who went on to become not only a showman but something of a charlatan. When he came to write his autobiography, Phelps idealized his first year at Harvard in terms that suggest what made him attractive to many students: he recalls it as the last year in which he was exclusively a student and proclaims it as one of the happiest of his life.[36] He had access, he observes, to the Harvard Library. He enjoyed the atmosphere in which William James, George Santyana, and other philosophers were giving public lectures. He got to know Norton, then in his prime. He managed to give himself wholly to the study of literature. Best of all, he was able to work with the Dean of Harvard College. 'One of the best things in my life', he wrote, 'was my intimate friendship with Briggs.'[37] The feeling was not entirely mutual. Years later, after Phelps had become well known as an inspirational speaker and other universities were seeking to lure him away from Yale, Briggs, while expressing a certain admiration for Phelps's 'remarkable teaching' and 'power of interesting boys who would seem impossible', cautioned inquirers from the U.S. Naval Academy that Phelps had grown overly enamored of publicity; and he discreetly suggested that Phelps was not so substantial a scholar as they ought to be seeking.[38]

[35] Programs cited here and several other programs, with menus, for the annual Feast of the Metaphysicals are in located among the William Lyon Phelps Papers, Manuscripts and Archives, Yale University Library, Ms. Group 578, Series IV, Box 21, Folder 232. The folder also contains 'A Session of the Poets.'

[36] William Lyon Phelps, *Autobiography with Letters* (New York, and London: Oxford Univ. Press, 1939), 245–7.

[37] Ibid. 255.

[38] See Briggs's letter of 23 Aug. 1916 to Miss Wheeler, his long-time secretary, Biographical Material of Men Known Chiefly for Their Harvard Connection, HUG 1233.5, Harvard University Archives.

OTHER STUDENTS AND THEIR NOTES

Lecture notes from nineteenth-century college students are rarely to be found in anything like abundance in the archives of U.S. colleges and universities. The four notebooks written for Briggs's English 15 were saved by men who, when they wrote them, were all envisaging careers in education. They belonged, in other words, to the class of persons likeliest to preserve such materials; and this prompts us to wonder what the notes of their less diligent contemporaries may have been like. Still, these notes offer more than a window onto what Briggs had to say about Donne. In their differences from one another they provide an opportunity to contemplate how Briggs's students responded to his lectures—and to Donne's poems.

One set of English 15 notes, now in the Harvard Archives, was written into a notebook that belonged to Fred Norris Robinson, Harvard class of '91. Robinson, who studied for a time at Freiburg, wrote a Harvard Ph.D. thesis on Chaucerian syntax and was hired onto the faculty. He developed into an expert medievalist, worked closely with Briggs at Radcliffe, and became Chairman of the English Department. Although he frequently gave the standard courses on Bacon and on Milton, he never taught any courses in which he might have been required to decide what he wanted to say about Donne.

Robinson's name does not appear on the classlists for English 15 in any of the years that Briggs gave the course. His set of notes, only six and a half pages (compared to Phelps's twenty-seven), may have been copied over or digested from someone else. They are, in any event, straightforward. The materials on Donne are organized into paragraphs, often with topic sentences. They contain an unusual density of proper names, both those of writers who had influential views about Donne—Coleridge, De Quincey, Taine, and above all Saintsbury—and of poets whose work could be profitably compared with Donne's—Jonson and Herrick, Dryden and Wordsworth. In annotating the eleventh lecture for the course, on Carew, the notetaker dutifully recorded a sentiment that we know from other notebooks Briggs voiced often: 'Even today to read Donne is to be influenced for life. He has such daring, such penetration, such majesty at times, such strong personality.' There is little sign anywhere, however, that the notetaker was seeking to cooperate with Briggs in making this prediction good.[39]

---

[39] Notes on English 15 found on unnumbered pages in a notebook that belonged to Fred N. Robinson. The notebook is headed, and also contains, 'Notes on English A'; Curriculum Collection, HUC 8887.325.77, Harvard University Archives.

Lecture notes taken by Raymond Calkins, class of '90, provide still earlier access to English 15. A bright and conscientious junior at the time he heard Briggs's lectures in 1889, Calkins was much the youngest of the four witnesses to the course. He was garnering top grades in physics and chemistry, French and German; and he elected a large number of English courses. In fact, he created for himself the 'concentration' that would eventually be required at Harvard, once the administration acknowledged that the elective system was subject to the sorts of abuses illustrated in, say, T. S. Eliot's college career. After graduation Calkins taught German at Harvard and decided to study in the Divinity School, a place then known for the large number of agnostics and atheists in its student body. He went on to become a Congregationalist minister and eventually Pastor of the First Church in Cambridge, across from Harvard Yard. In the 1920s he was appointed Lyman Beecher Lecturer on preaching at Yale.

In Calkins's notes from Briggs's lectures on Donne and in two reports on his private reading, there is scant indication that he was on his way to becoming a preacher. Briggs had relatively little to say about Donne and religion, although in orienting the students to the third of Donne's satires he clearly made reference to what young Calkins heard as 'Calvanism' and 'Calvantic' religion. While Briggs claimed to have a high opinion of the Divine Poems, he treated them only briefly. Calkins's notes suggest that he expected students to read these works on their own—and that he left them to interpret them for themselves. Having given five lectures on Donne, Briggs ended by remarking that the Divine Poems 'are truly masterful' and that the Holy Sonnets in particular are 'full of ... intellectual struggle' and 'are worth reading over and over.' He did not go into detail. For the class that followed, he asked the students to 'Sum up [their] impressions of Donne' in a brief report.[40]

Although Calkins's response to this assignment is not with his other notes, he incorporated into his notebook two earlier reports, two pages each, on his reading of the Anniversaries. These are rough reading notes, dense with summary and paraphrase, with many quotations thrown in. What is striking is Calkins's paraphrase of the passage in the First Anniversary in which Donne remarks that 'New Philosophy calls all in doubt.' The *Variorum* shows that these lines received no particular attention before the 1930s, and no lecture notes from English 15 suggest that Briggs called attention to them. Calkins paraphrased the passage in a way that suggested its contemporary relevance: 'Without the heart, one perishes. So without religion the world would die. Philosophers are teaching the nothingness of religion, and she who might have

---

[40] Raymond Calkins, 'Notes on Eng. XVII cent. Literature', 2ᵛ, 9ᵛ, 9ʳ; Curriculum Collection, HUC 8889.324.15, Harvard University Archives.

counteracted this evil influence is dead.'[41] If Briggs might have been pleased to notice one of his students grappling with the intellectual, moral, and religious issues raised in Donne's poems, his actual lecturing nonetheless left plenty of room for the more detached approach characteristic of the likes of a Robinson.

One conspicuous difference between Calkins's notes and the three sets from 1892 reveals that Briggs reduced his five lectures on Donne to four. He simply dropped most of the first lecture, on 'Donne's Life.' It must have been easy to do. His initial lecture in 1889 was largely given to summarizing what was known about Donne's life, chiefly from his 'lovely biographer: Isaac Walton.' (Calkins first wrote 'Wharton' and later crossed it out and wrote in 'Walton.') The notes do not suggest that Briggs made any attempt to set up biographical questions that were to be answered by looking into Donne's poetry. Nor did he make remarks in subsequent lectures that intimated that biographical information offered a key to opening up the poems. Briggs simply regarded the *Life of Donne* as a charming book. He used it to motivate students' curiosity about the poems. This was the implicit purpose of the introductory lecture Calkins heard and of the lecture on Donne Briggs generally gave in English 28, as Eliot's recollection attests. Donne's biography greatly interested M. G. Brumbaugh, however. It was he who mined Briggs's lectures on Donne more extensively than anyone else.

THE FIRST Ph.D. DISSERTATION ON DONNE

Born during the Civil War and of the same generation as Gamaliel Bradford and Louise Guiney, Martin Brumbaugh was nearly thirty when he came to Harvard from central Pennsylvania. He had studied at a small institution founded by members of his family as a Normal College for the Church of the Brethren, familiarly known as Dunkers. After graduation he went into education and quickly rose to the position of superintendent of schools in Huntingdon County. He also began training teachers at institutes and 'Chautauquas' in Louisiana, where amidst the political shambles of Reconstruction nearly half the population over age ten was illiterate. When he came to Harvard in 1891, he was one of the first from his congregation to embark on an advanced degree, or (for that matter) to study at a non-denominational institution. Coming back to formal study after years of working independently, he was at first awed and disoriented in the specialized sphere of advanced literary studies. He knew a little of seventeenth-century literature: *The Compleat Angler* had long

---

[41] Raymond Calkins, 'Notes on Eng. XVII cent. Literature', 5^r.

been to him a 'second bible', and through it he had a passing familiarity with Donne.[42]

The opening pages of Brumbaugh's notebook for English 15 show him all in earnest to get things right.[43] He wrote down what Briggs said about 'Ben Johnson' and the satirist 'Marsden' and recorded an assignment to read Donne's 'First' (rather than 'Verse') Letters. He proved a quick study, however. Increasingly he used his notebook to write directions to himself for what he wanted to do outside class: 'read' this poem; 'find' that line, which Briggs had quoted. Three exercises that he composed on Donne read like personal letters to his teacher. In one he remarks, apropos the *First Anniversary*, 'One feels that the author saw life on its sad side and no other.' In another, where he has copied out striking passages from the Divine Poems, he concludes, 'It was a real pleasure, not a painful effort, to read him.' The longest exercise is a three-page essay on the Verse Epistles. Its starting point is the praises of Donne penned by Jonson, Carew, and Dryden; its ostensible purpose is to test whether their criticisms hold up when one attends to the group of poems that were manifestly Briggs's favorites. Here, in a rudimentary way, Brumbaugh put the old practice of choosing striking passages ('Letters are better than kisses'; 'Reason is the soul's left hand, Faith the right') at the service of developing a thesis of his own.

If Brumbaugh had had it in mind when he moved his family east to take an advanced degree from Harvard, it quickly became apparent that living in Cambridge was not going work. He needed to make his living by speaking engagements, and the frequent journeys his calendar required him to make back to his home state proved burdensome. In the autumn of 1892 he enrolled at the University of Pennsylvania, where the number of Ph.D. degrees awarded was increasing just beyond a trickle. The University was granting far more degrees in law, medicine, and dentistry than in the arts and sciences. In the fifteen or so months that Brumbaugh worked on his thesis, he also did extensive coursework and earned an AM. Besides courses on drama, versification, and nineteenth-century poetry offered by Schelling, he took a course on the novel with Josiah Penniman, who later became president of the University. He also enrolled in courses on metaphysics, on the history of ancient and medieval philosophy, on economics (with one of the founders of the Wharton School

---

[42] See Earl C. Kaylor, Jr., *Martin Grove Brumbaugh: A Pennsylvanian's Odyssey from Sainted Schoolman to Bedeviled World War I Governor, 1862–1930* (Madison, NJ: Fairleigh Dickinson Univ. Press; London: Associated Univ. Presses, 1996), 97. For biographical information about the period of Brumbaugh's graduate work, see chapter 5.

[43] Brumbaugh's notes on English 15 are in the Vault Collection at Juniata College; my thanks to my former research assistant Denise Bracken for finding them and to archivist Donald Durnbaugh for supplying a photocopy.

of Business), on English history, and on philology. While he was pursuing these studies he was offered, on the basis of the educational reform work he had been doing for many years, the Presidency of Louisiana State University. When he finished the Ph.D. he declined it. He accepted, instead, the Presidency of Juniata College in Huntingdon, where he had been an undergraduate. He nonetheless committed himself to regular commuting to Philadelphia by taking up, simultaneously, a teaching post at Penn. As the University's first professor of education, he published textbooks and lectured widely. After the Spanish-American War he served as the first commissioner of education in Puerto Rico. In 1915, he was elected Governor of Pennsylvania. His supporters liked to regard him as the Republicans' answer to Woodrow Wilson. By Donne scholars he was virtually forgotten.

Brumbaugh's thesis, 'A Study of the Poetry of John Donne', might have been a landmark if he had ever revised and published it. Its hundred-plus typewritten pages lack sharp focus and appear unfinished. No integrated line of argument emerges. Yet in the course of working with Brumbaugh, his director learned to admire Donne's poetry. In 1895 Schelling arranged for his student to give a paper on Donne at the annual meeting of the Modern Language Association, to be held at Yale just after Christmas; in the event, however, Brumbaugh was 'unavoidably prevented' from making it to New Haven. Meanwhile, Schelling published an anthology, *A Book of Elizabethan Lyrics*, and in it paid tribute to 'the Thesis of my late student, now my colleague.' Four years later, in a sequel, *A Book of Seventeenth Century Lyrics*, he drew upon Brumbaugh's analysis of what Dryden had said about Donne.[44] In 1905, the thesis still unpublished, Schelling persuaded Brumbaugh to allow him to hire a professional bibliographer, to bring the apparatus up to date with a view to publication. John L. Haney, a graduate of Penn who had published *A Bibliography of Samuel Taylor Coleridge*, was enlisted and did the job. In the following year, Wrightman F. Melton's Johns Hopkins thesis on Donne made appreciative reference to Brumbaugh's 'interesting work … soon to be published.'[45] In the event, however, Brumbaugh, who had recently been elected Superintendent of Philadelphia's schools, did not follow through with publication. A copy of Haney's expanded and still unpublished bibliography now rests, along with the dissertation itself, in the Vault Collection at Juniata.

As the first doctoral dissertation on Donne, Brumbaugh's unpublished work reflected the current state of knowledge about Donne in the early 1890s,

[44] Felix E. Schelling, *A Book of Elizabethan Lyrics* (Boston: Ginn and Co., 1895), 256; *A Book of Seventeenth Century Lyrics* (Boston: Ginn and Co., 1899), pp. xxv–xxvi.

[45] Wrightman F. Melton, 'The Rhetoric of John Donne's Verse', Ph.D. thesis, Johns Hopkins University, 1906; cited by Kaylor, *Martin Grove Brumbaugh*, 99–100.

just when published writing on his poetry was beginning to proliferate. Five interrelated features of the dissertation may be isolated:

1. In the period just after variorum editions of Shakespeare had gathered up the history of the Bard's reputation, Brumbaugh created the most nearly comprehensive bibliography of published writing on Donne's poetry that had ever been compiled. He made the most extensive study of the critical history and documented how for more than one hundred years Dryden and Johnson had influenced nearly everyone's reading of the poetry. Meanwhile, he exposed himself to the considerable body of biographical writing on Donne to which both Briggs and Schelling paid little attention.

2. Before there was any significant body of notes and glosses on Donne's poetry, Brumbaugh made a detailed study of the diction and imagery of dozens of poems. He distilled his findings into an 'introspective study' that elaborated a variation on the idea of a unified sensibility that Emerson, Thoreau, and other New England readers had valued in Donne's poetry: 'Donne seems more than any other writer in our language to think in the "bodiless realms of the intellect".' To him the body is a veil to the real person. He has a body. He is a soul.'[46] The essential, admirable, and ultimately quite limited 'Donne' was to be found in those verses where the poet imposed his personality on whatever he touched. Donne, knowing full well that the 'outer world' (54), the realm of the senses, is diffuse and inharmonious, adopted an 'exceedingly subjective' view of things (53). He took his 'greatest comfort' (53) in the idea that the soul, 'the only really worthy object of contemplation' (53), unifies everything, so that by inviting 'retreat from the commonplace and even from all sense-scenes' (56), Donne was able to discover harmony within himself. So struck was Brumbaugh by the idea that Donne had considered his own soul to be the source of unity and harmony in the universe—an idea that he illustrated with dozens of quotations drawn chiefly from the kinds of poems on which he had first chosen to write when he was studying with Briggs—that he concluded he had found out the reason that Donne had for so long eluded critics and readers (56).

3. Much more even than Bradford, Brumbaugh sought to identify recurring preoccupations in the poetry and to build up generalizations about its distinguishing characteristics. In the process he moderated his admiration for Donne and distanced himself from his subject. He came to urge,

---

[46] M. G. Brumbaugh, 'A Study of the Poetry of John Donne', Thesis Submitted to the Philosophical Faculty of the University of Pennsylvania (23 Dec. 1893), 51. Subsequent references are given in the text.

against the New England tradition of reading Donne, that although the best critics have proposed to consider him a 'thinker' (22), Donne's thinking actually displays a 'very narrow range of thought' (23). While Brumbaugh was prepared to acknowledge Donne's supremacy within this range, he criticized him for writing within a narrow sphere where he was divorced from social life and the world of action. 'Donne is so fully steeped with pantheism, or soul-identity', Brumbaugh concluded, 'that when he describes others, he instinctively assumes iden[t]ity of soul. He ... actually and dynamically animates other persons with his own spirit, and portrays them as Donne is, rather than as Donne might have found them to be' (60–1).

4. Inspired by Dowden's work on Shakespeare, and in the wake of the muddle that Grosart had made of the dating of Donne's poems, Brumbaugh sought to establish a definitive chronology for Donne's whole poetic output. Dowden's prestige was considerable at Harvard: he was the only modern critic whose name regularly made its way into the English Department's course descriptions, and Brumbaugh read his 'Shakspere' *Primer* for Child's course. Dowden's pre-eminence among scholars was owing to his having isolated the writing of the 'Romances' as the culminating period in Shakespeare's development. Having characterized the period when Shakespeare wrote the tragedies as one during which he had plunged into unhealthy morbidity, he proposed that the Bard nonetheless emerged to communicate in his final plays a supernatural vision and to develop a mature religion that was neither denominational or ecclesiastical.[47] When Brumbaugh read Dowden's essay on Donne, however, its subtlety escaped him. He seems to have been unable to take a cue from the discretion with which Dowden referred to the 'expense of spirit' in the poetry. Certainly, he was slow to accept the implications of Dowden's observation that 'When Donne writes in his licentious vein ..., he makes voluptuousness a doctrine and argues out his thesis with scholastic diligence.'[48] Instead Brumbaugh assumed that the sensuous love poems must refer to the poet's experiences with actual women. He insisted that 'all the poems that contain lines unworthy the better and truer Donne' were written very early (40). In an attempt to imitate Dowden's Shakespeare chronology, which dramatized a growth towards spiritual maturity, he sought to place some of the religious verse as late and to read it as revealing the essential

---

[47] See Gary Taylor, *Reinventing Shakespeare: A Cultural History, from the Restoration to the Present* (New York: Weidenfeld and Nicolson, 1989; New York: Oxford Univ. Press, 1991), 173–82.

[48] Dowden, 'Poetry of John Donne', 804.

Donne. He dated most of the other poetry early, and placed the satires, *Metempsychosis*, the Lincoln's Inn epithalamion, the love elegies, and in fact virtually all the love poems, in two prolific periods, 1589–94 and 1596–1600. He adduced all sorts of previously scattered claims in an attempt to prove that 'No love poetry was written after 1600' (except for Donne's wife) and concluded that 'Most of his Lyrics show a decidedly youthful touch, and may be safely assigned to the earliest years of his authorship, i.e. before 1590' (44). In view of Grosart's argument that most of the religious poetry was composed early, the Divine Poems posed more of problem. Brumbaugh dwelt on the importance of those 'shorter ones … known definitely to come after 1615.' He also praised the *La Corona* sonnets, which he took to be the poems Donne sent to Magdalene Herbert in 1607, as 'the deepest, most penetrative and matterful in the language' (46). Ultimately, he concluded that there were two occasionally overlapping but distinct periods in Donne's writing: in the First Anniversary, the epistles, and the Holy Sonnets (by which Brumbaugh means *La Corona*), 'we see Donne as he really wished to be, while in his Lyrics, Satires, &c., we see him as he resolved himself to be in order to win favor and fortune' (60). For all Brumbaugh's comprehensive reading of earlier criticism, and for all the attention he lavished on the poems themselves, there was no breakthrough here.

5. Unlike Briggs, who generally avoided consideration of Donne's licentiousness, Brumbaugh worried that the lascivious materials were indicative of the most significant interpretative problem to which the poems give rise, the relation of the experiences depicted in them to the author's own life. His disposition to pursue issues raised in Grosart's Preface and Memorial-Introduction was out of keeping with the approaches taken by his mentor at Harvard and by his thesis director at Penn.

FELIX SCHELLING AND THE LYRIC DONNE

Schelling was only four years Brumbaugh's senior, and he held unusual qualifications to be the first director of a dissertation on Donne. Like Kittredge of Harvard, he began directing dissertations without having earned a Ph.D. himself. By the early nineties he had, however, begun what would be a distinguished career as a writer. His *Two Essays on Robert Browning* (1890) shows that, shortly before Brumbaugh arrived, he was familiar with the standard charges against Donne and had not yet begun to think through them for himself.⁴⁹ *Poetic and Verse Criticism in the Age of Elizabeth* appeared in 1891, the first book in a new monograph series published by the University of Pennsylvania Press. Editions of Ben Jonson's *Timber* (1892) and of writings by George Gascoigne (1893) were published in Boston, by Ginn and Co., the same publisher that, at the instigation of Kittredge, was bringing out Phelps's thesis, *The Beginnings of the Romantic Movement* (1893).

In the Boston publishing house of Ginn and Co., Schelling found a home for his two substantial anthologies of sixteenth- and seventeenth-century lyric poetry. In preparing them he made extensive use of the Harvard Library. These volumes appeared respectively in 1895 and 1899 in the Athenæum Series, edited by Kittredge. With their publication Schelling accomplished something that no scholar who taught sixteenth- and seventeenth-century literature at Harvard did: his anthologies integrated the fruits of wide reading in British criticism with the experience of teaching in an American university and made Donne's poetry available to a many more readers than the three hundred odd copies of the Grolier Club edition could ever reach.

Schelling's emulation of British literary critics seems in some ways surprising. The son of an immigrant Swiss physician, he had grown up under his father's expectation that he would become a professional musician. His father, in fact, had abandoned his medical career and became director of the St Louis Conservatory of Music. In his mid-teens Felix was sent to New York for training in music and the modern languages, subjects in which he continued to take an interest when he went to Penn as an undergraduate. These interests remained alive through a period during which he took a law degree, began legal practice, and earned a Master's Degree in Comparative Philology. Like Phelps, he abandoned his aspirations to practice law and accepted an appointment at the University where he had taken his degrees.

In 1888, when Le Baron Russell Briggs was giving the first course on seventeenth century literature at Harvard, the Provost of the University of Pennsylvania entrusted Schelling with the task of organizing a modern English Department. Almost immediately he travelled to Britain to consult with the leading authorities about the new academic discipline. He visited the three writers of Macmillan's new literary history who lived in England: Brooke, Gosse, and Saintsbury.⁵⁰ From meeting with Brooke he brought back to

---

⁴⁹ Felix E. Schelling, *Two Essays on Robert Browning* ([Printed privately], 1890), 17–18.
⁵⁰ See Arthur Hobson Quinn, 'Felix E. Schelling—A Tribute', Archives of the University of Pennsylvania, UPT 50, S 322; cf. the abbreviated version published in *Schelling Anniversary Papers* (New York: Century, 1923), 5–6. In his *Primer of English Literature*, first published in 1876, Brooke presented Donne as the pre-eminent English satirist of the 1590s. He urged that '[t]hough his work was mostly done in the reign of James I., and though his poetical reputation, and his influence (which was very great) did not reach their height till after the publication in

Philadelphia a sense of British envy at the remarkable opportunity that lay before him. In 1889–90, some six years before Phelps's course on the modern novel provoked resistance from the senior faculty at Yale, he gave the first course on the novel for undergraduates in the United States. This was in keeping with a foundational principle that Schelling employed for organizing English Studies: start with matter that the students will find familiar, and with prose before poetry. Of course he did not expect that the study of literature would be confined to contemporary writing. By 1894, he had hired a faculty, created a department, and devised a curriculum. As the John Welsh Centennial Professor of History and Literature, he was giving courses on Elizabethan literature (with Saintsbury for reference), eighteenth-century literature (with Gosse as the principal text), English versification, prose authors, and modern and contemporary poets. He was, moreover, developing graduate seminars, teaching extension students, and creating new courses specially for teachers. He was also at work on the two anthologies that made Donne more widely available.

The picture of Donne that emerges from Schelling's anthologies bears almost no resemblance to the Donne whom Palgrave had excluded from *The Golden Treasury*. Printing poems that had been written before 1625, *A Book of Elizabethan Lyrics* included nine poems by Donne: the songs, 'Go and catch a falling star' and 'Sweetest love, I do not go'; 'Lover's Infiniteness', 'Love's Deity', 'The Dream', 'The Message', and 'The Funeral'; and the well known 'Valediction: Forbidding Mourning' along with 'Death, be not proud'.[51] In his Introduction, Schelling insisted that Donne 'is an Elizabethan in the strictest possible acceptation of that term', that is, not only as Saintsbury had used it to denote a spirit, but also chronologically. He presented Donne, in fact, as the most significant poet of the 1590s after Spenser and Shakespeare and declared that he was not the 'representative of a degenerate and false taste', nor 'the founder of a school', nor 'the product' of 'obvious ... literary influences.' Acknowledging Donne's difficulty, he compared it to Shakespeare's and proposed that it was due to his having 'shone and glowed with a strange light all his own.' Schelling admired Donne above all for his 'positive originality', a quality that Saintsbury had associated especially with the lyrics, and for the 'negative originality' by which Donne made an utter break with the dominant conventions.[52]

1633 of all his poems, he really belongs, by dint of his youthful sensuousness, of his imaginative flame, and of his sad and powerful thought, to the Elizabethans'; quoted from the reprint, *English Literature* (New York: Macmillan, 1897), 124.

[51] Schelling also printed as Donne's 'Absence, hear thou my protestation', a poem that was for a time incorporated into *The Golden Treasury*. It also appeared in Saintsbury's anthology of 1892, *Seventeenth Century Lyrics* (New York: Macmillan, 1892), 1–2.

[52] Schelling, Introduction, *Elizabethan Lyrics*, pp. xxi–xxii.

What was still more striking, the musically trained Schelling bestowed equal praise on the originality displayed in Donne's prosody, not least in the nearly incomparable freedom and art of his phrasing, declaring him '[b]y far the most independent lyrical metrist' of the period. Donne, he observed, was 'quite as much misunderstood on this side as on the side of his eccentricities of thought and expression.' Schelling endorsed, moreover, Gosse's recent claim that Donne 'invented his violent mode of breaking up the line into quick and slow beats' as a deliberate rebellion against Spenserian smoothness and thus 'intentionally introduced a revolution into English versification.' To this Schelling added a powerful contrast between the unprecedented verse forms devised by Donne and the classically conservative ones with which Jonson contented himself: 'for inventive variety, fitness, and success, the lyrical stanzas of Donne are surpassed by scarcely any Elizabethan poet.'[53]

The culmination of Schelling's Introduction proposed a radical alternative to the traditional ridicule of Donne's figures as evidence of a malignant foreign influence. Arguing that Spenser and Sidney were the 'exponent[s]' of 'the Italianate school of poetry in England', Schelling observed that Elizabethan poets inevitably worked with poetic conventions borrowed from Italy. Sidney and Spenser and Shakespeare infused the tradition with 'characteristics of a genuine vernacular utterance.' Donne was so original, however, that the 'Italian influence ... failed, as the classic influence too failed, to reach' him. Donne's originality, although it was emulated, was never matched, with the result that Jonsonian classicism became the dominant poetic mode, flowing through Herrick and Sandys until it reached Dryden and Pope.[54] A year after he had finished directing Brumbaugh's thesis, Schelling, having begun the task with a low opinion of Donne, was articulating in print a rationale for the way in which Briggs had organized his course on the seventeenth century. He effectively refined what Briggs began, bringing Donne into the mainstream by making available many poems that had long been off the literary map. His appreciation of the lyric Donne was one sign among a growing number that there was a market for a new edition of the poetry.

Schelling's vision of Donne was partly reproduced by another academic, Frederic Ives Carpenter of the University of Chicago. Carpenter's *English Lyric Poetry 1500–1700* (1897) printed most of the poems found in Schelling's anthology and added 'The Undertaking' and 'The Blossom.' Carpenter also situated Donne's lyric achievement squarely in the 1590s; and he proclaimed him 'a thoroughly original spirit and a great innovator', who gave the

[53] *Elizabethan Lyrics*, pp. xlvii, lxviii. Compare: Gosse, *The Jacobean Poets* (London: J. Murray; New York: Charles Scribner's Sons, 1894), 61–2; an earlier version appeared in *Littell's Living Age*, 5th ser., 84 (1893), 429–36.
[54] *Elizabethan Lyrics*, pp. lxviii–lxix.

conceit new weight by virtue of using it symbolically. These claims were not unprecedented. Carpenter went on to assert that, with the Shakespeare of the sonnets, Donne was one of the two great masters of 'passionate introspection', who introduced 'an intense and self-consuming subjectivity into English lyric poetry.' His presentation of Donne as a Hamlet-like exponent of *Weltschmerz* and a forerunner of the expressions of yearning found in Rousseau and Byron indicates that, more than Schelling, he was in touch with critical currents in writing about Donne flowing outside the Academy.[55] Both these anthologies of the mid-nineties show that, well before the re-evaluations of the poetic canon found in H. J. Massingham's *Treasury of Seventeenth Century English Verse* (1919) and Grierson's *Metaphysical Lyrics and Poems of the Seventeenth Century* (1921), a reconfiguration of the poems by which Donne's lyric achievements were to be understood was already under way.[56]

DECADENT, IMPRESSIONIST, SYMBOLIST DONNE

This book has not sought finally to adjudicate the rival claims of those who propose, on the one hand, that it is creative writers who make a predecessor canonical and of those who insist, on the other, that it is the school that determines canonical status. The terms in which this debate is often conducted seem to presuppose an either/or, while the messy, concrete history that we have been exploring suggests that it is undesirable to settle for a single or simple conclusion. What Donne's history between 1800 and 1900 shows is not that one or other group (poets, or teachers, or editors, or critics, or readers) has been decisive, but that at key moments (such as the 1890s) there was a synergy at work as various groups differentiated themselves from one another and formed temporary and permeable interpretative communities, which sometimes overlapped. For a time in the twentieth century it looked as if the affinities for Donne evinced in modernist poetry had clinched the case for creative writers as the ultimate arbiters of canonical status. Yet we have seen that there is a good deal to be said for Briggs and his students having been decisive agents in re-establishing the importance of Donne. What warrants further illustration before concluding is that many of the most interesting developments necessarily took place outside the classroom.

---

[55] *English Lyric Poetry 1500–1700*, with an Introduction by Frederic Ives Carpenter (London: Blackie and Son; New York: Charles Scribner's Sons, 1897), pp. lviii, lx, xlviii–xlix. This anthology was also published in Glasgow and Dublin.

[56] On the importance of Massingham's *Treasury*, see Ferry, *Tradition and the Individual Poem*, 122.

While academic specialists in the United States were making Donne's poetry an object of study, interest in that body of work was by no means merely academic. At Harvard, until the late nineties, students read Donne's poetry in copies of Grosart's edition kept on reserve in Gore Hall. Their reports for Briggs's courses on outside reading show that, despite the instructor's attempts to dissuade them, like schoolboys ferreting out the 'dirty' bits from an unexpurgated Ovid, they often made their way to the love elegies and 'Sappho to Philaenis.' In Britain the growing number of complaints about Walton's inadequate appreciation of the poems was an index of the fact that Donne was being more widely read than at any time since the seventeenth century, and often by readers who were fascinated by the materials to which Grosart's preface had, by extravagant circumlocution, provocatively called attention. In the mid-nineties the case for displacing the hero of Walton's narrative with a lyric poet was enhanced by the publication of the Muses' Library edition; and it was made explicit in a variety of essays that claimed Donne for movements that were stirring the cultural ferment.

The appearance of the Muses' Library edition, in two volumes, was long expected and disappointingly delayed. The task had been entrusted to Brinsley Nicholson, who as early as the 1870s had been known to be knowledgeable about Donne. When Nicholson died in 1892, the uncompleted project was reassigned to E. K. Chambers, recently down from Oxford and keen to demonstrate that Donne was worthy of comparison with Spenser.[57] Several features of this edition contributed to the growing interest in Donne's poems. Like the Grolier Club edition, which was virtually unknown in Britain, its title page abandoned the practice of referring to the author as 'Doctor' Donne, and its contents were arranged to restore first place to the Songs and Sonnets. In the introduction Saintsbury made a strong case for the eminence of the lyric Donne. For his part, Chambers, having consulted the seventeenth-century editions, provided an eclectic text and supplemented it with considerable data about the variants. He recognized, well in advance of what the editors of the *Variorum* have since made good, that many of the poems survive in more than one authorial version. He also composed numerous annotations, identifying, for instance, historical figures referred to or addressed in the poems. Elsewhere in the apparatus he included criticisms of Grosart's edition, both of its eccentric text and of its tendentious dating of many poems. The edition, part of a series of 'standard poets', made Donne's poetry more widely available than it had been for nearly a century. It was reprinted into the period

[57] See Chambers's Introduction to *English Pastorals* (London: Blackie and Son, 1895), pp. xvii–xix.

when Grierson began his attempt to teach Donne at Aberdeen. At Harvard it displaced Grosart as the textbook in which the students encountered Donne.

Still, the formal study of Donne in the universities remained largely out of touch with much of the most intriguing critical writing about his poetry. As euphemistic double entendre of the sort perfected by Oscar Wilde proliferated, some of Donne's greatest admirers sought to slow the interest that students might take in the more risqué aspects of the poetry by enlisting practices of euphemism and bowdlerization that had reached their high water mark in the 1880s. Like Algernon Swinburne, who famously said of Dr Bowdler that 'No man ever did better service to Shakespeare', Saintsbury and Gosse participated in expurgating books.[58] And Donne, although Saintsbury and Norton regarded him as an exponent of the highest spiritual love, came increasingly to be consulted as an authority on all varieties of love, above all on the range of moods and experiences connected, as Arthur Symons put it, with 'the whole pilgrim's progress of physical love.'[59] College teachers, operating *in loco parentis*, did not encourage students to trace this progress; they seem to have said nothing in their lectures about a new chorus of praise, sometimes ebullient, sometimes muted, that in British periodical literature proclaimed Donne a spokesman for 'decadence', an early 'impressionist', and a 'symbolist.' These interests formed part of a more general literary cultivation of a 'poetics of nostalgia' that looked both to the Celtic Twilight and the seventeenth century for models and inspiration.[60] Some of its rebelliousness, as W. B. Yeats acknowledged, was inspired by Donne. [61]

In the year after the Muses' Library edition came out, a zany and wholly unprecedented discussion of Donne appeared anonymously in the *Quarterly Review*. Its author nominated Donne as the first of 'the lineal fathers' of English 'impressionism' and found his most able descendents to be the author of *Tristram Shandy* and the poet who composed 'Endymion', 'Lamia', and 'Hyperion.' His essay contributed to a recanonization by celebrating the achievements of Donne and Sterne and Keats as the measure against which contemporary impressionists were to be judged adversely. Defining an impressionist as one who excites by suggestion rather than by representation,

[58] See Joss Marsh, *Word Crimes: Blasphemy, Culture, and Literature in Nineteenth-Century England* (Chicago: Univ. of Chicago Press, 1998), 218–19.

[59] Arthur Symons, 'John Donne', *Fortnightly Review*, new ser., 66 (1899), 741.

[60] See Murray G. H. Pittock, *Spectrum of Decadence: The Literature of the 1890s* (London: Routledge, 1993), chap. 3; for a helpful characterization of the general ethos, see Linda Dowling, *Language and Decadence in the Victorian Fin de Siècle* (Princeton, NJ: Princeton Univ. Press, 1986).

[61] See Yeats's recollections of the 1890s in 'The Tragic Generation', in *The Trembling Veil* (1922); repr., *Autobiographies: Reveries over Childhood and Youth and The Trembling of the Veil* (New York: Macmillan, 1927), 402–3.

he praised Donne's emphasis on 'experience' and 'method of sensuous suggestion.' He declared him 'unique in English literature' because he is 'the mere diarist of his own feelings' and the writer of love poetry that concerns nothing but the 'workings of his own heart and soul.'[62] This was to place positive value on virtually the same features that were cooling Brumbaugh's enthusiasm for Donne's poems. Discovery of the poet's intense egoism, while it curtailed the admiration that Brumbaugh had felt, proved a stimulant to new admiration among those who were busy about the work of inverting conventional thinking and morality.

Meanwhile others had begun discreetly to praise Donne's love poetry for qualities that had long been deplored. Bradford, although he assumed that he was disallowed from quoting indecent passages, recommended the love elegies and the lyrics as the poet's 'most satisfactory productions.' Charles Kains Jackson remarked for knowing readers, in a periodical that he edited and through which he disseminated 'Uranian' views, that these poems will 'repay attention' and are 'far from being dull.'[63]

Known as 'the pope' of a group of homosexuals in London and Oxford, Jackson was especially friendly with John Addington Symonds, the first English translator of Michelangelo's sonnets. In *The Artist and Journal of Home Culture*, one of the little magazines rarely found in university libraries, he introduced Donne as a 'surprisingly modern' poet who often wrote in 'a wholly decadent fashion.' His essay provided more than two dozen quotations to illustrate how many different sorts of interests could be pursued in reading through a volume of Donne's poems. The longest of his quotations came from 'Sappho to Philaenis', which he proposed as the original for Swinburne's 'Erotion' and presented as proof that Donne was 'the true successor of the Elizabethan Marlowe.' There were plenty of readers who understood the purport of these recommendations. Perhaps some did have an academic interest and wanted to fill in from Donne's youthful poems what Grosart had designated 'an unwritten chapter in Elizabethan history.'[64] Self-consciously 'decadent' poets

[62] 'Fathers of Literary Impressionism in England', *Quarterly Review*, 185 (1897), 173, 178–9. *The Wellesley Index of Victorian Periodicals* identifies the author as Walter Sydney Sichel (1855–1933). He was a London barrister, who contributed articles on politics, literature, and drama to many of the leading English periodicals. He later wrote a book on Sterne (1910).

[63] Charles Kains Jackson, 'John Donne: An Appreciation', *The Artist and Journal of Home Culture*, 15/172 (1894), 105–7; because of the brevity of the essay I have not cited individual page numbers. This piece was called to my attention by Ian Fletcher's essay, 'Decadence and the Little Magazines', in *Decadence and the 1890s*, Stratford-upon-Avon Studies 17, ed. Ian Fletcher (London: Edward Arnold, 1979), 188–91. Cf. also Karl Beckson, *London in the 1890s: A Cultural History* (New York: Norton, 1992), 188.

[64] Alexander. B. Grosart (ed.), *The Complete Poems of John Donne, D.D., Dean of St. Paul's*, The Fuller Worthies' Library, 2 vols. ([London: printed for private circulation], 1872–3), i, p. x.

found in Donne, in any event, an attractive precursor with close affinities to Pater.

Late Victorian aesthetes recognized, as John Carey has observed, that Donne and Pater had 'kindred visions.' Both writers convey intensely the press of perpetual change and motion, and both respond to 'life's destructiveness' by cultivating 'the art of vivid sensation' and taking pleasure in 'outraging the narrow-minded.' Jackson illustrated Donne's pleasure in this pose with quotations from 'The Sun Rising', 'Woman's Constancy', 'The Indifferent', and 'The Canonization.' His essay makes good Carey's speculation that the successors of Pater recognized in Donne 'a dandy and a libertine.' No doubt Carey was also right when he observed that the subversive epigram proved equally appealing to Donne and to Wilde.[65]

Donne's poetry also commanded the attention of the members of the Rhymers' Club, including Yeats and Lionel Johnson. As early as 1893 Symons's poetry showed signs that he had been reading Donne and regarded him as a fellow 'decadent.' The first of his four 'Variations upon love' begins with the line, 'For God's sake, let me love you, and give over.' Once Symons began to think of himself as a 'symbolist' poet, he sought to engage Donne's poems as a body of symbolist work. Traces of this engagement appear in poems written in 1899 and 1900 when Symons was working on the study published as *The Symbolist Movement*. *The Loom of Dreams* (1901) contains several poems that voice a desire for transcendence and explore the difficulties of achieving it. 'The Ecstasy', 'The Alchemy', 'The One Desire', and 'The Regret' are more conspicuously reminiscent of Donne than virtually any other poems that had been written since the seventeenth century.[66]

The intensity with which Symons read Donne in 1899 was occasioned at least in part by the publication of *The Life and Letters*, which he reviewed. Symons had been friendly with Gosse for many years, and in 1891 had written to him revealing that he had been the anonymous reviewer of Saintsbury's *Essays in English Literature*. He asked that Gosse not reveal this to the author, whom he had praised for the 'high second-rate quality' of his work.[67] Reviewing Gosse for the *Fortnightly* in his own name, he had a delicate balancing act to perform. He largely disposed of Gosse's work in his opening paragraph,

---

[65] John Carey, *John Donne: Life, Mind, and Art* (Oxford: Oxford Univ. Press, 1980), 179–80.

[66] See *The Collected Works of Arthur Symons*: i-ii: *Poems* (London: Martin Secker, 1924; repr., New York: AMS Press, 1973), i. 244; ii. 127–8, 136, 135, 147.

[67] Symons's letter of 29 June 1891 to Gosse is printed and glossed in *Arthur Symons: Selected Letters, 1880–1935*, ed. Karl Beckson and John M. Munro (Iowa City, IA: Univ. of Iowa Press, 1989), 81–2.

praising it as 'perhaps' a 'solid and serious contribution' that 'we may well believe ... will remain the final authority on so interesting and so difficult a subject.' Yet Symons also judged that Gosse had not shown 'Donne as he really was.' His achievement was simply having made the letters of this 'very ambiguous human being' available, so that we can 'form our own opinion.'[68]

Symons did for Donne's life what Leslie Stephen might have wished: he removed the fiction of a dramatic conversion that was to be located at some key juncture. To Symons's way of thinking, Donne was above all an 'intellectual adventurer', who was 'interested in everything' (735): Copernicus, Tycho Brahe, and Galileo; travel and foreign literature; the body and disease, life and death. His career could be divided into three stages: the youthful soldier, traveller, lover and poet, 'unrestrained' in his pursuit of 'passionate adventures'; the 'lawyer' and 'theologian, seeking knowledge and worldly advancement'; then the explorer of 'saintly living and dying' (737–8). The 'principle of development' that occasioned 'growth' from one stage to the next was his 'curious, insatiable brain searching', with a 'fundamental uncertainty of aim', for 'something worthy of himself to do' (738). Symons's largest compliment to Gosse was to steal from him the idea that Donne found what he was looking for only after his wife's death. He then transmuted the stolen goods back into a variation on Walton's paradigm that was more acceptable to a modern sensibility: the object of Donne's quest turns out to be 'himself, the ultimate of his curiosities', and that 'self' was the Dean of St Paul's (739). This was as close to an integrated picture of Donne's life and writings as anyone had to offer.

For Symons, Donne's 'self' is known to us not through a narrative, the explanatory framework into which biographers sought to fit the writings, but through the letters and other writings, above all 'a bundle of manuscript verses' that the Dean 'could bring himself neither to print nor to destroy' and so left behind for posterity (739). A more subtle reader than Gosse, Symons ascribed the survival of the poems to Donne's own agency. The poems were relics, indirectly provided to aftertimes by Donne himself. Whatever they might suggest about his experiences beyond the written words, their principal significance was what they reveal about the workings of a remarkable imagination. The poems show what it would be like to love with one's 'whole nature', in a way that makes of reason not passion's adversary but its 'ally' (741). Symons invoked Wordsworth's definition of poetry in order to insist that, with a wonderful 'arrogant egoism' (740) matched only by Browning, Donne had written his poems before 'tranquility' set in to recollect 'emotion'

---

[68] Symons, 'John Donne', 734. Further citations appear after quotations in the text.

and convert it into art (744). The beauties to be found in Donne's verse, he argued, were produced as if by accident, for Donne was wholly concerned to capture the 'truth' of passion. He accomplished this through a 'frightful faculty of seeing through his own illusions' and wrote with a consummate detachment from himself, often making himself the principal object of his own satire (742). Symons thus endorsed Dryden's judgment that Donne was the 'greatest wit, though not the best poet of our nation', that is 'the greatest intellect' (744). To this he provocatively added, against Dryden,[69] that 'If women most conscious of their sex were ever to read Donne', they would see that he 'shows women themselves, in delight, anger, or despair' and not as an 'abstract angel'; and 'they would say, He was a great lover; he understood' (743).

SOME RESIDUE

Symons's reading of the poetry did not make an immediate impact. For many, the dominant terms for approaching Donne remained those that stymied Brumbaugh and those in which Norton, summing up the current state of Donne studies at the end of the nineteenth century, framed the central problem: 'The main perplexity in the reading of Donne arises, indeed,' Norton proposed, 'from no difficulty of the text, but from uncertainty how far the poems are the expression of genuine feeling, or dramatic utterances of feigned emotion and fictitious sentiment.'[70] Symons offered an alternative, however, to Gosse's attempt to create a narrative that defines the meaning and the significance of the poetry; and he pointed a way forward. His treatment of the poems as the expressions of a great intellect passionately set on getting at truth accorded with what was most promising in the early teaching of Donne. Dean Briggs of course was not about to present Donne as a great cynic about love. Yet a clever student might have seen pretty much what Symons was seeing in the poetry at the *fin de siècle* when he explored the maladies of love in *Amoris Victima* (1897). Eventually, one of Briggs's students, acutely aware that Donne had been receiving 'close attention from some of the most interesting younger poets' and having himself been transformed, as he acknowledged, by reading

[69] Having quoted from Dryden's dedication for 'Eleonora: A Panegyrical Poem', Symons then alluded to *A Discourse of the Original and Progress of Satire* (1693). For the relevant pages, see *The Poems of John Dryden*, ed. James Kinsley (Oxford: Clarendon, 1958), ii. 583, 604.
[70] Charles Eliot Norton, 'The Text of Donne's Poems', *Studies and Notes in Philology and Literature*, v: *Child Memorial Volume* (Boston: Ginn, 1896), 18.

Symons's book on *The Symbolist Movement*,[71] would distill into his influential essays what had been best about the early teaching of Donne at Harvard.

T. S. Eliot did not invent Donne. He recognized the value of freeing his writing from the historical and nationalist contexts that had framed the approaches by which most readers had come to it for more than two hundred years; and he heralded a re-entry of Donne's poetry into living literary history. By the middle of the twentieth century, as formalist approaches to literature began to flourish, some of Donne's poems became especially popular in the classroom. The broader contexts that have made up the subject of this book were largely forgotten. And while a great deal of historical scholarship has turned its attention to Donne, much of it has proceeded as if it were possible, and desirable, to ignore the history that has been recounted here. Sustained examination of how Donne was lodged in nineteenth-century literary culture reveals, however, that many concerns that inform our inquiries are shot through with assumptions that, while we do not exactly share them with the Victorians, contribute significantly to the ways in which we are likely to think about his marriage, his career, and his politics. Inevitably, they also affect the perspectives from which we read the writer's remarkable and unremarkable works.

Through most of the twentieth century it would have seemed odd to break off a study of Donne's place in literary culture around the year 1900. In order fully to account for the appearance of Grierson's edition of 1912 and Eliot's essay on 'The Metaphysical Poets', so the argument might go, we must examine the story within a long nineteenth century in which Victorianism did not really end until sometime around the First World War. I have sympathy with an objection to leaving the years 1901–12 out of full-scale consideration. The rumblings involving Donne in these years engaged several vital, sometimes overlapping, interpretative communities: he was attracting active interest within a gay subculture in Oxford and in Boston, a jovial feast in his honor was celebrated annually at Yale, Londoners were expecting a book on him from Desmond MacCarthy, Herbert Grierson was beginning to teach his poetry at Aberdeen, and Rupert Brooke was writing poems of love and grief that earned him a reputation as 'our Donne Redivivus.' All these currents and others warrant further probing. Nonetheless, the central argument of the book is concluded: whereas in the first half of the nineteenth century, thanks largely to the great popularity of Walton's *Lives*, the word 'Donne' was used principally to refer to a historical figure, an eloquent

---

[71] See Eliot's review of Peter Quennell's *Baudelaire and the Symbolists*, in *The Criterion*, 9 (Jan. 1930), 357.

preacher from the time of King James I, during the Victorian period the word came increasingly to refer to the varied body of writings that this man had left behind. In the 1890s, as the love poetry in particular found many new readers, the number of alternative Donnes multiplied. A much expanded horizon had opened myriad possibilities for reading Donne's œuvre with greater pleasure and understanding, some of which have since been realized.

Bibliography

Editions of the Writings of John Donne, 1779–1912

These items are arranged chronologically.

BELL, JOHN (ed.), *The Poetical Works of Dr John Donne, Dean of St Paul's, London,* 3 vols., in The Poets of Great Britain Complete, from Chaucer to Churchill (Edinburgh: Mundell and Son, 1779).

ANDERSON, ROBERT (ed.), 'The Poetical Works of Dr. John Donne ... To which is prefixed the Life of the Author', in *A Complete Edition of the Poets of Great Britain. Volume the Fourth. Containing Donne, Daniel, Browne, P. Fletcher, B. Jonson, Drummond, Crashaw, & Davenants* (London: James Evans, 1793; Boston, MA, for Messrs. Thomas and Andrews E. Larkin, Junr. and David West; Worcester, MA, for Mr. Isaiah Thomas; Providence, RI, for Messrs. Carter and Wilkinson, [n.d.]).

CHALMERS, ALEXANDER (ed.), 'Poems of Donne', in *The Works of the English Poets from Chaucer to Cowper* (London: J. Johnson et al., 1810). v. 115–219.

SANFORD, EZEKIEL (ed.), *The Works of the British Poets with the Lives of the Authors* (Philadelphia: Mitchell, Ames, and White, 1819), iv. 135–95.

ALFORD, HENRY (ed.), *The Works of John Donne, D.D., Dean of Saint Paul's, 1621–1631. With a Memoir of His Life,* 6 vols. (London: John W. Parker, 1839).

ANONYMOUS (ed.), *Selections from the Works of John Donne, D.D.* (Oxford: D. A. Talboys, 1840).

ANONYMOUS (ed.), *Devotions, with Two Sermons. I. On the Decease of Lady Danvers Mother of George Herbert. II. Deaths Duel—His Own Funeral Sermon [by John Donne DD Dean of St Paul's]. To which is prefixed His Life by Izaak Walton* (London: William Pickering, 1840).

ANONYMOUS (ed.), *Donne's Devotions* (Oxford: D. A. Talboys, 1841).

JESSOPP, AUGUSTUS (ed.), *Essays in Divinity by John Donne, D.D.* (London: John Tupling, 1855).

[LOWELL, JAMES RUSSELL (ed.)], *The Poetical Works of Dr. John Donne, with a Memoir* (Boston: Little, Brown, 1855).

GROSART, ALEXANDER B. (ed.), *The Complete Poems of John Donne, D.D.,* The Fuller Worthies' Library, 2 vols. (London: [printed for private circulation], 1872–3).

[LOWELL, JAMES RUSSELL, NORTON, CHARLES ELIOT, and BURNETT, MABEL (eds.)], *The Poems of John Donne from the Text of the Edition of 1633,* rev. James Russell Lowell, with the Various Readings of the Others Editions of the Seventeenth Century, and with a Preface, an Introduction, and Notes by Charles Eliot Norton, 2 vols. (New York: Grolier Club, 1895).

CHAMBERS, E. K. (ed.), *Poems of John Donne,* with an Introduction by George Saintsbury, The Muses' Library, 2 vols. (London: Lawrence and Bullen; George Routledge and Sons; New York: Charles Scribner's Sons; E. P. Dutton, 1896).

GOSSE, EDMUND (ed.), *The Life and Letters of John Donne Dean of St. Paul's*, 2 vols. (London: Heinemann; New York: Dodd, Mead, 1899; repr., Gloucester, MA: Peter Smith, 1959).

GRIERSON, HERBERT J. C. (ed.), *The Poems of John Donne*, edited from the Old Editions and Numerous Manuscripts with Introductions and Commentary, 2 vols. (Oxford: Clarendon Press, 1912).

Unpublished Manuscript Sources

ANONYMOUS, [Notes on English 28] (1900), Curriculum Collection, HUC 8899.324.28, Harvard University Archives.

ARNOLD, OLIVER HENRY, 'Prof. Robinson P. Dunn's Course of English Literature' (*c.*1863), ii, Lecture notes taken by students, MS-1M-2, Brown University Archives.

BEERS, HENRY A., 'Shakespere's Contemporaries', uncatalogued typescript, Za Beers 58, Beinecke Library, Yale University.

BIERSTADT, ALBERT MORTON, [Notes on English 28] (1909), Curriculum Collection, HUC 8908.324.28, Harvard University Archives.

BRIGGS, L. B. R., 'ENGLISH 15. 1897–98', in J. H. Gardiner, 'English 15. Opening', English Authors I, HUG 1415.24, Harvard University Archives.

——Letter of 23 Aug. 1916 to Miss Wheeler, Biographical Material of Men Known Chiefly for Their Harvard Connection, HUG 1233.5, Harvard University Archives.

BRUMBAUGH, M. G., 'A Study of the Poetry of John Donne', Thesis Submitted to the Philosophical Faculty of the University of Pennsylvania (23 Dec. 1893).

——[Notes on English 15 (at Harvard)], Archives Vault Collection, Juniata College, Huntingdon, PA.

BURNETT, MABEL, undated letter to Charles Eliot Norton, Norton Papers, bMS Am 1088 (898), Houghton Library, Harvard University.

CALKINS, RAYMOND, 'Notes on Eng. XVII cent. Literature' (1890), Curriculum Collection, HUC 8889.324.15, Harvard University Archives.

CULVER, BRIAN, ' "My Face in Thine Eye": John Donne's Poetry and the Institution of English Studies, *c.*1850–1950', Ph.D. dissertation (New York University, 1998).

'Expensive Books purchased, 1887–88 to 1919–20', Harvard University Library Records, UA III.50.28.87.3, Harvard University Archives.

FIELD, BARRON (ed.), 'The Songs and Sonnets of Dr. John Donne: With Critical Notes by the late Samuel Taylor Coleridge', MS Eng 966, Houghton Library, Harvard University.

GARDINER, J. H., 'Donne. Jonson', English Authors I, HUG 1415.24, Harvard University Archives.

——'English 15. Opening', English Authors I, HUG 1415.24, Harvard University Archives.

——'English 32^2, Summary', English Authors I, HUG 1315.24, Harvard University Archives.

HARVARD UNIVERSITY, Library charging records, 1834–7, UA III.50.15.60, Harvard University Archives.

—— Student Records, 'Eliot, Thomas Stearns', UA III.15.75.12 and UAV 161.272.5. Harvard University Archives.

KITTREDGE, GEORGE LYMAN, Commonplace Book, Curriculum Collection, HUC 8878.315, Harvard University Archives.

LOWELL, JAMES RUSSELL, 'Poetic diction', bMS Am 765 (905), Houghton Library, Harvard University.

MAIKOSKI, MATTHEW JOSEPH, 'Gamaliel Bradford: Psychographer', Ph.D. dissertation, University of Pittsburgh, 1954.

MELTON, WRIGHTMAN F., 'The Rhetoric of John Donne's Verse', Ph.D. thesis, Johns Hopkins University, 1906.

MYRICK, ARTHUR B., [Notes on English 15^2], Curriculum Collection, HUC 8899.324.15, Harvard University Archives.

NEILSON, WILLIAM ALLAN, 'Lectures on Historical English Literature by Prof. [David] Masson' (1889), ii. 161–2, in [Division] 32. Personal Papers, Series 1, Box 14, Smith College Archives.

—— [Lecture Notes for English 32^a, Harvard University], in [Division] 32. Personal Papers of William Allan Neilson, Series III, Box 19, Folder 339, Smith College Archives.

NORTON, CHARLES ELIOT, Annotations in a copy of Edmund Gosse, *The Life and Letters of John Donne Dean of St. Paul's*, 2 vols. (London: William Heinemann; New York: Dodd, Mead, 1899), *EC.D7187.W899gb, Houghton Library, Harvard University.

—— Letter of 8 Aug. 1907 to William James, bMS Am 1092 [626–634], Houghton Library, Harvard University.

PHELPS, WILLIAM LYON, [Reading notes, i], William Lyon Phelps Papers, YRG 47, RU 159, Box 6, Folder 39, Manuscripts and Archives, Yale University Library.

—— [Reading notes, iii], William Lyon Phelps Papers, Ms. Group 578, Series III, Box 16, Folder 199, Manuscripts and Archives, Yale University Library.

—— 'Briggs's History and Principles of English Versification, 1890–91', William Lyon Phelps Papers, MS Group 578, Series III, Box 17, Folder 202, Manuscripts and Archives, Yale University Library.

—— 'English Literature of the 17th Century' (1892), William Lyon Phelps Papers, MS Group 578, Series III, Box 17, Folder 202, Manuscripts and Archives, Yale University Library.

PHILLIPS, JAMES DUNCAN, [Notes on English 28] (1895), Curriculum Collection, HUC 8894.324.28, Harvard University Archives.

POTTER, M. A., Lecture Notes in Comparative Literature 7 (c.1907), Curriculum Collection, HUC 8907.214.70, Harvard University Archives.

Programs for 'The Feast of the Metaphysicals', Ms. Group 578, Series IV, Box 21, Folder 232, William Lyon Phelps Papers, Manuscripts and Archives, Yale University Library.

QUINN, ARTHUR HOBSON, 'Felix E. Schelling—A Tribute', UPT 50, S 322, Archives of the University of Pennsylvania.

RACKEMANN, FRANCIS M., Notes on English 28 (1906), Curriculum Collection, HUC 8905.325.28, Harvard University Archives.

ROBINSON, FRED N[ORRIS], [Notes on English 15] (1892), Curriculum Collection, HUC 8887.325.77, Harvard University Archives.

'A Session of the Poets', William Lyon Phelps Papers, Ms. Group 578, Series IV, Box 21, Folder 232, Manuscripts and Archives, Yale University Library.

STEPHEN, LESLIE, Letter of 13 Feb. 1888 to Dr Jessopp, ALS, 4 p, Garber Collection, Case Western Reserve University Library.

STERLING, HELEN KATHRYN, 'Unpublished Marginalia by Samuel Taylor Coleridge in a Volume of John Donne's Poetry', MA thesis, University of Nevada, 1954.

WILDER, WILLIAM R., Notes on 'Lecture Twelfth' for the course on English Literature given by James Ormsbee Murray (1878), the Lecture Notes Collection AC#-052, University Archives, Department of Rare Books and Special Collections, Princeton University Library.

Printed Sources

ALFORD, HENRY, *The School of the Heart and Other Poems*, 2 vols. (London: Longman and Co.; Cambridge: J. and J. J. Deighton, 1835).

_____ 'On Poetry in General', *Dearden's Miscellany*, 1 (Jan. 1839), 1–11.

_____ (ed.), Preface and 'Life of Dr. Donne', *The Works of John Donne, D.D., Dean of Saint Paul's, 1621–1631. With a Memoir of His Life* (London: John W. Parker, 1839), i, pp. v–viii, ix–xxix.

_____ 'Mr. Alford in Reply to Strictures on His Edition of Donne', *The British Magazine and Monthly Register of Religious and Ecclesiastical Information*, 16 (1839), 60–1.

_____ 'Wordsworth', *Dearden's Miscellany*, 3 (Feb. 1840), 93–108.

_____ 'Wordsworth's Sonnets', *Dearden's Miscellany*, 3 (Apr. 1840), 245–53.

_____ *Life, Journals and Letters of Henry Alford, D.D.*, ed. [Frances Alford] (London: Rivingtons, 1873).

ALLEN, PETER, *The Cambridge Apostles: The Early Years* (Cambridge: Cambridge Univ. Press, 1978).

AMIGONI, DAVID, *Victorian Biography: Intellectuals and the Ordering of Discourse* (London: Harvester Wheatsheaf; New York: St. Martin's, 1993).

ANONYMOUS, 'Coleridge's *Literary Remains*', *Quarterly Review*, 59/18 (July and Oct. 1837), 1–32.

ANONYMOUS, 'Robert Browning', *Putnam's Monthly Magazine*, 7/40 (Apr. 1856), 372–81.

ANONYMOUS, Review of F. J. Child's British Poets Series, *North American Review*, 84/171 (Jan. 1857), 240–53.

ANONYMOUS, 'A New Edition of John Donne', *The Dial* [Chicago], 20/237 (1896), 280.

ANONYMOUS, Review of *The Life and Letters of John Donne*, *Book Reviews*, 7 (1899), 482–3.

ANONYMOUS, 'Memorial to Norton: Books of Late Professor Are Exhibited', *Boston Evening Transcript* (16 Nov. 1908).

ANONYMOUS, 'Rare Volumes of Charles E. Norton', *Boston Sunday Herald* (22 Nov. 1908).

ARMSTRONG, ISOBEL, 'Browning and Victorian Poetry of Sexual Love', in Isobel Armstrong (ed.), *Robert Browning*, Writers and Their Background (London: Bell, 1974; Athens, OH: Ohio Univ. Press, 1975), 267–98.

ARNOLD, THOMAS, *Chaucer to Wordsworth: A Short History of English Literature from the Earliest Times to the Present Day* (London: Thomas Murby, [1868]).

BAKER, HERSCHEL, *William Hazlitt* (Cambridge, MA: Belknap Press of Harvard Univ. Press, 1962).

BALD, R. C., *John Donne: A Life* (Oxford: Oxford Univ. Press, 1970; repr. with corrections, Oxford: Clarendon, 1986).

BECKSON, KARL, *London in the 1890s: A Cultural History* (New York: Norton, 1992).

BEECHING, H. C., 'The Life of Donne', *Athenæum*, 3761 (25 Nov. 1899), 723.

——— 'The Life of Donne', *Athenæum*, 3762 (2 Dec. 1899), 760.

——— 'The Life of Donne,' *Athenæum*, 3764 (16 Dec. 1899), 836.

——— 'Izaak Walton's Life of Donne: An Apology', *Cornhill Magazine*, 3rd ser., 8 (1900), 249–68.

——— *Religio Laici* (London: Smith, Elder, 1902).

BEER, GILLIAN, *George Eliot* (Bloomington, IN: Indiana Univ. Press, 1986).

BEERS, HENRY A., *An Outline Sketch of English Literature* (New York: Chautauqua Press, 1886).

——— *From Chaucer to Tennyson: English Literature in Eight Chapters with Selections from Thirty Authors* (New York: Chautauqua Press, 1890).

——— *The Connecticut Wits, and Other Essays* (New Haven, CT: Yale Univ. Press; London: Humphrey Milford, Oxford Univ. Press, 1920).

BELLEW, J. C. M., *Poets' Corner: A Manual for Students in English Poetry* (London: Routledge and Sons, 1868).

BENET, DIANA TREVIÑO, 'Sexual Transgression in Donne's Elegies', *MP*, 92 (1994), 14–35.

BLACKBURN, VERNON, Introduction, in W. E. Henley (ed.), *Lives of Doctor Donne*, etc., by Izaak Walton, English Classics (London: Methuen, 1895), pp. vii–xxvi.

BLAKENEY, R. P., *Popery in its Social Aspect: Being A Complete Exposure of the Immorality and Intolerance of Romanism* (Edinburgh: M'Gibbon; London: Protestant Educational Institute, [c.1854]).

BLISS, PHILIP (ed.), *Athenæ Oxonienses: An Exact History of All the Writers and Bishops Who Have Had Their Education in the University of Oxford*, by Anthony à Wood, 3rd edn, 4 vols. (London: F. C. and J. Rivington, et al., 1813–20).

BLOOM, HAROLD, *The Visionary Company: A Reading of Romantic Poetry* (1961; rev. and enlarged edn, Ithaca, NY: Cornell Univ. Press, 1971).

BODENHEIMER, ROSEMARIE, *The Real Life of Mary Ann Evans: George Eliot, Her Letters and Fiction* (Ithaca, NY: Cornell Univ. Press, 1994).

BONNELL, THOMAS F., 'John Bell's *Poets of Great Britain*: The "Little Trifling Edition" Revisited', *MP*, 85 (1987), 128–52.

BOSWELL, JAMES, *Life of Johnson* (1791; London: Oxford Univ. Press, 1953).

BOTTING, ROLAND B., 'The Reputation of John Donne during the Nineteenth Century', *Research Studies of the State College of Washington*, 9 (Sept. 1941), 139–88.

BRADFORD, GAMALIEL, 'The Poetry of Donne', *Andover Review*, 18/106 (1892), 350–67; repr. *A Naturalist of Souls: Studies in Psychography* (New York: Dodd, Mead, 1917), 25–59.

——— *The Journal*, ed. Van Wyck Brooks (Boston: Houghton Mifflin, 1933).

BRISTOW, JOSEPH, *Robert Browning* (London: Harvester Wheatsheaf; New York: St. Martin's Press, 1991).

BRITTIN, NORMAN A., 'Emerson and the Metaphysical Poets', *American Literature*, 8 (1936), 1–21.

BROOKE, STOPFORD, *[Primer of] English Literature* (New York: Appleton, 1876); repr. as *English Literature* (New York: Macmillan, 1897).

BROUGHTON, TREV LYNN, 'Froude: The "Painful Appendix" ', *Carlyle Studies Annual: Carlyle at 200. Lectures I* (Normal, IL: Illinois State Univ. Department of English, 1995), 65–80.

——— *Men of Letters, Writing Lives: Masculinity and Literary Auto/Biography in the Late Victorian Period* (London: Routledge, 1999).

BROWNING, ROBERT, *The Complete Works*, gen. ed. Roma A. King, Jr, Jack W. Herring, et al., 13 vols. (Athens, OH: Ohio Univ. Press, 1969–).

BUCHANAN, R. W., *The Fleshly School of Poetry and Other Phenomena of the Day* (London: Strahan, 1872).

BULLEN, J. B., *The Myth of the Renaissance in Nineteenth-Century Writing* (Oxford: Clarendon Press; New York: Oxford Univ. Press, 1994).

BYATT, A. S., *Possession: A Romance* (London: Chatto and Windus, 1989; New York: Random House, 1990).

CAMERON, KENNETH WALTER, *Thoreau's Harvard Years: Materials Introductory to New Explorations. Record of Fact and Background* (Hartford, CT: Transcendental Books, 1966).

CAMPBELL, THOMAS, *Specimens of the British Poets; ... and an Essay on English Poetry*, 7 vols. (London: John Murray, 1819).

CAREY, JOHN, *John Donne: Life, Mind, and Art* (Oxford: Oxford Univ. Press, 1980).

CARLYLE, ALEXANDER, and CRICHTON–BROWNE, SIR JAMES, *The Nemesis of Froude: A Rejoinder to James Anthony Froude's 'My Relations with Carlyle'* (London and New York: John Lane, 1903).

CARPENTER, FREDERIC IVES (ed.), *English Lyric Poetry 1500–1700* (London: Blackie and Son; New York: Charles Scribner's Sons, 1897).

Catalogue of the Valuable and Very Choice Library of the Late Sir John Simeon, Bart., M.P. (London: Dryden Press, 1871).

CATTERMOLE, RICHARD (ed.), *The Literature of the Church of England Indicated in Selections from the Writings of Eminent Divines*, 2 vols. (London: John W. Parker, 1844).

CHALMERS, ALEXANDER, Preface, *The Works of the English Poets from Chaucer to Cowper*, 21 vols. (London: J. Johnson et al., 1810), i, pp. v–x.

CHAMBERLAIN, JACOB CHESTER, and LIVINGSTON, LUTHER S. (eds.), *A Bibliography of the First Editions in Book Form of the Writings of James Russell Lowell* (New York: [Privately Printed], 1914).

CHAMBERLAIN, THOMAS, *A Help to Knowledge, Chiefly Religious, in Extracts*, new edn., (Oxford: James Burns, 1840).

CHAMBERS, E. K. (ed.), *English Pastorals* (London: Blackie and Son, 1895).

CHARTERIS, EVAN, *The Life and Letters of Sir Edmund Gosse* (New York: Harper and Brothers, 1931).

CHESSBOROUGH, 'Donne's Poems, First Edition', *N&Q*, 3rd ser., 3 (18 Apr. 1863), 308–9.

CHRISTIANSEN, JEROME C., 'Coleridge's Marginal Method in the *Biographia Literaria*', *PMLA*, 92 (1977), 928–40.

CLARK, J. SCOTT CLARK, 'Special Introduction', *History of English Literature*, by H. Taine, rev. edn (New York: Colonial Press, 1900), i, pp. iii–viii.

COLERIDGE, SAMUEL TAYLOR, *Literary Remains*, ed. Henry Nelson Coleridge, 4 vols. (London: Pickering, 1836–9).

—— 'Coleridgiana. Mss. Notes of Coleridge in the Books of Charles Lamb, Now for the First Time Published', *Literary World*, 326 (30 Apr. 1853), 349–50; 328 (14 May 1853), 393.

—— *Coleridge on the Seventeenth Century*, ed. Roberta F. Brinkley (Durham, NC: Duke Univ. Press, 1955).

—— *Letters*, ed. Earl Leslie Griggs, 6 vols. (Oxford: Clarendon, 1956–71).

—— *The Collected Works*, Bollingen Series, 75, ed. Kathleen Coburn et al. (London: Routledge and Kegan Paul; Princeton, NJ: Princeton Univ. Press, 1969–).

—— *The Notebooks*, iii: *1808–1819 Text*, ed. Kathleen Coburn (London: Routledge and Kegan Paul; Princeton, NJ: Princeton Univ. Press, 1973).

—— *Selected Letters*, ed. H. J. Jackson (Oxford: Clarendon, 1987).

COLLIER, JOHN PAYNE, *The Poetical Decameron, or Ten Conversations on English Poets and Poetry, Particularly of the Reigns of Elizabeth and James I*, 2 vols. (Edinburgh: Archibald Constable, 1820).

COLLINS, JOHN CHURTON, *The Study of English Literature: A Plea for its Recognition and Organization at the Universities* (London: Macmillan, 1891).

CONNOLLY, REV EDWARD S. J. (ed.), *The English Reader* (New York: Benziger Brothers, 1887).

CONWAY, MONCURE, 'Robert Browning', *Victoria Magazine*, 2 (1864), 304–7.

CORSER, THOMAS, *Collectanea Anglo-Poetica: or, a Bibliographical and Descriptive Catalogue of a Portion of a Collection of Early English Poetry*, Part v, published by the Chetham Society, 91 (1873).

COURT, FRANKLIN E., *Institutionalizing English Literature: The Culture and Politics of Literary Study, 1750–1900* (Stanford, CA: Stanford Univ. Press, 1992).

—— 'The Early Impact of Scottish Literary Teaching in North America', in Robert Crawford (ed.), *The Scottish Invention of English Literature* (Cambridge: Cambridge Univ. Press, 1998), 134–63.

—— *The Scottish Connection: The Rise of English Literary Study in Early America* (Syracuse, NY: Syracuse Univ. Press, 2001).

CPL. [T. R. O'FLAHERTIE], 'Dr. John Donne', *N&Q*, 4th ser., 2 (26 Dec. 1868), 614.

—— 'Dr. John Donne', N&Q, 4th ser., 5 (11 June 1870), 565.

CRAIK, GEORGE L., *Sketches of the History of Literature and Learning in England*, 6 vols. (London: Charles Knight, 1844–5).

――*A Compendious History of English Literature*, 2 vols. (1845; repr. New York: Charles Scribner, 1863).

CUNNINGHAM, GEORGE GODFREY, *History of England in the Lives of Englishmen* (1834; London and Edinburgh: A. Fullarton, 1853).

D., C., 'T. E. Tomlins', *N&Q*, 10th ser., 6 (27 Oct. 1906), 338.

D., M. M., 'Essay on the Genius of Cowley, Donne and Clieveland', *European Magazine and London Review*, 82 (1822), 44–8, 108–12.

DEAN, DENNIS R., 'John W. Parker', in Patricia J. Anderson and Jonathan Rose (eds.), *Dictionary of Literary Biography*, cvi: *British Literary Publishing Houses, 1820–1880* (Detroit: Bruccoli Clark Layman, 1991), 233–6.

DELAURA, DAVID J., 'The Context of Browning's Painter Poems: Aesthetics, Polemics, Historics', *PMLA*, 95 (1980), 367–88.

[DE QUINCEY, THOMAS], 'Elements of Rhetoric', *Blackwood's Magazine*, 24 (Dec. 1828), 885–908.

DICK, CHARLES HILL, Introduction, *Lives of Doctor Donne*, etc., by Izaak Walton, The Scott Library (London: Walter Scott, [1899]), pp. v–xiv.

DISRAELI, ISAAC, *Amenities of Literature* [1841], new edn, ed. B[enjamin] Disraeli, 2 vols. (Boston: William Veazie; New York: Hurd and Houghton, 1864).

DONNE, JOHN, *The Sermons*, ed. George R. Potter and Evelyn M. Simpson, 10 vols. (Berkeley and Los Angeles: Univ. of California Press, 1953–62).

DOWDEN, EDWARD, 'The Poetry of John Donne', *Fortnightly Review*, new ser., 47 (1890), 791–808; repr. *Eclectic Magazine of Foreign Literature, Science, and Art*, 52 (1890), 234–44; *Littell's Living Age*, 186 (1890), 195–205; *New Studies in Literature* (London: Kegan Paul, Trench, and Trübner; Boston: Houghton Mifflin, 1895), 90–120.

DOWLING, LINDA, *Language and Decadence in the Victorian Fin de Siècle* (Princeton, NJ: Princeton Univ. Press, 1986).

DRYDEN, JOHN, *The Poems*, ed. James Kinsley, 4 vols. (Oxford: Clarendon, 1958).

DUNCAN, JOSEPH, *The Revival of Metaphysical Poetry: The History of a Style, 1800 to the Present* (Minneapolis, MN: Univ. of Minnesota Press, 1959).

DUYCKINCK, EVERT A., 'Dr. Donne', *Arcturus*, 2/1 (1841), 19–26.

ELFENBEIN, ANDREW, *Byron and the Victorians* (Cambridge: Cambridge Univ. Press, 1995).

[ELIOT, GEORGE] (Evans, Mary Ann), Review of *Men and Women*, *The Westminster Review*, 65 (Jan. 1856), 290–6.

――*Letters*, ed. Gordon S. Haight, 9 vols. (New Haven, CT: Yale Univ. Press, 1954–1978).

――*George Eliot's Middlemarch Notebooks: A Transcription*, ed. with an Introduction by John Clark Pratt and Victor A. Neufeldt (Berkeley, CA: Univ. of California Press, 1979).

――*Middlemarch*, ed. David Carroll (1871–2; Oxford: Clarendon, 1986).

[ELIOT, THOMAS STEARNS], 'The Metaphysical Poets', *Times Literary Supplement*, 1031 (20 Oct. 1921).

_____ 'John Donne', *Nation and Athenaeum*, 33/10 (9 June 1923), 331–2.

_____ Review of Peter Quennell's *Baudelaire and the Symbolists*, *The Criterion*, 9 (Jan. 1930), 357–9.

_____ 'Donne in Our Time', in Theodore Spencer (ed.), *A Garland for John Donne: 1631–1931* (Cambridge, MA: Harvard Univ. Press, 1931; repr. Gloucester, MA: Peter Smith, 1958), 1–19.

_____ *Selected Essays* (London: Faber and Faber, 1932).

_____ *The Use of Poetry and the Use of Criticism: Studies in the Relation of Criticism to Poetry in England* (Cambridge, MA: Harvard Univ. Press, 1933; repr. New York: Barnes and Noble, 1959).

_____ *To Criticize the Critic, and Other Writings* (London: Faber and Faber; New York: Farrar, Straus and Giroux, 1965).

EMERSON, RALPH WALDO, *Essays*, With a Preface by Thomas Carlyle (London: J. Fraser, 1841).

_____ *Letters and Social Aims* (Boston: Houghton Mifflin, 1875).

_____ (ed.), *Parnassus* (Boston: James K. Osgood, 1875).

_____ 'The American Scholar' (1837), *The Complete Works*, i: *Nature Addresses and Lectures*, ed. Edward Waldo Emerson (Boston: Houghton, Mifflin, 1904), 79–115.

_____ *The Letters*, i, ed. Ralph L. Rusk (New York: Columbia Univ. Press, 1939).

_____ *The Journals and Miscellaneous Notebooks*, ed. William H. Gilman et al., 16 vols. (Cambridge, MA: Belknap Press of Harvard Univ. Press, 1960–82).

FAIRBANKS, HENRY G., *Louise Imogen Guiney* (New York: Twayne, 1973).

FARNHAM, WILLARD, Foreword, in George R. Potter and Evelyn M. Simpson (eds.), *The Sermons of John Donne* (Berkeley and Los Angeles: Univ. of California Press, 1962), x, pp. vii–ix.

FARR, EDWARD (ed.), *Select Poetry Chiefly Sacred of the Reign of King James the First* (Cambridge: Deighton; London: John W. Parker, 1847).

FENWICK, GILLIAN, *Leslie Stephen's Life in Letters: A Bibliographical Study* (Aldershot, Hants: Scolar Press; Brookfield, VT: Ashgate Publishing, 1993).

_____ *Women in the Dictionary of National Biography* (Aldershot, Hants: Scolar Press; Brookfield, VT: Ashgate Publishing, 1994).

FERRY, ANNE, *Tradition and the Individual Poem: An Inquiry into Anthologies* (Stanford, CA: Stanford Univ. Press, 2001).

[FIELD, BARRON], 'Samuel Taylor Coleridge, Esq.', in *The Annual Biography and Obituary: 1835*, xix (London: Longman et al., 1835), 320–78.

FISH, STANLEY, *Is There a Text in This Class? The Authority of Interpretive Communities* (Cambridge, MA: Harvard Univ. Press, 1980).

FLETCHER, IAN, 'Decadence and the Little Magazines', in Ian Fletcher (ed.), *Decadence and the 1890s*, Stratford-upon-Avon Studies, 17 (London: Edward Arnold, 1979), 173–202.

FLYNN, DENNIS, 'Jasper Mayne's Translation of Donne's Latin Epigrams', *JDJ*, 3 (1984), 121–30.

_____ ' "Awry and Squint": The Dating of Donne's Holy Sonnets', *JDJ*, 7 (1988), 35–46.

FLYNN, DENNIS, *John Donne and the Ancient Catholic Nobility* (Bloomington, IN: Indiana Univ. Press, 1995).

FOUCAULT, MICHEL, *The History of Sexuality*, i: *An Introduction*, trans. Robert Hurley (New York: Vintage Books, 1980).

F[REEMANTLE], W[ILLIAM] H[ENRY], 'Alford, Henry', in *DNB* (Oxford: Oxford Univ. Press, 1917).

FULLER, MARGARET, *Woman in the Nineteenth Century* (New York: Greeley and McElrath, 1845).

FURST, CLYDE BOWMAN, 'The Life and Poetry of Dr. John Donne, Dean of St. Paul's', *Citizen* [Philadelphia], 2 (1896), 229–37; repr. *A Group of Old Authors* (Philadelphia: George W. Jacobs, 1899), 11–57.

GARNETT, RICHARD, 'Mr. Gosse's Life of Donne', *The Bookman*, 10 (1899), 582–4.

GILFILLAN, GEORGE, *Specimens with Memoirs of the Less-Known British Poets*, 3 vols. (Edinburgh: James Nichol, 1860).

GILL, STEPHEN, *Wordsworth and the Victorians* (Oxford: Clarendon, 1998).

GILL, THEODORE (ed.), Introduction, *The Sermons of John Donne: Selected and Introduced* (Canada: Meridan Books, 1958), 5–28.

GODWIN, WILLIAM, *Thoughts on Man, His Nature, Productions, and Discoveries* (London: Effingham Wilson, 1831).

GOSSE, EDMUND W., 'Donne, John', *Encyclopaedia Britannica*, 9th edn (Boston: Little, Brown, 1877).

—— *Seventeenth Century Studies* (London: Kegan Paul, Trench, 1883).

—— *Six Lectures Written to be Delivered Before the Lowell Institute in December, 1884* (London: Chiswick Press, 1884).

—— *Reply to the Quarterly Review* ([Cambridge: privately printed], Oct.–Nov., 1886).

—— 'The Poetry of John Donne', *The New Review*, 9 (1893), 236–47; repr. *Littell's Living Age*, 5th ser., 84 (1893), 429–36.

—— *The Jacobean Poets* (London: J. Murray; New York: Charles Scribner's Sons, 1894).

—— *A Short History of Modern English Literature* (1897; repr. London: William Heinemann; New York: D. Appleton, 1898).

—— (ed.), *The Life and Letters of John Donne Dean of St. Paul's*, 2 vols. (London: Heinemann, 1899; repr. Gloucester, MA: Peter Smith, 1959).

—— 'Donne', *Encyclopaedia Britannica*, 11th edn (Cambridge: Cambridge Univ. Press, 1910–11).

[—— ——], *Father and Son: A Study of Two Temperaments* (London: W. Heinemann, 1907); published in the United States with the author's name and under the title *Father and Son: Biographical Recollections*, 3rd edn (New York: Charles Scribner's Sons, 1908).

GRANQVIST, RAOUL, *The Reputation of John Donne 1779–1873*, Studia Universitatis Upsaliensia, 24 (Stockholm: Almqvist and Wiksell, 1975).

—— 'Izaak Walton's *Lives* in the Nineteenth and the Early Twentieth Century: A Study of a Cult Object', *Studia Neophilologica*, 54 (1982), 247–61.

—— 'A "Fashionable Poet" in New England in the 1890s: A Study of the Reception of John Donne', *JDJ*, 4 (1985), 337–49.

_____ 'Edmund Gosse: The Reluctant Critic of John Donne', *Neuphilogische Mitteilungen*, 87 (1986), 262–71.

_____ 'The Reception of Edmund Gosse's *Life of John Donne*', *English Studies*, 67 (1986), 525–38.

GREENE, ROBERT A., 'Whichcote, Wilkins, "Ingenuity," and the Reasonableness of Christianity', *Journal of the History of Ideas*, 42 (1981), 227–52.

GREY, ROBIN, *The Complicity of Imagination: The American Renaissance, Contests of Authority, and Seventeenth-Century English Culture* (Cambridge: Cambridge Univ. Press, 1997).

GRIERSON, HERBERT J. C. (ed.), Preface, *The Poems of John Donne*, 2 vols. (Oxford: Clarendon, 1912), i, pp. iii–xiii.

_____ 'The Text and Canon of Donne's Poems', *The Poems of John Donne*, 2 vols. (Oxford: Clarendon, 1912), ii, pp. lvi–cliii.

_____ (ed.), *Metaphysical Lyrics and Poems of the Seventeenth Century, Donne to Butler* (Oxford: Clarendon, 1921).

GRIFFIN, JOHN, '*The Contemporary Review*', in *British Literary Magazines: The Victorian and Edwardian Age, 1837–1913* (Westport, CT: Greenwood, 1983), 77–82.

_____ 'Tractarians and Metaphysicals: The Failure of Influence', *JDJ*, 4 (1985), 291–301.

GRISWOLD, RUFUS W. (ed.), *The Sacred Poets of England and America* (New York: D. Appleton, 1859).

GROSART, ALEXANDER B., 'Dr. Donne', *N&Q*, 4th ser., 5 (28 May 1870), 504.

_____ (ed.), Memorial-Introduction, *The Complete Poems of Robert Southwell, S.J.*, The Fuller Worthies' Library ([London: printed for private circulation], 1872), pp. xxxv–c.

_____ 'Essay on the Life and Writings of Donne', *The Complete Poems of John Donne, D.D.*, The Fuller Worthies' Library, 2 vols. ([London: printed for private circulation], 1872–3), ii, pp. ix–lvi.

_____ Preface, *The Complete Poems of John Donne, D.D.*, The Fuller Worthies' Library, 2 vols. ([London: printed for private circulation], 1872–3), i, pp. ix–xiv.

_____ (ed.), *Poems*, by Sir John Davies (London: Chatto and Windus, 1876).

GUILLORY, JOHN, 'Canon', in Frank Lentricchia and Thomas McLaughlin (eds.), *Critical Terms for Literary Study*, 2nd edn (Chicago: Univ. of Chicago Press, 1995), 233–49.

GUINEY, LOUISE IMOGEN, *A Little English Gallery* (New York: Harper and Brothers, 1894).

_____ 'Donne as a Lost Catholic Poet', *The Month*, 136 (1920), 13–19.

_____ *Letters*, ed. Grace Guiney, with a Preface by Agnes Repplier, 2 vols. (New York: Harper and Brothers, 1926).

HAIGHT, GORDON S., *George Eliot: A Biography* (Oxford: Oxford Univ. Press, 1968).

_____ 'George Eliot's "eminent failure", Will Ladislaw', in Ian Adam (ed.), *This Particular Web: Essays on Middlemarch* (Toronto: Univ. of Toronto Press, in association with the Faculty of Arts and Science of the Univ. of Calgary, 1975), 22–42.

HALES, JOHN W., 'John Donne', in Thomas Humphry Ward (ed.), *The English Poets: Selections with Critical Introductions*, i: *Chaucer to Donne* (London and New York: Macmillan, 1880).

HALLAM, HENRY, *Introduction to the Literature of Europe in the Fifteenth, Sixteenth, and Seventeenth Centuries*, iii (1837; repr. Paris: Baudry's European Library, 1839).

HARDING, ANTHONY JOHN, ' "Against the stream upwards": Coleridge's Recovery of John Donne', in Lisa Low and Anthony John Harding (eds.), *Milton, the Metaphysicals, and Romanticism* (Cambridge: Cambridge Univ. Press, 1994), 204–20.

HARE, AUGUSTUS J. C., *Biographical Sketches* (London: George Allen, 1895).

HARRIS, ROBIN S., *English Studies at Toronto: A History*, with a foreword by H. Northrop Frye (Toronto: Univ. of Toronto Press, 1988).

HARVARD UNIVERSITY, *Annual Reports of the President and Treasurer of Harvard College* (Cambridge, MA: Harvard University, various years); accessible online via a link on the Harvard University Archives web page.

—— *Official Register of Harvard University, Department of English 1905–06*, 2/26 (Cambridge, MA: Harvard University, 30 June 1905).

HASKIN, DAYTON, 'A History of Donne's "Canonization" from Izaak Walton to Cleanth Brooks', *JEGP*, 92 (1993), 17–36.

—— 'Coleridge's Marginalia on the Seventeenth-Century Divines and the Perusal of Our Elder Writers', *JDJ*, 19 (2000), 311–37.

—— 'No Edition Is an Island: The Place of the Nineteenth-Century American Editions within the History of Editing Donne's Poems', *TEXT: An Interdisciplinary Annual of Textual Studies*, 14 (2002), 169–207.

HAZLITT, W. CAREW, 'John Donne: Poems by Him in an Early MS', *N&Q*, 4th ser., 2 (21 Nov. 1868), 483–4.

—— 'Donne', in *Collections and Notes 1867–1876* (London: Reeves and Turner, 1876), 131.

HAZLITT, WILLIAM, *The Complete Works*, ed. P. P. Howe, 21 vols. (London: Dent, 1930–4).

HEINRICHS, JAY, 'How Harvard Destroyed Rhetoric', *Harvard Magazine*, 97/6 (July–Aug. 1995), 37–42.

HEWISON, P. E., 'George Saintsbury', in Steven Serafin (ed.), *Dictionary of Literary Biography*, cxlix: *Late Nineteenth- and Early Twentieth-Century British Literary Biographers* (Detroit: Bruccoli, Clark, Layman, 1995), 210–18.

HILL, W. SPEED, '*The Donne Variorum*: Variations on the Lives of the Author', *Huntington Library Quarterly*, 62 (1999), 445–54.

HODGSON, JOHN A., 'Coleridge, Puns, and "Donne's First Poem": The Limbo of Rhetoric and the Conceptions of Wit', *JDJ*, 4 (1985), 181–200.

HONE, WILLIAM (ed.), *The Every-day Book and Table Book; or, Everlasting Calendar of Popular Amusements*, 3 vols. (1826; London: Tegg and Son, 1835).

HOWARTH, HERBERT, *Notes on Some Figures behind T. S. Eliot* (Boston: Houghton Mifflin, 1964).

HUNT, LEIGH, Supplement to [his] *London Journal*, 49/7 ([1835]); repr. in *The Town: Its Memorable Characters and Events*, new edn (London: Gibbings, 1893).

____ *The Correspondence*, ed. [Thornton Leigh Hunt], 2 vols. (London: Smith, Elder, 1862).

____ 'An Essay on the Sonnet', in Leigh Hunt and S. Adams Lee (eds.), *The Book of the Sonnet*, 2 vols. (London: Sampson, Low; Boston: Roberts Brothers, 1867), i. 3–91.

____ and FIELD, BARRON], 'Is It Justifiable to Reprint the Pruriencies of Our Old Poets?', *The Reflector*, 1/2 (1811), 365–74.

'In Memoriam William Minto', *Alma Mater* [Aberdeen University Magazine] (4 Mar. 1893).

JACKSON, CHARLES KAINS, 'John Donne: An Appreciation', *The Artist and Journal of Home Culture* 15/172 (1894), 105–7.

JACKSON, H. J., ' "Turning and turning": Coleridge on Our Knowledge of the External World', *PMLA*, 101 (1986), 848–56.

____ 'Writing in Books and Other Marginal Activities', *UTQ*, 62 (1992–3), 217–31.

[JAMESON, ANNA BROWNELL MURPHY], *The Loves of the Poets*, 2 vols. (London: Henry Colburn, 1829).

JAMESON, MRS [ANNA], *Memoirs of the Early Italian Painters and the Progress of Painting in Italy*, 2 vols. (London: Charles Knight, 1845).

JESSOPP, AUGUSTUS, 'Some Notice of the Author and His Writings', *Essays in Divinity by John Donne, D.D.* (London: John Tupling, 1855), pp. ix–lxxiv.

____ *One Generation of a Norfolk House: A Contribution to Elizabethan History* (1878; 3rd edn, London: T. Fisher Unwin, 1913).

____ Introduction, *The Œconomy of the Fleete: An Apologeticall Answeare of Alexander Harris (Late Warden There) unto XIX Articles Sett Forth Against Him by the Prisoners* (Westminster: Camden Society, 1879), pp. vii–lii.

____ 'Donne, John', in *DNB* (London: Smith, Elder, 1888).

____ 'Letters and Letter-Writers', repr. in *Studies by a Recluse in Cloister, Town, and Country* (London: T. Fisher Unwin; New York: G. P. Putnam's Sons, 1893), 215–57.

____ *John Donne Sometime Dean of St. Paul's A.D. 1621–1631* (London: Methuen, 1897).

JOHNSON, SAMUEL, 'Cowley', in *Lives of the English Poets (1779–81)*, ed. George Birkbeck Hill, 3 vols. (Oxford: Clarendon, 1905), i. 1–69.

JONSON, BENJAMIN, *Ben Jonson*, i: *The Man and His Works*, ed. C. H. Herford and Percy Simpson (Oxford: Clarendon, 1925).

KAYLOR, EARL C., JR, *Martin Grove Brumbaugh: A Pennsylvanian's Odyssey from Sainted Schoolman to Bedeviled World War I Governor, 1862–1930* (Madison, NJ: Fairleigh Dickinson Univ. Press; London: Associated Univ. Presses, 1996).

KEMPE, ALFRED JOHN (ed.), *The Loseley Manuscripts* (London: John Murray, 1836).

KEMPE, JOHN EDWARD, Introduction, *The Classic Preachers of the English Church: Lectures Delivered at St. James's Church in 1877* (London: John Murray, 1877), pp. v–xxiv.

KENDALL, KENNETH E., *An Index to Leigh Hunt's Magazine, The Reflector* (Gainesville, FL: [printed privately], 1970).

KEYNES, GEOFFREY, *A Bibliography of Dr. John Donne, Dean of Saint Paul's*, 4th edn (Oxford: Clarendon, 1973).

KING, ALICE, 'John Donne', *Argosy* [London], 32 (1881), 299–305.

KIPPIS, ANDREW, 'Donne', *Biographica Britannica*, 2nd edn (London: John Nichols, 1793), v. 331–7.

KNIGHT, WILLIAM, 'Biographical Introduction', *The Literature of the Georgian Era*, by William Minto (1894; New York: Harper and Brothers, 1895), pp. ix–lvi.

LANDOR, WALTER SAVAGE, *Imaginary Conversations of Literary Men and Statesmen*, 2nd series., ii (London: James Duncan, 1829).

—— *The Works*, 2 vols. (London: E. Moxon, 1846).

LANGFORD, JOHN ALFRED, 'An Evening with Donne', *The Literature of Working Men: A Supplement to The Working Man's Friend and Family Instructor* (Dec. 1850), 18–21.

LARSON, CHARLES, 'Alexander Grosart's Donne and Marvell: "Glorious Old Fellows" in the Nineteenth Century', in William F. Gentrup (ed.), *Reinventing the Middle Ages and the Renaissance: Constructions of the Medieval and Early Modern Periods* (Turnhout: Brepols, 1998), 187–99.

LEARS, T. J. JACKSON, *No Place of Grace: Antimodernism and the Transformation of American Culture 1880–1920* (New York: Pantheon, 1981).

LEGOUIS, PIERRE, *Andrew Marvell: Poet, Puritan, Patriot*, 2nd edn (Oxford: Clarendon, 1968).

LEVINE, LAWRENCE W., *Highbrow/Lowbrow: The Emergence of Cultural Hierarchy in America* (Cambridge, MA: Harvard Univ. Press, 1988).

[LEWES, GEORGE HENRY], 'Donne's Poetical Works', *The National Magazine and Monthly Critic*, 2/9 (Apr. 1838), 374–8.

LEWISOHN, LUDWIG, *Cities and Men* (New York: Harper and Brothers, 1927).

LIGHTFOOT, J. B., 'Donne, the Poet-Preacher', in John Edward Kempe (ed.), *The Classic Preachers of the English Church: Lectures Delivered at St. James's Church in 1877* (London: John Murray, 1877), 1–26.

LILLY, WILLIAM S., 'New Light on the Carlyle Controversy', *Fortnightly Review*, 79 (1903), 1000–9.

LOHRLI, ANNE (ed.), *Household Words: A Weekly Journal 1850–1859* (Toronto: Univ. of Toronto Press, 1973).

[LOWELL, JAMES RUSSELL], 'Sketch of Wordsworth's Life', *The Poetical Works of William Wordsworth* (Boston: Little, Brown, 1854), i, pp. ix–xl.

[——] 'The Life of Keats', *The Poetical Works of John Keats* (Boston: Little, Brown, 1854), pp. vii–xxxvi.

—— 'Library of Old Authors', *My Study Windows* (Boston: James R. Osgood, 1871).

—— *Lectures on the English Poets* (Cleveland, OH: Rowfant Club, 1897).

—— *The Complete Works*, i: *Literary Essays* (Boston: Fireside Edition, 1899).

—— *Literary Criticism of James Russell Lowell*, ed. Herbert F. Smith (Lincoln, NE: Univ. of Nebraska Press, 1969).

MAHONEY, JOHN L., *The Logic of Passion: The Literary Criticism of William Hazlitt* (1978; repr. New York: Fordham Univ. Press, 1981).

MAITLAND, FREDERIC W., *The Life and Letters of Leslie Stephen* (London: Duckworth, 1906).

MAITLAND, THOMAS [BUCHANAN, ROBERT], 'The Fleshly School of Poetry: Mr. D. G. Rossetti', *Contemporary Review*, 18 (1871), 334–50.

MALLETT, PHILLIP, 'Edmund Gosse', in *The Dictionary of Literary Biography*, cxliv: *Nineteenth-Century British Literary Biographers* (Detroit: Bruccoli Clark Layman, 1994), 127–46.

MAROTTI, ARTHUR, *John Donne, Coterie Poet* (Madison, WI: Univ. of Wisconsin Press, 1986).

MARSH, JOSS, *Word Crimes: Blasphemy, Culture, and Literature in Nineteenth-Century England* (Chicago: Univ. of Chicago Press, 1998).

MARSHALL, W. GERALD, 'Time in Walton's *Lives*', *SEL*, 32 (1992), 429–42.

MARTIN, JESSICA, *Walton's Lives: Conformist Commemorations and the Rise of Biography* (Oxford and New York: Oxford Univ. Press, 2001).

MASSON, DAVID, *The Life of John Milton: Narrated in Connexion with the Political, Ecclesiastical, and Literary History of His Time*, i: *1608–1639* (Cambridge: Macmillan, 1859); rev. edn (1881; repr. Gloucester, MA: Peter Smith, 1965).

MASSON, ROSALINE ORME (ed.), *Three Centuries of English Poetry Being Selections from Chaucer to Herrick*, gen. preface by David Masson (London: Macmillan, 1876).

MATTHEW, H. C. G., *Leslie Stephen and the New Dictionary of National Biography*, The Leslie Stephen Lecture, 25 Oct. 1995 (Cambridge: Cambridge Univ. Press, 1997).

McCULLOUGH, PETER, 'Donne and Andrewes', *JDJ*, 22 (2003), 165–201.

McELDERRY, B. R., JR, 'Walton's *Lives* and Gillman's *Life of Coleridge*', *PMLA*, 52 (1937), 412–22.

MELCHIORI, BARBARA, 'Browning in Italy', in Isobel Armstrong (ed.), *Robert Browning*, Writers and Their Background (London: Bell, 1974; Athens, OH: Ohio Univ. Press, 1975), 168–83.

MENAND, LOUIS, *The Metaphysical Club* (New York: Farrar, Straus and Giroux, 2001).

MILMAN, HENRY HART, *Annals of S. Paul's Cathedral* (London: John Murray, 1868).

MINTO, WILLIAM, *A Manual of English Prose Literature, Biographical and Critical Designed Mainly to Show Characteristics of Style* (1872; rev. edn, Edinburgh: Blackwood and Sons, 1881).

—— *Characteristics of English Poets from Chaucer to Shirley* (1874; 2nd edn, Edinburgh: William Blackwood and Sons, 1885).

—— 'John Donne', *The Nineteenth Century*, 7 (May 1880), 845–63.

—— 'Wordsworth's Great Failure', *The Nineteenth Century*, 26 (1889), 435–51.

MORLEY, HENRY, *A First Sketch of English Literature* (London: Cassell, Petter, and Galpin, [1872/3]).

M[ORRIS], J[OHN], 'The Martyrdom of William Harrington', *The Month*, 20 (1874), 411–23.

[MORRIS, WILLIAM], Review of *Men and Women*, *Oxford and Cambridge Magazine*, 1/3 (Mar. 1856), 162–72.

Murray's Handbook of Northern Italy (London: John Murray, 1842).

MURRAY, HEATHER, 'English Studies in Canada to 1945: A Bibliographic Essay', *English Studies in Canada*, 17 (1991), 436–67.

NAJARIAN, JAMES, *Victorian Keats: Manliness, Sexuality, and Desire* (Basingstoke and New York: Palgrave, 2002).

NETHERCOT, ARTHUR H., 'The Reputation of John Donne as Metrist', *Sewanee Review*, 30 (1922), 463–74.

NEWMAN, JOHN HENRY, *The Via Media of the Anglican Church*, 2 vols. (London: Longmans, Green, 1901).

——— *The Letters and Diaries of John Henry Newman*, v: *Liberalism in Oxford January 1835 to December 1836*, ed. Thomas Gornall, S.J. (Oxford: Clarendon, 1981).

NICHOLSON, BRINSLEY, 'Donne, or Sir John Davies', *Athenaeum*, 2518 (29 Jan. 1876), 161–2.

NOCKLES, PETER BENEDICT, *The Oxford Movement in Context: Anglican High Churchmanship, 1760–1857* (Cambridge: Cambridge Univ. Press, 1994).

[NORTON, CHARLES ELIOT], 'Memoir of Shelley', *The Poetical Works of Percy Bysshe Shelley*, ed. Mrs Shelley, 3 vols. (Boston: Little, Brown, 1855), i, pp. xi–xlv.

——— *Notes of Travel and Study in Italy* (1859; Boston: Ticknor and Fields, 1860).

——— *The New Life of Dante: An Essay, with Translations* (Cambridge, MA: Riverside, 1859).

——— 'Feminine Poetry', *The Nation*, 22/556 (24 Feb. 1876), 132–4.

——— 'Editorial Note', *The Letters of James Russell Lowell*, 2 vols. (New York: Harper and Brothers, 1893), i, pp. iii–v.

——— 'James Russell Lowell', *Harper's New Monthly Magazine* 86/516 (May 1893), 846–57.

——— Preface and Introduction, *The Poems of John Donne from the Text of the Edition of 1633*, rev. James Russell Lowell, 2 vols. (New York: Grolier Club, 1895), i, pp. vii–ix, xvii–xxxii.

——— 'The Text of Donne's Poems', *Studies and Notes in Philology and Literature*, v: *Child Memorial Volume* (Boston: Ginn, 1896), 1–19.

——— 'Gosse's Life of Donne', *The Nation*, 70/1806–7 (8, 15 Feb. 1900), 111–13, 133–5.

——— Preface, *The Love Poems of John Donne* (Boston: Houghton Mifflin, 1905), pp. v–ix.

——— *Henry Wadsworth Longfellow; a Sketch of his Life … together with Longfellow's Chief Autobiographical Poems* (Boston: Houghton Mifflin, 1906).

——— *Letters*, with biographical comment by his daughter Sara Norton and M. A. De Wolfe Howe, 2 vols. (Boston: Houghton Mifflin, 1913).

NOVARR, DAVID, *The Making of Walton's Lives* (Ithaca, NY: Cornell Univ. Press, 1958).

O'MALLEY, JOHN W., *Praise and Blame in Renaissance Rome: Rhetoric, Doctrine, and Reform in the Sacred Orators of the Papal Court, c.1450–1521* (Durham, NC: Duke Univ. Press, 1979).

OZICK, CYNTHIA, 'A Critic at Large: T. S. Eliot at 101', *The New Yorker*, 65/40 (20 Nov. 1989), 119–44, 149–54.

PALGRAVE, FRANCIS (ed.), *The Golden Treasury of the Best Songs and Lyrical Poems in the English Language* (Cambridge and London: Macmillan, 1861).

PALMER, D. J., *The Rise of English Studies: An Account of the Study of English Language and Literature from its Origins to the Making of the Oxford English School* (London: Oxford Univ. Press, for the University of Hull, 1965).

PARRISH, STEPHEN MAXFIELD, *Currents of the Nineties in Boston and London: Fred Holland Day, Louise Imogen Guiney, and Their Circle* (New York: Garland, 1987).

PASK, KEVIN, *The Emergence of the English Author: Scripting the Life of the Poet in Early Modern England* (Cambridge: Cambridge Univ. Press, 1996).

[PATMORE, COVENTRY], 'English Metrical Critics', *North British Review*, 27 (1857), 127–61.

[_____ ?],'Gallery of Poets. No. 1.—John Donne', *Lowe's Edinburgh Magazine*, 1 (1846), 228–36.

PAYNE, WILLIAM MORTON (ed.), *English in American Universities* (Boston: D. C. Heath, 1895).

PAZ, D. G., *Popular Anti-Catholicism in Mid-Victorian England* (Stanford, CA: Stanford Univ. Press, 1992).

PETERSON, RICHARD S., 'New Evidence on Donne's Monument: I', *JDJ*, 20 (2001), 1–51.

PHELPS, WILLIAM LYON PHELPS, *Autobiography with Letters* (London and New York: Oxford Univ. Press, 1939).

PITTOCK, MURRAY G. H., *Spectrum of Decadence: The Literature of the 1890s* (London: Routledge, 1993).

QUINN, ARTHUR HOBSON, 'Felix E. Schelling', *Schelling Anniversary Papers* (New York: Century, 1923), 3–17.

REED, JOSEPH W., JR, *English Biography in the Early Nineteenth Century 1801–1838* (New Haven, CT: Yale Univ. Press, 1966).

REID, J. C., *The Mind and Art of Coventry Patmore* (London: Routledge and Kegan Paul, 1957).

RICKS, CHRISTOPHER, *Essays in Appreciation* (Oxford: Clarendon, 1996).

ROBERTS, JOHN R., *John Donne: An Annotated Bibliography of Modern Criticism 1912–1967* (Columbia, MO: Univ. of Missouri Press, 1973).

_____ *John Donne: An Annotated Bibliography of Modern Criticism 1968–1978* (Columbia, MO: Univ. of Missouri Press, 1982).

_____ *John Donne: An Annotated Bibliography of Modern Criticism 1979–1995* (Pittsburgh, PA: Duquesne Univ. Press, 2004).

[ROBERTSON, J. C.], 'The Rev. H. Alford's Edition of Donne', *The British Magazine and Monthly Register of Religious and Ecclesiastical Information*, 15 (1839), 534–7.

_____ 'Notes on the Life and Works of Dr. Donne', *The Gentleman's Magazine*, new ser., 16 (1841), 25–32.

ROSSETTI, D. G., 'The Stealthy School of Criticism', *Athenæum*, 2303 (16 Dec. 1871), 792–4.

RUSKIN, JOHN, and NORTON, CHARLES ELIOT, *The Correspondence*, ed. John Lewis Bradley and Ian Ousby (Cambridge: Cambridge Univ. Press, 1987).

RYAN, ROBERT M., *The Romantic Reformation: Religious Politics in English Literature, 1789–1824* (Cambridge: Cambridge Univ. Press, 1997).

S., A., 'T. E. Tomlins', *N&Q*, 10th ser., 6 (22 Sept. 1906), 228–9.

SAINTSBURY, GEORGE, *A History of Elizabethan Literature* (London: Macmillan, 1887).

—— (ed.), *Seventeenth Century Lyrics* (New York: Macmillan, 1892).

—— Introduction, *Poems of John Donne*, The Muses' Library, ed. E. K. Chambers, 2 vols. (London: Lawrence and Bullen; George Routledge and Sons; New York: Charles Scribner's Sons; E. P. Dutton, 1896), i, pp. xi–xxxiii.

[SALA, GEORGE A.], 'Dumbledowndeary', *Household Words*, 5/117 (19 June 1852), 312–17.

SATTELMEYER, ROBERT, *Thoreau's Reading: A Study in Intellectual History with Bibliographical Catalogue* (Princeton, NJ: Princeton Univ. Press, 1988).

SCHELLING, FELIX E., *Two Essays on Robert Browning* ([Printed privately], 1890).

—— (ed.), *A Book of Elizabethan Lyrics* (Boston: Ginn, 1895).

—— (ed.), *A Book of Seventeenth Century Lyrics* (Boston: Ginn, 1899).

SCHERR, JOHANNES, *A History of English Literature*, trans. M. V. (London: Sampson, Low, 1882).

SCHIPPER, J[AKOB], *Englische Metrik in historicischer und systematischer Entwickelung dargestellt*, 3 vols. (Bonn: Emil Strauss, 1880–88), ii: *Neuenglische Metrik* (1888).

SHARROCK, ROGER, 'Wit, Passion and Ideal Love: Reflections on the Cycle of Donne's Reputation', in Peter Amadeus Fiore (ed.), *Just So Much Honor: Essays Commemorating the Four-Hundredth Anniversary of the Birth of John Donne* (University Park, PA: Pennsylvania State Univ. Press, 1972), 33–56.

SHAWN, WALLACE, *The Designated Mourner* (London: Faber and Faber, 1996).

SHOWALTER, ENGLISH, JR, 'Authorial Self-Consciousness in the Familiar Letter: The Case of Madame de Graffigny', *Yale French Studies*, 71 (1987), 113–30.

[SICHEL, WALTER SYDNEY], 'Fathers of Literary Impressionism in England', *Quarterly Review*, 185 (1897), 173–94.

SIMEON, SIR JOHN (ed.), 'Unpublished Poems of Donne', *Bibliographical and Historical Miscellanies*, The Philobiblon Society, 3 (London: Printed by Charles Wittingham, 1856–7).

SIMPSON, EVELYN M., *A Study of the Prose Works of John Donne*, 2nd edn (Oxford: Clarendon, 1948).

SMITH, A. J. (ed.), *John Donne: The Critical Heritage* (London: Routledge and Kegan Paul, 1975).

—— and PHILLIPS, CATHERINE (eds.), *John Donne: The Critical Heritage*, ii (London: Routledge, 1996).

SOCIETY FOR THE COLLEGIATE INSTRUCTION OF WOMEN [Radcliffe College], *Annual Reports of the Treasurer and Secretary* (Cambridge, MA: Radcliffe College, various years); accessible online via a link on the Harvard University Archives web page.

SOUTHAM, B. C., 'General Editor's Preface', in A. J. Smith (ed.), completed with introductory and editorial material by Catherine Phillips, *John Donne: The Critical Heritage*, ii (London and Boston, MA: Routledge, 1996), p. v.

SOUTHEY, ROBERT, *Southey's Common-Place Book*, ed. John Wood Warter, 1st ser. (New York: Harper and Brothers, 1849).

——*Southey's Common-Place Book*, ed. John Wood Warter, 4th ser. (London: Longman, Brown, 1850).

SPALDING, WILLIAM, *The History of English Literature* (New York: D. Appleton, 1853).

STALLYBRASS, PETER, 'Editing as Cultural Formation: The Sexing of Shakespeare's Sonnets', *MLQ*, 54 (1993), 91–103.

STANWOOD, P. G., 'Donne's Earliest Sermons and the Penitential Tradition', in Raymond-Jean Frontain and Frances Malpezzi (eds.), *John Donne's Religious Imagination: Essays in Honor of John T. Shawcross* (Conway, AR: UCA Press, 1995), 366–79.

STEINBERG, LEO, *The Sexuality of Christ in Renaissance Art and in Modern Oblivion*, 2nd edn, rev. and expanded (1983; Chicago: Univ. of Chicago Press, 1996).

STEPHEN, LESLIE, 'Matthew Arnold and the Church of England', *Fraser's Magazine*, new ser., 2 (1870), 414–31.

——'National Biography', *National Review*, 27 (1896), 51–65.

——'John Donne', *National Review*, 34 (1899), 595–613.

——*Studies of a Biographer*, 4 vols. (London: Duckworth; New York: G. P. Putnam's Sons, 1898–1902).

——'Some Early Impressions', *National Review*, 42 (1903–4), 208–24.

——*Selected Letters*, ed. John W. Bicknell, 2 vols. (Basingstoke: Macmillan; Columbus, OH: Ohio State Univ. Press, 1996).

——'Proposed Method for the *Dictionary of National Biography*', in *Selected Letters*, Appendix I, ii. 545–7.

STORER, HORATIO ROBINSON, *Is It I? A Book for Every Man* (Boston: Lee and Shepard, 1867).

SULLIVAN, ERNEST W., II, *The Influence of John Donne: His Uncollected Seventeenth-Century Printed Verse* (Columbia, MO: Univ. of Missouri Press, 1993).

——'*Poems*, by J.D.: Donne's Corpus and His Bawdy, Too', *JDJ*, 19 (2000), 299–309.

SUMMERS, CLAUDE J., 'Donne's 1609 Sequence of Grief and Comfort', *SP*, 89 (1992), 211–31.

——Review of *The Variorum Edition of the Poetry of John Donne*, Vol. 6, in *Early Modern Literary Studies*, 1/3 (Dec. 1995), 6.1–10.

SWINBURNE, ALGERNON CHARLES, *George Chapman: A Critical Essay* (London: Chatto and Windus, 1875).

SYMONS, ARTHUR, 'John Donne', *Fortnightly Review*, new ser., 66 (1899), 734–45.

——*The Collected Works*, i-ii: *Poems* (London: Martin Secker, 1924; repr. New York: AMS Press, 1973).

——*Selected Letters, 1880–1935*, ed. Karl Beckson and John M. Munro (Iowa City, IA: Univ. of Iowa Press, 1989).

TAINE, H[IPPOLYTE], *Histoire de la Littérature Anglaise* (1863), trans. H. Van Laun as *History of English Literature* (Edinburgh: Edmonston and Douglas, 1871).

TANSELLE, G. THOMAS, 'Reflections on Scholarly Editing', *Raritan*, 16/2 (Fall 1996), 52–64.

TAYLOR, GARY, *Reinventing Shakespeare: A Cultural History, from the Restoration to the Present* (New York: Weidenfeld and Nicolson, 1989; Oxford Univ. Press, 1991).

TENISON, E. M., *Louise Imogen Guiney: Her Life and Works, 1861–1920* (London: Macmillan, 1923).

THOMSON, A. W. (ed.), *Wordsworth's Mind and Art* (Edinburgh: Oliver and Boyd, 1969).

THOREAU, HENRY DAVID, *Thoreau's Literary Notebook in The Library of Congress: Facsimile Text*, ed. Kenneth Walter Cameron (Hartford, CT: Transcendental Books, 1964).

—— *Walden*, ed. J. Lyndon Shanley (Princeton, NJ: Princeton Univ. Press, 1971).

—— *The Selected Works of Thoreau*, Cambridge Edition, ed. Walter Harding (Boston: Houghton Mifflin, 1975).

—— *Journal*, i: *1837–1844*, gen. ed. John C. Broderick (Princeton, NJ: Princeton Univ. Press, 1981); *Journal*, ii: *1842–1848* (1984).

THWAITE, ANN, *Edmund Gosse: A Literary Landscape, 1849–1928* (Chicago: Univ. of Chicago Press, 1984).

TILLOTSON, KATHLEEN, 'Donne's Poetry in the Nineteenth Century (1800–1872)', in *Elizabethan and Jacobean Studies Presented to Frank Percy Wilson in Honour of his Seventieth Birthday* (Oxford: Clarendon, 1959), 307–26.

[TOMLINS, THOMAS EDLYNE] (ed.), *The Life of John Donne, D.D. Late Dean of St. Paul's Church, London*, by Izaak Walton, with some original notes by an Antiquary [Tomlins] (London: Henry Kent Causton, [1852]).

TOWNSEND, KIM, *Manhood at Harvard: William James and Others* (New York: Norton, 1996; London: Harvard Univ. Press, 1998).

TRENCH, RICHARD (ed.), *Household Book of English Poetry* (London: Macmillan, 1868).

TRIMBLE, ESTHER J. (ed.), *A Hand-book of English and American Literature* (Philadelphia: Eldredge and Brother, 1883).

TURNER, JAMES, *The Liberal Education of Charles Eliot Norton* (Baltimore, MD: Johns Hopkins Univ. Press, 1999).

Typical Selections from the Best English Authors (Oxford: Clarendon, 1869).

VANDERBILT, KERMIT, *Charles Eliot Norton: Apostle of Culture in a Democracy* (Cambridge, MA: Belknap Press of Harvard Univ. Press, 1959).

VENABLES, EDMUND, 'Kaye, John', in *DNB* (London: Smith, Elder, 1892), xxx. 252–3.

VICKERS, BRIAN, Reviews of *The Variorum Edition of the Poetry of John Donne*, Vol. 6 and Vol. 8, respectively, in *Analytical & Enumerative Bibliography*, new ser., 10 (1999), 37–42; 107–11.

VINCENT, ARTHUR, Letter of 4 Dec. 1899, *Athenæum*, 3764 (16 Dec. 1899), 836.

VISWANATHAN, GAURI, *Masks of Conquest: Literary Study and British Rule in India* (New York: Columbia Univ. Press, 1989).

VON ARX, JEFFREY PAUL, *Progress and Pessimism: Religion, Politics, and History in Late Nineteenth Century Britain* (Cambridge, MA: Harvard Univ. Press, 1985).

WALDRON, F. G. (ed.), *The Shakespearean Miscellany* (London: Knight and Compton, 1802).

WALKER, ERIC C., 'Wordsworth as Prose Biographer', *JEGP*, 89 (1990), 330–44.

WALLIS, FRANK H., *Popular Anti-Catholicism in Mid-Victorian Britain*, Texts and Studies in Religion, 60 (Lewiston, NY: Edward Mellen Press, 1993).

WALTON, IZAAK, *The Lives of Dr John Donne, Sir Henry Wotton, Mr Richard Hooker, Mr George Herbert*, 4th edn (London, 1675).

WARREN, DALE, 'Gamaliel Bradford: A Personal Sketch', *South Atlantic Quarterly*, 32 (1933), 9–18.

WARRINGTON, BERNARD, 'William Pickering', in Patricia J. Anderson and Jonathan Rose (eds.), *British Literary Publishing Houses, 1820–1880*, cvi: *Dictionary of Literary Biography*, (Detroit: Bruccoli Clark Layman, 1991), 245–50.

WENDELL, BARRETT, *The Temper of the Seventeenth Century in English Literature*, Clark Lectures given at Trinity College, Cambridge in the Year 1902–3 (London: Macmillan; New York: Charles Scribner's Sons, 1904).

WHALLEY, GEORGE, 'The Harvest on the Ground: Coleridge's *Marginalia*', *UTQ*, 38 (1968–9), 248–76.

WHIPPLE, EDWIN PERCY, 'Minor Elizabethan Poets', *Atlantic Monthly*, 22/129 (July 1868), 26–35.

_____ *The Literature of the Age of Elizabeth* (Boston: Fields, Osgood, 1869).

[WILLIAMS, ROBERT F.], *Shakspeare and his Friends; or, 'The Golden Age' of Merry England*, 3 vols. (London: Henry Colburn, 1838).

[WILLMOTT, ROBERT ARIS], *Conversations at Cambridge* (London: John W. Parker, 1836), 1–36.

_____ (ed.), *Letters of Eminent Persons: Selected and Illustrated* (London: John W. Parker, 1839).

WINSHIP, GEORGE PARKER, 'The Norton Collection in the Library', *Harvard Alumni Bulletin*, 23 (May 1921), 706–7.

WITTREICH, JOSEPH ANTHONY, JR, *The Romantics on Milton: Formal Essays and Critical Asides* (Cleveland, OH: Press of Case Western Reserve Univ., 1970).

WOLFFE, JOHN, *The Protestant Crusade in Great Britain, 1829–1860* (Oxford: Clarendon Press, 1991).

WOOLF, VIRGINIA, 'Donne after Three Centuries' (*c*.1932), in *Collected Essays*, i, ed. Leonard Woolf (London: Hogarth, 1967).

WOOLFORD, JOHN, 'Periodicals and the Practice of Literary Criticism, 1855–64', in Joanne Shattock and Michael Wolff (eds.), *The Victorian Periodical Press: Samplings and Soundings* (Leicester: Leicester Univ. Press; Toronto: Univ. of Toronto Press, 1982), 109–42.

WORDSWORTH, CHRISTOPHER (ed.), 'Doctor John Donne', in *Ecclesiastical Biography; or Lives of Eminent Men, Connected with the History of Religion in England; From the Commencement of the Reformation to the Revolution; Selected and Illustrated with Notes*, 6 vols. (London: F. C. and J. Rivington, 1810), iv. 403–79.

_____ *Memoirs of William Wordsworth*, ed. Henry Reed, 2 vols. (Boston: Ticknor, Reed, and Fields, 1851).

WORDSWORTH, WILLIAM, *The Ecclesiastical Sonnets ... A Critical Edition*, ed. Abbie Findlay Potts (New Haven, CT: Yale Univ. Press, 1922).

Wordsworth, William, *The Poetical Works: Miscellaneous Sonnets*, etc., ed. E. de Selincourt and Helen Darbishire, 2nd edn (Oxford: Clarendon, 1954).

_____ and Wordsworth, Dorothy, *The Letters*, arranged and ed. Ernest de Selincourt, 2nd edn, 8 vols. (Oxford: Clarendon; New York: Oxford Univ. Press, 1967–93).

Wu, Duncan, *Wordsworth's Reading 1770–1799* (Cambridge: Cambridge Univ. Press, 1993).

Wyke, Clement H., 'Edmund Gosse as Biographer and Critic of Donne: His Fallible Role in the Poet's Rediscovery', *Texas Studies in Literature and Language*, 17 (1975–6), 805–19.

Yale University, *Catalogue of the Officers and Students of Yale College* (New Haven, CT: Yale Univ., annually).

Yeats, W. B., *Autobiographies: Reveries over Childhood and Youth and The Trembling of the Veil* (New York: Macmillan, 1927).

Y[eowell], J., [untitled note], *N&Q*, 2nd ser., 4 (1857), 49.

Zouch, Thomas (ed.), *Lives of Dr. John Donne*, etc., by Izaak Walton (York, 1796).

Acknowledgements

Some pleasures that we store up while reading and writing are multiplied in the memories that harvest them: amidst experiences of a shared love of learning, these acknowledgements express a gratitude that blurs the boundaries between life's scholarly and affective dimensions.

For nearly three decades Gary Stringer has been a principle of stability in Donne Studies. He has held together a large band of scholars, and he was good enough early on to bring me into their company. I owe a great deal to my co-workers on the Donne Variorum project and to members of the John Donne Society, especially to Al Labriola, a model of constancy. By a similar token, many colleagues at Boston College have intelligently encouraged my work, including Rosemarie Bodenheimer, Amy Boesky, John Mahoney, Andrew Sofer, Dennis Taylor, Andrew Von Hendy, Judith Wilt, and the late J. Robert Barth. Mary Crane has repeatedly supported the project, not least by a skepticism that kept asking (all but one time indirectly), Why Donne? Mick Smyer provided a space to do the writing; and the University has supported the work with a sabbatical leave and several small grants. The most timely support—and the best gift of time—came from the John Simon Guggenheim Foundation, at a juncture when I had been cavalierly presuming that a single year free from other duties would be enough to finish the book. As it turned out, the best fruit of that fellowship year was a deepening awareness of what I would need to learn.

While periods apart from ordinary teaching duties enabled me to do the writing, experiences in the archives with graduate students and in the classroom with undergraduates have renewed a sense of what's at stake in the work. I take great pleasure in remembering hours upon hours spent with student research assistants, including Jason Alberti, Denise Bracken, Matthew Brunell, and Emily Cersonsky, who saw the manuscript to completion.

Invitations to speak on this or that aspect of the subject have kept things moving. I thank Annabel Patterson for the opportunity to participate in Yale's graduate Renaissance Colloquium and John Guillory for inviting me to speak at Harvard's Barker Center. Members of the Thoreau Society, including Kevin Van Anglen and Tammy Beams, prodded me to learn all sorts of things I had not known about New England literary culture. Among those who have asked me to speak at the annual convention of the Modern Language Association, I thank Heather Jackson for having helped me to see how my subject relates to larger configurations than I had been glimpsing. The organizers of the annual conference of the John Donne Society, especially Jeanne Shami, have brought me into the heart of the most knowledgeable and appreciative of audiences, whose remembered presence informs virtually every part of this book.

Learned colleagues who have responded to drafts of one or more chapters have made welcome demands. They include Trev Lynn Broughton, the late David DeLaura, Karen Edwards, Jonathan Post, Ramie Targoff, and Jim Turner. Raoul Granqvist's foundational scholarship on Donne's reception got me looking at all sorts of materials and provoked many of the questions that have kept me interested; all who have worked on the Variorum have benefited from his indispensable spadework. Tom Hester read through the whole from start to finish and helped me to see where to end. Tom Perridge of Oxford University Press patiently and clearly answered many queries. Long, leisurely talks with Achsah Guibbory and with Dennis Flynn have enhanced my pleasure in reading Donne and in thinking about what makes him appealing to very different kinds of readers. And through many years the late Anne Ferry's unsurpassed standards and her generous interest, and David Ferry's exacting enthusiasm, have informed a friendship that has nourished these endeavors.

Inasmuch as my mother trained as a librarian, it is unsurprising that she should share my pleasure in having written a book that owes its existence to what dozens of members of that profession have preserved and made accessible. It has been a joy to work in the company of the professional staffs at Harvard University, in particular Susan Halpert and Betty Falsey at the Houghton Library and Robin McElheny, Barbara Meloni, and Brian Sullivan in the Harvard Archives. The work of these librarians and archivists has made possible nearly all the scholarly projects in which I have been involved over many years. At Boston College, Brendan Rapple and other members of the library staff have been unfailingly helpful; those working in the Interlibrary Loan office have seen to it that even the magnificent holdings of the Harvard libraries can be productively supplemented. My thanks, too, to archivists at Brown, Case Western Reserve, Johns Hopkins, Princeton, and Yale Universities, at the University of Pennsylvania, at Juniata College and Smith College, and elsewhere for helping me to find relevant materials. I gratefully acknowledge the permissions that their institutions have given me to quote from the holdings that are specified in the footnotes.

Some of the argument of the book was rehearsed in 'New Historical Contexts for Appraising the Donne Revival from A. B. Grosart to Charles Eliot Norton', published in *ELH*, 56 (1989), 869–95, and in various essays that appeared in the *John Donne Journal*. The latter pieces include 'Reading Donne's *Songs and Sonnets* in the Nineteenth Century', 4 (1985), 225–52; 'John Donne and the Cultural Contradictions of Christmas', 11 (1992), 133–57; 'Coleridge's Marginalia on the Seventeenth-Century Divines and the Perusal of Our Elder

Writers', 19 (2000), 311–37, and 'Impudently Donne', 20 (2001), 281–7. In addition, several sentences incorporated into the book first appeared in 'No Edition Is an Island: The Place of the Nineteenth-Century American Editions within the History of Editing Donne's Poems', published in *TEXT*, 14 (2002), 169–207. The research reported in this last piece undergirds several features of the larger argument in the book. My thanks to the Johns Hopkins University Press, to M. Thomas Hester of the *John Donne Journal*, and to the University of Michigan Press for permission to redeploy these materials. It is a pleasure also to acknowledge that, while I was working on the book, some main lines of the argument were digested in the essay called 'Donne's Afterlife' that I contributed to *The Cambridge Companion to John Donne*, ed. Achsah Guibbory (Cambridge: Cambridge University Press, 2006), 233–46.

The book is dedicated to the four persons with whom I have lived while writing it, all of whom I look forward to waking up each morning.

Index of References to John Donne's Works

General Index